Music Fundamentals, Methods, and Materials for the Elementary Classroom Teacher

Music Fundamentals, Methods, and Materials for the Elementary Classroom Teacher

THIRD EDITION

Michon Rozmajzl

Boise State University

René Boyer-Alexander

University of Cincinnati

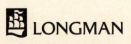 LONGMAN

An imprint of Addison Wesley Longman, Inc.

New York • Reading, Massachusetts • Menlo Park, California • Harlow, England
Don Mills, Ontario • Sydney • Mexico City • Madrid • Amsterdam

Editor-in-Chief: Priscilla McGeehon
Acquisitions Editor: Virginia L. Blanford
Development Editor: Barbara Conover
Supplements Editor: Joy Hilgendorf
Full Service Production Manager: Patti Brecht
Project Coordination, Text Design, and Electronic Page Makeup: Nesbitt Graphics, Inc.
Cover Design Manager: Nancy Danahy
Cover Designer: Joseph DePinho
Cover Photos: PhotoDisc, Inc.
Senior Print Buyer: Hugh Crawford
Printer and Binder: Courier/Stoughton, Inc.
Cover Printer: Coral Graphic Services, Inc.

For permission to use copyrighted material, grateful acknowledgment is made to the copyright holders on page 388, which is hereby made part of this copyright page.

Library of Congress Cataloging-in-Publication Data
Rozmajzl, Michon.
     Music fundamentals, methods, and materials for the elementary
classroom teacher / Michon Rozmajzl, René Boyer-Alexander. —3rd
ed.
          p.   cm.
     Includes index.
     ISBN 0-8013-3081-5
     1. School music—Instruction and study–United States.   I. Boyer
-Alexander, René.   II. Title.
MT1.R85   1999
372.87'044—dc21   99-24347
                                                                          CIP

Copyright © 2000 by Addison Wesley Longman, Inc.

Please visit our website at http://www.awlonline.com

ISBN 0-8013-3081-5

12345678910—CRS—02010099

Music is one of the greatest gifts that we as a society pass on to our children. This book will serve to guide, enhance, and replenish the classroom teachers' understanding and appreciation of how music can be creatively taught so that it becomes an integral part of our children's lives.

Enjoy!

Contents

List of Songs   xi

Preface   xvii

Section I   Teaching the Elements of Music to Children   1

1 *Children and Music*   *1*
Why Teach Music to Children?   1
National Standards for Arts Education   2
Learning Theory Applied to Music Education   3

2 *Teaching Rhythm to Children*   *6*
Introduction   6
Beat/Pulse   6
Rhythm   8
Quarter Note, Eighth Note, Two Eighth Notes   9
Quarter Rest   11
Grouping Beats   13
Time Signature or Meter Signature   15
Sixteen Notes and Rest, Half Note and Rest, Whole Note and Rest   17
Tie   23
Dotted Notes   25
Simple Meter   28
Compound Meter   31
Asymmetrical or Irregular Meters   34
Mixed or Changing Meters   35
Other Rhythms: Triplet, Syncopation, Polyrhythms   36
Anacrusis (Pick-up)   43
Additional Rhymes for Rhythm Activities   47
Introducing the Structural Components of Rhythm: Suggested Sequencing by
    Grade Level   48
Written and Performance-Related Assessments Through Cooperative Learning Activities:
    Rhythm   49

3 *Teaching Melody to Children*   *51*
Introduction   51
Pitch: High/Low   51
Staff   53
Clef Signs   55
Grand Staff   56
Musical Alphabet   56
Note Stems   60
Unorganized and Organized Pitches   61
Contour   62
Steps, Skips, and Repeated Notes   64
Melodic Intervals   65
Whole Steps and Half Steps   69
Accidentals   70
Enharmonic Equivalents   72
Major Scales and Key Signatures   73
Minor Scales and Key Signatures   79

Pentatonic Scale   87
Chromatic Scale   90
Transposing   92
Introducing the Structural Components of Melody: Suggested Sequencing by
   Grade Level   104
Written and Performance-Related Assessments Through Cooperative Learning Activities:
   Melody   105

4 *Teaching Timbre to Children*　　　　　　　　　　　　　　　　　*106*
Introduction   106
Environmental and Body Sounds   106
Tone Color of Rhythm Instruments   108
Electronic Sounds   110
Vocal Sounds   111
Orchestral Sounds   112
Written and Performance-Related Assessments Through Cooperative Learning Activities:
   Timbre   119
Listening Selections   119

5 *Teaching Expressive Elements to Children*　　　　　　　　　　　*121*
Introduction   121
Tempo   121
Dynamics   123
Articulation   128
Slur   130
Fermata   132
Introducing Expressive Elements: Suggested Sequencing by Grade Level   134
Written and Performance-Related Assessments Through Cooperative Learning Activities:
   Expressive Elements   134

6 *Teaching Form to Children*　　　　　　　　　　　　　　　　　*135*
Introduction   135
Phrase   135
Sectional Forms: Binary, Ternary, Rondo, Theme and Variations, and Strophic   142
Introduction, Interlude, and Coda   152
Repeat Signs   154
Sequence   157
Introducing the Structural Components of Form: Suggested Sequencing by Grade Level   160
Written and Performance-Related Assessments Through Cooperative Learning Activities:
   Form   161

7 *Teaching Texture to Children*　　　　　　　　　　　　　　　　*162*
Introduction   162
Monophonic Texture   162
Polyphonic Texture   164
Homophonic Texture   169
Introducing the Structural Components of Texture: Suggested Sequencing by Grade Level   172
Written and Performance-Related Assessments Through Cooperative Learning Activities:
   Texture   173

8 *Teaching Harmony to Children*　　　　　　　　　　　　　　　*174*
Introduction   174
Aural Harmonic Awareness   174
Preparation for Harmony   174
Singing Rounds   177
Melodic Ostinato   178
Singing in Thirds and Sixths   178
Partner Songs and Descants   179

Bordun   182
Chordal Accompaniment   183
Chord Inversions   191
Introducing the Structural Components of Harmony: Suggested Sequencing by Grade Level   195
Written and Performance-Related Assessments Through Cooperative Learning Activities: Harmony   196

Section II   Developing Musical Skills   199

9 *The Singing Voice*   199
Adult Voice   199
Vocal Mechanism   200
Adult Voice Classifications   200
Voice Registers   201
Characteristics of the Child's Voice at the Primary Level   203
Characteristics of the Child's Voice at the Upper Elementary Level   204
Solving Vocal Problems in the Older Student   204
Helping Children Find Their Singing Voice   206
Physical Characteristics of Good Singing   209
Objectives and Guidelines for Singing at the Elementary Level   210
Teaching a Song by Rote   211
Teaching a Song by Note   214
Written and Performance-Related Assessments Through Cooperative Learning Activities:
    Singing Voice   222

10 *Playing Musical Instruments*   223
Playing Classroom Instruments   223
Playing the Orff Barred Instruments   236
Playing the Soprano Recorder   243
Playing the Autoharp   258
Playing the Guitar   261
Playing Keyboard Instruments   267
Written and Performance-Related Assessments Through Cooperative Learning Activities:
    Instruments   273

11 *Listening Activities and Materials*   274
Goals for Listening Activities   274
Guidelines for Listening   274
Organizing Listening Activities   275
Written and Performance-Related Assessments Through Cooperative Learning Activities:
    Listening   293

12 *Movement and Children*   294
Preparing for Movement Activities   294
Beginning Movement Activities   295
Categories of Movement   297
Movement and Space   299
Movement and Improvisation   301
Movement and Dynamics   302
Circle Games   302
Folk Dances   306
Written and Performance-Related Assessments Through Cooperative Learning Activities:
    Movement   312

Section III   Organizing Musical Experiences   313

13 *Lesson Planning*   *313*
Characteristics of the Group   313
What Shall I Teach?   313
How Shall I Teach?   319
Cooperative Learning   319
How Will I Know I Taught It?   320
What Materials Shall I Use?   327

Section IV   Teaching Music in Specialized Areas   329

14 *Integrating Music Across the Curriculum*   *329*
Social Studies (Grade 3)   329
Mathematics (Grades 1 and 2)   331
Literature (Grades 5 and 6)   332
Cultural Studies/Literature/Drama/Poetry/Science (Grades 5 and 6)   335
Selected Pieces of Music for Integrated Activities   342
U.S. and World History   342
Science   345
Physical Education   346
Related Arts   346
Integration of the Arts   349
Written and Performance-Related Assessments Through Cooperative Learning Activities:
   Specialized Areas   350

15 *Special Education and Mainstreaming*   *351*
Learners Who Present Variations in the Music Settings   351
Mainstreaming   351
Inclusion   351
Who Are Learners Who Present Variation?   352
Inclusion in the Music Classroom   355
Musical Adaptations for Use in the "Inclusive" Setting   358
Classroom Management in an All-Inclusive Setting   372
Written and Performance-Related Assessments Through Cooperative Learning Activities:
   Learners Who Present Variations in the Music Setting   373

Glossary   374

Appendix A   Chapter Correlation for National Standards for Arts Education   380

Appendix B   Instructional Materials   382

Credits   388

Index   389

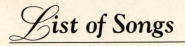

List of Songs

Song	Composer/Type/Country	Chapter	Page	Key/Tonal Center	Major/Minor/Pentatonic	Meter
A-Hunting We Will Go	English Game Song	12	310	G	Major	2/4
*Above the Plain	Czechoslovakian Folk Song	14	348	F	Major	2/4
Achshav	Israeli Folk Song	10, 12	249, 308	G	Major	2/4
*Al Citron	Latin American	12	304	G	Major	2/4
All Through the Night	Welsh Folk Song	3	78	G	Major	4/4
America	Smith/Carey	3	94	G	Major	3/4
America the Beautiful	Bates/Ward	3/6	93, 150	C	Major	4/4
Animals in the Zoo	Boyer-Alexander	15	365	F	Major	2/4
Arirang	Korean Folk Song	8	176	G	Pentatonic	3/4
Au Clair de la Lune	French Folk Song	8	188	F	Major	4/4
Autumn Comes	English Folk Song adapted to German text	3	86	d	Minor	6/4
Away in a Manger	Müller	3	99	G	Major	3/4
Battle Hymn of the Republic	Howe/Steffe	3	94	B♭	Major	4/4
Bingo	Scottish Folk Song	3	78	E	Major	2/4
*Bingo	East St. Louis Version	12	309	G	Major	6/8
Bluebird	Game Song	3, 6	88, 155	D/C	Pentatonic	4/4, 2/4
Boatman, The	African-American Song	10	245	G	Pentatonic	4/4
Bounce High	Traditional	3, 8	70, 71, 176	D/F	Pentatonic	2/4
Bow Wow Wow	Game Song	6, 8	138, 177	F	Pentatonic	4/4
Button	American Game Song	9	218	F	Pentatonic	2/4
C-Saw	Boyer-Alexander	3	75	C	Major	3/4
Candles of Hanukkah	Jewish Folk Song	8	185	D	Minor	4/4
Chan-Mali-Chan	Malay Folk Song	3	101	F	Major	2/4
*Cherry Bloom (Sakura)	Japanese Folk Song	5	129	b	Pentatonic	2/2
Chickama Craney Crow	Southern Game Song	3	90	F	Pentatonic	6/8
Chop Sticks	American Folk Tune	10	256	C	Major	3/4
Chumbara, Chumbara	Canadian Folk Song	10	230	C	Major	4/4
Church Bells	Boyer-Alexander	3	66	C	Major	6/8
Circle Round the Zoo	American Street Song	3, 12	89, 304	D	Pentatonic	4/4, 2/4
Clementine	American Folk Song	8	183, 186	G	Major	3/4
Clown, The	French Folk Song	5	122	D	Major	3/4
Cockles and Mussles	Irish Folk Song	8	192	G	Major	3/4
Come, Ye Thankful People, Come	Alford/Elvey	3	98	G	Major	4/4
Come Boating With Me	McDowell/Italian Folk Song	5	128	D	Major	3/4

*Songs preceded by an asterisk indicate inclusion on the CD accompanying the text.

Song	Composer Type/Country	Chapter	Page	Key/ Tonal Center	Major/Minor Pentatonic	Meter
Cradle Hymn	J. S. Bach	10	247	G	Major	4/4
Dancing Leaves	Rozmajzl	3	66	C	Major	2/4
Dog and Cat	American Folk Song	3	89	G	Pentatonic	4/4
Dona Nobis Pacem	Latin Hymn/Round	7	165	F	Major	3/4
*Down By the Station	Southern Folk Song	8	175	F	Major	4/4
*Draw Me a Bucket of Water	African-American	12	305	D	Major	4/4
Dreams	Hughes/Boyer-Alexander	10	241	d	Minor	3/4
Ermuntre Dich, Mein Schwacher Geist	J. S. Bach	7	170	G	Major	3/4
Farmer in the Dell, The	English Game Song	10	258	G	Major	6/8
*Follow the Drinking Gourd	Spiritual	14	330	e	Minor	4/4
For Health and Strength	Old English Round	3	99	F	Major	4/4
Frère Jacques (Are You Sleeping?)	French Round	7, 8	164, 165, 184	G/F	Major	4/4
Ghost of Tom	Traditional Round	5	124	e	Minor	4/4
Go Down, Moses	Spiritual	3	86	g	Minor	4/4
Good Mornin' Blues	Boyer-Alexander	11	292	F	Major	4/4
Good News	Spiritual	10	245	G	Pentatonic	4/4
Go To Sleep	Canadian Lullaby	3	63	D	Pentatonic	4/4
Grandma Grunts	Traditional	10	245	G	Pentatonic	4/4
Greatest Love of All, The	Creed/Mosser	15	369	A	Major	4/4
*Halloween Is Coming	Boyer-Alexander	3	80	f/F	Minor/Major	4/4
Hensel and Gretal Dance	Wette/Humperdinck	6	155	D	Major	2/4
*Hawaiian Rainbows	Hawaiian Folk Song	10	254	D	Major	2/2
Head and Shoulders	East St. Louis	15	364	E♭	Pentatonic	2/4
Hey, Ho! Nobody Home	English Round	7	166	e	Minor	4/4
Hey, Betty Martin	American Folk Song	10	229	G	Major	4/4
Hickory, Dickory Dock	Mother Goose/Elliot	5	130	C	Major	6/8
Hoo, Hoo!	Crowninshield	5	125	G	Major	4/4
Hop Old Squirrel	African-American	6	156	F	Pentatonic	2/4
Hot Cross Buns	England	10	245	G	Pentatonic	4/4
How Do You Do Ev'rybody	Boyer-Alexander	12	299	G	Major	4/4
How Many Miles to Babylon?	American Game Song	10	246	G	Pentatonic	4/4
*Hummingbird, The	American Folk Melody	10	234	D	Major	3/4
*Ida Red	Kentucky Folk Song	10	242	F	Pentatonic	2/4
If I Had a Hammer	Harp/Seeger	15	368	E♭	Major	4/4
I Got a Letter	South Carolina	5	122	e	Pentatonic	4/4
*I'm Gonna Sing	Spiritual	9	212	G	Major	4/4
Jig Jog Jig Jog	Edmonds	5	125	C	Major	4/4
Jim Along Josie	American Folk Song	3, 10	89, 248	B♭/G	Pentatonic	2/4
Johnny Has Gone for a Soldier	Revolutionary War Song	3	85	a	Minor	4/4
Jolly Miller, The	New England Song	6	139	G	Pentatonic	2/2
Jolly Old Saint Nicholas	Traditional Carol	7	170	G	Major	2/4

Song	Composer Type/Country	Chapter	Page	Key/Tonal Center	Major/Minor Pentatonic	Meter
Joshua Fought the Battle of Jericho	Spiritual	8	189	d	Minor	4/4
*Land of the Silver Birch	Canadian Folk Song	9	219	d	Pentatonic	2/4
*La Piñata	Mexican Folk Song	3, 10	77, 255	B♭, C	Major	2/4
Laughing Song	Sweden	9	221	C	Major	4/4
Lavender's Blue	England	8	180	D	Major	6/8
Let's Take a Walk	Boyer-Alexander	15	365	F	Major	2/4
*Lightly Row	Germany	6	158	F	Major	2/4
Little Bunny Foo Foo	Traditional	9	206	F	Major	2/4
Little Dappled Cow, The	Traditional	10	251	C	Major	4/4
'Liza Jane	American Folk Song	3	87	C	Pentatonic	2/4
Loch Lomond	Scotland	5	132	G	Major	4/4
London Bridge	England	5, 6	124, 154	F	Major	2/4
Looby Loo	American Folk Song	12	303	F	Major	6/8
*Look at Me	Boyer-Alexander	15	366	C	Major	4/4
Love Somebody	American Folk Song	10	260	F	Major	2/4
Lucy Locket	American Game Song	9	218	C	Pentatonic	2/4
Magic Penny, The	Reynolds	9	213	E♭	Major	4/4
Make New Friends	Round	7, 10	166, 263	E♭/D	Major	4/4
Mango Walk	Jamaican Calypso	10	253	F	Major	2/2
Marching	Hungary	6	137, 152	F	Pentatonic	2/4
*Martin Luther King	Boyer-Alexander	10	272	C	Major	4/4
*Mary Ann	Calypso	10	231	F	Major	2/2
Mein Hut (My Hat)	German Folk Song	8	187	C	Major	3/4
Merrily We Roll Along	Traditional	10	263	D	Pentatonic	4/4
Mill Wheel	Traditional	8	178	C	Pentatonic	2/4
Mister Rabbit	African-American	5	131	G	Pentatonic	2/4
Moon Shine	Boyer-Alexander	3	66	C	Major	3/4
Most Done Ling'ring Here	African-American	5	133	g	Pentatonic	2/4
Mulberry Bush	English Game Song	7, 12	167, 303	F	Major	6/8
*Music Alone Shall Live	German Round	7	168	F	Major	3/4
My Home's in Montana	Cowboy Song	10	265	C	Major	3/4
New River Train	American Folk Song	3	78	C	Major	2/4
*Nighttime	Dalton/Hungarian Folk Song	5	121	e	Minor	4/4
*Nobody Knows the Trouble I've Seen	Spiritual	6	145, 156	G	Major	4/4
Now Let Me Fly	Spiritual	9	219	G	Pentatonic	2/4
Oats, Peas, Beans	English Game Song	10	247	G	Major	6/8
O, Christmas Tree	German Traditional	3	102	F	Major	3/4
*O Hanukkah	Jewish Traditional	3	103	d	Minor	4/4
Oh, Rocka My Soul	Hairston/Spiritual	7	171	F	Major	4/4
Oh, Susanna	Foster	6, 10	136, 250	F	Major	2/4

Song	Composer Type/Country	Chapter	Page	Key/ Tonal Center	Major/Minor Pentatonic	Meter
Old Brass Wagon	American Dance Song	12	307	G	Pentatonic	2/4
One, Two, Tie My Shoe	American Traditional	9	216	F	Pentatonic	2/4
*On Top of Old Smokey	American Folk Song	10	264	D	Major	4/4
Oranges and Lemons	English Folk Song	9, 10	220, 270, 271	C	Major	3/4
Over My Head	Spiritual	10	254	G	Major	4/4
Over the River	Traditional	3	98	C	Major	6/8
Pat Works on the Railway	American Railway Song	3	92	b	Minor	6/8
Paw Paw Patch	American Singing	3	79	D♭	Major	2/4
Pito Pito	Mexican Game Song	10	239	C	Major	4/4
Poor Little Kitty Cat	American Folk Song	6, 10	140, 248	G	Pentatonic	4/4
Pourquoi	American Folk Song	10	250	C	Pentatonic	4/4
Red River Valley	American Folk Song	12	311	G	Major	4/4
Riding in the Buggy	Play-Party Song	6, 10	144, 250	C	Pentatonic	2/4
Ring Around the Rosy	American Game Song	9	218	C	Pentatonic	2/4
Rock-a-My Soul	Spiritual/Boyer-Alexander	9	205	E♭	Major	2/2
Rock of Ages	Gottlieb/Jewish Traditional	3	102	E♭	Major	4/4
Rocky Mountain	Southern Folk Song	6	136	C	Pentatonic	2/4
Round and Round We Go	Überliedfest	12	308	e	Minor	4/4
Row, Row, Row Your Boat	American Round	8	182, 184	C	Major	6/8
*Sailing on the Ocean	Game Song	3	66	F	Pentatonic	2/4
San Sereni	Hispanic Children's Song, Puerto Rican Variant	8	179	D	Major	2/4, 6/8
*Santa Lucia	Oliphant/Cottrau	3	91	C	Major	3/8
Scarborough Fair	England	10	253	F	Major	3/4
Scotland's Burning	Traditional	6	153	G	Pentatonic	2/4
Shake Them 'Simmons Down	Southern Play–Party Song	12	307	G	Pentatonic	2/4
*Shenandoah	American Chantey	3	79	E♭	Major	4/4, 3/4
*Shoo, Fly	Reeves/Campbell	6	143	D	Major	2/4
Silent Night	Mohr/Gruber	3	99	C	Major	6/8
Simple Gifts	Shaker Tune	10	252	G	Major	2/2
Sing Together	English Round	10	259	G	Major	6/8
Skin and Bones	Southern Folk Song	3	97	e	Pentatonic	6/8
Skip To My Lou	American Singing Game	7	166	F	Major	4/4
Sleep, Baby, Sleep	Germany	5	124	F	Major	4/4
St. Paul's Steeple	English Folk Song	10	233	C	Major	4/4
Star-Spangled Banner	Key/Smith	3	95	B♭	Major	3/4
Star Light	American Folk Song	9	216	C	Pentatonic	2/4
Stars Shinin'	Texas	10	251	C	Major	4/4
Sweet Betsy from Pike	American Folk Song	10	259	C	Major	3/4
There's a Brown Girl in the Ring	Jamaican Folk Song	8	197	C	Major	4/4
There Was an Old Witch	Traditional	3	97	d	Pentatonic	4/4
This Land Is Your Land	Guthrie	3	96	G	Major	2/4

Song	Composer Type/Country	Chapter	Page	Key/ Tonal Center	Major/Minor Pentatonic	Meter
This Old Man	England	7	167	F	Major	2/4
*This Train, Oh When the Saints Swing Low	Spiritual/ Boyer-Alexander	8	181	G	Major	4/4
Three Rogues, The	Ohio Folk Song	5	126, 127	G	Major	2/2
*Tinga Layo	West Indies	8	187, 190	C	Major	4/4
Tom Dooley	American Ballad	10	263	D	Major	4/4
Touch a Star	Boyer-Alexander	3	66	C	Major	6/8
Turn! Turn! Turn!	Ecclesiastes/Seeger	6	157	C	Major	4/4
Twelve Days of Christmas, The	English Traditional	3	100	F	Major	4/4
Viva La Musica	Praetorius	10	252	G	Major	4/4
Wayfaring Stranger	Spiritual	3	85	d	Minor	3/4
*Welcome Song	Boyer-Alexander	14	332	F	Major	4/4
When That I Was a Tiny Little Boy	Elizabethan Song	5	131	d	Minor	2/4
When the Train Comes Along	American Folk Song	9	220	C	Pentatonic	4/4
Where Is Thumbkin?	American Folk Song	3	77	F	Major	4/4
Wind the Bobbin	Winding Game	5	129	G	Pentatonic	4/4
Willum	Traditional	3	85	e	Minor	2/4
*Young Man Who Wouldn't Hoe Corn, The	American Frontier Ballad	10	249	e	Pentatonic	2/4

In addition to the songs asterisked in the List of Songs, a number of vocal, instrumental, and orchestral selections discussed in the text are included on the CD that accompanies the text.

Selection	Composer	Chapter	Page	Example of
Poem Electronique	Varèse	4	110	Electronic music
"Habanera" from Carmen	Bizet	4	111	Mezzo-soprano voice
"Mephisto's Serenade" from Faust	Gounod	4	111	Bass voice
From Flight of the Bumblebee	Rimsky-Korsakov	4	113	Violin
From Stars and Stripes Forever	Sousa	4	115	Trombone
From "In the Hall of the Mountain King," Peer Gynt Suite No. 1	Grieg	4	117	Bassoon
From Capriccio Espagnol	Rimski-Korsakov	4	118	Castanets
"Trio" from Eine Kleine Nachtmusik	Mozart	4	119	Binary Form (AABB)
Mazurka No. 24	Chopin	6	146	Ternary form
"Waltz" from Masquerade Suite	Khachaturian	6	147	Waltz
"Heiden Röslein"	Schubert	6	151	Stanza repetition
"Alleluia"	Gregorian chant	7	162	Monophonic texture
Little Fugue in G Minor	Bach	7	168	Polyphonic texture
Opening, Also Sprach Zarathustra	Strauss	11	277	Call chart listening activity (Timbre)
"Ecce gratum" from Carmina Burana	Orff	11	278	Call chart listening activity (Form)

Selection	Composer	Chapter	Page	Example of
"Ballet of the Unhatched Chicks" from *Pictures at an Exhibition*	Moussorgsky	11	287	Call chart listening activity (Timbre)
From *Maple Leaf Rag*	Joplin	11	290	Ragtime form
"Frightening," from *Scenes of Childhood*	Schumann	11	275	Call charts using pictures
From *American in Paris*	Gershwin	14	342	American music
From *The Planets*	Holst	14	345	Excerpt for science curriculum

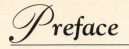

Preface

As more and more institutions of higher education require earlier and more extensive preclinical experiences for the elementary classroom teacher, there is an increase in the need for well-sequenced textbooks with readily useable methods and materials. *Music Fundamentals, Methods, and Materials for the Elementary Classroom Teacher*, Third Edition, provides a thorough presentation of the basic fundamentals of music required of a musically knowledgeable teacher. Fundamentals are presented within the context of pedagogical techniques intended for use when teaching children. It is the authors' intent that as college students proceed through Section I, "Teaching the Elements of Music to Children," they will come to an understanding of the fundamentals of music by using the same sequence that they, as teachers, would use to present the material to children.

WHO WILL USE THIS TEXT

This text has been written for the elementary education student who has had little or no previous background in music. Often, the anticipation of studying music fundamentals and methods is characterized by both anxiety and excitement. Although prospective teachers may appreciate the need for having a strong background in music, they are often fearful of not being "talented" enough for the task. This text is designed to eliminate much of this anxiety by providing students with carefully sequenced procedures that move slowly and take little for granted.

Because music fundamentals are presented within the context of methods that can be used with children, this text can also serve as a resource for elementary music majors, students in special education, and early childhood majors.

CHANGES IN THE THIRD EDITION

Many of the suggestions made by reviewers of both the second edition and final draft of the third edition have been incorporated in the third edition. These suggestions have been an invaluable guide in approaching the revision of this text. One of the primary requests made by reviewers—especially from those who currently use the book—was "Don't change the format." The highly praised format of the first two editions has been left intact for this third edition. At the same time, improvements have been made to the layout, especially for easier reading of the visuals.

Several important changes have been made to the content:

- **Inclusion of the National Standards for Arts Education.** Chapter 1, "Children and Music," includes a detailed discussion of the National Standards for Arts Education, and throughout the text, appropriate reference is made to the Standards. For example, Chapter 9, "The Singing Voice," cites specific requirements as to reading and notating music, and the Cooperative Learning Activities at the end of each chapter now incorporate the Written and Performance-Related Assessments suggested by the National Standards.
- **Expanded coverage of Orff method.** Chapter 10, "Playing Musical Instruments," contains a new, lengthy discussion of Orff Barred instruments and includes three specific lesson plans using the Orff method.

- **Extensive revision of Chapter 14, "Integrating Music Across the Curriculum."** Each section of Chapter 14 represents a specific grade level, and its lesson plan reflects the National Standards criteria of Goal, Objectives, Concepts, Materials, Procedure, and Assessment. A new section on The Power of Rhythm focuses on the integration of arts across the curriculum with a presentation about the music and folklore of Africa.
- **Extensive revision of Chapter 15, "Special Education and Mainstreaming."** Chapter 15 has been extensively revised to reflect the latest guidelines and strategies for working with the complex diversities that teachers encounter in inclusive classroom settings.
- **New songs and listening selections.** Throughout the text many songs and listening selections have been added, with special attention to those reflecting the growing multicultural environment of the classroom.
- **A CD packaged with the book.** Perhaps most exciting, this edition includes a CD which provides audio versions of many of the selections mentioned in the book. Prospective teachers will find this an invaluable tool—both in their own current learning and in their future teaching.

The following section explains how these new elements enhance the organization of the text and describe, for new users, how that organization can be used most effectively.

HOW THIS TEXT IS ORGANIZED

This text has been written primarily for classes in which fundamentals and methods of music are taught *simultaneously*. To meet the needs of this type of multipurpose course, the text has been divided into four sections.

Section I: Teaching the Elements of Music to Children Chapters 2–8 include step-by-step procedures formulated to help the prospective classroom teacher understand the structural components relating to each of the basic elements of music. These musical components are introduced and reinforced through musical experiences that are comprehensive, yet easily understood by nonmusicians.

Chapters 2–8 have several noteworthy features. Each new music component is highlighted in a **Focus** box, prior to its sequential presentation, for easy identification and retrieval. Following each Focus is one or more **Learning** statements that specify the aspect of the Focus that will be presented. **Strategies** for teaching each new music component follow the Learning statements. The purpose of these step-by-step teaching procedures is twofold: they provide methodology that college students can use when teaching music in their own classroom; and they provide the means whereby college students with limited or no musical background will also come to understand the material that is being taught. Thus, even though these Strategies contain methods that can be used with children, they are also the methods through which college students will grow in their understanding of the structural components of each music element. **Visuals** that will help clarify the Strategies have been included. These will not only help the college students understand the material being presented but will also give direction to the preparation of charts, overheads, flash cards, and handouts in their own elementary classrooms.

The **music selections** included in each chapter have been chosen for their appeal to children and their potential for clearly demonstrating each Learning under consideration. An emphasis on songs representing a variety of countries and ethnic groups also influenced the choice of the selection, as did the need for a variety of tonal centers and time signatures. Songs—with their origins, tonal centers, and time sequences—have been classified in the preceding List of Songs. **Sequencing charts** have been included at the end of each chapter where they serve a practical purpose; namely, Chapters 2, 3, 5, 6, 7, and 8. Classroom teachers often find it difficult to decide at what grade level a particular learning should be introduced. Choices must be made based on what is known about child growth and development, which is summarized in Chapter 1. With this goal in mind, each new music component identified in a Focus box has been sequenced according to the grade where it might be first introduced. This sequence should serve only as a guide. It can be adjusted to meet the needs of a class, to accommodate a different sequence used in the elementary school's adopted music series, or to parallel the sequence used by the music specialist in the school.

Written and performance-related assessments as evidenced through **cooperative learning activities** have been included for Chapters 2–12, 14, and 15. These can be used in two ways: (a) the college class can be divided into groups to work through the activities; and/or (b) each college student or group of students can select one or more activities to develop into a handout that can be used by elementary students in a cooperative learning setting. In an actual classroom setting with children, the cooperative learning activities may be used as performance-assessment tools. Each is designed to provide a simple but authentic testing of student understanding and growth.

Readers will note the absence of any musical score in the chapter on teaching rhythm. This is intentional because at this point in their learning, most college students have difficulty reading music. The music score is introduced in Chapter 3 on melody, where students begin to read pitches placed on a staff.

Although key signatures are usually not indicated in music using the pentatonic scale, we have given every song included in the text, even pentatonic songs, a key signature. Students beginning their study of music usually have fewer problems identifying the tonal center of pentatonic songs if a key signature is indicated.

Section II: Developing Musical Skills   This section focuses on the learning of minimum musical skills required of teachers who plan to incorporate a music program into their classroom curriculum. The music skills of playing instruments, singing, listening, and moving are essential to the better understanding and reinforcement of music elements and their structural components presented in Section I.

Section III: Organizing the Musical Experience   In this section, students are guided through the mechanics of preparing, sequencing, and evaluating the music activities contained in the daily music lesson. Attention is given to the ways in which the formulation of goals and objectives can lead a teacher more successfully through the lesson planning process.

Section IV: Teaching Music in Specialized Areas   This section addresses two important aspects of the elementary music program: integrating music with other subjects; and mainstreaming special education students. Background information and teaching strategies are included in both of these chapters.

A glossary, two appendixes (Appendix A, Chapter Correlation for National Standards for Arts Education, and Appendix B, Instructional Materials), and an index are included at the end of the text.

HOW TO USE THIS TEXT

This text can be as flexible as the user wishes it to be. Some teachers may choose to adjust the overall order of the chapters, if this better serves the needs of a particular class. For example, the chapters on timbre and movement could be taught before the chapter on rhythm. Some teachers will want to present portions of the chapters involving skills development much sooner, at appropriate points throughout Chapters 2–8. For instance, it might help the development of music reading skills if the soprano recorder was introduced in Chapter 3, when studying melody. Some teachers may also want to introduce solmization in Chapter 3.

Because this text is written primarily for college students enrolled in classes that combine music fundamentals and methods, the format used here was considered the most appropriate; that is, teaching the elements of music one at a time, rather than combining elements according to elementary grade levels. It must be emphasized, however, that when teaching music to children, appropriate components of several music elements should be addressed in each music lesson. This point is clarified in Chapter 13 on lesson planning.

Technical music terminology has been italicized at the place where it is defined in the text. The same terms can be found in the glossary, for easy reference.

Fifty-one familiar recorded music selections (both songs and orchestral excerpts) included in the text can be found on the compact disc that accompanies the text. Other recordings can be found on Bowmar, Folkway, or RCA Adventures in Music recordings or on recordings in the local library.

Finally, the most important approach for teaching music that is used in this book comes from the authors' basic philosophy: What is taught in a music lesson should flow from the musical example being used. Whenever possible, the elements of music and their structural components should not be taught in isolation from the music in which they occur. Children should experience the music first. Afterward, a structural component, such as a triplet or a phrase, can be identified and labeled for conscious learning. Practice and further exploration of the learning will follow, with the use of culturally diverse musical examples that should ensure a lasting effect on the students' musical education.

ACKNOWLEDGMENTS

The authors would like to acknowledge the following reviewers: Anthony Arnone, Ripon College; Kimberly Jo Burns, Ball State University; Richard Dugger, University of New Orleans; Nancy Ferguson, University of Arizona; Dianne Hardy, Dickinson State University; Ramona Holmes, Seattle Pacific University; Margaret Kelly, Illinois State University; Sandra Mathias, Capital University; Jan McCrary, Ohio State University, Louise Patrick, Eastern Michigan University; Janet Robbins, West Virginia University; Marg Schmidt, St. Cloud State University; Charlotte Smelser, University of Kentucky; Richard Sorensen, Western Oregon University; and Cynthia Taggart, Michigan State University.

Michon Rozmajzl
René Boyer-Alexander

Music Fundamentals, Methods, and Materials for the Elementary Classroom Teacher

Teaching the Elements of Music to Children

Children and Music

WHY TEACH MUSIC TO CHILDREN?

Classroom teachers are very important people in the lives of children. They are responsible for contributing to the total development of each child in their classrooms. Not only will they help students develop their intellectual potential, but they must provide opportunities for social, ethical, emotional, physical, and aesthetic development as well. Aesthetic development involves growth in a person's sensitivity to the expressive qualities found in things: in the lines of a car, in a sunset, in a Picasso painting, or a Mozart symphony. Expressive qualities are those qualities that call forth an "ah-h" from the perceiver. Because these qualities are present in music, growth in music awareness is as important as the three "Rs" to a child's being able to enter into the full experience and enjoyment of life. Not only music educators make this claim, but also such prominent educators as Maxine Greene,[1] professor emeritus at Columbia University's Teachers College and G. Larson[2] have stressed the importance of the arts in the school curriculum. Music is for everyone and should be accessible to every child in the elementary classroom. More specifically, the following postulates are among the most important reasons why music should be included in every child's daily classroom activities:

1. The enjoyment and understanding of music gives expression to the deepest movements of the human spirit. The human need for expression is second only to our needs for food, water, and companionship. Learning to respond sensitively through music helps to satisfy this need.
2. Growth in musical understanding can result in the development of basic musical skills needed for making future choices for enriching the quality of life during all stages of development. Today's child is tomorrow's audience. To be able to appreciate music more fully as listener and observer at concerts or in one's own home when using the stereo or television is an exciting potential.
3. Through the study of music, the imagination and creativity of a child can be developed for more creative living in our mechanized society. The development of these attributes is valuable, not only in the arts, but in all areas of endeavor.
4. Our music tells us not only who we are, but also points to who we can be. It is part of our cultural memory, making connections among the folk songs of Appalachia, the emotional contexts of the blues, the spirituality of a hymn or Mozart Mass, the courage reverberating through Copland's *Lincoln Portrait*, or the determination of the Western settlers as portrayed in the songs of our

[1]Greene, "Why Ignore Forms of Art?" *Education Week* (February 19, 1997).
[2]Larson, "American Canvas" (1997), Washington, D.C.: National Endowment for the Arts, p. 97.

country's cowboys, miners, and railroad workers. Our children should be made aware of the many ways music has captured and preserved our history.

5. An important part of our nation's multiethnic and multinational heritages will be transmitted from generation to generation through education in music. Whether or not the traditions of our diverse culture are respected, valued, and passed on depends on our ability to take part in the rituals associated with those traditions. The learning of patriotic songs and of singing games and dances associated with the varied aspects of our folk culture depends heavily on classroom musical activities.

6. Participating in creatively planned musical activities helps build a child's self-esteem and understanding of others. Making a circle, singing together in tune, and playing instruments in harmony represent a few of the many musical activities that require and promote discipline and sensitivity towards self and others.

7. Knowledge about the arts, especially music, is important for understanding more fully many of the other subject areas within the general education curriculum. Examining the derivation of African American spirituals and the symbolism found in their texts and performance techniques is just one example of how music contributes to a better understanding of the subject of history as it relates to slavery in America. Foreign languages and cultures, physics of sound production, and literature are subject areas integrally linked to music.

8. Music education reinforces a student's understanding of the use of nonverbal symbols for communication. Because the symbol systems of language, music, and mathematics are unique to the human mind, the concept of literacy needs to be expanded beyond the use of words.

NATIONAL STANDARDS FOR ARTS EDUCATION

All human beings engage in fundamental music processes such as performing, creating, and responding to music. Learning music concepts, especially through singing, playing instruments, moving to music, and creating music, empowers students to gain musical skills and knowledge. Reading and notating music allow students to explore music independently and with others. Listening to, analyzing, and evaluating are also important building blocks in developing musical competencies. "Because music is a basic expression of human culture, every student should have access to a balanced, comprehensive, and sequential program of study in music" (National Standards for Arts Education, p. 26).

The passage of **Goals 2000: Educate America Act** permitted the arts to be written into federal law. The law acknowledged that the arts are a core subject, as important as English, mathematics, social studies, science, and foreign language. Title II of the act addresses the issue of education standards. A National Education Standards Improvement Council, whose job was to work with appropriate organizations to determine the criteria for certifying voluntary content standards, defined three objectives:

1. to ensure that the standards are internationally competitive,

2. to ensure that they reflect the best knowledge about teaching and learning, and

3. to ensure that they have been developed through a broad-based, open adoption process.

The national standards have since allowed classroom and music teachers to approach the teaching of music based on a well-designed outline of musical competencies. These competencies allow for flexibility in planning and at the same time provide children with the knowledge and skills that will equip them to enter society, work productively, and make contributions as citizens.

Nine national content standards for music in the public schools exist today, consisting of: (1) singing alone, and with others, a varied repertoire of music, (2) performing on instruments, alone and with others, a varied repertoire of music, (3) improvising melodies, variations, and accompaniments, (4) composing and arranging music within specified guidelines, (5) reading and notating music, (6) listening to music, (7) evaluating music and music performance, (8) understanding relationships among the other arts and disciplines outside the arts, and (9) understanding music in relation to history and culture.

national content standards

LEARNING THEORY APPLIED TO MUSIC EDUCATION

How children learn at each stage in their development determines what they are capable of doing physically and neurologically. Children grow in their love for music and become increasingly more secure working with musical concepts and skills when musical activities are well planned for successful completion. To accomplish these objectives, teachers must be well schooled in how children learn and what children are capable of doing and understanding during each of their growth stages.

The categories given below are approximate and presuppose an awareness that some children develop either more slowly or more quickly than other children. Implications for teaching music follow the discussion of growth traits in each developmental stage.

Nursery School and Kindergarten (ages 4 and 5)

Four- and five-year-old children are growing rapidly, but their large muscles are better developed than the smaller ones. They are constantly active and tend to fatigue quickly. Their voices are small and pitch is generally underdeveloped. These children love repetitious activities; they are capable of varying spans of attention depending on their interest. They are imitative and talkative, with a great deal of exaggeration. Both age groups learn best by manipulating concrete objects; much of their learning is nonverbal. They are inquisitive, creative, spontaneous, and ask many questions. They are able to group things according to similarities. Although they tend to be individualistic and self-centered, five-year-olds are more capable of working in groups than four-year-olds.

Four- and five-year-olds enjoy organizing sounds that express a story or accompany a song. Action songs and finger plays appeal to their imaginative natures. Their favorite chants and songs usually have silly words and much rhyme. They need many opportunities to match pitches and to order the direction of musical sounds in terms of going up, going down, and staying the same. They are able to classify sounds as to high and low, loud and soft, fast and slow, smooth and disconnected. They can reproduce sounds and patterns both vocally and with instruments. These children are able to play simple, repeated instrumental accompaniments to their songs and to improvise on simple classroom instruments. They show rapid improvement in stepping to the basic beat; five-year-olds can also learn simple dance steps.

First- and Second-Grade Children (ages 6 and 7)

The voice of the six-year-old is light and generally high in pitch. Although six-year-olds are usually active and restless, seven-year-olds tend to alternate between active and quiet activities and desire periods of privacy. Both age groups are eager to learn; they are inventive, imaginative, imitative, and curious. They like to construct things out of many kinds of odd materials. They learn through manipulation of concrete materials, but the reasoning powers of the seven-year-old are developing rapidly. Seven-year-olds seem to have less confidence than when they were six, but both age groups look for positive feedback and encouragement. Group activities are becoming increasingly more popular.

These children enjoy singing, but six-year-olds tend to want to shout at first. They are easily encouraged, however, to sing tunefully, with a pleasant tone, and will imitate a teacher's sensitive approach to word meanings and varying moods found in songs. Both age groups are able to distinguish beat and rhythm. They are capable of creating and playing simple accompaniments on rhythm and melody instruments. Group participation in partner and folk dances is enjoyed, but repetition for perfection is welcomed more by the seven-year-old. The seven-year-old's singing is becoming very accurate and is characterized by a pleasing, light tone. This age group can perform simple rounds and can hold its own pitch while the teacher sings or plays a contrasting part. Seven-year-olds are ready to begin reading and writing music.

Third- and Fourth-Grade Children (ages 8 and 9)

The attention span of eight- and nine-year-olds is expanding. They are more co-ordinated and can enjoy activities involving small-muscle movements. They have greater control of their singing voice, which is improving in quality and range. They are sensitive to criticism and seek praise from adults. The peer group rises in importance, along with secret codes and same-sex activities. They are interested in patriotism and in other cultures, with the nine-year-old's interest expanding into the areas of hero worship and folklore. These children enjoy news and gossiping, collecting a wide variety of objects, and role playing. They have greater abilities for self-evaluation and for distinguishing right from wrong; however, they often become depressed when their outcomes don't measure up to their expectations. Eight- and nine-year-olds still learn best through manipulating concrete materials and through guided, active participation, but they are capable of mastering symbolic systems because they can classify objects and ideas abstractly.

Eight- and nine-year-olds are now physically able to progress rapidly when learning to play the piano and other instruments. They are interested in sounds produced by instruments and how these instruments are constructed. The harmonic sense of nine-year-olds is also developing; they enjoy singing in harmony or adding harmonic accompaniment to their songs. They can easily sing while playing a second part. Folk songs, games, and dances are particularly interesting to these age groups, as well as music materials from a wide variety of cultures. These students are increasingly able to understand the abstractions of music notation; they readily respond to reading and writing challenges through games and performances. Both choral and instrumental group activities are particularly enjoyable to these students. Although they won't normally choose partners of the opposite sex for dances or games, once partners have been assigned, students seem to enjoy these types of musical activities.

Fifth- and Sixth-Grade Children (ages 10 and 11)

Peer group approval and "belonging" begin to take top priority for ten- and eleven-year-olds. Although these students work well both alone and in groups, they are often unpredictable, defiant, and overcritical of themselves and others. Eleven-year-olds, particularly girls, grow rapidly with corresponding awkwardness and self-consciousness. Some sixth-grade boys will also experience the beginnings of the changing voice. Fifth and sixth graders are capable of refining the mental and physical skills that were developing in their middle elementary years; skills requiring minute coordination are mastered now. Abstract thinking is well developed, and numbers and musical notation can be more easily manipulated mentally. These students are able to conserve information; that is, information will be recognized as being the same even though its context changes. Ten- and eleven-year-olds seem to have insatiable curiosity and are open to learning many new things.

These students like to sing and are interested in a wide variety of songs; mystery, adventure, humor, outer space, and family life are all attractive themes. However, some students may be self-conscious because of physical changes in their bodies, and so will hesitate to sing. Some of these students have a vocal range of two octaves; music for the changing voice, however, must be chosen carefully. Singing in harmony is both challenging and satisfying. The desire of fifth- and sixth-grade children to know how and why makes the learning of music theory an enjoyable process. These students are becoming increasingly more interested in popular music and are avid listeners of this type of recorded music. Working with the songs and dances of national groups being studied in social science is also satisfying to these students.

With this background in how children learn, we are ready to consider a variety of techniques that can be used when teaching music to children.

INTRODUCTION

Rhythm is the most important of all musical elements. It is found in nature, in art and architecture, in speech, in movement, and in everyday life. Rhythm is that abstract phenomenon that unifies language, music, movement, and life itself. The recurrence of day and night, the change of seasons, the rotation of our planet on its axis, the progression from life to death, and the flow of the tides are all symbolic of the powerful presence that rhythm has in our environment.

There is rhythm in physiology: the beat of the pulse, regular breathing, the throbbing of the heart. In athletics rhythm is evident in the consistent strokes used to operate a rowboat or canoe and in the strides of a runner or hurdler.

Rhythm is generally accepted as the first type of musical expression used by primitive people. Rhythmic music no doubt served these civilizations as an accompaniment to the action of their dances, which were part of their religion as well as their entertainment.

Rhythm in music suggests a similar flow of motion with recurring high points or emphases and intervening points of relaxation. In this more restricted sense, *rhythm* can be defined as the varied lengths of sounds and silences over a basic pulse.

> *The whole of man's life stands*
> *in need of a right rhythm.*
> *—Plato*

FOCUS
Beat/Pulse

LEARNING   In our environment and in our own bodies, we experience the repetition of sounds and movements.

Strategies

Listen to sounds in the classroom that repeat—clock, wristwatch, heartbeat.
Recall repeated movements in the environment outside the classroom—shoveling snow, rowing a boat, stirring a cake, or hammering.
Feel your heart beating. Tap the recurring pattern that is felt.
Walk to your heartbeat. The teacher imitates the walk on a drum. The remaining students join in imitating the first student's walk.

Hint: Students should be given a specific signal, such as a double rap on the drum, to signify silence or cessation of movement during locomotor activities.

LEARNING   *Beat* is the underlying, unchanging, repeating pulse found in most music.

Strategies

While chanting the words of a familiar rhyme, have students tap their thighs (called *patching*) or shoulders to the underlying pulse, as in **Visual R1.**

	One,	two,	three,	four,
Say:	One,	two,	three,	four,
Tap:	X	X	X	X
	Ma-ry	at the	kitchen	door.
	X	X	X	X
	Five,	six,	se-ven	eight
	X	X	X	X
	Ma-ry	at the	gar-den	gate.
	X	X	X	X

Reinforce the awareness of beat by tapping it while chanting many rhymes or while singing a familiar song, such as "Hot Cross Buns," found in **Visual R2.** Notice that once the beat is established, it continues to be felt even if no words are sung or spoken.

VISUAL R2

	Hot	cross	buns;	
Sing:	Hot	cross	buns;	
Tap:	X	X	X	X
	Hot	cross	buns.	
	X	X	X	X
	One a	pen-ny	two a	pen-ny,
	X	X	X	X
	Hot	cross	buns.	
	X	X	X	X

Listen to short musical selections that have a strong, steady beat. Have students walk in a variety of ways or play rhythm instruments to the beat of these selections.

Provide students with many opportunities to read beat by creating charts containing pictorial representations known as *icons*. Children enjoy icons that relate to what is being said or sung. There should be an icon for every beat. Point to each beat while chanting or singing. Students should also practice pointing to each beat of the rhyme or song. See **Visual R3.**

VISUAL R3

☆	☆	☆	☆	☆	☆	☆	☆
Star-	light,	star-	bright	first	star I	see to-	night.
☆	☆	☆	☆	☆	☆	☆	☆
Wish I	may,	wish I	might,	have the	wish I	wish to-	night.

👟	👟	👟	👟
Cob-bler,	cob-bler,	mend my	shoe.
👟	👟	👟	👟
Get it	done by	half past	two.

LEARNING — *Rhythm* in music is the length of sound or silence in relation to the underlying beat.

Strategies

Have students chant a familiar rhyme. First say the rhyme while tapping the beat. Then repeat the rhyme while tapping the rhythm of each sound; that is, tap every syllable that is spoken. Place the words of the rhyme on the chalkboard or on a chart. Have a student mark each beat where it occurs in the rhyme. Then decide which sounds are long and which are short. Long and short sounds can be designated in a variety of ways, such as ——— for a long sound and — — for short sounds. Children enjoy using icons to designate long and short durations also. Place the long and short duration symbols above the words as students decide where they belong. See **Visual R4.**

VISUAL R4

Duration:	___	___	__	_	_
Say:	One,	two,	tie	my	shoe;
Beat:	X	X	X		X

Duration:	___	___	__	_	_
Three,	four,	shut	the	door;
X	X	X		X

Three,   four,   shut   the   door;
  X   X   X   X

Five,   six,   pick   up   sticks;
  X   X   X   X

Sev-en,   eight,   set   them   straight;
   X   X   X   X

Nine,   ten,   big   fat   hen.
  X   X   X   X

or

Duration:	⅄	⅄	⅄ ⅄	⅄
Say:	See,	saw,	up and	down,
Beat:	X	X	X	X
Duration:	⅄ ⅄	⅄ ⅄	⅄ ⅄	⅄
Say:	In the	air and	on the	ground.
Beat:	X	X	X	X

Have students practice moving their fingers along the long and short lines as they say the chant. Students should repeat these activities many times, using a variety of rhymes and songs.

With repeated experiences, students will also grow in their ability to distinguish between the even, steady nature of beat in contrast to the uneven, short and long combinations found in the rhythms of the sounds they are experiencing. To reinforce both beat and rhythm, divide the class into two groups. While saying a familiar rhyme or singing a song, have one group tap the beat and the other group tap the rhythms.

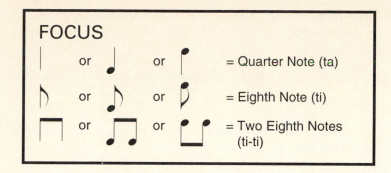

or ♩ or ♩	= Quarter Note (ta)
♪ or ♪ or ♪	= Eighth Note (ti)
⊓ or ♫ or ♫	= Two Eighth Notes (ti-ti)

LEARNING

Long sounds experienced in the rhymes chanted or sung above can be identified as *quarter notes;* short sounds can be called *eighth notes.*

Two short sounds (eighth notes) equal one long sound (quarter note).

Eighth notes are often used in pairs.

Rhythm syllables (ta, ti) are sometimes used as tools to facilitate the verbalizing of rhythm symbols.

Strategies

Using a "shorthand" notation called *stick notation* (| and ⊓), show students how the symbols used for long and short sounds (——, — —) can be replaced with musical symbols, called *notes.* The musical symbol for a long sound (——) is the quarter note (|); two short sounds (— —) become eighth notes (⊓). See **Visual R5.**

VISUAL R5

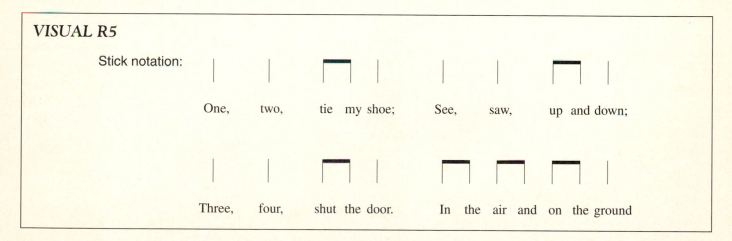

Stick notation:

One,   two,   tie my shoe;   See,   saw,   up and down;

Three,   four,   shut the door.   In the air and on the ground

Stick notation is a convenient shorthand method for designating notes and can be used at all grade levels. However, students should also be able to recognize and reproduce *standard notation,* identifying each of its parts:

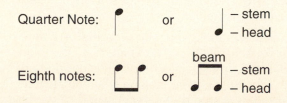

Quarter Note: ♩ or ♩ – stem / – head

Eighth notes: ♫ or ♫ beam – stem / – head

Although pairs of eighth notes are easier to read, students should know that eighth notes can stand alone with head, stem, and flag. Flags are always placed to the right of the note:

Students will find the replacing of stick notation with standard notation a simple process, as in **Visual R6.**

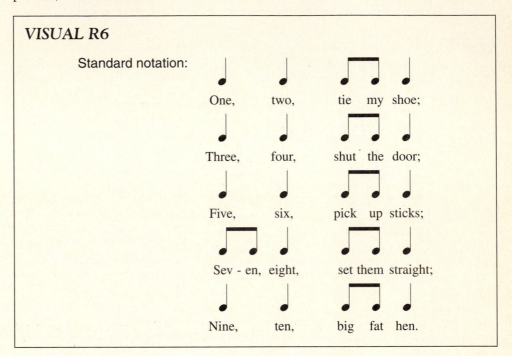

VISUAL R6

Standard notation:

One,   two,   tie my shoe;

Three,   four,   shut the door;

Five,   six,   pick up sticks;

Sev - en, eight,   set them straight;

Nine,   ten,   big fat hen.

Because it is harder and slower to use standard notation, stick notation is usually used when notating rhythm activities. Standard notation becomes essential when students begin reading and placing notes on a staff.

Students should have many opportunities to move in a variety of ways to quarter- and eighth-note rhythms. Place around each student's neck a circle containing the symbol of either two eighth notes or a quarter note:

As the teacher plays quarter notes on a drum, students wearing the quarter-note symbols should step to that rhythm. When the drum sounds eighth notes, students wearing the eighth-note symbols should respond. Later, the drum can be replaced with a melody instrument.

To reinforce a student's awareness of the duration of different sounds, teachers often use different *rhythm syllables* or "nicknames" to designate different rhythms. There is no standard rhythm syllable system, but the one presented here is used by many teachers. Choose a rhyme or song that the students know well. Work out its rhythms, deciding where there is one sound to the beat and where there are two sounds. Give to the quarter note the nickname *ta* and to the eighth note, *ti* (pronounced "tēē"). Have students verbalize the rhythms using nicknames, as in **Visual R7.**

VISUAL R7

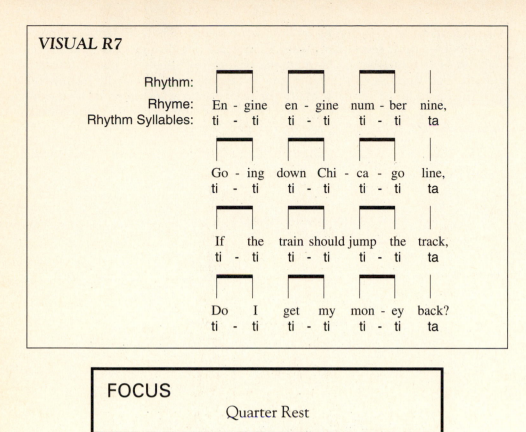

Rhythm:				
Rhyme:	En - gine	en - gine	num - ber	nine,
Rhythm Syllables:	ti - ti	ti - ti	ti - ti	ta

	Go - ing	down Chi -	ca - go	line,
	ti - ti	ti - ti	ti - ti	ta

	If the	train should	jump the	track,
	ti - ti	ti - ti	ti - ti	ta

	Do I	get my	mon - ey	back?
	ti - ti	ti - ti	ti - ti	ta

FOCUS

Quarter Rest

LEARNING Music contains both sounds and silence. Silence is represented by musical symbols called *rests*.

The quarter note (♩) has a corresponding rest of equal duration called the quarter rest: 𝄽

Strategies

Have students sing "Hot Cross Buns." Provide a chart showing the words of the song, the rhythm, and the beats, as in **Visual R8.**

VISUAL R8

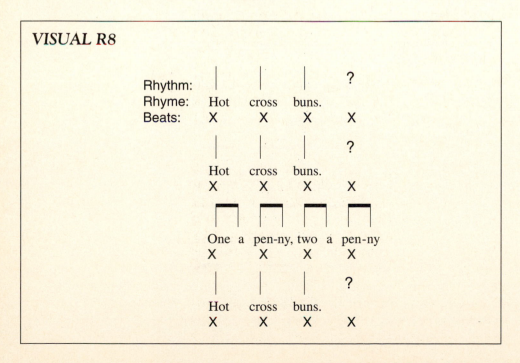

Rhythm:				?
Rhyme:	Hot	cross	buns.	
Beats:	X	X	X	X

				?
	Hot	cross	buns.	
	X	X	X	X

	One a	pen-ny, two a	pen-ny	
	X	X	X	X

				?
	Hot	cross	buns.	
	X	X	X	X

Ask students what is happening on beat 4 (no sound). Show students the musical symbol—quarter rest—that is used to indicate one beat of silence, as in **Visual R9.** Now find other beats where the quarter rest should be placed (beats 8 and 16). Verbalize the rhythms using the nicknames. Tap or clap for each note; open the hands for each rest. Initially, the teacher may want the students to verbalize softly the word "rest" when it appears. Once the concept is understood, however, the rest should be represented by total silence.

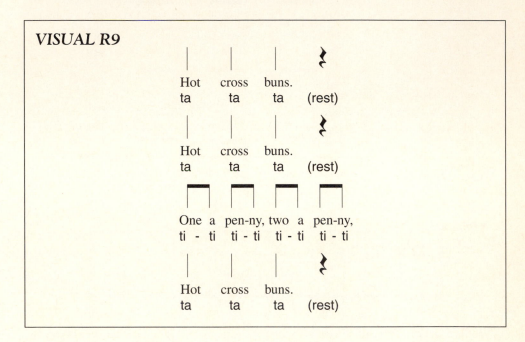

VISUAL R9

Create *rhythmic ostinati*—short repeated rhythm patterns—to accompany the students' rhymes. These ostinati can be spoken, clapped, or played on rhythm instruments. Using the rhyme "Burnie Bee," given in **Visual R10,** have one group of students speak and clap the ostinato four times while the other group speaks and claps the rhyme.

Rhythm ostinato:

Bee,   Bur-nie bee

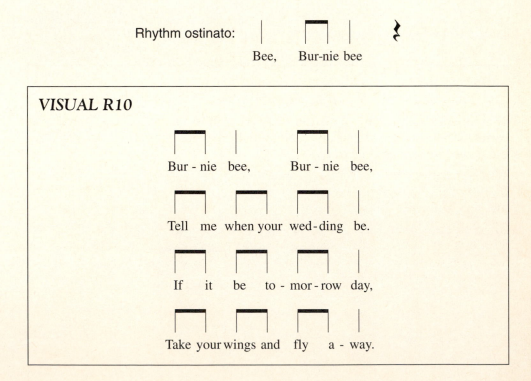

VISUAL R10

Grouping Beats

LEARNING A series of basic beats can be organized into groups by the placing of accents: > . An *accent* is a symbol placed above or below a note head to emphasize the sound of that note.

Strategies

The natural inflections of speech are a primary source for studying the accent of sound. Place on the chalkboard a list of names containing two and three syllables, whose normal accent is on the first syllable of each name. See **Visual R11.**

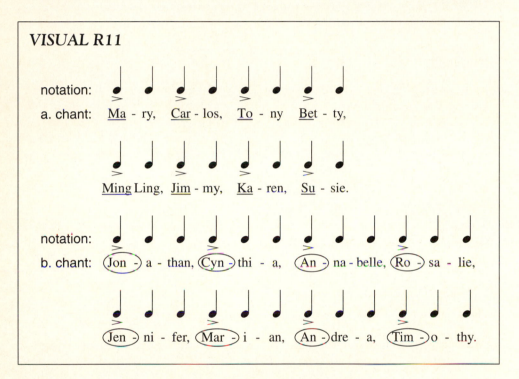

VISUAL R11

notation:

a. chant: Ma - ry, Car - los, To - ny Bet - ty,

Ming Ling, Jim - my, Ka - ren, Su - sie.

notation:

b. chant: Jon - a - than, Cyn - thi - a, An - na - belle, Ro - sa - lie,

Jen - ni - fer, Mar - i - an, An - dre - a, Tim - o - thy.

Chant the names, marking the emphasized syllable by underlining or circling it.

Transfer each syllable into a quarter note, placing an accent on those notes that correspond to the stressed syllables. Note that the placement of accents organizes the notes into groups of 2s and 3s.

While chanting the names, have students clap the accented syllables and tap their shoulders for the unaccented syllables. Students can also walk while chanting, gently stressing the accented syllables in their step.

Chant or sing "Bounce High, Bounce Low." Have students form a circle with the teacher in the center. Bounce the ball to each child in turn; the child bounces it back to the teacher in the center. The ball should always bounce on the accented beat. See **Visual R12.**

VISUAL R12

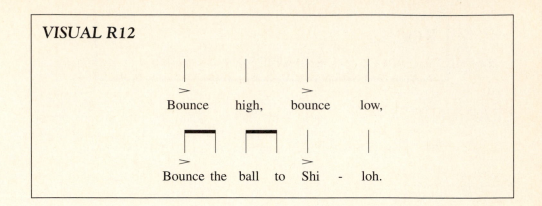

```
   |        |        |        |
   >                 >
Bounce   high,    bounce    low,

 ┌──┐    ┌──┐      |        |
   >                 >
Bounce the ball   to Shi  -  loh.
```

LEARNING   Accented groups may be separated by the placement of a *bar line*. The area between bar lines is called a *measure*. A *double bar* designates the end of either a musical section or the complete work.

Strategies

Chant or sing "Bounce High, Bounce Low" while clapping the beat. Repeat, clapping the rhythms. Now sing and clap the rhythm one line at a time. Have students decide which beats have one sound (quarter note) and which have two sounds (eighth notes). Notate the rhythms on the chalkboard. Have students discover where the accents should be placed. See **Visual R13**.

VISUAL R13

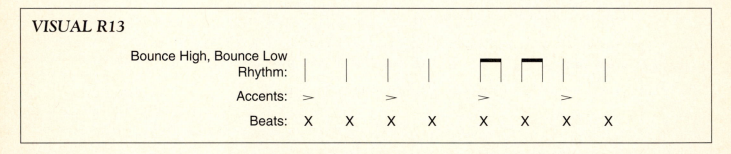

```
Bounce High, Bounce Low
          Rhythm:   |   |   |   |   ┌──┐┌──┐  |   |

         Accents:   >       >       >       >

           Beats:   X   X   X   X   X   X   X   X
```

Show students that a bar line can be placed in front of each accented note to separate one group from another, as in **Visual R14.** Two bar lines (double bar) are used to show the end of the song or rhyme. The space between two bar lines is called a measure.

VISUAL R14

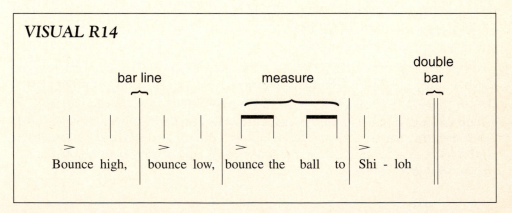

```
                                              double
          bar line        measure              bar

   |   |  |   |  ┌──┐ ┌──┐ |   |   ‖
   >         >        >            >
Bounce high, |bounce low, |bounce the ball  to Shi - loh ‖
```

Give students many experiences with placing accents, bar lines, and double bars where they belong. **Visual R15** can be made into charts or handouts for this purpose. Once students become proficient in forming groups of two beats each, they can be challenged to work with groups of three and four beats each.

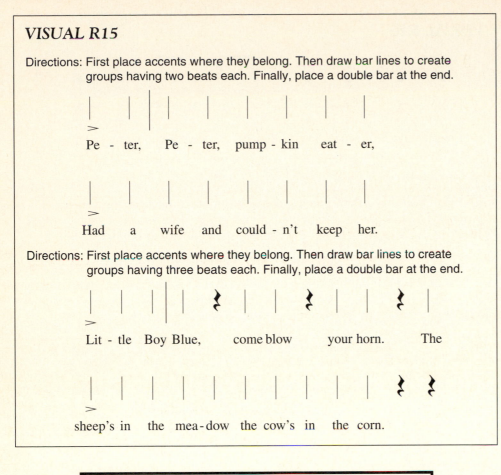

Directions: First place accents where they belong. Then draw bar lines to create groups having two beats each. Finally, place a double bar at the end.

Pe - ter,   Pe - ter,   pump - kin   eat - er,

Had   a   wife   and   could - n't   keep   her.

Directions: First place accents where they belong. Then draw bar lines to create groups having three beats each. Finally, place a double bar at the end.

Lit - tle   Boy Blue,   come blow   your horn.   The

sheep's in   the mea - dow   the cow's in   the corn.

FOCUS

Time Signature or Meter Signature

2 or $\frac{2}{4}$ 3 or $\frac{3}{4}$ 4 or $\frac{4}{4}$

LEARNING

A *time signature* or *meter signature*, found at the beginning of a musical work, is a symbol containing two numbers, one above the other. The lower number dictates which rhythm symbol will be used to establish the basic pulse in the music. The top number designates the number of beats allowed per measure.

Strategies

Sing or chant the song "Bounce High, Bounce Low." Place the rhythms on the board and mark the beats. Place the accents and then separate the rhythms into groups of two, as was done previously. Ask the students how many beats are in each measure. Number them. Show the students that a symbol can be used to indicate that every measure has two beats: 2. Place 2 to the left of the rhythms. See **Visual R16.**

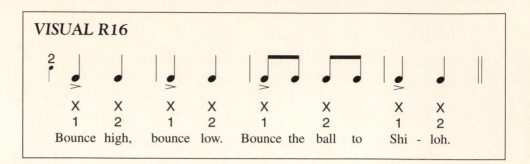

VISUAL R16

Bounce high, bounce low. Bounce the ball to Shi - loh.

Students should have repeated experiences numbering the beats of different songs and chants and then placing the appropriate time signatures to the left of the notes. In later grades, chants and songs grouped in 3s and 4s can be added. When the students are ready, 2 3 4 can be replaced with 2/4, 3/4, and 4/4.

Charts of worksheets can be created to reinforce an understanding of time signatures. **Visual R17** contains three examples that can be used at different grade levels, whenever each is appropriate. By numbering each beat, the student proves that there really are two, three, or four beats in every measure.

VISUAL R17

Directions: Number the beats in each measure. Then decide what the time signature should be and place it to the left of the rhythms.

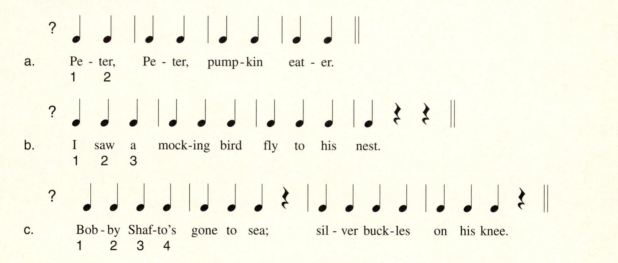

a. Pe - ter,   Pe - ter,   pump-kin   eat - er.
    1   2

b. I saw a mock-ing bird fly to his nest.
    1   2   3

c. Bob - by Shaf-to's gone to sea;   sil - ver buck-les on his knee.
    1   2   3   4

LEARNING   Time signatures can be translated into hand and arm movements called *conducting patterns*. Each movement tells us where each beat within the time signature occurs.

Strategies

Students should conduct a variety of music having 2/4, 3/4, and 4/4 time signatures. Use the conducting patterns shown in **Visual R18.** In each conducting pattern, the first beat is always the *downbeat*; the last beat is always the *upbeat*.

Demonstrate the 2/4 conducting pattern as shown in Visual R18. Identify the first beat (usually the accented beat) as the downbeat and the last beat as the upbeat. Apply the 2/4 conducting pattern to "Bounce High, Bounce Low" and to "Hot Cross Buns." Sing "America" while conducting in 3/4. Conduct in 4/4 while singing "Row, Row, Row Your Boat." Find other familiar songs in this book that are written in 2/4, 3/4, and 4/4 meters and practice conducting them while singing the songs.

VISUAL R18

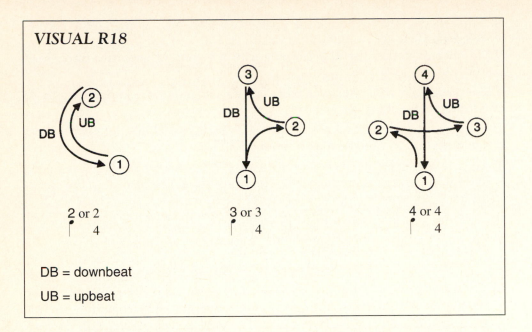

2 or 2
        4

3 or 3
        4

4 or 4
        4

DB = downbeat

UB = upbeat

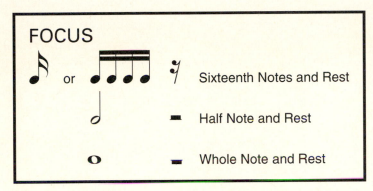

FOCUS

Sixteenth Notes and Rest

Half Note and Rest

Whole Note and Rest

LEARNING A whole note contains four quarter notes.

A half note contains two quarter notes.

A quarter note contains four sixteenth notes.

The same equivalents are present in the corresponding rests.

Strategies

To teach additional note values and their corresponding rests, use the same procedures as those that were applied to the teaching of the quarter note and rest and the eighth note. Those procedures are summarized here:

1. Choose a familiar rhyme/song that contains a good example of the rhythm structure being taught.
2. Place the words of the rhyme/song on the chalkboard.
3. Chant/sing the words and clap the beat while the teacher or a student marks the beats under the appropriate syllables.
4. Clap the rhythms and chant/sing the words while the teacher or a student points to the beats.
5. Work out how many sounds or silences occur on each beat of the known rhythms in the rhyme/song, and place the appropriate notation above each syllable.
6. Teacher presents the new rhythm structure and writes it on the chalkboard in its proper place.
7. Teacher gives the new rhythm both its real name and its rhythm syllable, if it has one.

8. Students clap the rhythm of the rhyme/song while saying/singing the rhythm syllables.
9. Teacher reinforces the new learning with a variety of activities throughout the school year.

These procedures will take more than one day to complete, so don't try to do everything in one short lesson.

To reinforce the strategies listed in the nine procedures above, let's apply them to a new rhythm learning, sixteenth notes: ♫♫ .

1. Choose a song having a good example of ♫♫ . "Love Somebody" is a good choice. It can be chanted or sung. The words should be placed on the chalkboard:

> Love somebody, yes I do.
> Love somebody, yes I do.
> Love somebody, yes I do.
> Love somebody but I won't tell who.

2. Once students learn the rhyme/song well, they should chant/sing it while the teacher or a student marks each beat as it occurs, as in **Visual R19.**

VISUAL R19

| Love | some-bod-y, | yes | I do, |
| X | X | X | X |

| Love | some-bod-y, | yes | I do. |
| X | X | X | X |

| Love | some-bod-y, | yes | I do, |
| X | X | X | X |

| Love | some-bod-y, but I | won't | tell who. |
| X | X | X | X |

---

3. Repeat the rhyme/song and clap its rhythms while the teacher or a student points to each beat.
4. Work out how many sounds or silences are voiced on each beat for all the known rhythms. Place the appropriate rhythm symbols on the chalkboard, as in **Visual R20.**

VISUAL R20

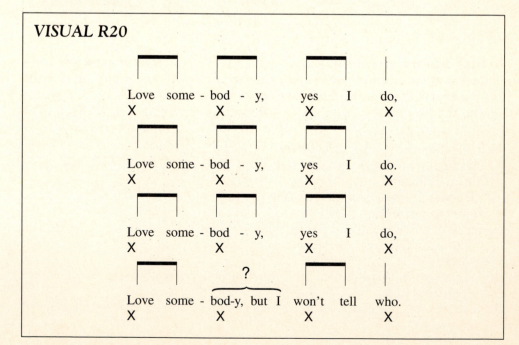

---

5. Ask students how many sounds are in "bod-y but I." There are four sounds to this beat. Show how these sounds should be written: 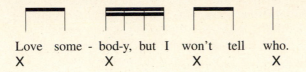. Rewrite the last line of the rhyme/song, inserting the four sixteenth notes:

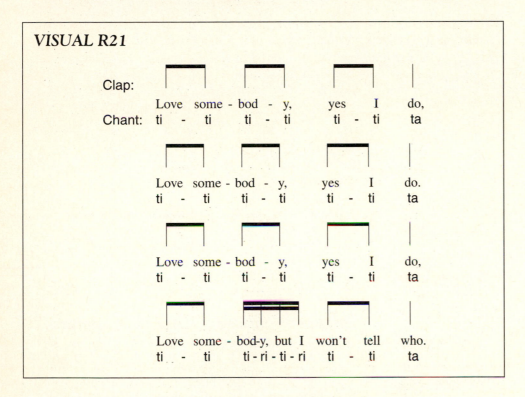

Love some - bod-y, but I won't tell who.
X   X   X   X

6. Tell students that these are sixteenth notes. They often come in fours, but not always. If the note stands alone, it has two flags = ♬. This should be compared to a single eighth note with one flag = ♪. The rhythm syllables for the four-sixteenth-note group are: ti-ri-ti-ri.

7. Students should clap the rhythms of the rhyme/song while chanting/singing the rhythm syllables, as in **Visual R21.**

VISUAL R21

Clap:

Love some - bod - y,   yes   I   do,
Chant: ti - ti   ti - ti   ti - ti   ta

Love some - bod - y,   yes   I   do.
ti - ti   ti - ti   ti - ti   ta

Love some - bod - y,   yes   I   do,
ti - ti   ti - ti   ti - ti   ta

Love some - bod-y, but I won't tell who.
ti - ti   ti - ri - ti - ri   ti - ti   ta

---

8. Reinforce the new learning by discovering ▦ in other rhymes and songs included within this book. After examining the song, try tapping out the new rhythm using nonsense rhythm syllables (ti-ri-ti-ri). Try adding the words to the rhythm. Next, create simple accompaniments that can be played on rhythm instruments that use this rhythm. Add the accompaniment to another song of your own choosing. Songs using ▦ include:

Sailing on the Ocean   p. 67
Paw Paw Patch   p. 79
When That I Was a Little Tiny Boy   p. 131
Riding in the Buggy   p. 144
Old Brass Wagon   p. 307
A-Hunting We Will Go   p. 310

Use similar procedures to teach the remaining rhythm symbols found in **Visual R22.**

Appropriate portions of Visual R22 can be displayed at each grade level in the form of a chart. Place on the chart only those symbols that the students know. Add new symbols as they are taught.

VISUAL R22

Whole note:	o						
Whole rest:	▬						
Duration Syllables:	ta	-	a	-	a	-	a
Counting:	1		2		3		4

Half note:	𝅗𝅥		𝅗𝅥	
Half rest:	▬		▬	
Duration Syllables:	ta	- a	ta	- a
Counting:	1	2	3	4

Quarter note:	♩	♩	♩	♩
Quarter rest:	𝄽	𝄽	𝄽	𝄽
Duration Syllables:	ta	ta	ta	ta
Counting:	1	2	3	4

Eighth note / Eighth rest:

Duration Syllables:	ti	-	ti	ti	-	ti	ti	-	ti	ti	-	ti
Counting:	1		&	2		&	3		&	4		&

Sixteenth note / Sixteenth rest:

Duration Syllables:	ti - ri - ti - ri	ti - ri - ti - ri	ti - ri - ti - ri	ti - ri - ti - ri
Counting:	1 ee & a	2 ee & a	3 ee & a	4 ee & a

Note: Stick notation can be used for all the above note values except for the half note and the whole note.

Students should use speech to reinforce their understanding of rhythm values. Exercises similar to **Visual R23** may be helpful. Students should be encouraged to find additional words, relating to the categories specified, that will match the rhythms given.

VISUAL R23

Categories (2/4)	𝅗𝅥	♫ ♫	♫ ♩	♩ ♩	♩ ♫
FRUITS	Plum	Wa- ter- me- lon	Tan- ger- ine	Grape- fruit	Straw- ber- ry
VEGETABLES	Bean	A- vo- ca- do	Broc- co- li	Car- rot	Green pep- per
NAMES	John	Mi-chael An-drew	Ma- ry Ann	Pe- ter	Rose- ma- ry
FLOWERS	Rose	Wa- ter li- ly	Daf- fo- dil	Sweet pea	Snap- dra- gon
ANIMALS	Dog	Spot-ted leop-ard	Por- cu- pine	Ti- ger	Black stal- lion
TREES	Oak	Weep-ing wil- low	Sil- ver ash	Ma- ple	Horse chest- nut
TOYS	Drum	Bean- ie Ba- by	Choo-choo train	Doll house	Red wa- gon

Students should be given metered experiences that reinforce their understanding of notational equivalences, such as those in **Visual R24.** To learn the rhythms, students should say the rhythm syllables and count each measure aloud (refer to Visual R22). To reinforce their understanding, students should perform these activities using percussion instruments and body rhythms. Later, divide the class into five groups, each group performing a different line of rhythm.

VISUAL R24

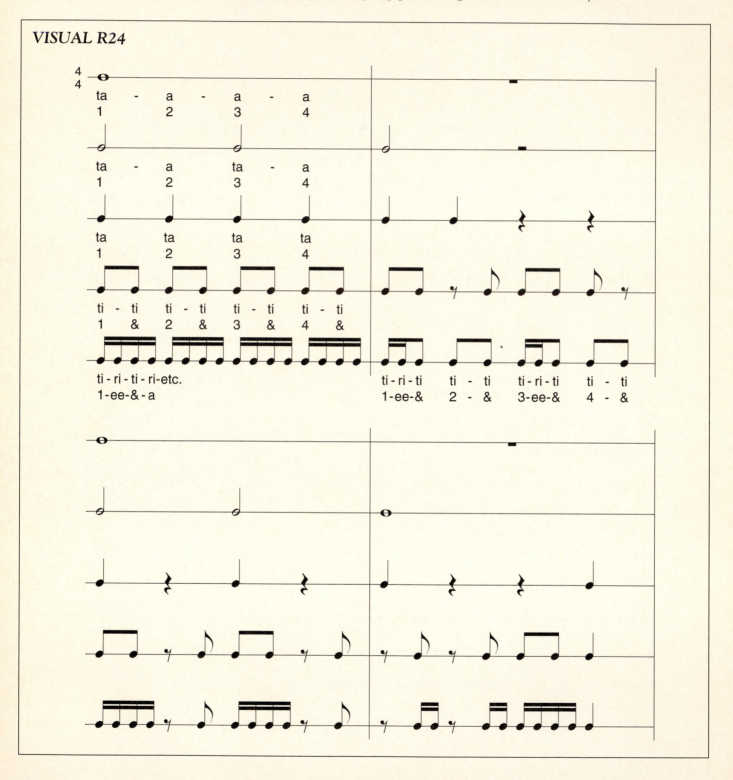

Flash cards, such as those in **Visual R25,** can be reproduced on larger cards for drill, to reinforce the use of rhythmic patterns in 4/4. Similar cards can be constructed to reinforce rhythms in 2/4 and 3/4. These patterns can also be used as ostinati to accompany songs or rhythmic activities.

VISUAL R25

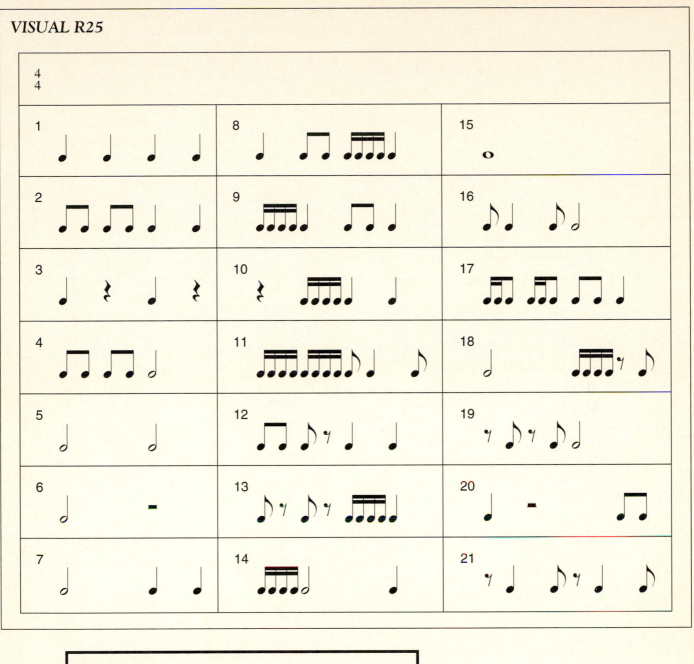

FOCUS

Tie

LEARNING A curved line joining two rhythm symbols sung or played on the same pitch results in a *tie*. When two notes are tied, the first note is held for its duration as well as the duration of the note to which it is tied: ♩♩ .

Strategies

Have students sing "Are You Sleeping" as the teacher points to the beats.

    Are you sleeping, are you sleeping,
Brother John, Brother John.
Morning bells are ringing. Morning bells are ringing.
Ding, ding, dong. Ding, ding, dong.

Sing the song again while clapping the word rhythms. Now work out the rhythms for the first two lines of the song, as in **Visual R26.**

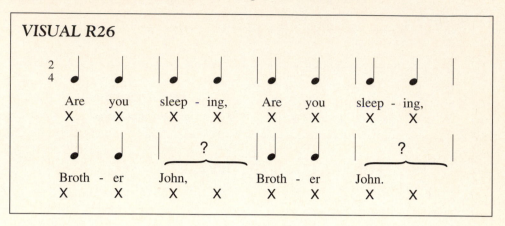

VISUAL R26

Ask the students how many beats are felt while singing the word "John" in measures 6 and 8. Show how to extend a sound through the use of a tie ♩♩. Rewrite measures 6 and 8, using the tie. Explain how to verbalize this pattern = ta-a. See **Visual R27.**

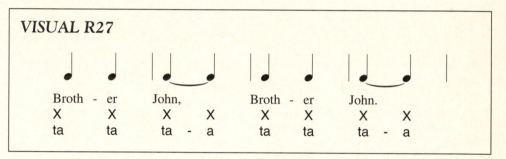

VISUAL R27

Place the last two lines of the song on the chalkboard. Work out the rhythms for these lines. Are there any more ties in these lines? Give each note its rhythm syllable, as in **Visual R28.** Sing "Are You Sleeping" again, using the rhythm syllables rather than the words. Clap the rhythms while singing the rhythm syllables.

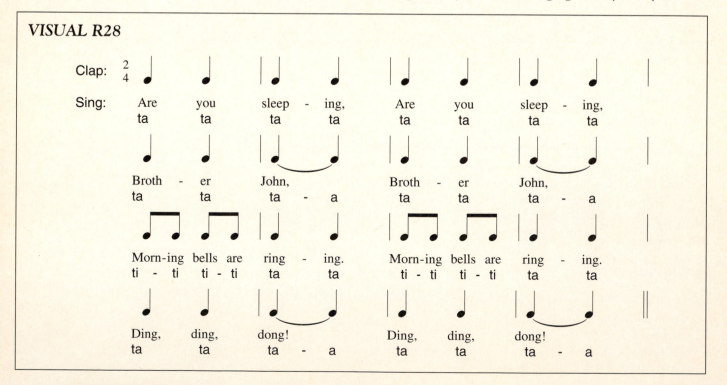

VISUAL R28

Students should understand that only the first note of the tie is "attacked." The sound is then held the length of both notes in the pattern. Both notes of the tie do not have to be of the same value. Other combinations are possible, such as ♩♫ or ♩♩ . Notes can also be tied across the bar line: ♩♩ .

Sing songs having other examples of the tie to reinforce this learning.

Many teachers use the tie to teach both the half and the whole note. ♩♩ easily becomes ♩ (half note); ♩♩ becomes ○ (whole note). This is a particularly good procedure because it leads students from what they know (tie) to the unknown (half note or whole note).

Once students have experienced the tie in the context of several songs, flash cards or a felt board can be used to reinforce the learning, using such patterns as those in **Visual R29.**

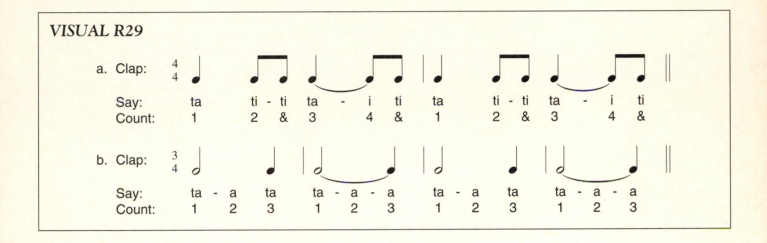

VISUAL R29

a. Clap:

Say:	ta	ti	-	ti	ta	-	i	ti	ta	ti	-	ti	ta	-	i	ti
Count:	1	2	&	3	4	&			1	2	&	3	4	&		

b. Clap:

Say:	ta	-	a	ta	ta	-	a	-	a	ta	-	a	ta	ta	-	a	-	a
Count:	1		2	3	1		2		3	1		2	3	1		2		3

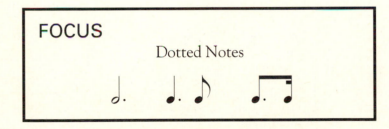

FOCUS

Dotted Notes

LEARNING   A dot following a note or rest adds to that note or rest one half of its value. These symbols are called *dotted notes* (♩·) and *dotted rests* (𝄽·).

Strategies

Have students sing "America." Place on the chalkboard the rhythms for the first six measures, as in **Visual R30.**

VISUAL R30

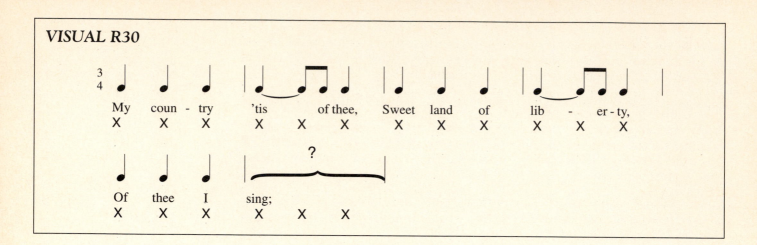

Students should sing the song again while the teacher points to the beats. Now have the students clap the rhythms as they sing the words. Ask the students how many beats should be given to "sing" in measure 6. When they respond "three," ask them how we could notate this. Some students may suggest a half note tied to a quarter note = ♩♩ . Place this rhythm in measure 6. Now work out the rhythm syllables for the first six measures, and sing them while clapping the rhythm. See **Visual R31**.

VISUAL R31

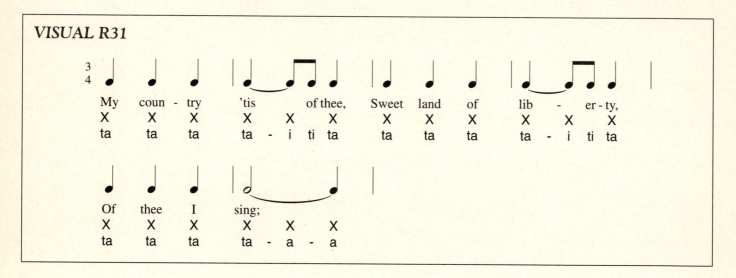

At the next lesson, show students that another way to write ♩♩ in measure 6 is to put the quarter note into a dot. The result is a dotted half note ♩. verbalized ta-a-a. Explain that a dot to the right of any note is always equal to the next smaller value of the note it is with. Replace the pattern ♩♩ in measure 6 with the new pattern ♩.. See **Visual R32.** Sing the rhythm syllables once more while clapping the rhythms.

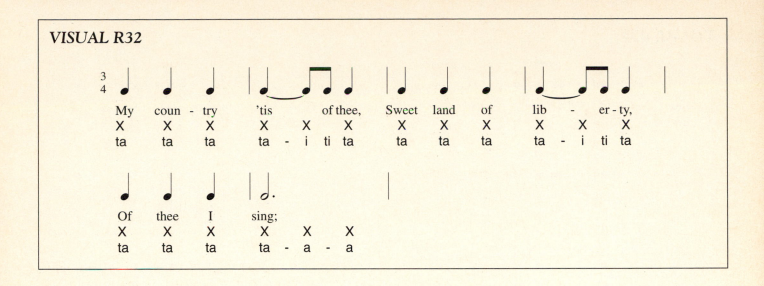

"America" can also be used to teach the dotted quarter note, ♩. . Place **Visual R32** on the chalkboard once more and ask the students for another way to write the tied notes in measures 2 and 4. Since the quarter note is tied to a note having the next smaller value (an eighth note), that eighth note can become a dot beside the quarter note. Rewrite the measures, as in **Visual R33,** and place the rhythm syllables under the notes. Sing the syllables while clapping the rhythms.

VISUAL R33

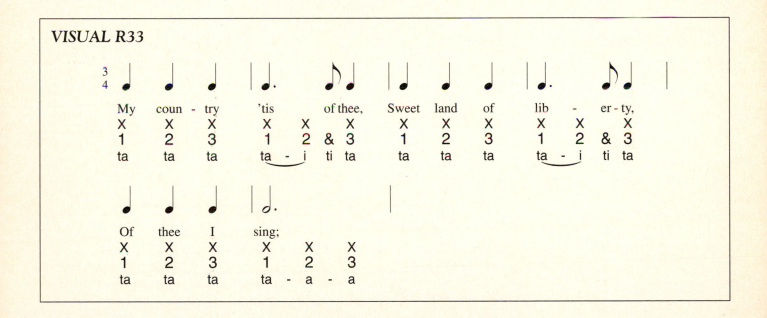

Charts showing dotted note equivalents can be used to reinforce this learning. Three different charts are given in **Visual R34.** Each example should be used at the appropriate grade level, when the students are ready for it.

VISUAL R34

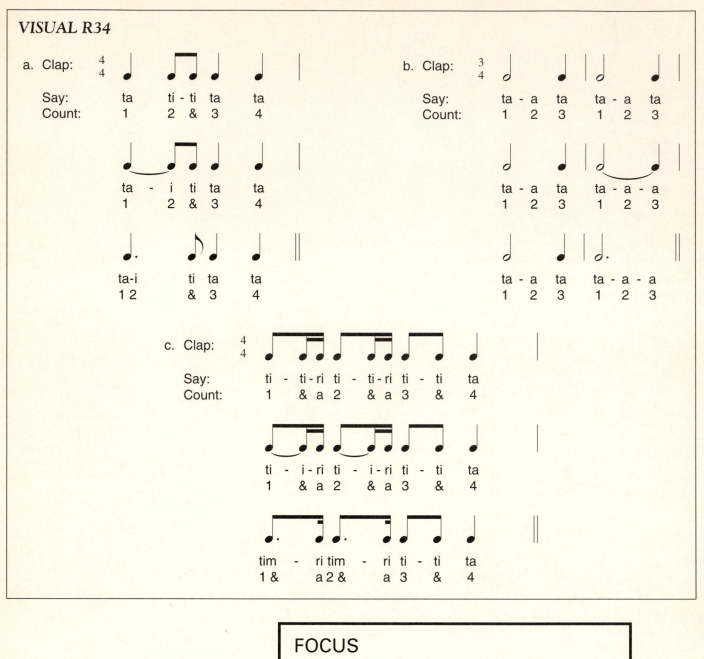

FOCUS

Simple Meter

LEARNING When the upper number of the time signature or meter signature is a 2, 3, or 4, the musical composition is in *simple meter*.

Strategies

The quarter note is not the only note that serves as the *beat note*; that is, as the note that receives one full beat within a measure. Both eighth and half notes are also commonly used as beat notes in music. Students should have repeated experiences with music written in meters where either the eighth or the half note receives one full beat. The most commonly used of these meters are 3/8 and 2/2.

Note that 4/4 is often referred to as *common time*, expressed by the symbol ¢. 2/2 is commonly referred to as *alla breve* or *cut time*, and may be notated ¢.

Meter in 2s is often referred to as *duple meter*; in 3s, as *triple meter*; and in 4s, as *quadruple meter*. **Visual R35** summarizes these learnings.

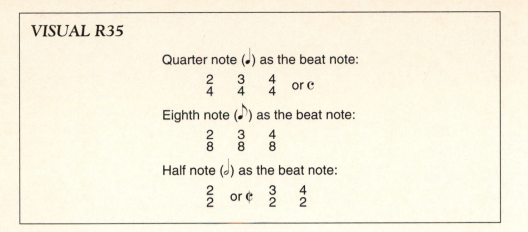

VISUAL R35

Quarter note (♩) as the beat note:

$$\frac{2}{4} \quad \frac{3}{4} \quad \frac{4}{4} \quad \text{or } \mathbf{c}$$

Eighth note (♪) as the beat note:

$$\frac{2}{8} \quad \frac{3}{8} \quad \frac{4}{8}$$

Half note (♩) as the beat note:

$$\frac{2}{2} \quad \text{or } \mathbf{¢} \quad \frac{3}{2} \quad \frac{4}{2}$$

Practice charts and flash cards can be produced that reinforce the learning of beat notes in simple meter, as in **Visual R36.**

VISUAL R36

Note: In 3/4 time, there must be the equivalent of three quarter notes $\left(\frac{3}{♩}\right)$ in each measure.

In 3/8 time, there must be the equivalent of three eighth notes $\left(\frac{3}{♪}\right)$ in each measure.

In 3/2 time, there must be the equivalent of three half notes $\left(\frac{3}{♩}\right)$ in each measure.

Marking the beat notes highlights these learnings.

LEARNING Simple meter is present when the beat note can be divided into two equal parts, creating a ratio of 2:1.

Strategies

Sometimes summary charts are helpful tools to use for reinforcing learnings that have been previously experienced within a music context. To this end, a chart can be created, similar to that in **Visual R37,** showing the ratio of 2:1 which characterizes simple meter.

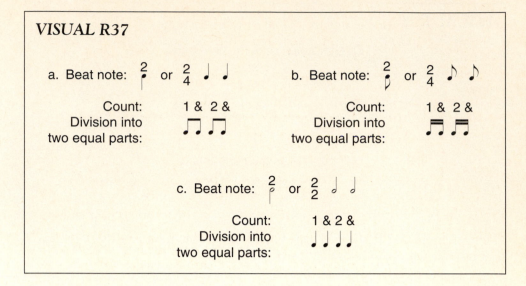

Students should clap patterns using a variety of simple meters, such as those found in **Visual R38.**

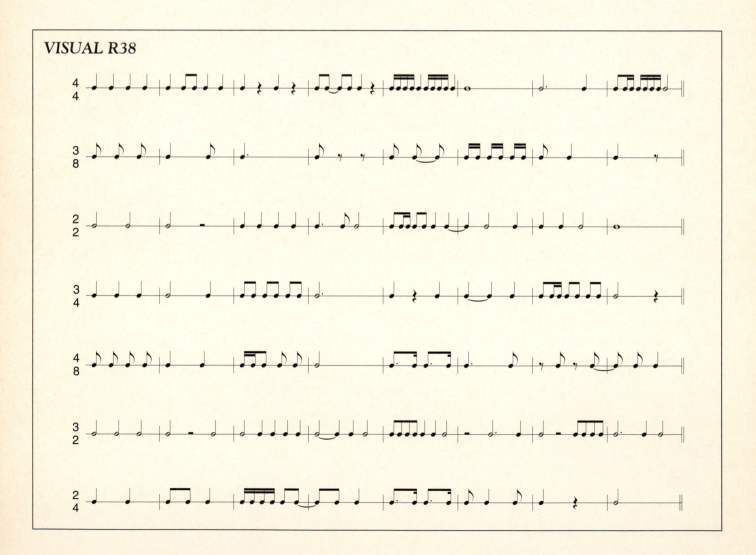

Students should have practice conducting the patterns in Visual R38 as well as a variety of songs in simple meters. Whether the beat note is a quarter, a half, or an eighth note, the conducting patterns in Visual R18 can be used for all simple meters. The conducting pattern used for 2/4 is also used for 2/8 and 2/2; the pattern used for 3/4 is also used for 3/8 and 3/2; and the 4/4 pattern is used for 4/8 and 4/2.

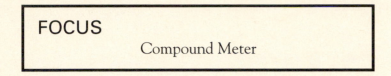

FOCUS

Compound Meter

LEARNING   When the upper number of the time or meter signature is a multiple of three, the musical composition is in *compound meter*. Compound meter is present when the beat note can be divided into three equal parts, creating a ratio of 3:1.

Strategies

Choose a rhyme or song that the students know well, such as "Hickory Dickory Dock." Write the words of the rhyme on the chalkboard, with both beats and rhythms indicated, as in **Visual R39.**

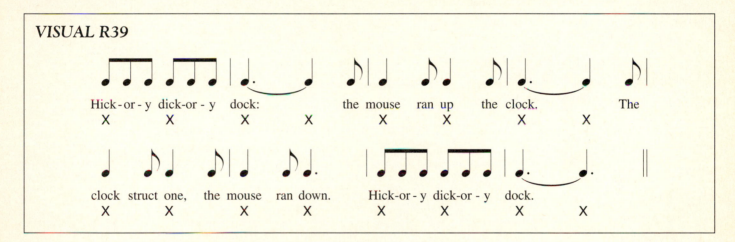

VISUAL R39

Have students chant the rhyme while the teacher points to the beats. Now, point to the beats again while students clap the rhythm of the words. Ask the students what kind of note will get the beat in this rhythm. If they say "eighth note," mention that this response might be possible, but the beat (**X**) has not been marked to designate the eighth note as receiving one full beat. The correct response, of course, is the dotted quarter note (♩.), because ♪♪♪ is equivalent to ♩. in total counts. Because there is no number to represent ♩ in a time signature, we commonly use 6/8 to show this meter.

Have students sing familiar songs in 6/8 found in the text. Clapping the beat and/or rhythm while singing will help to reinforce this new time signature.

After students have had other experiences with songs in 6/8 meter, explain that music having the dotted quarter note (♩.) as the beat note is said to be in compound meter. Other common time signatures in compound meter are 9/8 and 12/8. A chart summarizing this information can be exhibited, such as that in **Visual R40.**

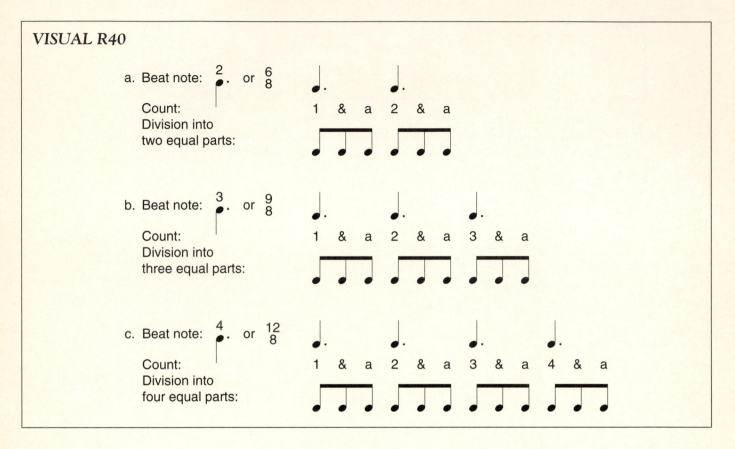

VISUAL R40

a. Beat note: ...
 Count:
 Division into
 two equal parts:

b. Beat note: ...
 Count:
 Division into
 three equal parts:

c. Beat note: ...
 Count:
 Division into
 four equal parts:

Students should know that, in compound meter, the eighth note does function as the beat note when the music is performed very slowly. This can be emphasized by showing students a chart, similar to **Visual R41.**

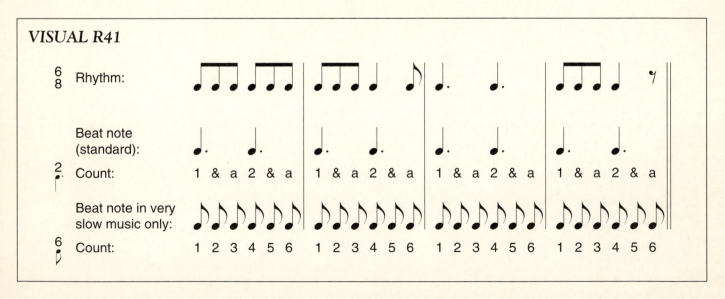

VISUAL R41

When students understand the difference between a slow and a fast 6/8, or any other compound meter, they should conduct "Hickory Dickory Dock" using both a fast and a slow 6/8 conducting pattern, as shown in **Visual R42.**

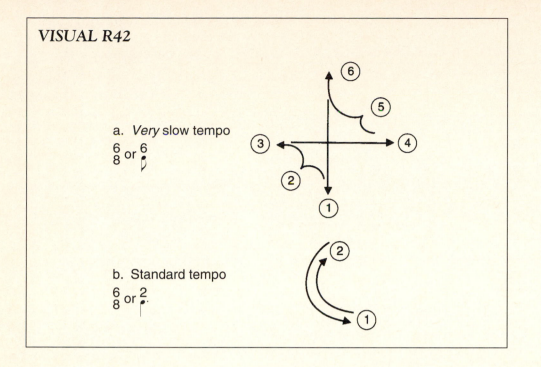

VISUAL R42

a. *Very* slow tempo
6/8 or 6♪

b. Standard tempo
6/8 or 2♩.

Students should have practice in conducting music written in common compound meters. The conducting patterns shown in Visual R18 are used for both simple and compound meters. Because compound meters in 6 (6/8) are grouped in 2s (two beat notes per measure), 6/8 meter is conducted with two arm movements; because compound meters in 9 are grouped in 3s (three beat notes per measure), 9/8 meter is conducted in three movements. Similarly 12/8 is grouped in 4s (four beat notes per measure) and uses four arm movements. A very slow tempo, however, would necessitate conducting each eighth note, rather than the dotted quarter note.

Note that other compound meters are possible, such as 6/4, 9/4, 12/4, 6/2, 9/2, and 12/2, but these meters are seldom used by most composers.

Patterns such as those in **Visual R43** can be used to reinforce reading music in common compound meters. Clapping and other body movements can be used when practicing these patterns.

VISUAL R43

Flash cards, such as those in **Visual R44,** can be reproduced on larger cards for drill to reinforce the use of rhythmic patterns in 6/8. Similar cards can be constructed to reinforce rhythms in other compound meters, if desired.

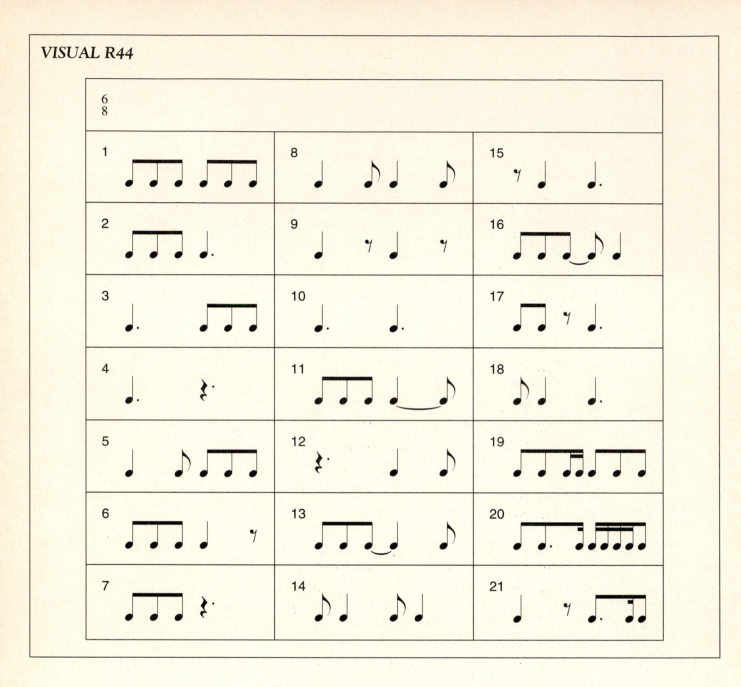

FOCUS
Asymmetrical or Irregular Meters

LEARNING Meters that are not duple, triple, or quadruple are called *asymmetrical* or *irregular meters*, such as 7/8 or 5/4.

Strategies

Echo clap rhythms in a variety of asymmetrical meters. Use different body sounds to emphasize the shifting accents as in **Visual R45.**

Place on the chalkboard a variety of rhythmic patterns in different asymmetrical meters, as in **Visual R46.** These patterns are usually subgrouped into 2s and 3s. Appropriate speech can be added to reinforce the shifting accents, and rhythm instruments can be played to emphasize the accented note in each rhythmic grouping.

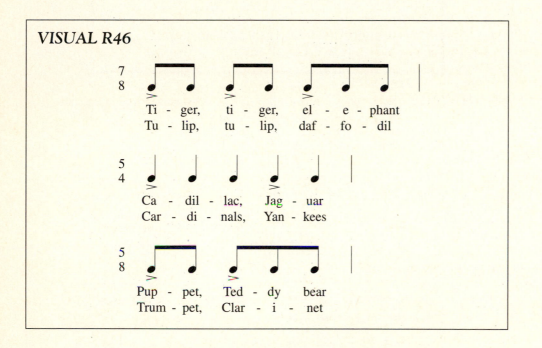

FOCUS
Mixed or Changing Meters

LEARNING When the meter signature changes often, even from one measure to the next, *mixed* or *changing meters* result.

Strategies

Have students chant patterns or sing songs using mixed meters, such as those found in **Visual R47.**

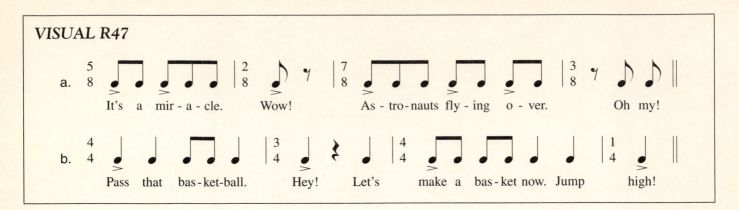

Students can notate their own rhythms, using mixed meters, and create texts to accompany their rhythms.

FOCUS

Other Rhythms: Triplet, Syncopation, Polyrhythms

LEARNING   A note (not a dotted note) divided into three equal parts becomes a *triplet*, chanted tri-o-la.

Strategies

Have students chant a well-known rhyme or song such as "Jack Be Nimble." Place a copy of the rhyme with the beats marked on the chalkboard. Point to the beats as the students clap them and say the rhyme. Repeat while students clap the rhythms of the words. Work out the rhythms, as in **Visual R48.**

VISUAL R48

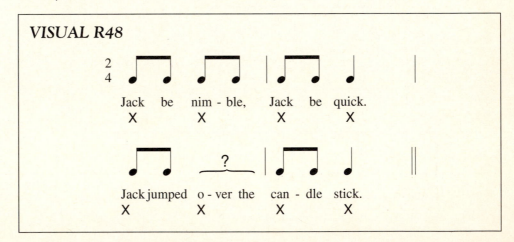

Have students say the rhyme once more, concentrating on how many sounds are heard on the second beat of measure 3. Show how these three sounds should look: . Identify the symbol as a *triplet*, whose nickname is *triola*.

Notice that a triplet is identified by the presence of the number "3" and usually by a curved line. Rewritten, measure 3 would look like this:

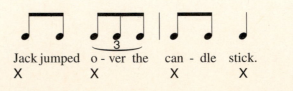

Students should understand that a triplet is not always equal to one full beat. The three notes in a triplet are equal to two notes of the same value:

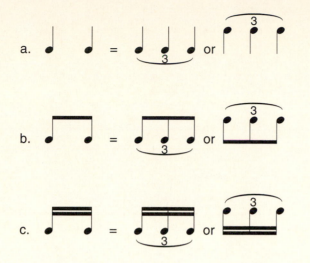

Have students create chants using the triplet figure, as in **Visual R49.**

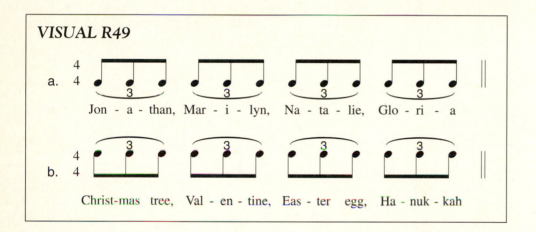

VISUAL R49

a. 4/4

Jon - a - than, Mar - i - lyn, Na - ta - lie, Glo - ri - a

b. 4/4

Christ-mas tree, Val - en - tine, Eas - ter egg, Ha - nuk - kah

Students should perform, by singing, saying, clapping, or patsching, a variety of rhythmic patterns incorporating the triplet figure, as in **Visual R50.** Remember to say the rhythm syllables when performing the patterns.

VISUAL R50

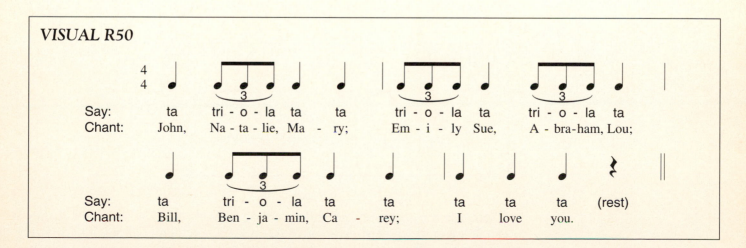

4/4

Say: ta   tri - o - la ta   ta   tri - o - la ta   tri - o - la ta
Chant: John, Na - ta - lie, Ma - ry;   Em - i - ly Sue,   A - bra-ham, Lou;

Say: ta   tri - o - la ta   ta   ta   ta   ta   (rest)
Chant: Bill, Ben - ja - min, Ca - rey;   I   love you.

LEARNING *Syncopation* (♪ ♩ ♪), chanted "ti ta ti" or "syn-CO-pa," occurs when the accent of a rhythm pattern does not coincide with the normal metrical accent.

Strategies

Choose a rhyme or song containing a good example of syncopation, such as "A Needle and Thread." See **Visual R51.**

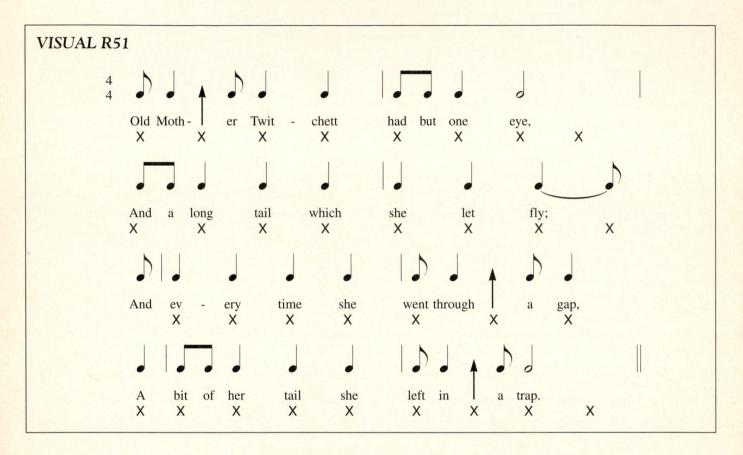

VISUAL R51

Put only the words and beat symbol (**X**) on the board. Point to the beats while the students clap them and chant the rhyme. Repeat this activity, but now ask the students to clap the word rhythms. Place above the words the rhythms for the first two measures of the rhyme, as in **Visual R52.**

VISUAL R52

Chant these measures again while pointing to each beat. Ask students if they can discover which rhythms are incorrect. Chant several more times if necessary. Once they've discovered that measure 1 is not correct, have them verbalize why this is so. Ask them how we can change measure 1 so that it looks right. Some-one will probably suggest

ti ti - i ti ta ta
Old Moth - er Twit - chett

which would be correct. Replace the incorrect measure 1 with the new measure containing the tie. Then chant the measures using both the words of the chant and the rhythm syllables. Ask students if they know another way to write ♩. They will probably suggest using a quarter note.

Now rewrite measure 1 using the syncopated pattern:

ti ta ti ta ta
Old Moth - er Twit - chett

Chant measures 1 and 2, using the correct syncopated pattern. Clap the rhythms while saying the rhythm syllables.

At a subsequent lesson, students can discover other syncopated patterns in this rhyme.

Give students many opportunities to chant and sing rhymes and songs contain-ing syncopated patterns. ♪♩♪ is the most common syncopated pattern, but other patterns can also occur in music, such as those found in **Visual R53.** No-tice the "short-long-short" nature of syncopation, as highlighted in this visual.

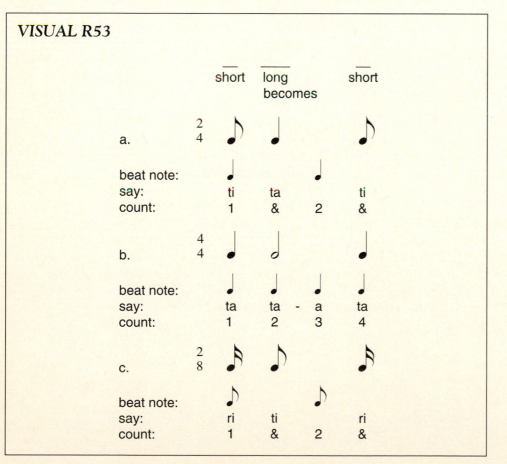

VISUAL R53

Syncopated rhythmic ostinati can be created to accompany simple rhymes and songs, as in **Visual R54.** These can be played with body percussion—clapping, tapping, and so on—or with rhythm instruments.

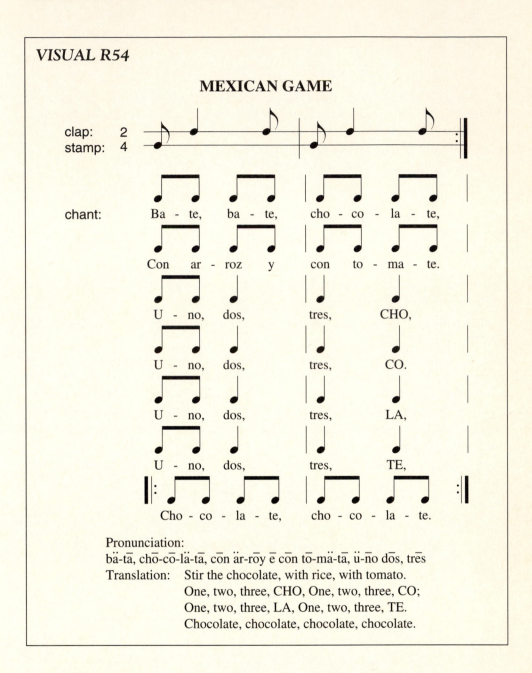

VISUAL R54

MEXICAN GAME

clap: 2
stamp: 4

chant: Ba - te,   ba - te,   cho - co - la - te,

Con ar - roz y con to - ma - te.

U - no, dos, tres, CHO,

U - no, dos, tres, CO.

U - no, dos, tres, LA,

U - no, dos, tres, TE,

Cho - co - la - te, cho - co - la - te.

Pronunciation:
bä-tā, chō-cō-lä-tā, cōn är-roy ē cōn tō-mä-tā, ü-nō dōs, trēs
Translation: Stir the chocolate, with rice, with tomato.
One, two, three, CHO, One, two, three, CO;
One, two, three, LA, One, two, three, TE.
Chocolate, chocolate, chocolate, chocolate.

Within the rhyme "A Needle and Thread," syncopation was taught through the use of a tie, as shown in example "a" of **Visual R55.** This visual contains additional patterns that demonstrate how rests and tied notes can create syncopated rhythms.

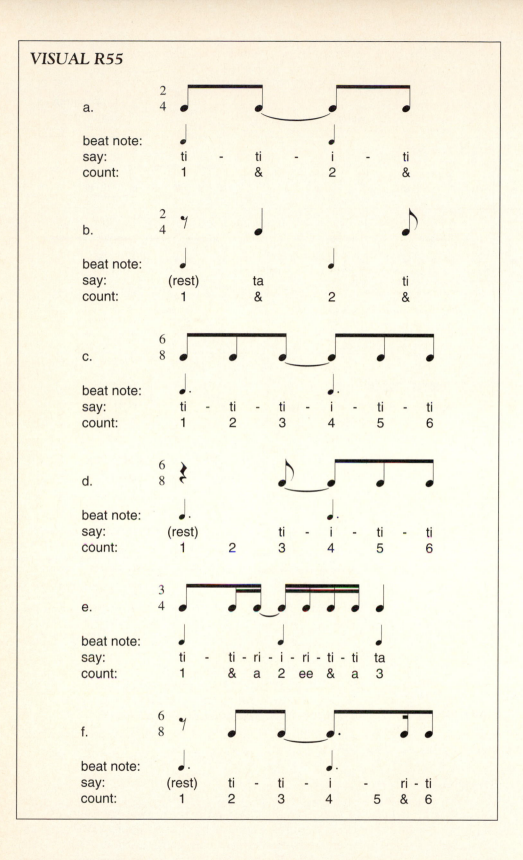

Students should be encouraged to discover the syncopated patterns in the flash card examples in Visuals R25 and R44.

Flash cards, such as those in **Visual R56,** can be reproduced on larger cards for drill, to reinforce the use of rhythmic patterns containing ties, triplets, syncopation, and dotted notes.

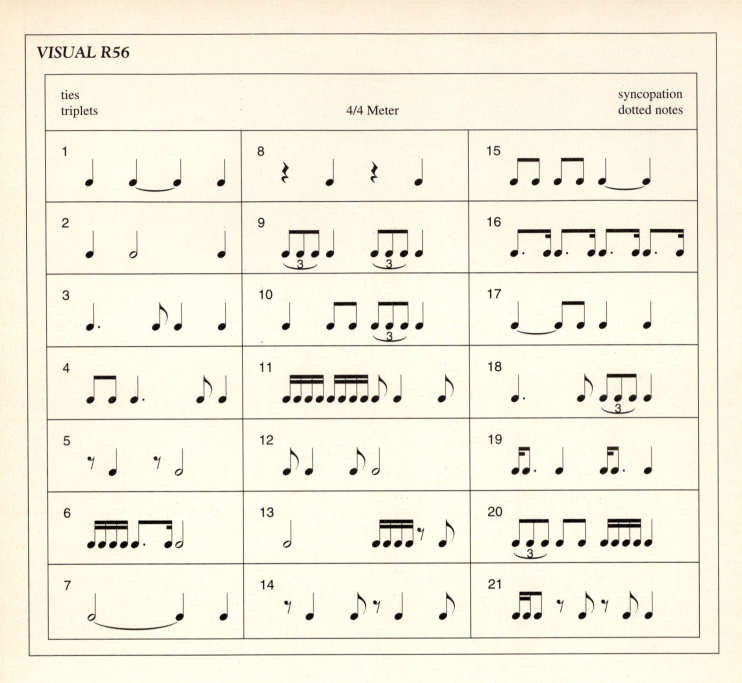

LEARNING

Polyrhythms are combinations of two or more independent rhythms, occurring simultaneously, whose metrical accents do not coincide.

Strategies

Establish a basic pulse or time line, as in **Visual R57.** Repeat the numbers several times, placing the accent at different points by circling appropriate numbers. Uncircled numbers represent rests or silences, characteristic tools used to effect polyrhythms. Divide students into three groups, each group having a different time line. Assign a different percussion instrument to each group of students; for example, cow bell, claves, and guiro.

Students perform only the circled numbers in their time line, but all three lines are performed simultaneously so that polyrhythm results.

VISUAL R57

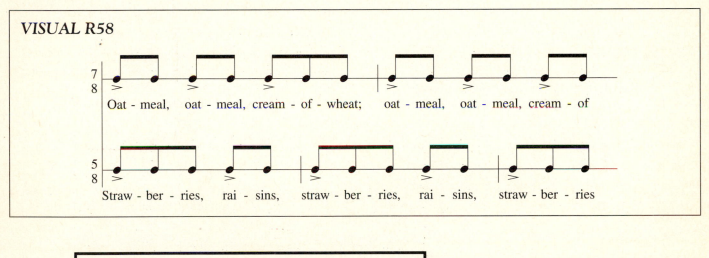

Different polyrhythm ostinati can be written to accompany songs, recordings, or creative movement exercises.

Polyrhythms can also be produced by combining two or more asymmetrical meters as in **Visual R58.** Adding speech will reinforce the accented groupings, but eventually the chant can be replaced with body percussion or rhythm instruments.

VISUAL R58

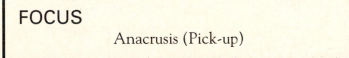

FOCUS

Anacrusis (Pick-up)

LEARNING   When musical compositions begin with an incomplete measure of one or more notes, these notes are called an *anacrusis* or *pick-up*. A composition beginning with an anacrusis will have an incomplete final measure; the combination of the final measure and the anacrusis equals a complete measure.

Strategies

Place on the chalkboard the rhythm for "The Old Woman Under the Hill," found in **Visual R59.** Chant the rhyme several times, with half the class clapping the dotted-quarter-note beat (♩.) and the other half clapping the rhythms. Ask students how many eighth notes are in the last measure. When they respond "5," ask them how many there should be. Following their response, ask where the sixth beat is. Someone will note the lone eighth note at the very beginning of the piece. Identify this note as the pick-up or anacrusis. Mark the counting for both the anacrusis and the last measure, as in **Visual R59,** noting that the anacrusis, added to the last measure, will form one complete measure.

VISUAL R59

There was an old wo-man lived un-der a hill;

And if she's not gone, she lives there still.

Find other examples of rhymes and songs in the text that begin with an anacrusis.

Visual R60 contains a rhythmic composition beginning with an anacrusis. Have students learn the rhythms well. Then perform the work as a two-, three-, or four-part rhythmic canon, adding body percussion or rhythm instruments. A *rhythmic canon* is a composition in which the same rhythm is performed by different people or groups, each beginning at a different time, as indicated by the numbers 1, 2, 3, and 4.

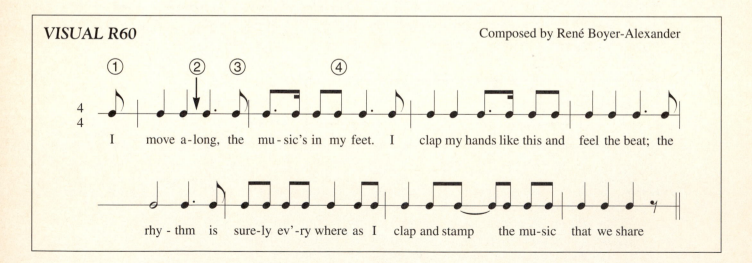

VISUAL R60

Composed by René Boyer-Alexander

I move a-long, the mu-sic's in my feet. I clap my hands like this and feel the beat; the

rhy - thm is sure-ly ev'-ry where as I clap and stamp the mu-sic that we share

Visuals R61, R62, R63 can be used for review of rhythmic structures or as motivators for student creativity.

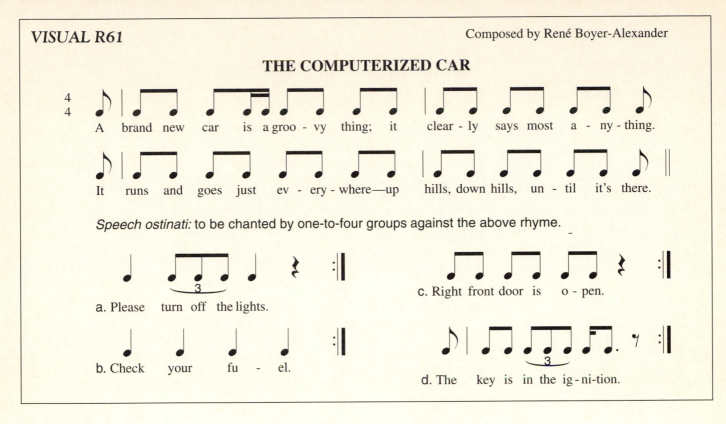

The symbol ‖ is a repeat sign. When this symbol occurs, go back to the beginning and perform the rhythms again.

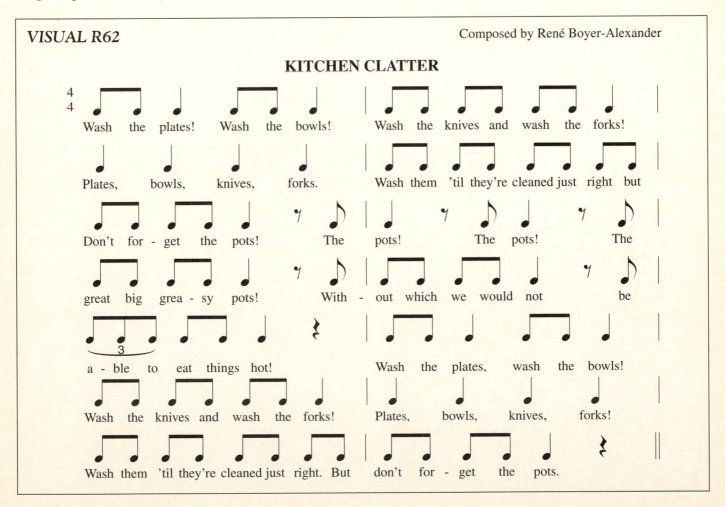

Composed by René Boyer-Alexander

THE SYNCOPATED RONDO

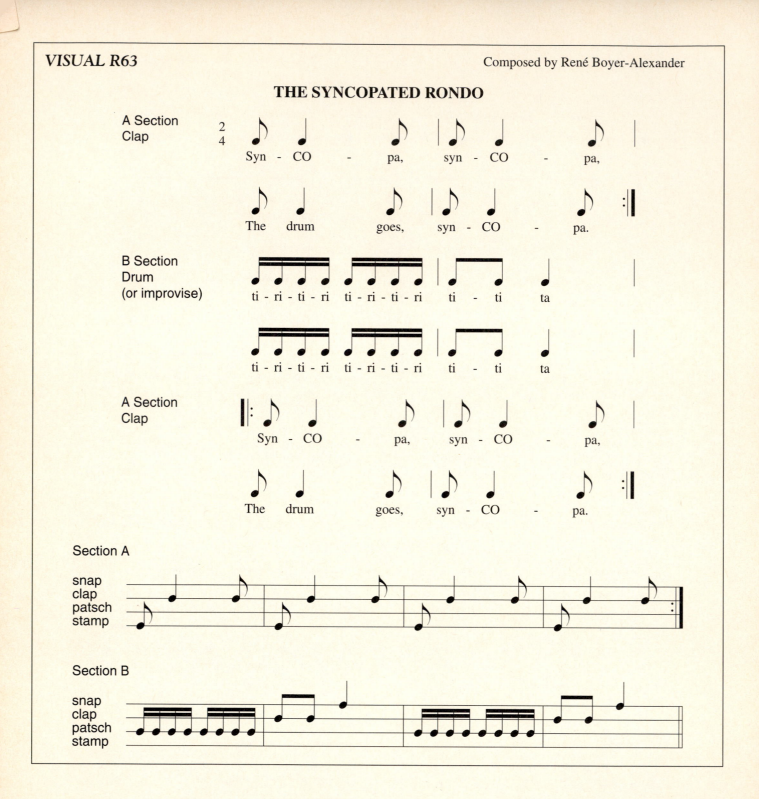

ADDITIONAL RHYMES FOR RHYTHM ACTIVITIES

Icka backa soda cracker
　　Icka backa boo!
Icka backa soda cracker
　　Out goes you!

Donkey, donkey, old and gray,
　　Open your mouth and gently bray;
Lift your ears and blow your horn,
　　To wake the world this sleepy morn.

Cross-patch, draw the latch,
　　Sit by the fire and spin;
Take a cup and drink it up;
　　Then call your neighbors in.

Cobbler, cobbler, mend my shoe
　　Give it one stitch, give it two,
Give it three stitch, give it four;
　　If it needs it, give it more.

Fudge Fudge, call the judge,
　　Mama's got a baby.
Not a girl, not a boy,
　　Just a plain old baby.

Teddy Bear, Teddy Bear, turn around,
　　Teddy Bear, Teddy Bear, touch the ground!
Teddy Bear, Teddy Bear, do a clap,
　　Teddy Bear, Teddy Bear, touch your lap!

To market, to market, to buy a fat pig.
　　Home again, home again, jiggety jig.
To market, to market, to buy a fat hog.
　　Home again, home again, jiggety jog.

Pease porridge hot,
　　Pease porridge cold,
Pease porridge in the pot,
　　Nine days old.
Some like it hot,
　　Some like it cold,
Some like it in the pot,
　　Nine days old.

Diddle Diddle Dumpling, my son John,
　　Went to bed with his stockings on.
One shoe off and one shoe on,
　　Diddle Diddle Dumpling, my son John.

Jack and Jill went up the hill
　　To fetch a pail of water.
Jack fell down and broke his crown,
　　And Jill came tumbling after.

	Translation
Dale, dale, dale	Hit it, hit it, hit it
no pierdas el tino;	Don't lose your good aim.
mide la distancia	Measure out the distance,
que hay en el campo	From here to there.

INTRODUCING THE STRUCTURAL COMPONENTS
OF RHYTHM
Suggested Sequencing by Grade Level

Kindergarten

1. silence and sound
2. steady beat
3. short and long sounds

Grade One

1. ♩ ♫ 𝄽
2. accent
3. 2/4 meter
4. bar line, measure, double bar
5. ostinato

Grade Two

1. tied notes
2. ♩ ▬
3. 4/4 meter

Grade Three

1. ♬♬
2. ♩♫ and ♫♩
3. 3/4 meter
4. ○ ▬
5. ♩.
6. ♪ ♩ ♪ = syncopation

Grade Four

1. ♩. ♪ and ♪ ♩.
2. anacrusis (pick-up)
3. 6/8 meter
4. ﹀
5. ♩ ♩ ♩ and ♪ ♩ ﹀ = more difficult syncopation

Grade Five

1. ♩. ♩ and ♫.
2. asymmetrical meters
3. mixed meters
4. ﹀

Grade Six

1. triplet
2. polyrhythms
3. ¢ meter

WRITTEN AND PERFORMANCE-RELATED ASSESSMENTS THROUGH COOPERATIVE LEARNING ACTIVITIES: RHYTHM

1. Give each group a different rhyme. Students read through the rhyme to discover on which syllables the beat initially falls; the best symbol (X) is placed under those syllables. Students then work out the rhythms of the words and place them above each syllable. After the teacher checks their solutions, students practice together the rhythms of the rhyme on instruments of their choice. It may be helpful if they chant the rhythm syllables while performing the rhythms.

2. Give each group a work sheet with a series of four-beat rhythm patterns on the left side of the page and a list of first lines of familiar songs or rhymes on the right. Students must match each rhythm pattern to the words having the same pattern. When finished, each student in the group should clap the rhythms correctly and say the rhythm syllables for each rhythm pattern.

3. Give students a list of rhythm patterns. They must discover what familiar rhyme or song uses each pattern in its opening phrase.

4. Give each group a different rhyme in either 2/4, 3/4, or 4/4 meter. Students must
   a. mark the accents in each phrase and decide what time signature to place at the beginning of the rhyme
   b. place the bar lines
   c. number each beat of the rhyme
   d. clap the rhythms while counting aloud each beat

5. Give each group Visual R23. The group must find at least one additional word to place under each rhythm pattern in every cateogry.

6. Give each group a set of flash cards containing different combinations of known rhythms. Each card contains a four-beat pattern. Every student must be able to clap the rhythms on each card while saying the rhythm syllables.

7. Distribute six blank flash cards, a felt marker, a work sheet, and a pencil to each group. Group members are to create six flash cards, each containing four beats. Every card should contain one dotted note: ♩., ♩., or ♩. ♪ , plus whatever other notes/rests are chosen to complete the four beats (ex.: ♩. ♪♫ ♩). Patterns should be written on the worksheet first and checked by the teacher before members draw them on the cards. When the cards are completed, each group member should correctly clap the rhythm pattern on each card while saying the rhythm syllables. (This activity can be used with other rhythm combinations such as ♫♫, ♫♫, and ♫♫, or ♫♫, ♩. ♩, and ♫..) On another day, after cards are completed, each group's cards can be exchanged with those of another group to use in clapping and verbalizing.

8. Ask each group to create two measures of rhythms in an irregular meter. A specific meter—7/8, 5/4, or 5/8—is assigned to each group. After completing the two measures, each group sets a word chant to its rhythms. Accents should be placed to show the groups of 2s and 3s within each measure. Each group should be able to chant to its rhythm while clapping the accents.

9. Each group must create four measures of rhythms within mixed meters. 2/4 and 3/4, 3/4 and 5/4, or 2/4 and 4/4 are assigned to each group. When finished, the group should be able to perform the rhythm on rhythm instruments while saying the rhythm syllables or chanting words set to the rhythms.

10. Assign several rhythm patterns in Visual R56 to each group. Group members must place the numbers 1 through 4 on the beats where they occur. Members should decide how to perform together each pattern by stamping, patching, clapping, and/or snapping. After practicing its routines, the

group performs its rhythms for the class while counting aloud the beat numbers.

11. Give each group Visual R62. Groups should develop a kitchen ostinato which can accompany "Kitchen Clatter." Use spoons, glasses, plates, bowls, pots, pans, and other kitchen utensils as instruments. Students should bring their "instruments" to the next class so they can perform their compositions.

Teaching Melody to Children

Chapter 3

INTRODUCTION

A melody consists of a linear succession of sounds and silences ordered in time. By its very nature, melody cannot be separated from rhythm. Each musical sound in a melody has two fundamental qualities, pitch and duration. When 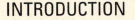 used in succession, pitch-plus-duration values form melodies.

When pitches change in a melody, they give the melody direction, sometimes moving upward, sometimes moving downward, and other times staying the same. The upward and downward motion of a melody, the ease or tension that results when a melody changes direction, and the rate of change in a melody's direction contribute to the expressiveness of the melodic line.

The concept of the nature of a melody has changed over the centuries to encompass a variety of characteristics. Although early composers of Western music wrote melodies that were unaccompanied and rhythmically free, without bar lines and measures, composers today are much more diversified in their approach to the melodic line. Some melodies may be smooth and connected, whereas others tend to be irregular and unpredictable. For most of us, however, melody will always be the most memorable element in the music we love—the "tune."

> *It is the melody which is the charm of music,*
> *and it is that which is most difficult to produce.*
> *The invention of a fine melody is a work of genius.*
> *—Joseph Haydn*

FOCUS
Pitch: High/Low

LEARNING   *Pitch* is the relative highness or lowness of a musical sound. Sounds in our environment are high, medium, low, or the same in relation one to another.

Strategies

Identify environmental sounds that are high: siren, bird chirping, whistling teapot, bell ringing; identify sounds that are low: foghorn, lion growling, frog croaking.

Have students explore and identify extreme highs and lows of melodic instruments, such as the piano, resonator bells, or xylophone. Draw a wavy line on the chalkboard to represent the ocean. When students hear a high sound, they can place a star in the sky; when hearing a low sound, they can put a starfish in the ocean, as in **Visual M1.** Other visuals, such as a plane and a whale, could be used. This activity can also be reversed. When a student places a star in the sky, another student plays a high sound on a melody instrument.

VISUAL M1

or

Children can express their awareness of high and low through body movements, such as standing on tiptoe or reaching upward when they hear high sounds and crouching down low when they hear low sounds.

Once students can identify the highs and lows of a single instrument, such as the piano, expand their listening abilities by playing different instruments that are either high or low; for example, the triangle versus the drum; soprano glockenspiel versus the bass xylophone.

Creative dramas can be developed to help students identify and manipulate high, medium, and low sounds, as in "I Can't Pay the Rent," which follows. Children's stories, nursery rhymes, and fairy tales can also be developed into dramas.

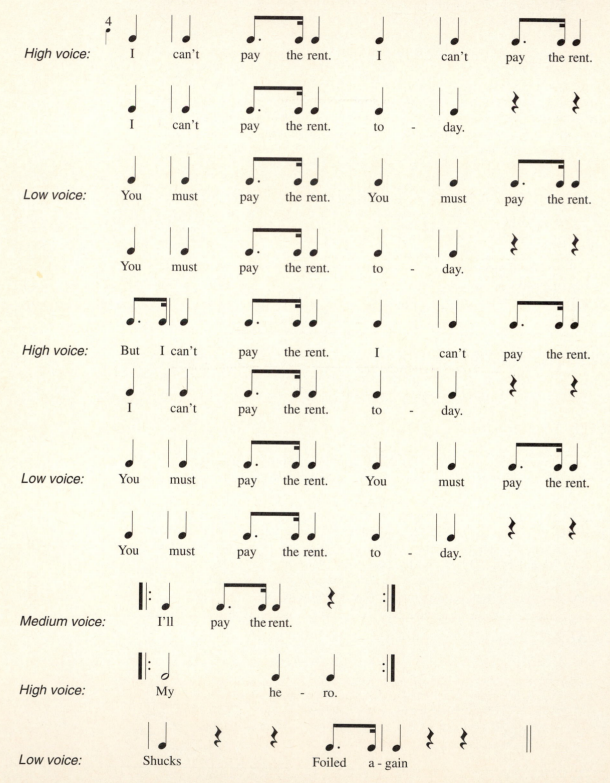

I Can't Pay the Rent

Provide a paper napkin or tissue for each student. Have the student twist the napkin in the middle to produce a hair bow, a mustache, or a bow tie. Divide the class into three groups, each group representing a character in the drama. Each group recites its own line of the drama, placing the napkin in the appropriate place on the body, corresponding to the high-, medium-, or low-pitched voice of the character speaking:

Your "High"-ness   Your "Medium"-ness   Your "Low"-ness

For variety, the rhythm of the speakers' lines can be transferred to high, medium, and low melodic instruments, such as the soprano glockenspiel, the alto xylophone, and the bass xylophone. These instruments can be played before, during, or after each spoken line to reinforce the relatively high, medium, or low voices.

After completing the drama, place a single line across the chalkboard. Provide students with small replicas of your "High"-ness, "Medium"-ness, and "Low"-ness. Ask the students which replica should be placed high, above the line; low, below the line; or on the line in the middle. Explain that these replicas represent musical symbols called notes. Placing notes above, below, or on lines helps us show which pitches are high, medium, and low.

FOCUS
Staff

LEARNING   Pitches are usually represented by symbols called *notes*, which are placed on a staff. A *staff* consists of five parallel lines and four spaces.

Strategies

Draw a staff on the chalkboard and number the lines and spaces from bottom to top as in **Visual M2.** The first line is always the bottom line, representing the lowest pitch on the staff.

VISUAL M2

5th line
4th line   4th space
3rd line   3rd space
2nd line   2nd space
1st line   1st space

Using the chalkboard or felt board, provide multiple experiences for students to become familiar with the staff by having them place notes on designated lines and spaces. The teacher may also reverse this procedure by having students identify notes already placed on the staff, as in **Visual M3.** Be sure that students are aware that, when recording a series of notes, the notes move from left to right on the staff, just as their printing or writing moves from left to right on the page.

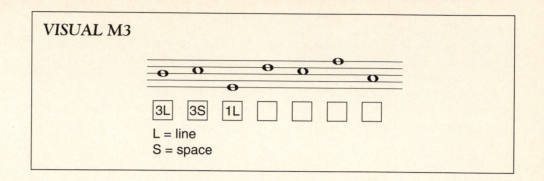

VISUAL M3

L = line
S = space

LEARNING Because a staff has only five lines and four spaces where a pitch can be placed, extra lines are often added above and below the staff to accommodate additional pitches. These lines are called *ledger lines*.

Strategies

Ledger lines are taught to children only as they are needed. The manner in which they ascend and descend is presented in **Visual M4** as a source of needed information for the adult learner at this point. Note that a ledger line is slightly wider than the width of a note head. Remember that the lowest pitch is always on the lowest ledger line.

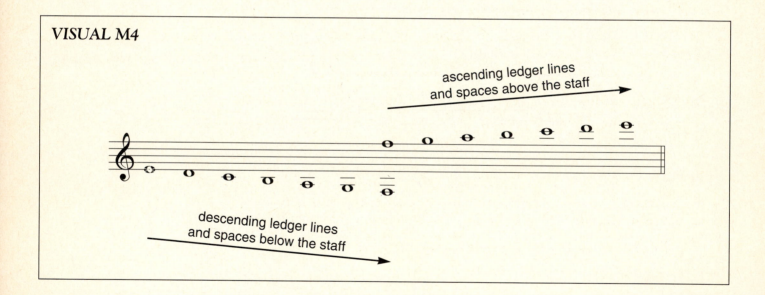

VISUAL M4

ascending ledger lines
and spaces above the staff

descending ledger lines
and spaces below the staff

Ledger lines that extend far beyond the staff can be notated more simply by using 8va, the common abbreviation for 8 *ottava*, rather than multiple ledger lines. *8va* means that the notes should be played eight zones (an *octave*) higher or lower than written. See **Visual M5.**

VISUAL M5

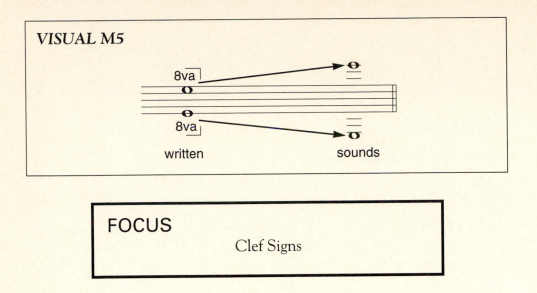

written   sounds

FOCUS

Clef Signs

LEARNING The placement of a *clef sign* on the far left side of a staff indicates the relative highness or lowness of pitches. A *treble clef sign* usually denotes pitches that are considered high in contrast to the *bass clef sign*, which usually denotes lower pitches.

Strategies

Place on the chalkboard either a treble or a bass clef sign, depending on which is being taught. Identify the clef sign, as in **Visual M6.**

VISUAL M6

Treble clef   Bass clef

On the chalkboard, carefully demonstrate a step-by-step procedure for drawing the treble or the bass clef sign, as in **Visual M7.** Because the final scroll movement encircles the second line (called "G"), the treble clef is often referred to as G *clef*. The bass clef is often referred to as F *clef* because the two dots to the right of the bass clef sign are placed on either side of the F line.

VISUAL M7

Students should practice drawing treble and bass clef signs.

The treble and the bass clefs have been presented here together. It should be noted, however, that the bass clef is usually not presented to children until the upper grades.

LEARNING
When the treble and bass clefs are placed on two staves joined by a vertical line and a brace at the left, the *Grand Staff* is formed.

Strategies

Since the bass clef is usually taught to children in the upper grades, the Grand Staff, as seen in **Visual M8,** would also be presented to older children.

VISUAL M8

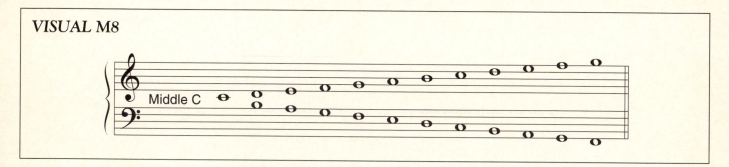

Middle C

The Grand Staff is used for the notation of keyboard music and is useful for other purposes, since it is capable of representing a great range of pitches. The treble clef sign, however, is the most commonly used clef sign in children's song literature. Therefore it will be emphasized in the strategies that follow.

The note placed on the first ledger line above the bass staff represents the same pitch as the note placed on the first ledger line below the treble staff. This note is called *Middle C*. Middle C derives its name from its location approximately in the middle of the Grand Staff.

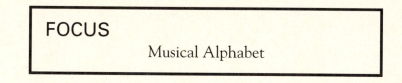

┌─────────────────────────────────────┐
│ FOCUS   │
│   Musical Alphabet   │
└─────────────────────────────────────┘

LEARNING
With the addition of the treble clef sign to the staff, pitches can now be assigned specific names. Their names will change, however, if a clef sign other than the treble clef is used.

Pitches take their name from the first seven letters of the alphabet: A, B, C, D, E, F, G. These seven letters are known as the *musical alphabet*.

Strategies

Place a staff on the chalkboard. Explain to the students that each line and space has its own name, taken from the first seven letters of the alphabet. Place these letters on the chalkboard, as in **Visual M9.** Now place the treble clef on the staff and remind students that this clef will always tells us where "G" can be located. Sing the song "Hot Cross Buns." Under the staff write the first three words of the song and place the note G above the word "cross." Again, see Visual M9.

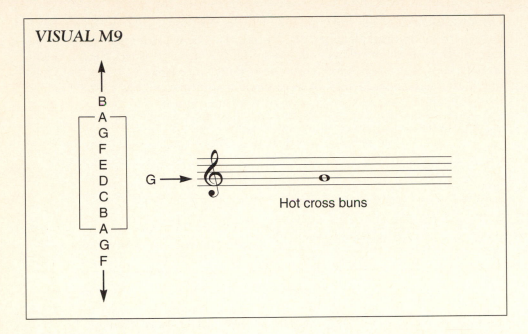

If the word "cross" is sung on G, then there are only two more pitches to learn. Sing the three pitches for "hot cross buns" and ask students if the pitch for "buns" is higher or lower than the pitch for "cross." Since it is just a little lower, its name will be the alphabet letter that comes just before G; that is, its name is F. This can easily be seen by checking the alphabet ladder to the left of the staff. Place F on the staff. Sing the three pitches for "hot cross buns" one more time. Ask students if the pitch for "hot" is higher or lower than the pitch for "cross." The students will know it is a little bit higher. By checking the alphabet ladder again, the students will be able to identify the pitch for "hot" as "A." Sing just the first three pitches of the song again, but instead of singing the words, have the students sing the alphabet names: A, G, F.

On another day, place the words to the whole song on the chalkboard and work out the rest of the pitches, as in **Visual M10.** Then sing both the song words and the alphabet names of the pitches.

VISUAL M10

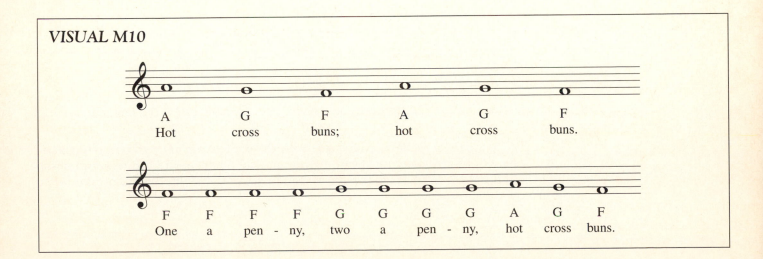

On subsequent days, use the same song to discover the location of the pitches in the rest of the musical alphabet. See **Visual M11.** Sing "Hot Cross Buns" beginning on B (example b below) and, later, on E (example c below). Since students already know the pitches for "cross" and "buns" in example b, they only have one more pitch to discover = B. In example c, all three pitches must be named. In this example students should notice that lines can be added—for the pitch C—if more than the five staff lines are needed. At this time, the ledger line for middle C should be introduced.

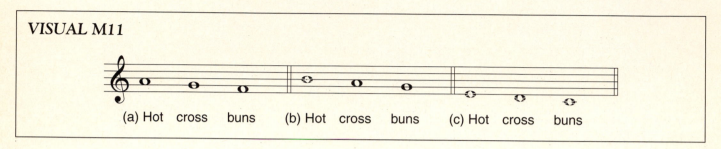

VISUAL M11

(a) Hot cross buns   (b) Hot cross buns   (c) Hot cross buns

Now the musical alphabet is complete. All seven letters have been used.

Students need to sing and play many songs containing the musical alphabet. One of the best ways to learn to read pitches and rhythms from a staff is through the playing of the soprano recorder. At this point, adult students may want to parallel their learning of melodic concepts by turning to the chapter on "Playing Musical Instruments" and learning to play the recorder by proceeding through the sequence provided.

Once students have learned the musical alphabet—often referred to as *absolute pitch names*—a chart similar to that in **Visual M12** can be posted. This chart helps students realize that, once the seven letters of the musical alphabet have been used, they are repeated over and over again.

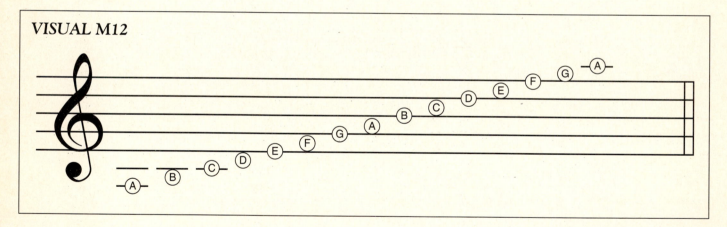

VISUAL M12

Help students become comfortable with the musical alphabet by providing experiences that reinforce it. Learning the musical alphabet in both its forward and backward sequences should be stressed. Asking students questions similar to these may be helpful:

What comes after D?
What comes before F?
What comes after G?
What comes before A?

Some teachers find that learning key words or phrases can be helpful to students in remembering the names of the lines and spaces of the staff. See **Visual M13.**

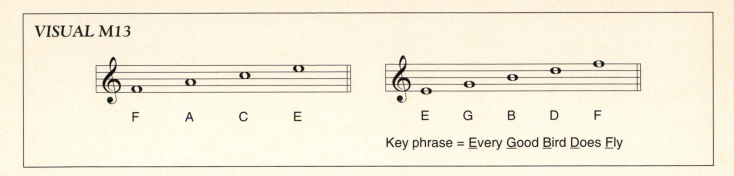

F   A   C   E

E   G   B   D   F

Key phrase = Every Good Bird Does Fly

Provide a number of worksheets containing exercises for naming only spaces and only lines. Worksheets containing a combination of lines and spaces should follow. Once students have facility naming notes placed on the staff, the naming of ledger lines should be added. Examples are provided in **Visual M14.**

VISUAL M14

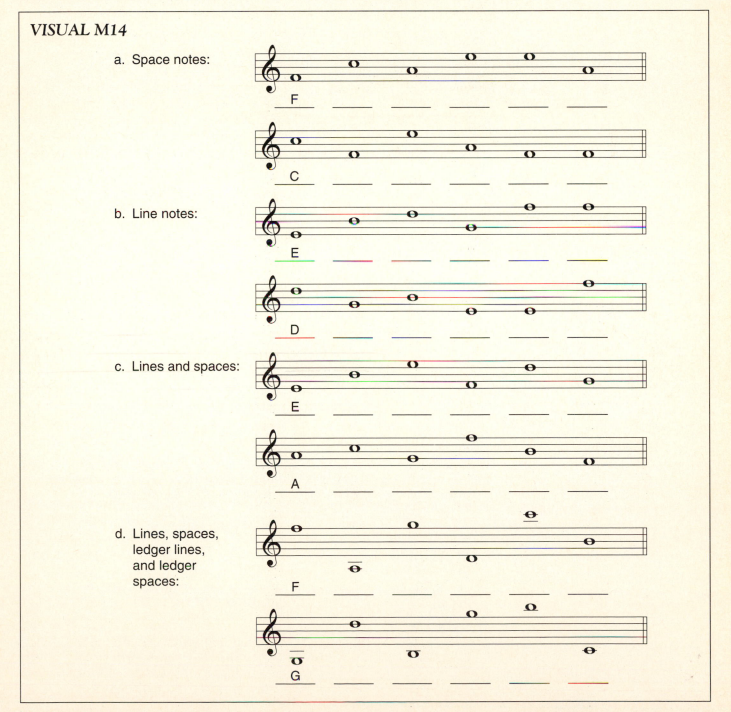

a. Space notes:

F _ _ _ _ _ _

C _ _ _ _ _ _

b. Line notes:

E _ _ _ _ _ _

D _ _ _ _ _ _

c. Lines and spaces:

E _ _ _ _ _ _

A _ _ _ _ _ _

d. Lines, spaces, ledger lines, and ledger spaces:

F _ _ _ _ _ _

G _ _ _ _ _ _

Students often find it helpful to name groups of notes that spell words, such as those in **Visual M15.**

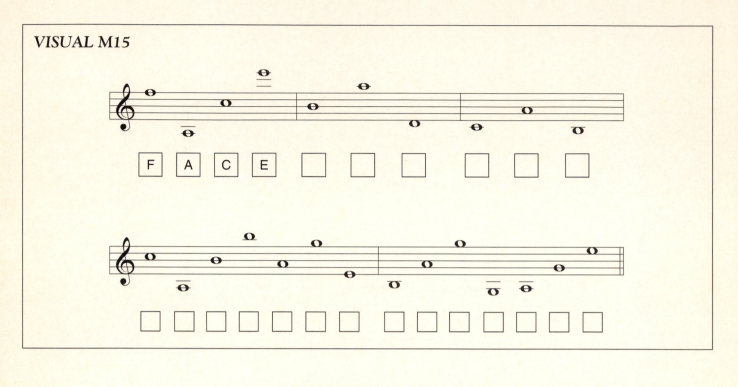

VISUAL M15

F A C E ▢ ▢ ▢ ▢ ▢ ▢

▢ ▢ ▢ ▢ ▢ ▢ ▢ ▢ ▢ ▢ ▢ ▢ ▢

FOCUS

Note Stems

LEARNING  When note heads with stems are placed on the staff, special rules must be followed. When the note head is placed on the third line or above, its stem must be placed downward to the left of the note head. When the note head is below the third line, the stem must extend upward to the right of the note head. The direction of all stems in beamed note groups is determined by the note farthest from the third line.

Strategies

Provide an example of a staff containing a series of notes whose stems are correctly placed according to the rules stated above. See **Visual M16.**

VISUAL M16

Have students take turns going to the chalkboard and placing stems on note heads provided by the teacher, as in **Visual M17.**

VISUAL M17

Place on the chalkboard examples of notes that have been beamed, as in **Visual M18.** Provide opportunities for students to create combinations of beamed note groupings.

VISUAL M18

Have students examine the placement of stems on note heads found in simple song literature.

FOCUS
Unorganized and Organized Pitches

LEARNING When musical ideas are created by adding rhythms to a linear succession of pitches and rests, a *melody* results.

Strategies

Show students the difference between unorganized and organized pitches, as in **Visual M19.**

VISUAL M19

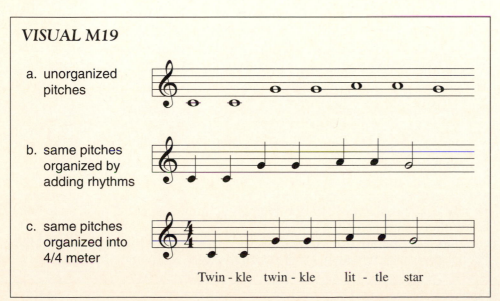

a. unorganized pitches

b. same pitches organized by adding rhythms

c. same pitches organized into 4/4 meter

Twin - kle   twin - kle   lit - tle   star

Provide experiences for students to manipulate pitches to form melodies. Have students study the unorganized linear succession of pitches as presented in **Visual M20.** The teacher may wish to have the entire class sing or play the pitches on a melody instrument until they discover the name of the song. When students know the name of the song, have them organize the pitches into a melody by changing the open note heads to appropriate rhythm symbols and adding bar lines and a time signature.

VISUAL M20

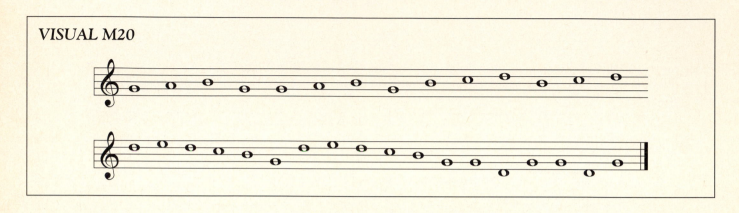

FOCUS

Contour

LEARNING   *Contour is the direction or shape of a melody.*

Strategies

Sitting in a circle, students should take turns vocalizing their names in a creative manner. The rest of the class should immediately repeat the name, using the same voice inflections. Simultaneously, the students should trace in the air the contour of the name. When the students are ready, the teacher—and later the students themselves—should reproduce the contours on the chalkboard, as in **Visual M21.**

VISUAL M21

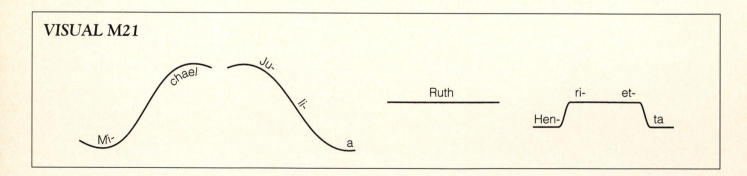

Be sure to emphasize that contours progress upward, downward, or stay the same. Using flash cards containing a variety of contours, have students vocalize the contours using improvised neutral sounds, words, or phrases, as in **Visual M22.** Flash cards can be turned in any direction to create additional contours.

VISUAL M22

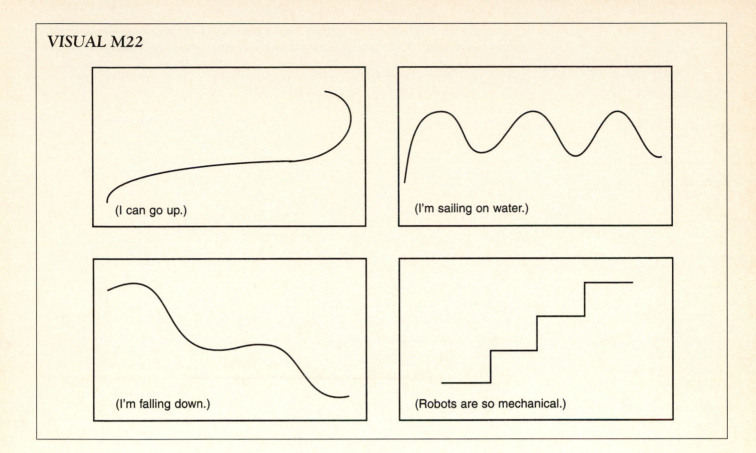

(I can go up.)

(I'm sailing on water.)

(I'm falling down.)

(Robots are so mechanical.)

Have students move their hands to the contours of familiar songs, such as "Go to Sleep," demonstrated in **Visual M23.**

VISUAL M23

Canadian Lullaby

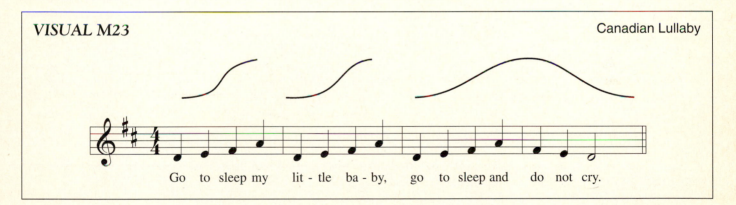

Go to sleep my lit - tle ba - by, go to sleep and do not cry.

Demonstrate an alternative way of showing contour by lining a melody, reproducing more exactly the direction of the line and the relative length of time each note is held, as in **Visual M24.**

VISUAL M24

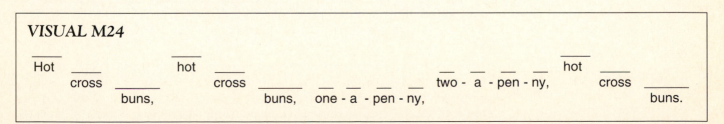

Hot ____ hot ____ __ __ __ __ hot ____
cross _____ cross _____ __ __ __ __ two - a - pen - ny, cross _____
buns, buns, one - a - pen - ny, buns.

Have a student place on the chalkboard a lined pattern to a familiar song while the class sings it. The finished product might resemble that in **Visual M25.**

VISUAL M25

"Mary Had a Little Lamb"

Place on the chalkboard the contour of a "mystery song" that the students can identify. Have students place the contour of their own "mystery song" on the board for the class to identify.

Students should create their own contours for members of the class to reproduce vocally or on a melodic instrument. Students can also do interpretive movement to different contours.

FOCUS
Steps, Skips, and Repeated Notes

LEARNING Pitches within a melody move by steps, skips, or repetition. Pitches *step* when they move from line to space or space to line on the staff; pitches *skip* when they move from line to line or space to space; *repetition* results when pitches stay on the same line or space of the staff.

Strategies

Place on the chalkboard or create a chart that shows notes that step, skip, and repeat, as in **Visual M26.**

VISUAL M26

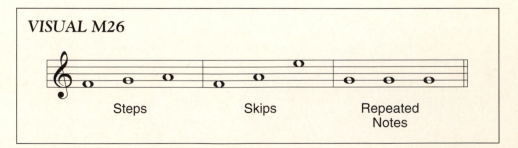

Steps   Skips   Repeated Notes

Reinforce the understanding of how melodies move by creating flash cards or overhead transparencies containing many examples of steps, skips, and repeated notes for students to identify, as in **Visual M27.** Students should sing or play the examples on a melodic instrument so that they identify the symbols with the sounds.

VISUAL 27

(Skipping Down)   (Stepping Up)

(Stepping Down)   (Repeated Notes)   (Skipping Up)

(Step Down; Skip Up)   (Step Up; Skip Down)

Students should have many opportunities to identify a mixture of steps, skips, and repeated notes found in their song literature. An approach to reinforcing these skills is provided in **Visual M28.** Students should verbalize how the song moves as shown in the visual.

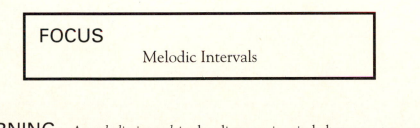

FOCUS

Melodic Intervals

LEARNING A *melodic inteval* is the distance in pitch between two notes sounded consecutively. Melodies contain a succession of melodic intervals.

Strategies

Put on the chalkboard the main intervals used within a melody or display them on a chart or overhead transparency, as in **Visual M29.**

B = begin   SU = step up
SD = step down   SkU = skip up
R = repeat   SkD = skip down

CHURCH BELLS

B   R   R   SD   R   R   SD   R   R   SD

Lis - ten,   oh   lis - ten,   now   what   do   you   hear?

SD   R   R   SD   R   R   SD   R   R   SD

Church   bells   are   ring - ing;   they   sound   loud   and   clear.

TOUCH A STAR

B   R   R   SU   R   R   SU   R   R   SU

Here   we   go   fly - ing   so   high   in   the   sky;

SU   R   R   SU   R   R   SU   R   R   SU

Up   to   the   stars   we   go,   just   you   and   I.

MOON SHINE

B   R   R   R   R   R   R   R   R   R   SkU

The   moon   when   it's   shin - ing,   so   round   and   so   high,

R   R   R   R   R   SkD   R   R   SkU   R   R   SkU

Is   a   Ja - pa - nese   lan - tern,   hung   up   in   the   sky.

DANCING LEAVES

B   R   SD   R   SD   SkU   SkD   R   SD   SU   SkD   SkD   SU   SkD   SU

Fall - ing   leaves   come   twirl - ing   down,   like   bal - le - ri - nas   whirl - ing   'round.

VISUAL M29

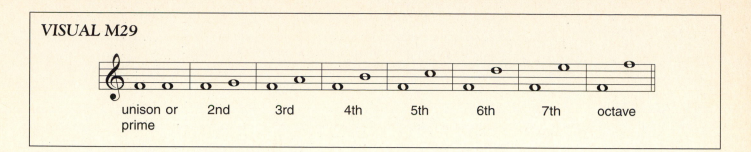

unison or prime   2nd   3rd   4th   5th   6th   7th   octave

Intervals are named by counting the number of lines and spaces involved in the interval. Both the lower and the upper notes are part of the interval and must be included in the count. Call the lower note "1"; then count each line and space, ending with the upper note, as in **Visual M30.**

VISUAL M30

interval of a 6th

Have students study their song literature to identify the intervals each song contains, as in **Visual M31.**

VISUAL M31

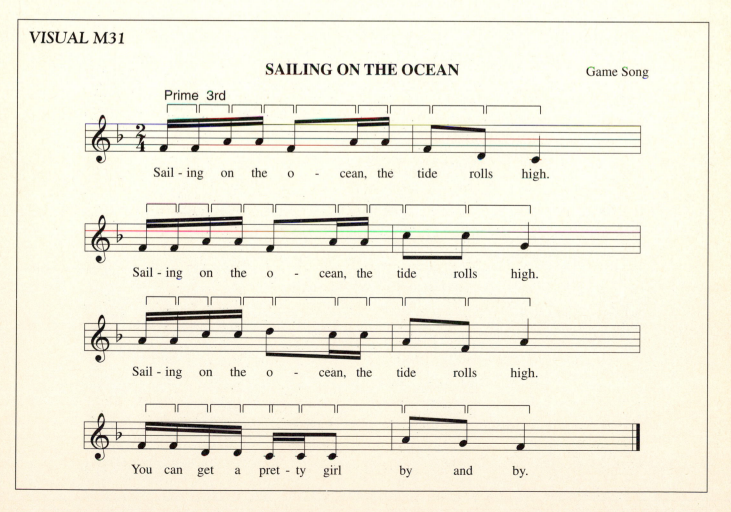

SAILING ON THE OCEAN   Game Song

Prime 3rd

Sail - ing on the o - cean, the tide rolls high.

Sail - ing on the o - cean, the tide rolls high.

Sail - ing on the o - cean, the tide rolls high.

You can get a pret - ty girl by and by.

To reinforce the learning of melodic intervals, provide worksheets, as in **Visual M32.** Each measure in this visual can be made into a flash card. Students should be challenged to play these intervals on melodic instruments.

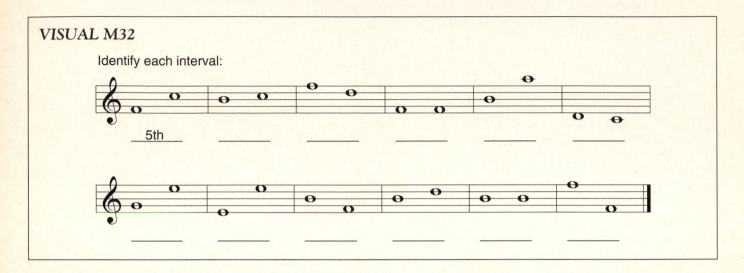

VISUAL M32

Identify each interval:

5th _____ _____ _____ _____ _____

_____ _____ _____ _____ _____

Provide worksheets for students to notate intervals above or below given notes, as specified by the teacher. See **Visual M33.**

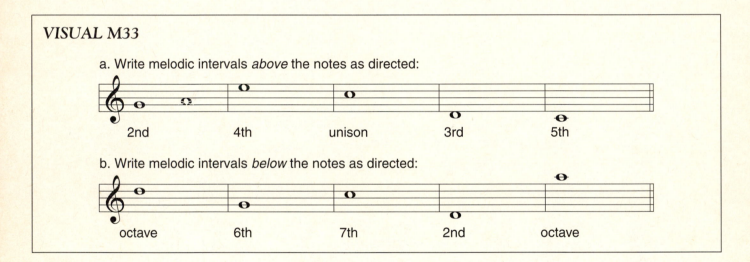

VISUAL M33

a. Write melodic intervals *above* the notes as directed:

2nd 4th unison 3rd 5th

b. Write melodic intervals *below* the notes as directed:

octave 6th 7th 2nd octave

Some intervals are larger than an octave. These intervals are commonly called *compound intervals.* See **Visual M34.**

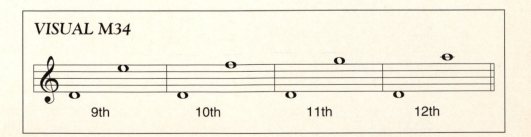

VISUAL M34

9th 10th 11th 12th

LEARNING The *half step* is the smallest interval used in most of the music of Western civilization. Two half steps combine to make a *whole step*.

Strategies

Place on a staff a series of adjacent notes, as in **Visual M35.** Each note appears to be equidistant from the preceding and following note. In this example, the notes on the staff are deceptive; between the notes E and F, and B and C, there is a half step, whereas between all other adjacent notes there is a whole step. When notes are placed on the staff in alphabetical sequence—either ascending or descending—the succession is said to be stepwise or *diatonic*. Visual M35 is a *diatonic sequence*.

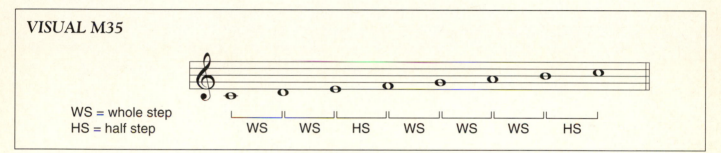

VISUAL M35

WS = whole step
HS = half step

WS   WS   HS   WS   WS   WS   HS

Provide a picture of a section of a piano keyboard. The white keys on the piano are a good example of a diatonic sequence. Show the relationship of the diatonic white keys to the diatonic series on the staff. See **Visual M36.**

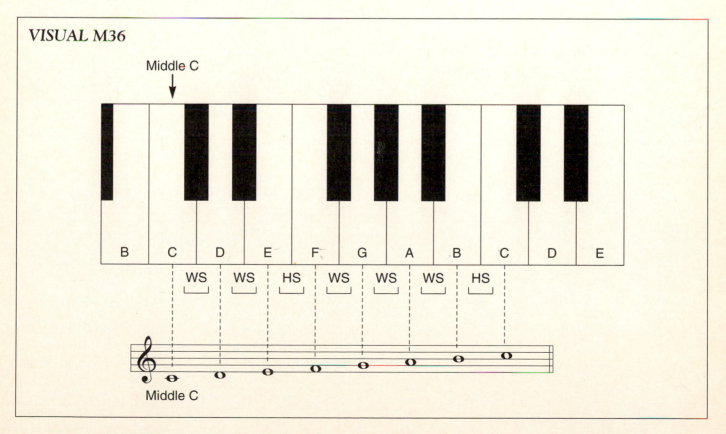

VISUAL M36

Middle C

B   C   D   E   F   G   A   B   C   D   E

WS   WS   HS   WS   WS   WS   HS

Middle C

Students should play on a piano or keyboard instrument each of the half and whole steps in the diatonic series. Middle C is the white key directly to the left of two black keys located in the middle of the piano keyboard.

Play a variety of whole steps and half steps; have students echo each interval vocally after it is played.

Provide students with opportunities to identify half steps and whole steps, as in **Visual M37.** The measures in Visual M37 can also be made into flash cards to provide another means for learning intervals. These melodic intervals should be sung and played on melodic instruments.

VISUAL M37

Identify each progression as half step (HS) or whole step (WS).

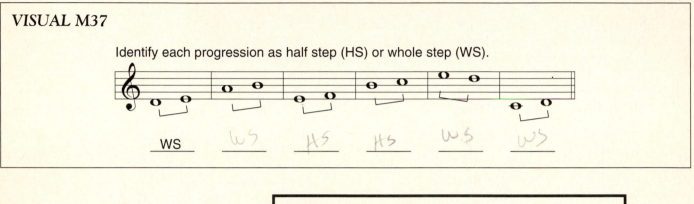

WS   WS   HS   HS   WS   WS

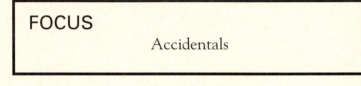

FOCUS

Accidentals

LEARNING   *Accidentals* are symbols that can be applied to any pitch to alter it in some way. There are three basic accidentals: a *sharp* (♯) raises the pitch of a note a half step; a *flat* (♭) lowers the pitch of a note a half step; a *natural* (♮) cancels a previous sharp or flat.

Strategies

Have students sing a song they know well, such as "Bounce High, Bounce Low." Place the song on the chalkboard, as in **Visual M38.**

VISUAL M38

Bounce high,   bounce low,   Bounce the ball to Shi - loh.

Now play the song on a melody instrument, exactly as it appears on the chalkboard. Ask the students if the song sounds correct. Sing and play the song again, so that the problem note F can be identified. Ask students if F should be played higher or lower. After their "high" response, show how a note can be raised one half step higher by placing a sharp sign (♯) to the left of the note, as in **Visual M39.**

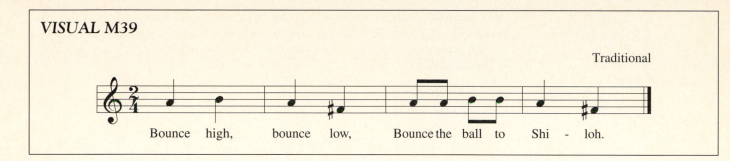

Traditional

Bounce high,   bounce low,   Bounce the ball to   Shi - loh.

Choose other songs to demonstrate how to lower a pitch one half step, by plac-ing a flat (♭) to the left of the note; demonstrate how a natural sign (♮) will can-cel either a sharp or a flat.

Provide visual experiences that demonstrate the effect that an accidental has when placed to the left of any pitch on a staff. Make accessible a picture of a pi-ano keyboard that has each key name clearly marked. Underneath the picture place a staff containing each note that directly correlates with each key on the piano as in **Visual M40.**

VISUAL M40

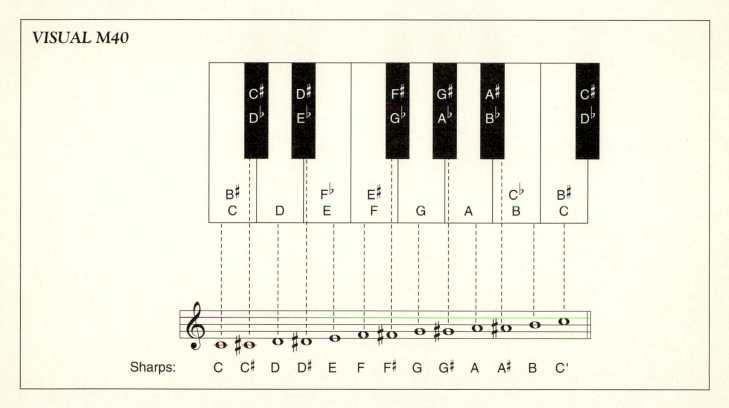

Sharps: C   C♯   D   D♯   E   F   F♯   G   G♯   A   A♯   B   C'

Explain that when a series of notes progresses from high to low, flats rather than sharps are used, as in **Visual M41.**

VISUAL M41

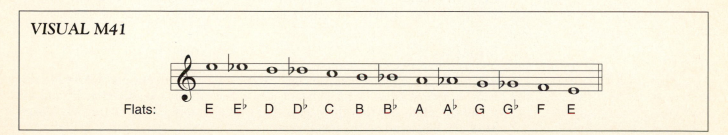

Flats: E   E♭   D   D♭   C   B   B♭   A   A♭   G   G♭   F   E

Have students identify notes altered by sharps, flats, and natural signs. See **Visual M42** for a sample worksheet. Note that, when identifying an altered note, the accidental is placed to the right of the note name: A♯, B♭, C♮. The measures in Visual M42 may also be reproduced as flash cards.

VISUAL M42

A♯

Provide some measures containing examples of notes that have been altered by accidentals, as in **Visual M43.** Note that accidentals remain in effect throughout the measure in which they occur; they are automatically cancelled (no natural sign needed) by a bar line. The only exception to this rule occurs when an altered note is tied across a bar line. The accidental remains in effect for the length of the tied note.

VISUAL M43

(F♯)   (F♮)

(B♭)   (B♮)   (B♭)   (B♮)

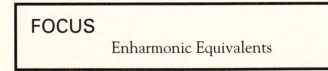

FOCUS

Enharmonic Equivalents

LEARNING   When two pitches have the same sound but are written with different letter names, these pitches are called *enharmonic*.

Strategies

Ask a student to play F♯ on the piano. Have a second student play G♭ within the same octave. Discuss what is heard. Once the students realize that F♯ and G♭ sound the same and that there are other similar combinations of pitches, **Visual M44** can be placed on the chalkboard.

VISUAL M44

Enharmonic pitches

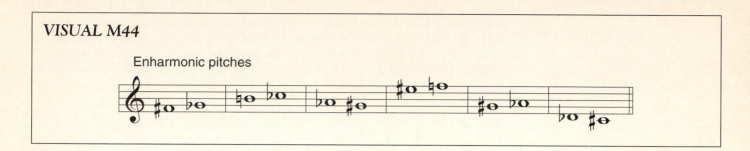

Have students write the enharmonic equivalents of designated pitches. A worksheet similar to that in **Visual M45** can be used.

VISUAL M45

FOCUS
Major Scales and Key Signatures

LEARNING A *scale* is an orderly ascending or descending arrangement of pitches within the limits of an octave. Common scales used by composers are the major, minor, pentatonic, and chromatic. Most melodies in children's song literature are derived from pitches belonging to one of these scales.

Strategies

Have students create a scale using each of the tones of any octave; limit the number of accidentals that may be used. The beginning tone and its upper octave may not be altered. Two arbitrary scales that may result are given in **Visual M46.**

VISUAL M46

Example 1

Example 2

LEARNING A *major scale* is composed of the following whole- and half-step relationships: W W H W W W H. A major scale can be built on any pitch. The starting pitch gives the scale its name.

Strategies

After students have played their scales on a melody instrument, have them compose a short, four- or eight-measure composition using only the tones of their scale. After listening to the original compositions, note that some scales worked better than others. Today, composers use scales that are versatile, that work well over and over again. Sing a familiar song using the major scale, such as "Touch a Star," found in Visual M28. Show how this song uses all the tones of a major scale beginning on C. As students say each tone, draw it on a staff, as in **Visual M47.** Analyze and label the half- and whole-step relationships occurring between the notes of the scale. Point out that half steps always occur between the scale degrees of 3 and 4, and 7 and 8 in a major scale. Have students sing the letter names of the scale, both ascending and descending.

VISUAL M47

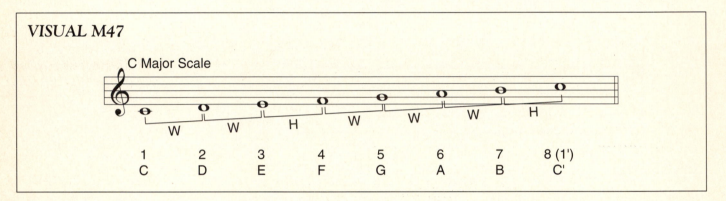

On the keyboard, the white keys from C to C' represent a major scale. Students can "build" a human scale by representing the keys contained in an octave of the keyboard. Each student representing a white key can play a resonator bell whose pitch corresponds to the student's place in the major scale.

Have students construct additional major scales beginning on any diatonic pitch. Mark each half and whole step, inserting accidentals where needed. See **Visual M48.** Remember, scales always end one octave above or below their beginning pitch.

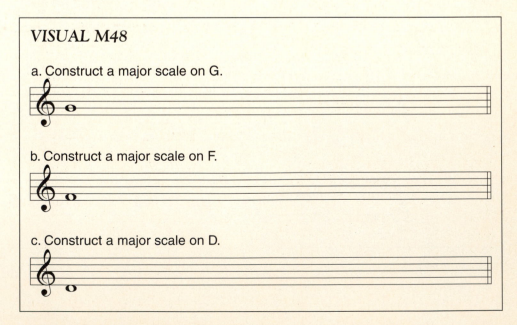

Have students sing "C-Saw" to demonstrate songs built on a major scale. Students can play the song on melody instruments. After students learn the song well, they can play it beginning on diatonic pitches other than C.

C-SAW

I   climb   up   the   moun - tain,   I   climb   up   the   hill;

I   keep   go - ing   high - er,   like   Jack   and   like   Jill.

And   now   I   climb   down,   it's   so   ea - sy   you   see.

I   keep   go - ing   low - er   'til I   reach   Mid - dle   "C".

LEARNING

A *key signature* is a sign, placed at the beginning of a song immediately following the clef sign, that tells the performer the names of the sharps or flats occurring in the music.

Strategies

Build an E-flat major scale, as in **Visual M49.** Note that accidentals have been placed before every E, A, and B. To ease the burden of having to place a flat sign on these three notes every time they occur, composers use a key signature instead. The key signature tells the performer to flat E, A, and B every time they occur in the music, unless the composer indicates otherwise.

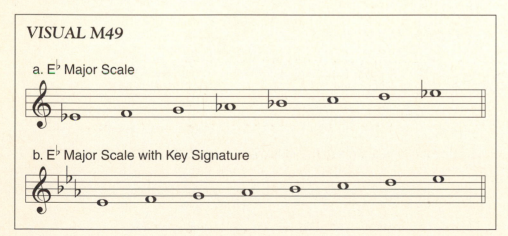

VISUAL M49

a. E♭ Major Scale

b. E♭ Major Scale with Key Signature

Since there are seven different pitches in every major scale, a key signature may have as many as seven sharps or flats. The absence of a key signature indicates that the composition may be in C major.

Provide a chart containing the key signatures for all the major scales, as in **Visual M50.** Notice that accidentals in key signatures always occur in the same order; that is, F♯ is always the first sharp; B♭ is always the first flat. Sharps and flats are always placed from left to right in the key signature. To remember the order in which the sharps and flats are placed on the staff, the following slogans may be useful:

sharps: <u>F</u>ine <u>c</u>ut <u>g</u>lass <u>d</u>ishes <u>a</u>re <u>e</u>asily <u>b</u>roken.
flats: <u>B</u>ill, <u>E</u>d, <u>a</u>nd <u>D</u>on <u>g</u>o <u>c</u>od <u>f</u>ishing.

Notice that the order of the flats is the reverse of the order of the sharps. Except for the key of F, a flat sign must always accompany the name of a flat key. Each measure in **Visual M50** can be made into a flash card to reinforce students' understanding of key signatures.

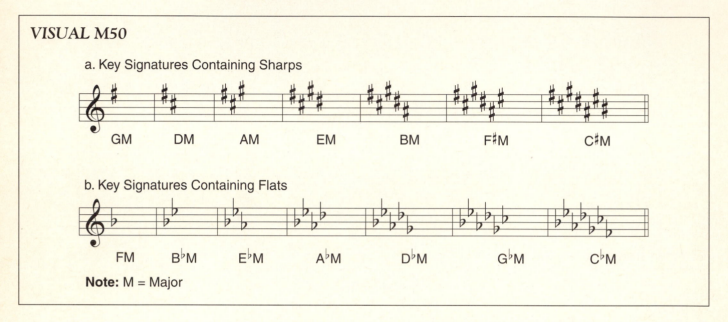

VISUAL M50

a. Key Signatures Containing Sharps

GM   DM   AM   EM   BM   F#M   C#M

b. Key Signatures Containing Flats

FM   B♭M   E♭M   A♭M   D♭M   G♭M   C♭M

Note: M = Major

Have students construct a variety of major scales and assign the proper key signature.

Provide worksheets that reinforce students' understanding of key signatures, as in **Visual M51.**

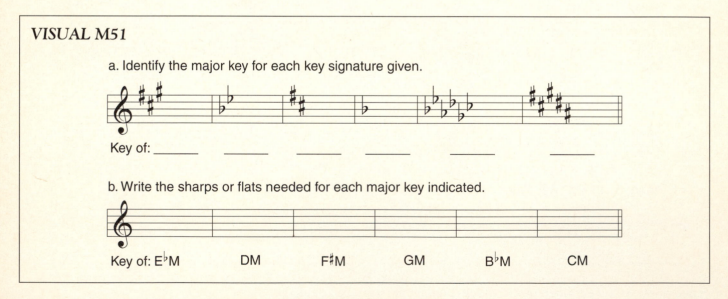

VISUAL M51

a. Identify the major key for each key signature given.

Key of: _____ _____ _____ _____ _____ _____

b. Write the sharps or flats needed for each major key indicated.

Key of: E♭M   DM   F#M   GM   B♭M   CM

In completing the exercises in Visual M51, students can use shortcuts. To discover the key of a composition having sharps in the key signature, refer to the last sharp in the signature. This sharp is the seventh scale degree in every major scale. The key, therefore, is the name of the pitch that is one half step higher. For example, if the last sharp is C♯, the key of the composition will be D major.

If the key signature consists of flats, refer to the last flat in the signature. This flat is the fourth scale degree in every major scale. Count down to "1," or the first scale degree, for the name of the key. For example, if the last flat is E♭, then the song is in B♭ major. Notice that, for key signatures having more than one flat, the second to the last flat will always be "1" or the name of the key. **Visual M52** diagrams these shortcuts.

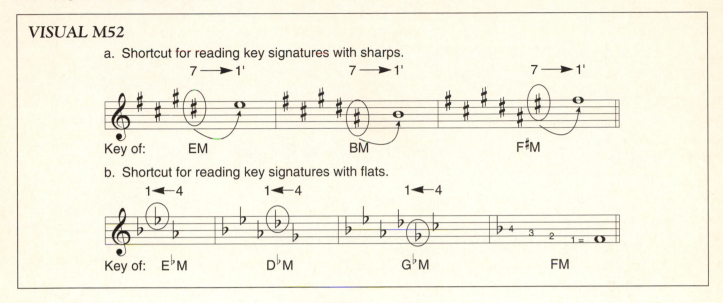

VISUAL M52

a. Shortcut for reading key signatures with sharps.

Key of: EM   BM   F♯M

b. Shortcut for reading key signatures with flats.

Key of: E♭M   D♭M   G♭M   FM

Have students compose songs in different major keys. To determine the key signature for a sharp key, begin writing the sharps in order until the sharp representing "7," for the key needed, appears. For flat keys, begin writing the flats in order until you reach the flat matching the key name desired. Add one more flat in the series to obtain the needed key signature.

Study the following songs and determine the major key in which each song is written.

LA PIÑATA

Key of ____ major

Mexican Folk Song

Da - le,   da - le,   da - le,   no   pier - das   el   ti - no;
Hit   it,   hit   it,   hit   it,   See   that   you   don't   miss   it!

mi - de   la   dis - tan - cia   que hay   en   el   ca - mi - no.
Try   to   find   the   dis - tance   so   that   you   can   find   it.

WHERE IS THUMBKIN?

Key of ____ major

American Folk Song

Where   is   Thumb-kin?   Where   is   Thumb-kin?   Here   I   am,   Here   I   am.

How   are   you   to-day,   Sir?   Ver - y   well   I   thank   you.   Run   a - way,   Run   a - way.

BINGO

Key of ____ major

Scotland

There was a farm-er had a dog and Bin-go was his

name - o.   B - I - N - G - O!   B - I - N - G - O!

B - I - N - G - O and Bin-go was his name - o.

NEW RIVER TRAIN

Key of ____ major

American Folk Song

I'm rid - in' that new riv - er train,_____ I'm rid - in' that

new ri - ver train,_____ That same old train that

brought me here, Gon - na take me back home a - gain._____

ALL THROUGH THE NIGHT

Key of ____ major

Welsh Folk Song

Sleep, my child, and peace at - tend thee, All through the night.
Guard - ian an - gels God will send thee, All through the night.

Soft the drow - sy hours are creep - ing, hill and vale in slum - ber steep - ing,

I, my lov - ing vig - il keep - ing, All through the night.

SHENANDOAH

Key of ____ major

American Chantey

Oh, Shen - an - doah, I long to hear you, A -

way, you roll - ing riv - er. Oh, Shen - an - doah, I long to

hear you. A - way, I'm bound to go, 'Cross the wide Mis - sour - i.

PAW PAW PATCH

Key of ____ major

American Singing Game

Where, oh where is pret - ty lit - tle Nel - lie?

Where, oh where is pret - ty lit - tle Nel - lie?

Where, oh where is pret - ty lit - tle Nel - lie?

Way down yon - der in the paw paw patch.

Look at a variety of key signatures in additional song literature written in major keys. Determine the key of each song.

FOCUS
Minor Scales and Key Signatures

LEARNING Every major scale has a corresponding minor scale using the same key signature. The *minor scale* is built on the sixth tone of the major scale. There are three types of minor scales: the natural, the harmonic, and the melodic, each having a slightly different pattern of whole and half steps.

Strategies

Sing a familiar song that uses a minor scale, such as "Halloween Is Coming." Then sing the song again, this time in the major mode. See **Visual M53.** Have students describe the differences in sound between the major and minor modes.

VISUAL M53

HALLOWEEN IS COMING

Song in F minor

Hal - low - een is com - ing, There're wit - ches in the air;

Light - ed jack - o' - lan - terns, Green gob - lins ev - ery - where. Boo!

Song in F Major

Hal - low - een is com - ing, There're wit - ches in the air;

Light - ed jack - o' - lan - terns, Green gob - lins ev - ery - where. Boo!

Send a student to the piano to play a diatonic scale beginning on A. Notate the scale on the chalkboard. Identify the whole- and half-step relationships between the notes, as in **Visual M54.** Number each note in the sequence. Students should recognize that the half steps now occur between 2 and 3, and 5 and 6, resulting in the pattern W H W W H W W. This pattern identifies the *natural minor scale*.

Have students sing the letter names of the scale, both ascending and descending.

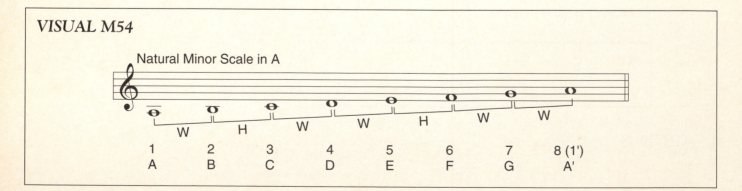

VISUAL M54

Natural Minor Scale in A

| W | H | W | W | H | W | W |

| 1 | 2 | 3 | 4 | 5 | 6 | 7 | 8 (1') |
| A | B | C | D | E | F | G | A' |

Students can build a human scale to represent the natural minor scale. Organize the students to represent the white keys on the keyboard from A to A'. Each student can play a resonator bell whose pitch corresponds to the student's place in the minor scale.

Have students build natural minor scales in a variety of keys, indicating each whole and half step. See **Visual M55.**

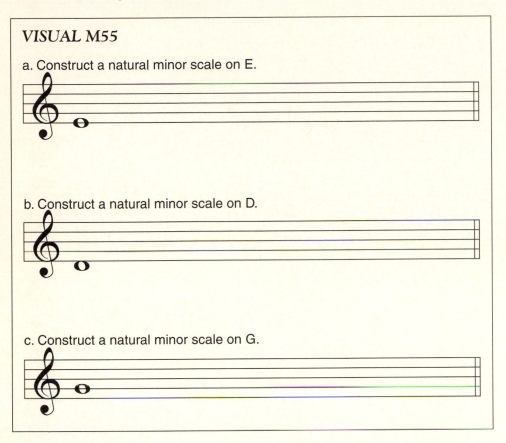

VISUAL M55

a. Construct a natural minor scale on E.

b. Construct a natural minor scale on D.

c. Construct a natural minor scale on G.

Often, there is little time to teach more than the natural minor to children. However, both the harmonic and melodic minor scales are given here for the adult student, as a source of information and for future reference, if needed.

Place an A minor scale on the chalkboard. Explain that, by altering the seventh degree of the natural minor scale, a second scale is created—the *harmonic minor scale*. See **Visual M56.**

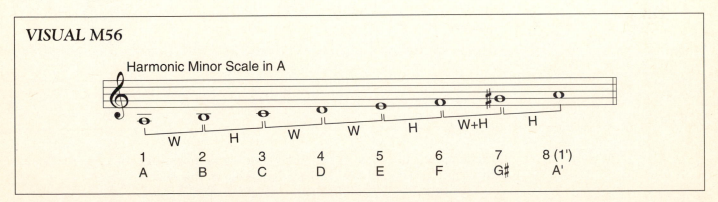

VISUAL M56

Harmonic Minor Scale in A

The addition of the accidental to the seventh degree of the scale results in a half-step relationship between 7 and 8 and one and one-half steps between 6 and 7. Play this scale on a melody instrument.

Students should construct harmonic minor scales in a variety of keys. See **Visual M57.**

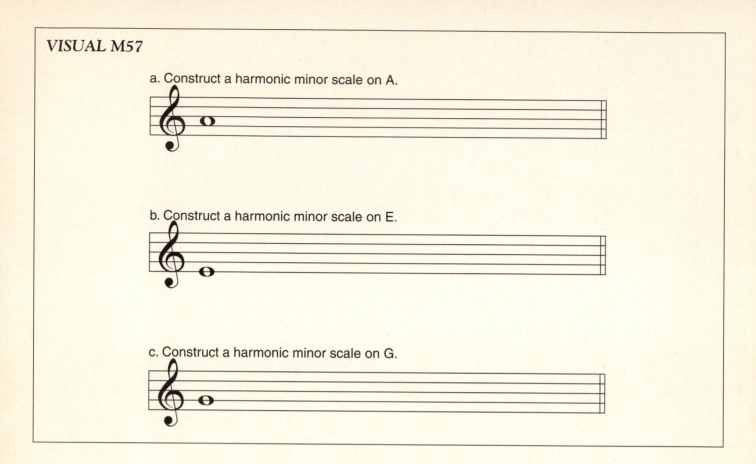

a. Construct a harmonic minor scale on A.

b. Construct a harmonic minor scale on E.

c. Construct a harmonic minor scale on G.

Again, place the A minor scale on the chalkboard. Explain that, by altering the sixth and seventh degrees of the natural minor, a third minor is created—the *melodic minor scale*. See **Visual M58.** The addition of the accidental to both the sixth and seventh degrees of the scale results in a whole step between 6 and 7 and a half step between 7 and 8. The raised sixth and seventh degrees are used only in ascending passages; for descending lines, the accidentals are cancelled, resulting in a scale identical to that of the natural minor. Play this scale on a melody instrument.

VISUAL M58

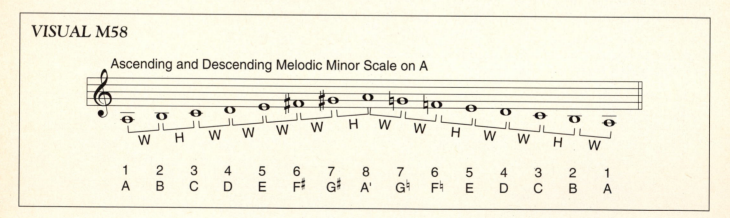

Ascending and Descending Melodic Minor Scale on A

Students should construct melodic minor scales in a variety of keys. See **Visual M59.** Letter names should be sung for pitches in this scale.

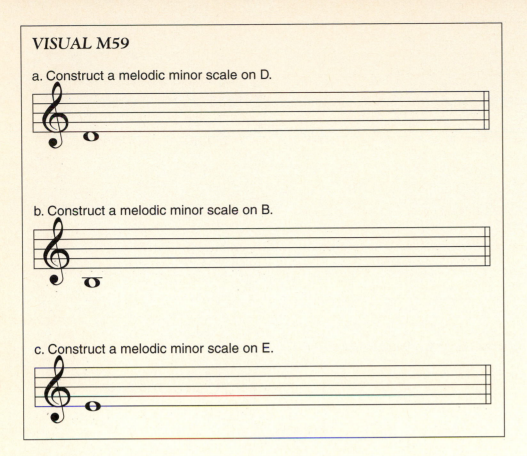

VISUAL M59

a. Construct a melodic minor scale on D.

b. Construct a melodic minor scale on B.

c. Construct a melodic minor scale on E.

LEARNING When a major and a minor key utilize the same key signature, the two keys are referred to as *relative*. There is a relative minor key for every major key.

Strategies

Have students play a C major scale and then an A minor scale. Notate these scales on the chalkboard. Observe that both scales use the same letter names and therefore possess the same key signature; the key signature of C major and A minor has no sharps or flats. See **Visual M60.**

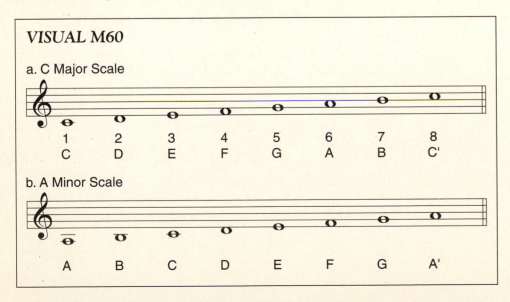

VISUAL M60

a. C Major Scale

| 1 | 2 | 3 | 4 | 5 | 6 | 7 | 8 |
| C | D | E | F | G | A | B | C' |

b. A Minor Scale

| A | B | C | D | E | F | G | A' |

Give students examples of relative major and minor keys sharing the same key signature, as in **Visual M61.** Note that the *key note* (starting note) of the relative minor key is located on the sixth degree of the major scale.

VISUAL M61

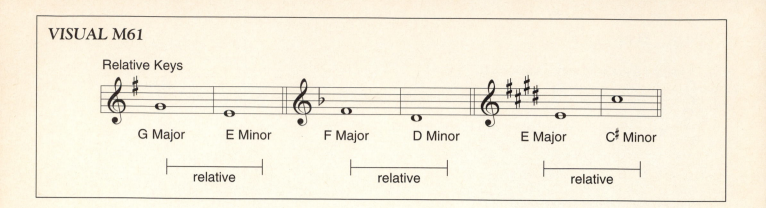

Relative Keys

G Major   E Minor   F Major   D Minor   E Major   C# Minor

relative   relative   relative

Provide exercises to reinforce the understanding of relative major and minor keys. See **Visual M62.** These measures can be reproduced as flash cards.

VISUAL M62

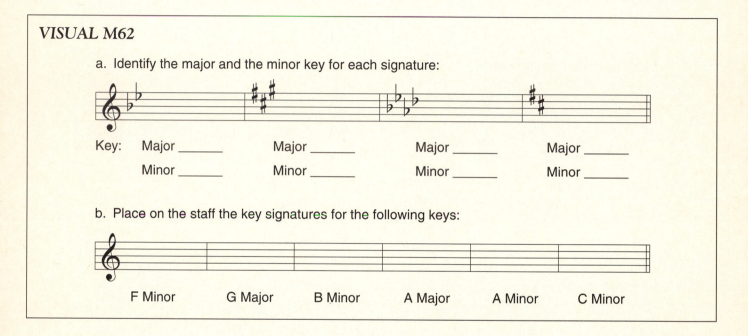

a. Identify the major and the minor key for each signature:

Key: Major _____   Major _____   Major _____   Major _____

Minor _____   Minor _____   Minor _____   Minor _____

b. Place on the staff the key signatures for the following keys:

F Minor   G Major   B Minor   A Major   A Minor   C Minor

Have students compose songs in different minor keys and notate their compositions.

Study the folowing songs and determine the minor key in which each song is written. To do this, students can apply the following guidelines:

a. Look at the key signature. This will tell you both the major and the relative minor keys in which the song could be written.

b. Look at the final note of the song to determine the key. The final note is usually the key note or "1."

Example   If a key has no sharps or flats, the song will probably be in C major or A minor. If the final note is C, then the key is probably C major; if the final note is A, then the key is probably A minor.

WAYFARING STRANGER

Key of _____ minor

Spiritual

I'm just a poor way-far-ing strang-er, A - trav-'ling through this world of woe;

But there's no sick-ness, toil nor dan-ger in that bright world to which I go.

JOHNNY HAS GONE FOR A SOLDIER

Key of _____ minor

Revolutionary War Song

There I sat on But-ter-milk Hill, Who could blame me cry my fill; And

ev - 'ry tear would turn a mill; John-ny has gone for a sol - dier.

WILLUM

Key of _____ minor

Traditional

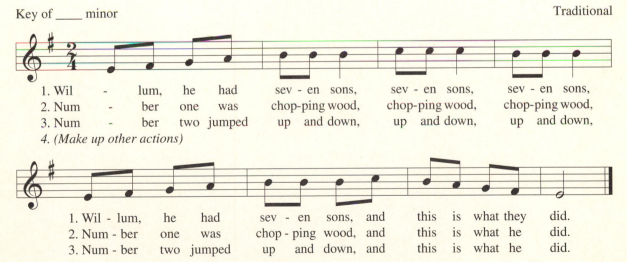

1. Wil - lum, he had sev - en sons, sev - en sons, sev - en sons,
2. Num - ber one was chop-ping wood, chop-ping wood, chop-ping wood,
3. Num - ber two jumped up and down, up and down, up and down,

4. (Make up other actions)

1. Wil - lum, he had sev - en sons, and this is what they did.
2. Num - ber one was chop - ping wood, and this is what he did.
3. Num - ber two jumped up and down, and this is what he did.

GO DOWN, MOSES

Key of ____ minor

Spiritual

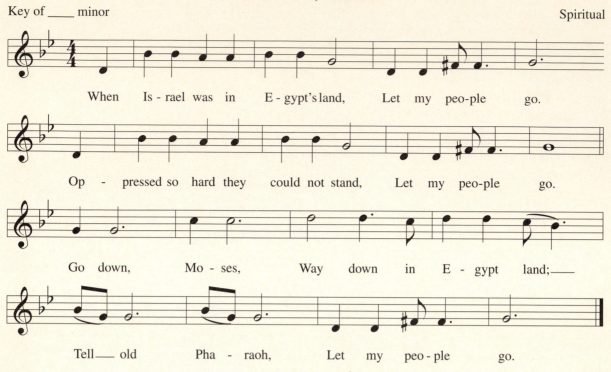

When Is-rael was in E-gypt's land, Let my peo-ple go.

Op - pressed so hard they could not stand, Let my peo-ple go.

Go down, Mo-ses, Way down in E-gypt land;

Tell old Pha-raoh, Let my peo-ple go.

AUTUMN COMES
HERBST IST KOMMEN

Text and melody: England, 16th century

English Folk Song adapted to German text

German text: Karl Haus/Franz Möckl

1. Au - tumn comes, the sum-mer is past, win-ter will
1. Herbst ist kommen, der Som-mer vor - bei, Win - ter - zeit
2. Au - tumn comes, but let us be glad, sing-ing an
2. Herbst ist kommen, laßt fröh - lich uns sein, singt auch zur

come too soon. Stars will shine clear - er, skies seem
ist nicht fern. Hel - ler am Him - mel des Ern - te -
au - tumn tune. Hearts will be light - er, nights be
Ern - te - zeit. Un - ter dem Him - mel des Ern - te -

near - er, un - der the Har - vest Moon.
mon - des leuch - tet nun Stern um Stern.
bright - er, un - der the Har - vest Moon.
mon - des wer - den die Her - zen weit.

LEARNING   Sometimes major and minor keys are coupled on the basis of their common key note rather than their common key signature. When this occurs, we refer to them as being *parallel keys*.

Strategies

Provide a chart containing examples of parallel major and minor keys, as in **Visual M63.** Note that parallel keys have the same letter name—EM and Em—but different key signatures.

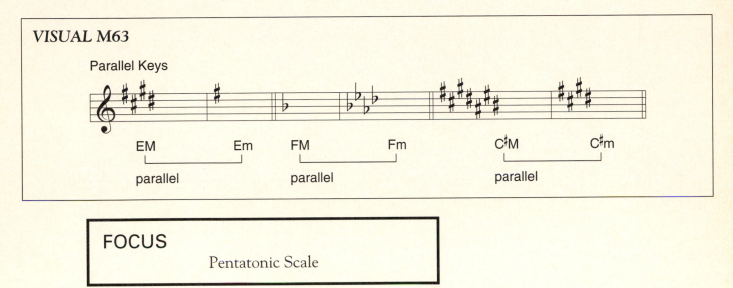

VISUAL M63

Parallel Keys

EM   Em   FM   Fm   C♯M   C♯m
└── parallel ──┘   └── parallel ──┘   └── parallel ──┘

FOCUS

Pentatonic Scale

LEARNING   Any scale that consists of a sequence of five tones within the octave is called a *pentatonic scale*. When the pentatonic scale is used in children's song literature, it is usually written in tonal pentatonic; that is, no half steps are present.

Strategies

Place a transparency of the song " 'Liza Jane" on an overhead projector.

'LIZA JANE

American Folk Song

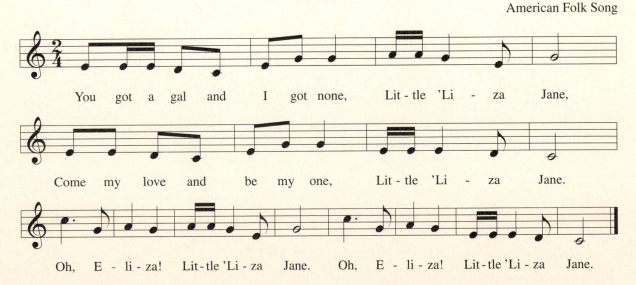

You got a gal and I got none, Lit - tle 'Li - za Jane,

Come my love and be my one, Lit - tle 'Li - za Jane.

Oh, E - li - za! Lit - tle 'Li - za Jane. Oh, E - li - za! Lit - tle 'Li - za Jane.

Sing through the song with the students. Analyze the piece to establish the location of the key note (C). Construct a scale using only the tones in this song, as in **Visual M64.** Discuss the makeup of this scale. The following questions may be helpful:

a. How many different tones are in this scale?   (5)
b. What are they?   (C D E G A)
c. Are there any half-step relationships in this song?   (No)

Students should conclude that this song is based on a pentatonic scale, built on C, that has five different tones and no half-step relationships.

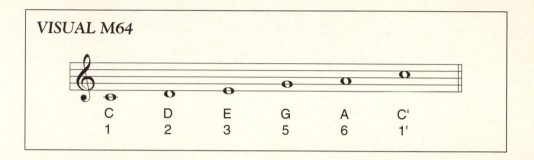

Examine the following songs and determine the pentatonic scale used. Write the scale on the staff beneath the song.

BLUEBIRD

Game Song

DOG AND CAT

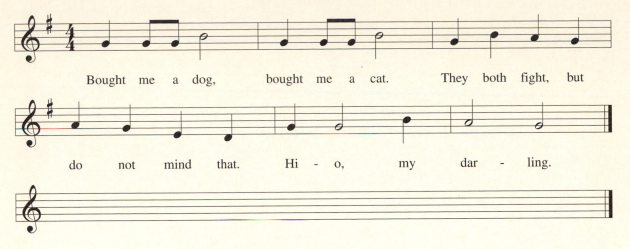

Bought me a dog, bought me a cat. They both fight, but

do not mind that. Hi - o, my dar - ling.

JIM ALONG JOSIE

American Folk Song

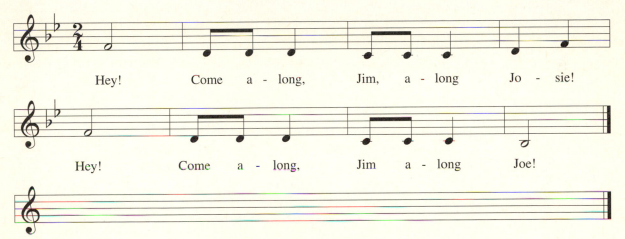

Hey! Come a - long, Jim, a - long Jo - sie!

Hey! Come a - long, Jim a - long Joe!

CIRCLE ROUND THE ZERO

American Street Song

Cir - cle round the ze - ro, Find your lov - in' ze - ro, Back, back, ze - ro,

Side, side, ze - ro, Front, front, ze - ro, Tap your lov - in' ze - ro.

CHICKAMA CRANEY CROW

Southern Game Song

Chick- a - ma Chick- a - ma   Cran - ey Crow,   Went to the well   to   wash his toe,

When he got there his   chick-en was gone. What   time, Old Witch?   One
Two *(etc. through 12)*

Have students compose their own pentatonic songs and play them on melody instruments. It is recommended that Orff instruments be used so that the half steps can be removed; this will facilitate the construction of the pentatonic scale.

FOCUS
Chromatic Scale

LEARNING   A *chromatic scale* is a scale whose tones are one-half step apart, resulting in twelve semi-tones. The chromatic scale progresses by half steps, encompassing one octatve; it can be built on any tone.

Strategies

Build a chromatic scale as in **Visual M65.** Note that, in its ascending form, the tones of a chromatic scale are raised (♯), and in its descending form, the tones are lowered (♭).

VISUAL M65

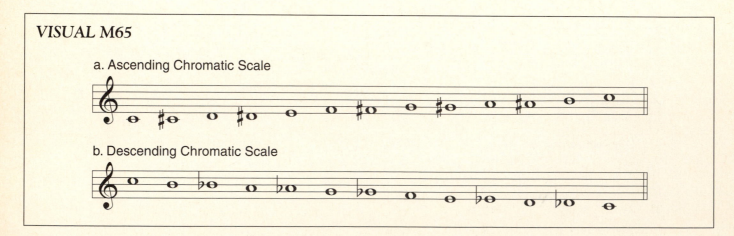

a. Ascending Chromatic Scale

b. Descending Chromatic Scale

Sing the song "Santa Lucia." Note that composers do not generally write an entire song using a chromatic scale; rather, portions of the chromatic scale are used. Discover where the composer has used chromaticism in "Santa Lucia," and highlight these areas.

SANTA LUCIA

Teodoro Cottrau
Tr. Thomas Oliphant

Teodoro Cottrau
Neapolitan Boat Song

FOCUS
Transposing

LEARNING *Transposing* is the technique of rewriting a song in a key different from that in which it was originally written. If a song is too high or too low for a child's voice, it can be transposed to a more comfortable key.

Strategies

Have the class sing the song "Pat Works on the Railway" in the key of B minor. They will immediately discover that the song is too high.

Help them transpose the song to a more comfortable key. To do this, number each tone of the song according to its place in the B minor scale, as in **Visual M66.**

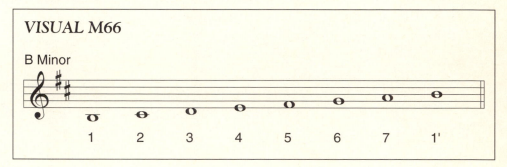

VISUAL M66

B Minor

1 2 3 4 5 6 7 1'

PAT WORKS ON THE RAILWAY

American Railroad Song

A more comfortable key might be E minor. To transpose to E minor or any other key, observe that notes in the new key must be used that correspond to the same scale degrees as in the original key; that is, if the song began on the first degree of the scale in E minor, then it must also begin on the first degree in E minor. See **Visual M67.**

Be sure that students understand that a song in a minor key can be transposed only to another minor key and that a song in a major key can be transposed only to another major key.

Have students transpose other short songs to different keys.

The following patriotic, Halloween, Thanksgiving, Christmas, and Hanukkah songs can be used to reinforce the melodic concepts learned in this chapter.

AMERICA THE BEAUTIFUL

Katherine Lee Bates   Samuel A. Ward

AMERICA

Samuel Francis Smith

Henry Carey

My coun - try, 'tis of thee, Sweet land of lib - er - ty,

Of thee I sing; Land where my fa - thers died, Land of the

Pil - grims' pride, From ev - 'ry moun - tain side Let free - dom ring

BATTLE HYMN OF THE REPUBLIC

Julia Ward Howe

William Steffe

Verse

Mine eyes have seen the glo - ry of the com - ing of the Lord;

He is tram - pling out the vin - tage where the grapes of wrath are stored;

He hath loosed the fate - ful light - ning of His ter - ri - ble swift sword;

His truth is march - ing on. Glo - ry, glo - ry hal - le -

Refrain

lu - jah! Glo - ry, glo - ry hal - le - lu - jah!

Glo - ry, glo - ry hal - le - lu - jah! His truth is march - ing on.

THE STAR-SPANGLED BANNER

Francis Scott Key

John Stafford Smith

Oh,— say can you see, by the dawn's ear-ly light,

What so proud-ly we hailed at the twi-light's last gleam-ing,

Whose broad stripes and bright stars, through the per-il-ous fight,

O'er the ram-parts we watched were so gal-lant-ly stream-ing?

And the rock-ets' red glare, The bombs burst-ing in air,

Gave proof through the night that our flag was still there.

Oh, say does that— Star - Span - gled Ban - ner— yet— wave—

O'er the land— of the free and the home of the brave?

THIS LAND IS YOUR LAND

Woody Guthrie   Woody Guthrie

SKIN AND BONES

Southern Folk Song

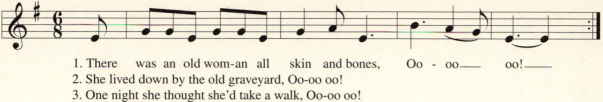

1. There was an old wom-an all skin and bones, Oo - oo—— oo!——
2. She lived down by the old graveyard, Oo-oo oo!
3. One night she thought she'd take a walk, Oo-oo oo!
4. She walked down by the old graveyard, Oo-oo oo!
5. She saw the bones a-layin' around, Oo-oo oo!
6. She went to the closet to get a broom, Oo-oo oo!
7. She opened the door and BOO!

THERE WAS AN OLD WITCH

Traditional

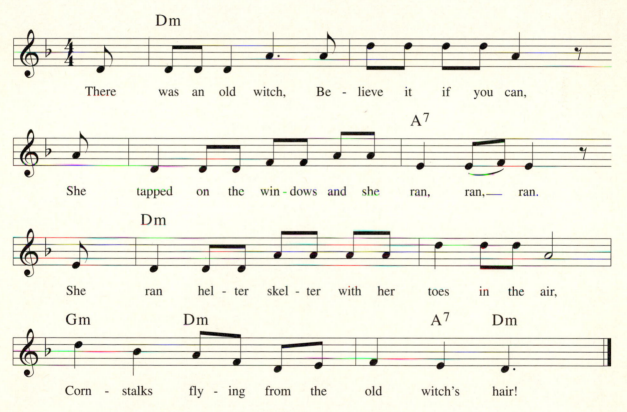

There was an old witch, Be - lieve it if you can,

She tapped on the win-dows and she ran, ran,— ran.

She ran hel-ter skel-ter with her toes in the air,

Corn - stalks fly-ing from the old witch's hair!

OVER THE RIVER AND THROUGH THE WOOD

Lydia Maria Childs

Traditional

O - ver the riv - er and through the wood, To grand-mo-ther's house we go:____

The horse knows the way to car-ry the sleigh, Through the white and drift-ed snow____

O - ver the riv - er and through the wood, Oh, how the wind does blow!____

It stings the toes and bites the nose, As o - ver the ground we go.

COME, YE THANKFUL PEOPLE, COME

Henry Alford

George J. Elvey

Come, ye thank - ful peo - ple, come, Raise the song of har - vest home;

All is safe - ly gath - ered in, Ere the win - ter storms be - gin;

God, our Mak - er, doth pro - vide For our wants to be sup - plied;

Come to God's own tem - ple, come, Raise the song of har - vest home.

FOR HEALTH AND STRENGTH

Old English Round

For health and strength and dai - ly food We praise Thy name, O Lord.

SILENT NIGHT

Josef Mohr

Franz Gruber

Si - lent night, ho - ly night! All is calm, all is bright.

'Round yon vir - gin Moth - er and Child Ho - ly In - fant so ten - der and mild,

Sleep in heav - en - ly peace,____ Sleep____ in heav - en - ly peace.

AWAY IN A MANGER

Carl Müller

A - way in a man - ger, no crib for a bed,

The lit - tle Lord Je - sus laid down His sweet head;

The stars in the sky____ looked down where He lay,

The lit - tle Lord Je - sus, a - sleep on the hay.

THE TWELVE DAYS OF CHRISTMAS

English Traditional

1. On the first day of Christ-mas my true love sent to me A par-tridge in a pear tree.

2. On the sec-ond
3. On the third— day of Christ-mas my true love sent to me
4. On the fourth—

Two tur-de-doves.
Three French— hens, And a par-tridge— in a pear tree.
Four call-ing birds

5. On the fifth day of Christ-mas my true love sent to me.

Five gold-en rings; Four— call-ing birds, three French hens,

Two— tur-tle-doves and a par-tridge— in a pear tree.

6. On the sixth day of Christ-mas my true love sent to me
7. On the seventh...
8. On the eighth...
9. On the ninth...
10. On the tenth...
11. On the eleventh...
12. On the twelfth...

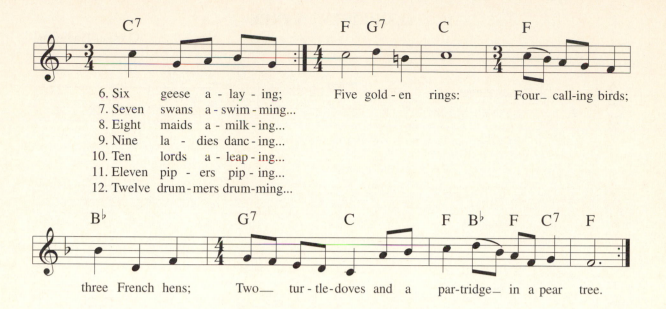

6. Six geese a-lay-ing;
7. Seven swans a-swim-ming...
8. Eight maids a-milk-ing...
9. Nine la-dies danc-ing...
10. Ten lords a-leap-ing...
11. Eleven pip-ers pip-ing...
12. Twelve drum-mers drum-ming...

three French hens; Two— tur-tle-doves and a par-tridge— in a pear tree.

CHAN MALI CHAN

Collected and recorded by René Boyer-Alexander

Malay Folk Song

Di ma-na di-a A-na kam-bin sa-ya, A-

na kam-bin sa-ya ke-ti pon - pa-yong.

Chan ma-li chan hoi! hoi! Chan ma-li chan hoi! hoi!

Chan ma-li chan ke-ti pon - pa-yong.

Rough translation: A donkey is traveling along the road. As he passes people he says, "Love me who has on a blue shirt. Love me who has no teeth, love me."

O, CHRISTMAS TREE

German Traditional

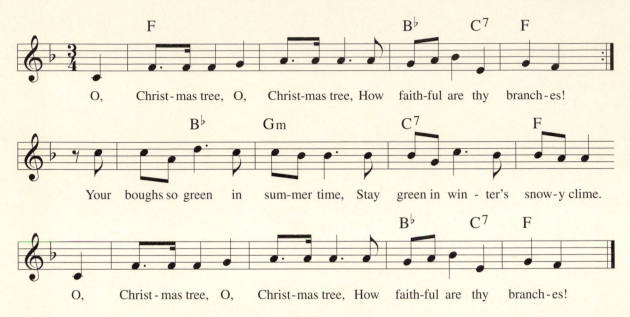

O, Christ-mas tree, O, Christ-mas tree, How faith-ful are thy branch-es!

Your boughs so green in sum-mer time, Stay green in win - ter's snow-y clime.

O, Christ-mas tree, O, Christ-mas tree, How faith-ful are thy branch-es!

ROCK OF AGES

M. Jastrow/G. Gottlieb

Jewish Traditional

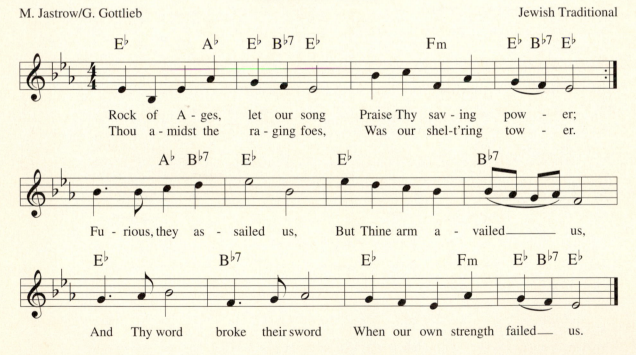

Rock of A - ges, let our song Praise Thy sav - ing pow - er;
Thou a - midst the ra - ging foes, Was our shel-t'ring tow - er.

Fu - rious, they as - sailed us, But Thine arm a - vailed_____ us,

And Thy word broke their sword When our own strength failed__ us.

O HANUKKAH

Jewish Traditional

O Ha - nuk - kah, O Ha - nuk - kah, come light the me - no - rah,

Let's have a par - ty, we'll all dance the ho - rah, Gath - er 'round the ta - ble, we'll

give you a treat, S'vi - vo - nim to play with, le - vi - vot to eat, And

while we are play - ing, The can - dles are burn - ing — low.

One for each night, they — shed a sweet light, To re -

1. mind us of days long a - go,

2. mind us of days long a - go.

INTRODUCING THE STRUCTURAL COMPONENTS
OF MELODY
Suggested Sequencing by Grade Level

Kindergarten

1. High, medium, low ranges
2. High and low pitches
3. Upward, downward, stay the same.

Grade One

1. Higher, lower
2. Staff
3. Notes
4. Sol, mi, la

Grade Two

1. Treble clef
2. Absolute note names
3. Middle C ledger line and D ledger space
4. Organized versus unorganized pitches
5. Pentatonic scale
6. Melodies move by step, skip, repeated notes

Grade Three

1. Sharps, flats, naturals
2. Direction of note stems

Grade Four

1. Ledger lines
2. 8va
3. Bass clef
4. Grand staff
5. Melodic intervals

Grades Five and Six

1. Whole steps and half steps
2. Major scales and key signatures in C, F, G
3. Minor scales and key signatures in A, D, E
4. Chromatic scale
5. Enharmonic equivalents
6. Transposing

WRITTEN AND PERFORMANCE-RELATED ASSESSMENTS THROUGH COOPERATIVE LEARNING ACTIVITIES: MELODY

1. Give each group a "note on a stick" (♀) and a staff containing a treble clef sign. Students take turns placing the note on different lines and spaces, while the group identifies that line or space by letter name. When the group feels ready, each student should be given a copy of Visual M14 to complete. Teacher checks responses.

2. Distribute to each group a sheet with several staffs on it, each staff containing a treble clef sign. Students place notes on the staff so that each measure spells a word, as in Visual M15. When finished, groups exchange papers and name the notes to discover the words they spell.

3. Give each group a staff containing note heads, similar to Visual M20. Students must first discover the name of the song. To do this, they may need to play the pitches on a barred instrument. Next, they should change the open note heads to the rhythms appropriate for the song, add bar lines, and finally, place the time signature. Teacher checks the finished product.

4. Give each group a paper containing a familiar melody lined out, as in Visual M25. When the group guesses the song, a member whispers its name to the teacher. If correct, the group exchanges papers with another group that has successfully guessed its assigned song. So that some groups are not sitting around waiting for others to finish, let groups who have finished guessing all songs try their hand at lining out the melodies of familiar songs of their choice. These can be used as "mystery songs" later, in follow-up activities.

5. Give each group three songs, each song in a different major key. The songs should be on separate sheets, with a blank staff at the bottom of the page. Group members must determine the key of the song, place the key signature on the score, and draw the corresponding major scale on the blank staff. Each student in the group must be able to play one of the three songs on a barred instrument. This activity can be repeated using songs in three different minor keys.

6. Have students compose their own songs. Give each group some staff paper. On the top staff, the teacher places the pentatonic scale to be used in the composition. If the teacher wants to limit the rhythms or the time signature that can be used, those should also be indicated. The staff is divided into the number of measures that the song should contain. When the group members have finished their song, they should test it on melody bells to see if they want to make any changes. Group members should then create a poem whose words can be set to the song. The group should be able to sing and play its song for the class.

This activity can be repeated using major or minor scales, or different rhythms and time signatures.

INTRODUCTION

There are sounds all around us. In our external environment, we hear sound when we listen to the ticking of a clock, chimes ringing in the clock tower, or the starting of an engine in a car or boat.

Even if our external environment were silent, we would still be surrounded by the sounds our own bodies make: breathing, sneezing, and coughing. Each of these sounds has distinctive qualities that distinguish one sound from the other. These qualities are referred to as *timbre* (tam-bur) or *tone color*.

Children instinctively recognize differences in tone color. The response that many infants and toddlers display when hearing the sound of their mother's voice in comparison to the voice of a stranger is evidence of their abilities to discriminate between sounds. As children grow and are guided in exploring sound, they begin to identify and ultimately place the origins of these sounds into different categories. They learn quickly, for example, to recognize the sounds of various animals, the sounds of nature, the sounds of people, and the sounds produced by different musical instruments. Guidance by the classroom teacher will help them discover and realize more subtle differences which exist between the various sounds in their environment. As their skill in recognizing tone color develops, their ability to discriminate, understand, and appreciate, not only music but also the host of sounds offered to them in their everyday environment, will take on added meaning.

> I sing!
> > I shout!
> Just listen as I move about.
> I stop . . . No sound.
> > Now listen . . .
> Silence.
> —René Boyer-Alexander

FOCUS
Environmental and Body Sounds

LEARNING   Sounds in our environment have their own characteristic qualities by which the sound and its source may be identified.

Strategies

Ask students to close their eyes and listen carefully, noticing any sounds they hear. For thirty seconds, let them listen to the natural sounds in the environment; then add a few sounds by doing such things as taking a step, rustling paper, pounding a desk, whistling, or sighing. At the end of the thirty seconds, signal children to open their eyes. List all the sounds they heard.

Discuss how sounds can be placed into categories according to their similarities and differences. **Visual TM1** provides an example of categories that may result from the discussion.

Mechanical Sounds	People Sounds	Sounds of Nature
automobile engines	breathing	thunder
boat engines	whistling	rain falling
blender	talking	wind
mixer	crying	trees rustling
airplane	laughing	insect sounds
furnace	moaning	waterfall
lawn mower	yawning	river flowing

At-Home Sounds	Music Sounds	Animal Sounds
telephone	piano	purring of a cat
door bell	singing	barking of a dog
clock ticking	violin	hissing of a snake
television	trumpet	chirping of a bird
radio	guitar	mooing of a cow

Have students discover how many ways sounds can be produced using their own bodies. Each sound can be assigned a symbol and included in a body-sound composition similar to the ones provided here.

Body-Sound Composition
(Can be performed in canon)

Group 1 Snap fingers

Group 2 Rub hands together

Group 3 Slap thighs

Group 4 Stamp feet

Mouth-Sound Composition

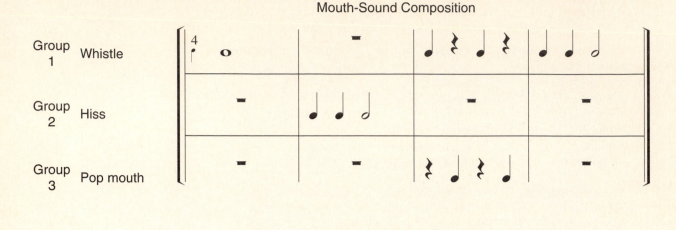

Group 1 — Whistle
Group 2 — Hiss
Group 3 — Pop mouth

FOCUS
Tone Color of Rhythm Instruments

LEARNING Rhythm instruments provide an excellent source for the exploration and understanding of timbre or tone color.

Strategies

Make available a variety of rhythm instruments that students can explore. Have students pay attention to the many ways sound can be produced on each instrument. (See Chapter 10 for a listing of frequently used rhythm instruments.) After this hands-on experience, identify each instrument by name and demonstrate how each is commonly used by musicians.

Have students group those rhythm instruments whose tone is produced in a similar manner. For example, students may choose to classify the rhythm instruments in the following way:

Rhythm Instrument Classification Chart

I. Instruments that are hit or struck:	triangle, drum, wood block, claves, cymbals
II. Instruments that are shook:	maracas, jingle bells, tambourine
III. Instruments that are scraped:	guiro, grooved tone block, grooved sticks
IV. Instruments that are rubbed:	sand blocks, drum head

Students can also develop categories that address the composition of the various rhythm instruments being used, as demonstrated below:

Skins	*Rattles*	*Metals*	*Woods*
hand drum	maracas	cow bell	claves
conga drum	jingle clogs	cymbals	wood block
bongo drum	bells	gong	guiro
		triangle	sticks

LEARNING   Some stories, nursery rhymes, and poems are enhanced by the addition of sound effects or sound imagery.

Strategies

Provide students with examples of poems and stories similar to the one outlined below. After students have read the poem or story thoroughly, the teacher can assign appropriate sound effects.

MONICA AND JOEY

Monica and Joey went for a walk. (*wood block*)
They came to a bridge and marched over it. (*drum*)
They came to a stream and swam across it. (*tambourine*)
They came to a field and brushed through it. (*sand blocks or cabasa*)
They came to a grassy hillside and walked down it. (*descending minor scale on bass xylophone*)
They came to a rocky hillside and walked up it. (*ascending major scale on piano or soprano xylophone*)
They came to a cave and looked in. (*triangle*)
A bear looked out . . . and growled at them! (*cymbals, vibra-slap, and guiro*)
Well, the bear did not have to growl twice. Monica and Joey turned and ran.
    Down the rocky hillside,
    Up the grassy hillside,
    Through the field,   } (*repeat sounds in reverse*)
    Across the stream,
    Over the bridge,
Into their house and slammed the door. (*slap stick*)
Whew!
Going for a walk is great, . . . but staying at home is even better!

Have students experiment with a variety of instruments that can be used to interpret each line in a poem; then evaluate their appropriateness to the poem. The two poems that follow can be used for this experience.

SEVEN DAYS INDOORS

One day a little dog decided to stay indoors because he refused to get his feet wet and . . .
That was the day it rained . . .
And the fog rolled in . . .
And the snow melted . . .
And there was a tornado . . .
And a hurricane . . .
And a breeze . . .
And a shower . . .
Then the sun came out, and all the flowers came up because it was Spring.
Because the sun was shining, the little dog decided to take a walk.
As he walked, the bright light of the sun began to dim.
And the stars came out . . .
And the moon came out . . .
And it was night . . .
And the wind began to blow gently through the trees.

ONLY THE MOON AND ME (excerpt)

By Richard J. Margolis

My stomach growls.
My throat gurgles.
My teeth click.
My fingers crack.
My toes thump.
My nose sniffs.
My lips pop.
Even my blinks make a sound.
I'm really very noisy,
in quiet way.

Have students add to the enjoyment of other stories such as "The Three Bears," "The Three Billy Goats Gruff," and "The Three Little Pigs" by adding appropriate instruments and sound effects.

After having explored the variety of rhythm instruments used in the classroom, students should refine their aural ability to distinguish various timbres by identifying rhythm instruments by sound alone. A number of approaches may be taken to help reinforce this skill. For example, all eyes might be closed while one student performs a short rhythmic pattern on a rhythm instrument. At the completion of the pattern, students would guess which instrument was playing. A screen might be provided to separate player from listeners. A correct response might provide an opportunity for an aurally perceptive listener to become the next player.

FOCUS
Electronic Sounds

LEARNING   Sound can be altered electronically to change its pitch, duration, or volume. An alteration in any of these aspects of sound opens up a plethora of timbre possibilities.

Strategies

Have students listen to any piece of music that has been altered electronically. "Tossed As It Is Untroubled" by John Cage might be a good starting piece. Discuss the sounds heard in the composition. Ask students to identify the instrument(s) or sound source that is being used. Have them describe the sounds used and talk about ways that these sounds may have been created. Have them give opinions as to how the addition of the new sounds affected them as listeners.

Have students listen to and discuss other examples of electronic music. A few choices might include:

a. *Piece for Tape Recorder* by Ussachevsky
b. *Poem Electronique* by Varèse
c. *Sounds of New Music* containing works by Cage, Cowell, and others

Have students create their own example of music that is electronically altered. The teacher may choose to have students observe the following guidelines:

1. Find some interesting sounds and record them on a reel-to-reel tape recorder.
2. Experiment with playing these sounds back at different speeds. Discuss how the sound is changed.
3. Create a tape loop by recording the sounds on a piece of tape. Use splicing tape to connect the ends of the recording tape.

4. Create other tape loops that have contrasting timbres and pitch levels. Create a sound collage by randomly connecting these tapes.
5. Play the tape loop at different speeds. Change the volume of sound. Use the pause button to create rhythmic interest.
6. Play the pieces for the rest of the class.
7. Talk about the sound sources used, how the sounds were modified or changed, and how the composition was organized.

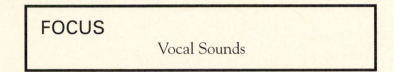

FOCUS

Vocal Sounds

LEARNING The categorization and development of an individual's singing voice are determined not only by the range of the voice but also by the quality of sound that it produces.

Strategies

Record the voices of two students singing the same song. Compare the two voices, describing their quality of tone. Urge students to provide adjectives to adequately describe what is heard. Their ability to verbalize will be helpful in better understanding the concept of timbre.

Have students compare the vocal sounds of adults and children. Describe similarities and differences in these voices.

Provide recordings of both male and female voices. Students should begin to recognize, identify aurally, and verbalize the differences in timbre that exist between these two groups of voices.

As students listen to music of other countries, they should discover that the timbre of the singing voice varies from culture to culture. Exposure to different cultural styles helps students become more musically sensitive to and appreciative of the great diversity of music characteristics of other countries.

Students should recognize that the adult voice may be classified according to similar and contrasting differences in range as well as differences in quality of sound, as seen in the following diagram:

Vocal Ranges

	Soprano	High
Female	Mezzo-soprano	Medium
	Alto	Low
	Tenor	High
Male	Baritone	Medium
	Bass	Low

Have students listen to examples of vocal performances that highlight each male and female vocal range. Some examples might include:

a. Soprano: "Depuis le jour," from *Louise* by Carpentier
b. Mezzo-soprano: "Habanera," from *Carmen* by Bizet
c. Alto: "Dido's Lament," from *Dido and Aeneas* by Purcell
d. Tenor: "Celeste Aïda," from *Aïda* by Verdi
e. Baritone: "Evening Star," from *Tannhäuser* by Wagner
f. Bass: "Mephisto's Serenade," from *Faust* by Gounod

LEARNING   A *symphony orchestra* consists of four major families of instruments: strings, brass, woodwinds, and percussion. The instruments in each family are grouped together because they share physical characteristics and have similarities in the way they produce tones.

Strategies

Make available many opportunities to view and hear orchestral instruments. Students need to hold and feel the instruments, as well as hear them played. The study of orchestral instruments should be presented over a period of time, not all at once.

Follow these hands-on experiences with visuals and sound recordings of the instruments.

Students should identify the physical characteristics of each instrument so that they can eventually draw conclusions as to why the instrument belongs to a particular family.

The Young Person's Guide to the Orchestra, by Benjamin Britten, is a composition featuring each orchestral instrument in turn. This recording can be used with older students as an introduction to or review of instrumental sounds.

LEARNING   The *string family* includes four basic instruments: violin, viola, cello, and double bass, also known as string bass or bass viol. Tone is produced when the strings vibrate. Strings are set in motion by plucking them, called *pizzicato*, or by drawing a bow across them with one hand. The other hand produces definite pitches by pressing one or more strings against the fingerboard. This action produces varying lengths of the string which, in turn, cause the pitch to ascend or descend. The harp also belongs to the string family.

The shorter and thinner the string on any stringed instrument, the higher the sound. Likewise, the longer and thicker the string, the lower the sound. The same principle can be applied to the size of all instruments; the smaller the instrument, the higher its pitch.

The violin is the soprano of the string family. Because of its small size, it produces the highest pitches. The tone color of the violin closely resembles the human voice and is capable of much versatility. The viola corresponds to the alto voice. It is slightly larger than the violin and has thicker strings. Both the violin and the viola are held under the chin.

Because of its size, the cello rests comfortably between the thighs while the player is in a seated position. A peg at the base of the instrument allows the instrument to stand upright on the floor. The tone of the cello is often described as mellow. The double bass is the largest of the four stringed instruments. Like the cello, it is connected to a peg which helps the player balance the instrument on the floor. Players either stand or sit on a high stool to play the bass. The thickness and length of the strings on the bass make it one of the lowest sounding instruments in the orchestra.

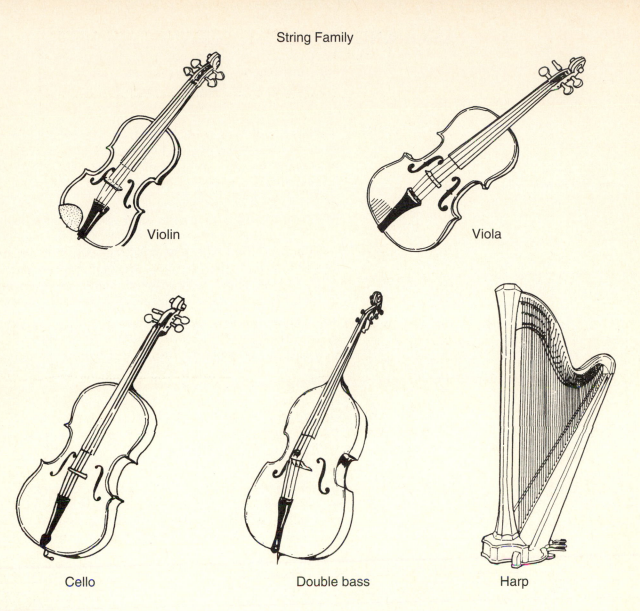

Violin

Viola

Cello

Double bass

Harp

Strategies

Provide students with opportunities to explore stringed instruments. Examine and discuss their general makeup. Examine the bow; explain that a substance called rosin is used on the bow to produce tension between the bow and string. The tension causes the string to vibrate and sound results.

Invite students from the school orchestra to demonstrate the playing of a stringed instrument. If available, invite a professional to perform for the students.

Have students listen to recordings of stringed instruments, such as these:

a. Violin:
(1) *Violin Concerto in E Minor* (Rondo) by Mendelssohn
(2) *Flight of the Bumblebee* by Rimsky-Korsakov

b. Viola:
(1) "Third Movement" (Song) from *Háry János Suite* by Kodály

c. Cello:
(1) "The Swan" from *Carnival of the Animals* by Saint-Saëns
(2) *Sonata No. 1 for Cello and Piano*, Op. 45 by Mendelssohn

d. Double bass:
(1) *Jimbo's Lullaby* by Debussy
(2) "Elephant" from *Carnival of the Animals* by Saint-Saëns

LEARNING

The *brass family* consists of four major instruments: trumpet, trombone, French horn, and tuba. Unlike the string family, brass instruments produce tone as a result of lips vibrating into either a cone-shaped or cup-shaped mouthpiece, causing the air being blown into the instrument to vibrate. Pitch is changed by pressing valves and tightening or loosening the lips; both will change the length of the air column being blown into the instrument. This process is consistent in the brass family except for the trombone. In place of valves, the trombone slide is pushed out or pulled in to shorten or lengthen the column of air.

The bright and brilliant tone color of the trumpet makes it one of the most popular instruments in the brass family. The trumpet has three valves which, singly or in combination, lower the natural pitch of the instrument. Because of its brilliance in tone, mutes made of metal, wood, and synthetic materials are inserted into its bell to change its tone quality.

The French horn has the reputation of requiring the most difficult technique of all the orchestral instruments. Both its tone quality and pitch are influenced by a technique called "stopping," which involves the insertion of the hand into the bell. The mellowness of tone that results affords the French horn opportunity to blend easily with other families of the orchestra as well as with its own.

The size of the instrument and the cup-shaped mouthpiece of the trombone are larger than those of the trumpet, causing its tone to be lower and perhaps more dignified and solemn. The trombone's sliding mechanism allows a player to glide quickly up and down, from one tone to another, through all degrees of pitches. This sliding technique is called *portamento*. There are four sizes of trombones; the tenor and the bass are the most popular.

The tuba is the lowest pitched instrument in the brass family. It exists in many shapes and sizes and may have as many as five valves. Because of its large size and weight, the tuba lacks versatility and is therefore often limited to providing support tones for the rest of the orchestra; however, the tube is capable of playing a legato, melodic line. Its tone color is deep and warm.

Brass Family

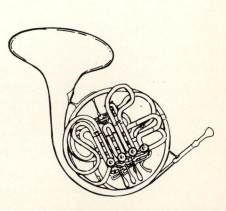

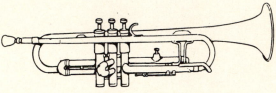

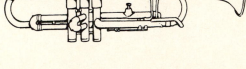

Trumpet

French horn

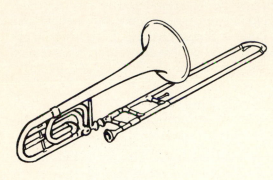

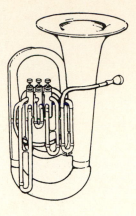

Trombone   Tuba

Strategies

Students should examine as many members of the brass family as possible. They should observe that cone- and cup-shaped mouthpieces are used. They should also note that the trombone's slide shortens or lengthens the air column. Valves perform this same function for the other brass instruments.

If possible, invite students from band or orchestra to demonstrate some of the instruments for the class.

Students should eventually be able to identify the brass instruments by sight and sound.

The following recordings can be used to help students identify the sound of each brass instrument:

a. Trumpet:
   (1) "Finale" from *William Tell Overture* by Rossini
   (2) *Pictures at an Exhibition* by Moussorgsky
b. French horn:
   (1) *Peter and the Wolf* (hunters' theme) by Prokofiev
   (2) *Symphony No. 5* (2nd movement) by Tchaikovsky
c. Trombone:
   (1) *Stars and Stripes Forever* by Sousa
   (2) *Equali for Four Trombones* by Beethoven
d. Tuba:
   (1) "Bydlo" from *Pictures at an Exhibition* by Moussorgsky
   (2) *Finlandia* by Sibelius

LEARNING

The *woodwind family* is one of the most diversified of the four instrumental groups because it contains seven major members: piccolo, flute, clarinet, oboe, English horn, bassoon, and contrabassoon. Different sounds are produced by the player closing holes, which lengthens the column of vibrating air, or opening holes, which sortens the vibrating column of air.

The woodwind family is divided into single-reed, double-reed, and no-reed members. The clarinet is a single-reed member. When it is played, its reed vibrates, creating a vibrating column of air which causes sound to result. On the oboe, English horn, bassoon, and contrabassoon, however, two reeds vibrate. The flute's and the piccolo's tones are produced by blowing a column of air over an open hole.

The flute and the piccolo are transverse instruments, meaning that they are held at a right angle to the body. The piccolo is the smallest member of the woodwind family and thus produces the highest pitches. Its tone, unlike the mellow and lyric quality of the flute, is almost piercing. Both instruments were originally made of wood and therefore were classified as woodwinds. Today, the piccolo and the flute are usually made of silver.

There are several sizes of clarinets, ranging from soprano to bass. The B-flat clarinet, however, continues to be one of the most popular among beginning players.

The oboe is similar in structure to the clarinet except for its double-reed. Its quality of tone is often described as being nasal yet plaintive. The double-reed mouthpiece requires a different embouchure or mouth placement than its single-reed counterpart.

The English horn is actually an alto oboe. It is longer than the oboe and contains a pear-shaped bell. It has a lower range of pitches and a somewhat melancholy tone quality.

The bassoon and contrabassoon possess large amounts of tubing which allows them to produce very low tones. The contrabassoon is the lowest sounding instrument in the orchestra. Both the bassoon and the contrabassoon are double-reed instruments. Their tone quality is both nasal and plaintive, like the oboe.

Although the saxophone has not been included as a traditional member of the orchestra, it is often scored in contemporary orchestral music. It is also traditionally used to play popular styles of music such as blues, jazz, and rock. The saxophone is a reed instrument made of metal.

Woodwind Family

No Reed

Single Reed

Piccolo

Flute

Soprano clarinet

Double Reed

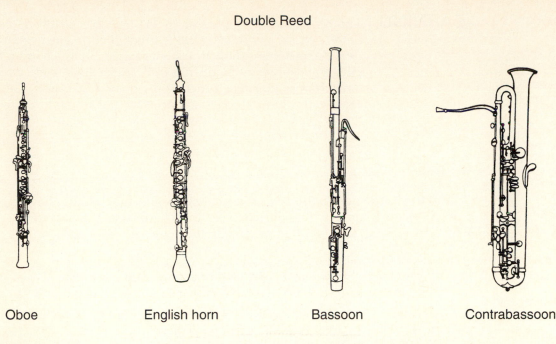

Oboe English horn Bassoon Contrabassoon

Strategies

Students should examine instruments of the woodwind family, giving special attention to the mouthpieces.

Have students from band and orchestra demonstrate their instruments. Reinforce this activity by inviting professional musicians to play for the class.

Students should compare the flute to its predecessor, the recorder. Discuss similarities and differences between the instruments.

Students should be given opportunities to recognize woodwind instruments when heard on recordings.

The following list provides some of the best known examples of woodwind instruments that can be used to acquaint children with woodwind sounds:

a. Flute:
    (1) *Afternoon of a Faun* by Debussy
    (2) "Dance of the Toy Flutes" from the *Nutcracker Suite* by Tchaikovsky
b. Piccolo:
    (1) *Stars and Stripes Forever* by Sousa
    (2) "Chinese Dance" from the *Nutcracker Suite* by Tchaikovsky
c. Clarinet:
    (1) *Peter and the Wolf* (the cat) by Prokofiev
    (2) "Cuckoo in the Deep Woods" from *Carnival of the Animals* by Saint-Saëns
d. Oboe:
    (1) *Peter and the Wolf* (the duck) by Prokofiev
    (2) "Bacchanale" from *Samson and Delilah* by Saint-Saëns
e. English horn:
    (1) "Largo" from *New World Symphony* by Dvoräk
    (2) *Roman Carnival Overture* by Berlioz
f. Bassoon:
    (1) "In the Hall of the Mountain King" from *Peer Gynt Suite No. 1* by Grieg
    (2) *Rondo for Bassoon and Orchestra No. 35* (Andante and Rondo) by Von Weber
g. Contrabassoon:
    (1) "Conversations of Beauty and the Beast" from *Mother Goose Suite* by Ravel

LEARNING
The *percussion family* consists of innumerable members, because, by rule, any surface that is struck is considered percussive. Percussion instruments can be categorized as having definite or indefinite pitch. Instruments having definite pitch are tuned to specific pitches, such as the piano, the timpani, and the chimes. Instruments that are indefinite in pitch are not tuned. These include the wood block, the triangle, and the tambourine.

Strategies

Call students' attention to the classroom rhythm instruments that they have used and indicate which ones are also members of the orchestral percussion family.

Play creative games that allow students to recognize aurally the sounds generated by the instruments. See Chapter 10 for concrete examples.

The following list of recordings can be used to acquaint students with the sounds of different instruments in the percussion family:

a. Castanets: *Capriccio Espagnol* by Rimsky-Korsakov
b. Timpani: *Symphony No. 1* (3rd movement) by Sibelius
c. Harpsichord: *Brandenburg Concerto No. 5* (1st movement) by Bach
d. Organ: *Toccata and Fugue in D Minor* by Bach
e. Piano: Works by Chopin, Listz, Schumann, Bach

Nocturnes, Preludes, Etudes, and Waltzes by Chopin
f. Celesta: "Dance of the Sugar Plum Fairies" from the *Nutcracker Suite* by Tchaikovsky
g. Bells: "Witches' Sabbath" from *Symphonie Fantastique* by Berlioz
h. Tambourine: "Tarantella" from *Fantastic Toy Shop* by Rossini

It is often helpful to summarize the information referring to orchestral instruments by providing students with a chart similar to that in **Visual TM2.**

VISUAL TM2

Families of the Orchestra

String Family		*Brass Family*	
Violin	Soprano	Trumpet	Soprano
Viola	Alto	French horn	Alto
Cello	Tenor	Trombone	Tenor
Double bass	Bass	Tuba	Bass

Woodwind Family
No Reed

		Percussion Family	
Piccolo	Soprano	*Definite Pitch*	
Flute	Soprano	Xylophone	Piano
		Marimba	Organ
		Celesta	Harpsichord
Single Reed		Timpani	Glockenspiel
Clarinet Family	Soprano, Bass		
Saxophone Family	Soprano, Alto,	*Indefinite Pitch*	
	Tenor, Baritone	Wood block	Triangle
		Maracas	Tambourine
Double Reed		Cymbals	Snare drum
Oboe	Soprano	Gong	Bass drum
English horn	Alto		Castanets
Bassoon	Bass		
Contrabassoon	Bass		

WRITTEN AND PERFORMANCE-RELATED ASSESSMENTS THROUGH COOPERATIVE LEARNING ACTIVITIES: TIMBRE

1. Have each group create a composition using body sounds. Decide whether the composition will include hand, foot, or mouth sounds or a combination of these three. Score the composition using the examples under Visual TM1 for a guideline. Perform the work for the class.
2. Ask each group to create a poem or make up a story that lends itself to instrumental sound effects. Decide which instruments will best enhance the literary work and prepare a performance of the poem or the story for the class.
3. Give each group a cassette tape and player. Each tape should be the same and contain excerpts of songs sung by different singers. Ask each group to list adjectives that characterize the timbre of each of the taped voices. Groups should try to identify each vocal range—soprano, tenor, and so forth. Return students to the large group and discuss the characteristics identified in the small groups.

   This activity can be repeated using tapes containing the sounds of different musical instruments.

4. Provide each group with a set of cards, each card containing the picture of a different orchestral instrument. Students should be able to identify each instrument by name, family, and/or range.
5. Distribute to each group a short, taped, instrumental composition; each tape is different. Students should listen to the tape and identify as many musical instruments as possible. Finally, students should list everything they know about the instruments heard.

   On another day, tapes can be exchanged and the activity repeated.

6. Assign children to teams and have each term prepare for a listening identification competition. Some of the standard classical literature that might be used in the competition are:

LISTENING SELECTIONS

1. *Peter and the Wolf* by Prokofiev
2. *Carnival of the Animals* by Saint-Saëns
3. *Flight of the Bumblebee/Tale of Tsar Saltan Suite* by Rimsky Korsakov
4. "March" from *The Comedians* by Dimitri Kabalevsky
5. "Spring" from *The Four Seasons* by Vivaldi
6. *Tubby the Tuba* by George Kleinsinger
7. "Children's Chorus" from *Carmen* by Bizet
8. *Children's Symphony* (3rd movement) by McDonald
9. *The Nutcracker* by Tchaikovsky
10. "In the Hall of the Mountain King" from *Peer Glynt Suite No. 1* by Grieg
11. Minuet and Trio from *Eine kliene Nachtmusik* by Mozart
12. "Viennese Musical Clock" from *Háry János Suite* by Kodály
13. "Puisque tout passe" from *Six Chansons* by Hindemith
14. *African Postal Workers*
15. *Clair de lune* by Debussy
16. *Symphony No. 94* by Joseph Haydn
17. *Appalachian Spring* by A. Copland
18. *Fanfare for the Common Man* by A. Copland
19. "Erlkönig" by F. Schubert

20. "Hoedown" from *Rodeo* by A. Copland
21. *"La Raspa"* (Mexican Folk Music)
22. *Pictures at an Exhibition* by Mussorgsky
23. *Jamaican Rumba*
24. *Lift Every Voice and Sing*
25. "On the Trail" from *Grand Canyon Suite* by Grofé
26. "Variations on Simple Gifts" from *Appalachian Spring* by Copland
27. *Bolero* by Ravel

Teaching Expressive Elements to Children Chapter 5

INTRODUCTION

Teachers of music are faced with many challenges as they progress from day-to-day lessons in music reading, performance, and appreciation. Thus far, this text has been concerned with the basic structural components of rhythm, melody, and timbre. Reading and singing songs well, however, include more than a working knowledge of duration symbols and pitch identification. At some point children must become aware of the expressive potential each song possesses. To perform a song well, children must solve the puzzles it contains: should this song be sung a little faster? a little slower? Would this song sound better if it were softer? louder? Could we improve this song by gradually getting louder or softer at some specific point? Should this song be sung smoothly or in a more detached manner? What instruments would best accompany this song? Such questions can help lead children to a more sensitive performance of music, whether sung or played on melodic or rhythmic instruments.

Music expresses that which cannot be said,
and which cannot be suppressed.
–Victor Hugo

FOCUS
Tempo

LEARNING The speed of the basic, underlying beat of a composition, ranging from very slow to very fast, is called *tempo*.

Strategies

Have students move to fast and slow music.

Sing songs containing words that suggest a slow tempo for performance, such as "Nighttime." Have students explain why they think the song should be sung slowly. Comments may center around the sunset time of day referred to in the song, when living things prepare for sleep, or the many words found in the song that indicate a serene mood, such as "sunset," "shadow," "nighttime," "sleeping," and "dreaming."

NIGHTTIME

Words: K. Dalton — Hungarian Folk Song

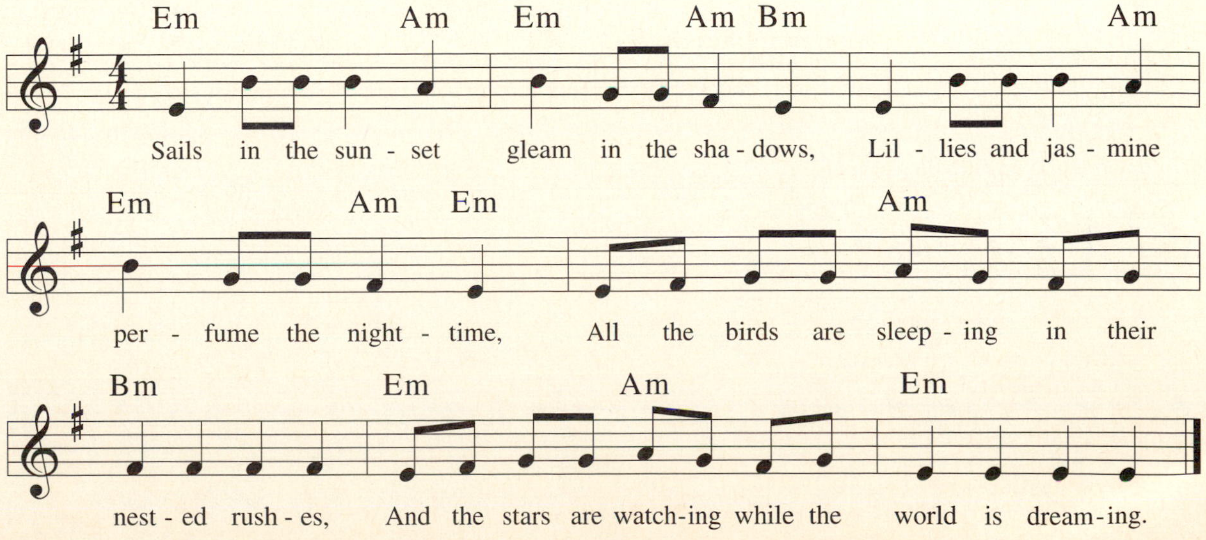
Em Am Em Am Bm Am
Sails in the sun - set gleam in the sha - dows, Lil - lies and jas - mine
Em Am Em Am
per - fume the night - time, All the birds are sleep - ing in their
Bm Em Am Em
nest - ed rush - es, And the stars are watch-ing while the world is dream-ing.

Sing songs containing words that suggest a fast tempo for performance, such as "The Clown." In discussing why this song would be sung more quickly than "Nighttime," students may discover such words as "jolly," "merriest," and "tumbling" which suggest a lively, animated mood.

THE CLOWN

French Folk Song

LEARNING

Some songs with measures containing notes of shorter duration, such as quarter or eighth notes, seem to move more quickly than other measures having half notes, even though the tempo of the basic beat does not change.

Strategies

Sing "I Got a Letter." Have students discover that measures 1 and 5 seem to be faster than the rest of the song because these measures contain mostly notes of shorter duration.

I GOT A LETTER

South Carolina

LEARNING Sometimes composers designate how a song should be performed by writing a tempo indication at the top of a song on the far left side above the staff.

Strategies

Look at the song "The Clown" and discover the tempo marking "gaily." Expain that often composers will use Italian words to designate tempo. Gradually introduce the most common Italian tempo markings contained in **Visual E1.**

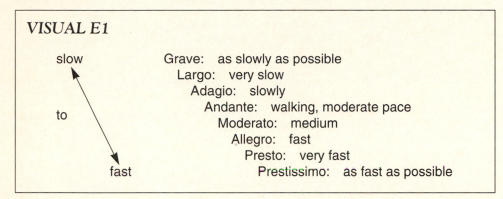

VISUAL E1

slow

to

fast

Grave: as slowly as possible
Largo: very slow
Adagio: slowly
Andante: walking, moderate pace
Moderato: medium
Allegro: fast
Presto: very fast
Prestissimo: as fast as possible

Have students examine the songs in their song book. Discover which songs have tempo markings. If the markings are in Italian, give their English meanings.

LEARNING Sometimes a piece becomes more expressive if a gradual change of speed occurs. The Italian word *ritardando* (abbreviated *rit.* or *ritard.*) designates a gradual slowing down; *accelerando* (abbreviated *accel.*) indicates a gradual increase in speed.

Strategies

Have students move to melodies that gradually change tempo.

Listen to "Little Train of the Caipira" from *Bachianas Brasileiras No. 2* by Villa-Lobos. Have students tap the beat to the opening measures of this composition to discover the accelerando. Similarly, tap the last measures of the piece which incorporate a ritardando. A call chart for this work can be found in Chapter 11.

Choose other recordings having gradual accelerandi or ritardandi (plural forms) and discover the tempo changes.

Choose songs where the addition of an accelerando or ritardando can be used to enhance the meaning of the song. Have children analyze the songs to discover what expressive marking can be used. Sing the songs using the accelerando or ritardando. For example, a ritardando could be used during the singing of the last two measures of "Nighttime"; the gradual slowing down would highlight the lullaby nature of the song to suggest that the world is falling asleep.

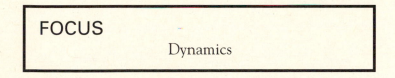

FOCUS

Dynamics

LEARNING The degree of volume in a musical composition is known as *dynamics*. Dynamics range from very soft to very loud.

Strategies

Have students explore body sounds that are soft and others that are loud.

Ask students to find things in the room that would make soft sounds and loud sounds.

Ask students what other sounds they have heard that are loud or soft. Sing songs, such as "Sleep, Baby, Sleep" and "Ghost of Tom," whose words suggest soft pitches. Have students explain why these songs should be sung softly.

SLEEP, BABY, SLEEP

GHOST OF TOM

Traditional Round

Students should move in an appropriate manner to melodies that are soft and those that are loud. Students can impersonate animals, stepping loudly for elephants and hippopotamuses, but using soft steps for rabbits and mice.

Sing songs whose words imply louder pitches, such as "London Bridge" and "Jig Jog Jig Jog." Students should be able to explain why they think these songs would be sung more loudly than "Sleep, Baby, Sleep."

LONDON BRIDGE

England

JIG JOG JIG JOG

Paul Edmonds

I want some-one to buy me a po-ny, Jig Jog Jig Jog Jig-a Jog Gee.

Not too fat and not too bo-ny, Jig Jog Jig Jog Jig-a Jog Gee.

For I want to go for a ride All a-round the coun-try-side, With a

Jig Jog Jig Jog Jig Jog Jig Jog Jig Jog Jig-a Jog Gee.

Have students choose instruments that could be used to accompany both soft and loud songs. Students should be able to express why they think some instruments would be appropriate for loud songs but not for songs performed softly.

LEARNING It is possible to increase the expressiveness of a song by changing the dynamic level at different points within the song.

Strategies

Sing "Hoo, Hoo!" Ask students if an echo is loud or soft. Decide how they should sing this song to make it as expressive as possible.

HOO, HOO!

Ethel Crowninshield

There's some-one liv-ing on a big high hill, I won-der who it can be?

There's some-one liv-ing on a big high hill, Who al-ways an-swers me.

Hoo hoo! Hoo hoo! Hoo hoo! Hoo hoo! I won-der who it can be?

Sing other songs that have words or phrases suggesting a change in dynamic level.

LEARNING Sometimes a song can be more expressive if a gradual change in dynamics occurs. The Italian word *crescendo* (abbreviated *cresc.*) designates a gradual increase in volume, symbolized by ◁ . *Decrescendo* (abbreviated *decresc.*) or *diminuendo* (abbreviated *dim.*) implies a gradual decrease in volume and is symbolized ▷ .

Strategies

Sing "The Three Rogues." Help students decide where a crescendo and a decrescendo could be placed to increase the song's musical interest.

THE THREE ROGUES

Ohio Folk Song

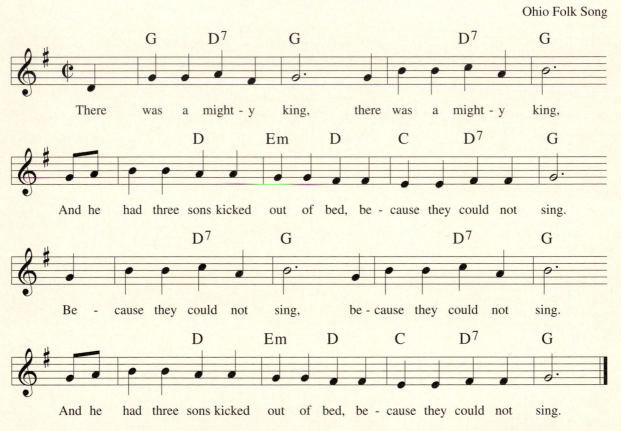

Listen to "In the Hall of the Mountain King" from *Peer Gynt Suite No. 1* by Grieg. Students should listen for the gradual crescendo used throughout the piece.

Listen to additional recordings containing gradual crescendos and decrescendos and discover the changes in dynamic level.

LEARNING Composers often use dynamic markings to indicate the degree of volume they feel will be most expressive at different points in a composition.

Strategies

Gradually introduce the most common dynamic markings contained in **Visual E2.**

VISUAL E2

soft   pp: very soft (pianissimo)
           p: soft (piano)
        mp: medium soft (mezzo piano)
to   mf: medium loud (mezzo forte)
         f: loud (forte)
loud   ff: very loud (fortissimo)

Have students discover dynamic markings found in the songs in their song book and explain how these markings affect the way the song should be performed. Begin with "Hoo, Hoo!" and discuss the markings found in measures 9–14.

Put "The Three Rogues" on the overhead projector and place dynamic markings on the score to correspond to the way students sang it earlier, with changing dynamic levels. It might look like **Visual E3.**

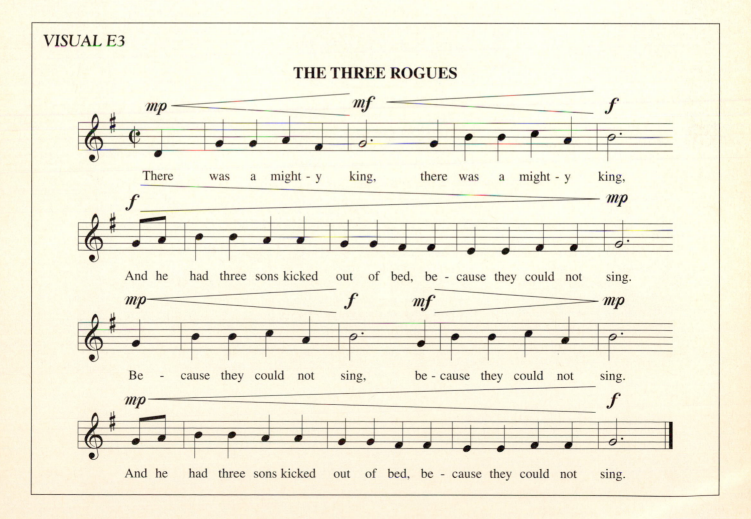

VISUAL E3

THE THREE ROGUES

LEARNING Articulation refers to whatever will provide an overall clarity in a musical performance. Two aspects of articulation are legato and staccato performances. *Legato* denotes a smooth, connected progression from note to note, without any perceptible interruptions. *Staccato* denotes a reduction in the value of notes which have a dot placed over or under them. Staccato notes sound disconnected.

Strategies

Have students move in a smooth, connected manner, denoting legato performance. Movements could include swimming, ice skating, and ballet dancing.

Have students imitate living things that move smoothly, such as swans on a lake, fish in the water, or birds in flight.

Have students listen and move to recordings that exemplify legato performance, such as "Cradle Song" from *Children's Games* by Bizet or "Ballet of the Sylphs" from *The Damnation of Faust* by Berlioz.

Sing legato songs that demonstrate smooth, connected tones, such as "Come Boating With Me" and "Cherry Bloom."

COME BOATING WITH ME

Lansing MacDowell

Italian Folk Song

CHERRY BLOOM
(SAKURA)

Japanese Folk Song

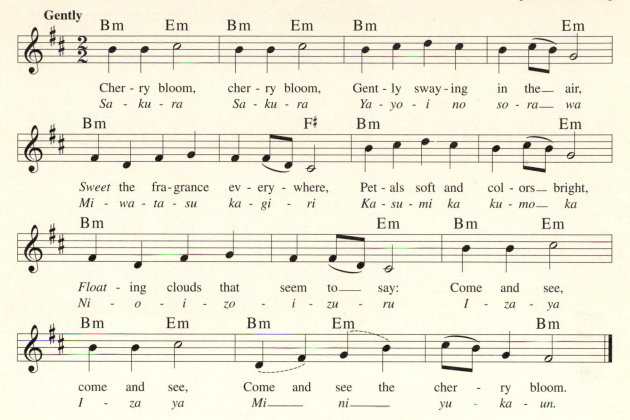

Gently

Cher - ry bloom,   cher - ry bloom,   Gent - ly sway - ing   in the— air,
Sa - ku - ra   *Sa - ku - ra*   *Ya - yo - i   no   so - ra— wa*

Sweet the fra - grance   ev - ery - where,   Pet - als soft and   col - ors— bright,
Mi - wa - ta - su   ka - gi - ri   Ka - su - mi ka   ku - mo— ka

Float - ing clouds that   seem to— say: Come and see,
Ni - o - i - zo - i - zu - ru   I - za - ya

come and see,   Come and see the   cher - ry bloom.
I - za - ya   Mi— ni—   yu - ka - un.

Have students move in a disconnected, staccato manner, using such movements as hopping, popping balloons, or touching a hot iron.

Students can imitate living things that move in a disconnected manner, such as kangaroos, rabbits, and woodpeckers.

Have students listen and move to recordings that contain examples of staccato performance, such as "Petite Ballerina" and "Pizzicato Polka" from *Ballet Suite No. 1* by Shostakovich.

Sing songs that have some staccato passages, such as "Wind the Bobbin," or contain staccato ostinati, such as "Hickory, Dickory, Dock." Have students explain why the songs or ostinati sound better sung staccato rather than legato.

WIND THE BOBBIN

Winding Game

Wind the bob - bin, ding dang   gon - na wind it tight,   ding dang.

Bob - bin a wound up,   Bob - bin a wound up,   Bob - bin a wound up,   Break it!

HICKORY DICKORY DOCK

Words from Mother Goose

Melody by: J. W. Elliot
Arr. M. Rozmajzl

Teaching Expressive Elements to Children

FOCUS

Slur

LEARNING   A *slur* is a curved line connecting two or more notes on different lines or spaces, as opposed to tied notes which share the same line or space. This symbol designates that the notes connected by the slur should be sung or played with a single breath. Often, a slur is used to connect two or more notes sharing a single syllable of text.

Strategies

Sing a number of songs containing slurs, such as "When That I Was a Little Tiny Boy" and "Mister Rabbit." Find the slur symbols in these songs; discover which slurs connect notes sharing the same, single syllable.

WHEN THAT I WAS A LITTLE TINY BOY

Elizabethan Song

MISTER RABBIT

African American

Study the songs in the students' music book and discover where slurs occur.

LEARNING A *fermata* (⌢) over a note indicates that the note should be held longer than its normal duration. The length of the fermata is determined by the musical director.

Strategies

Sing songs containing fermata such as "Lock Lomond" and "Most Done Ling'ring Here." Discuss how the performance of the fermata in these compositions can add to the expressiveness of the work.

LOCH LOMOND

Scotland

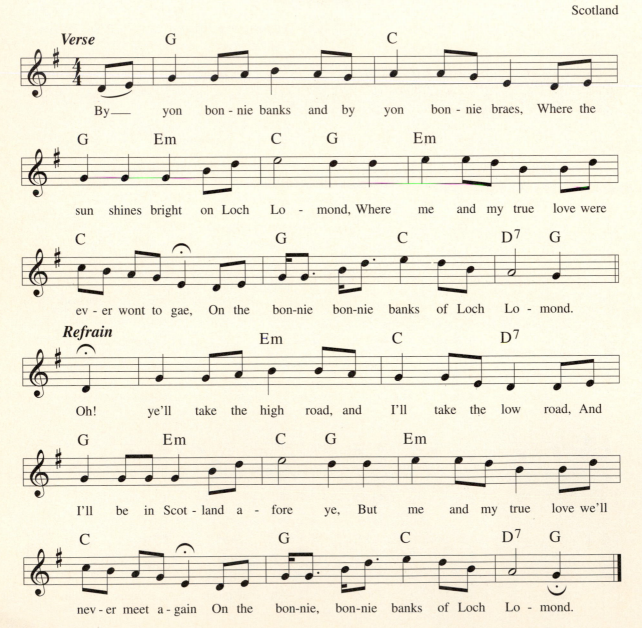

MOST DONE LING'RING HERE

African American

If you get there be - fore I do, Most done ling - 'ring here.

Look out for me I am com - ing too, Most done ling - 'ring here.

I'm goin' a - way, goin' a - way, I'm most done ling - 'ring here.

I'm goin' a - way to Ga - li - lee, and I'm most done ling - 'ring here.

INTRODUCING EXPRESSIVE ELEMENTS
Suggested Sequencing By Grade Level

Kindergarten

1. Loud/soft
2. Fast/slow

Grade One

1. Loud (f), soft (p)
2. Smooth, disconnected

Grade Two

1. Getting louder, getting softer
2. Getting faster and slower
3. Legato/staccato

Grade Three

1. ff, pp, mf, mp
2. fermata

Grades Four, Five, Six

Italian terminology and abbreviations

WRITTEN AND PERFORMANCE-RELATED ASSESSMENTS THROUGH COOPERATIVE LEARNING ACTIVITIES: EXPRESSIVE ELEMENTS

1. Give each group a different, familiar song.
   a. Students should sing through the song, determine its tempo using a term from Visual E1, and place the appropriate Italian tempo marking above the song on the left side.
   b. Students should sing through the song again and decide where an accelerando and/or a ritardando could be placed to enhance the song's performance.
   c. They should then practice the song with its expressive markings and perform it for the class.
   d. Students could also play the song on barred instruments.
2. Provide each group with a different, familiar song.
   a. Ask students to sing through their song and to decide what dynamic markings might be placed in the song to enhance the meaning of the words. Refer to Visual E2.
   b. Students should sing the song several times until they are satisfied with their choice of markings.
   c. They should then choose one to three instruments to use in accompanying the song. The instruments and the accompaniment should be appropriate to the song and its dynamic markings.
   d. Finally, students perform the song for the class.
3. Give each group a different, familiar song. Simple instrumental accompaniments should also be included on the manuscript. Students should sing through the song several times to decide what dynamic and tempo markings would enhance the song's performance. These markings should be added to both the vocal and the instrumental parts of the song. When satisfied, students should practice their song until they are able to perform it for the class.

Teaching Form to Children

Chapter 6

INTRODUCTION

Form, as a concept, is experienced by children in their earliest years. Nature provides an abundance of objects that have their own distinctive form. The form of a dandelion is different from that of a daisy; the shape of an oak tree is not the same as that of a weeping willow.

Music, too, has many forms that distinguish one composition from another. Music is not a haphazard coming together of various elements; it is an orderly arrangement of many interwoven relationships: Pitches are combined to form melodic and harmonic intervals; duration symbols are combined to form rhythm; and both intervals and rhythm are combined to form phrases. The manner in which music phrases are arranged within a composition contributes to its form. The *form* of a piece of music refers to its structure or design, to the way its expressive relationships are combined to provide both unity and variety within the music.

The basic, underlying principles of form in music are the concepts of "same" and "different." In a song, some musical parts are exactly the same, some are totally different, and others are only partially different. The repetition and contrast that exist from one part to the next help determine the total effect of the musical work.

> *In music there is no form without logic, there is no logic without unity.*
> —Arnold Schoenberg

FOCUS

Phrase

LEARNING A *phrase* is a musical line that contains a coherent grouping of pitches, similar to a sentence in language which contains a coherent grouping of words. Phrases are usually two to eight measures long, but more often four measures in length.

Strategies

Choose songs that the children know well. Sing each song, adding movements that will show where each new phrase of a song begins. For example, have students form a circle. Move to the right for phrase 1, to the left for phrase 2, and so on. Or pass a pillow or ball to the right on the first phrase; to the left on the second phrase, as in the song "Oh, Susanna."

OH, SUSANNA

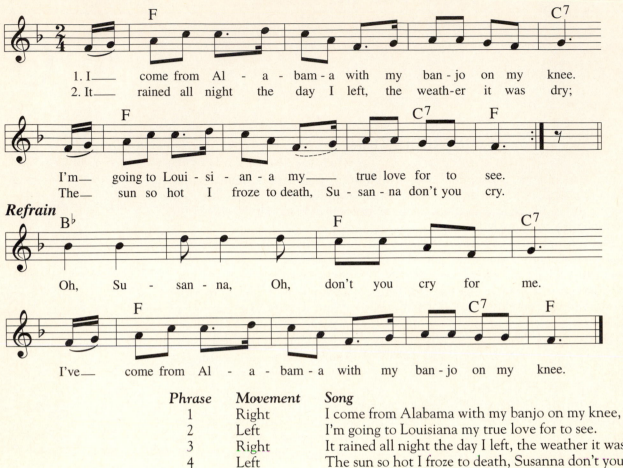

1. I come from Al - a - bam - a with my ban - jo on my knee.
2. It rained all night the day I left, the weath - er it was dry;

I'm going to Loui - si - an - a my true love for to see.
The sun so hot I froze to death, Su - san - na don't you cry.

Refrain

Oh, Su - san - na, Oh, don't you cry for me.

I've come from Al - a - bam - a with my ban - jo on my knee.

Phrase	Movement	Song
1	Right	I come from Alabama with my banjo on my knee,
2	Left	I'm going to Louisiana my true love for to see.
3	Right	It rained all night the day I left, the weather it was dry;
4	Left	The sun so hot I froze to death, Susanna don't you cry.
5	Right	Oh, Susanna, oh, don't you cry for me,
6	Left	I've come from Alabama with my banjo on my knee.

Students can also identify phrases by drawing in the air an appropriate picture—a sun, a star, a kite—suggested by a song. The student should begin drawing the picture at the beginning of phrase 1 and should complete it by the end of the phrase, so that the picture can be redrawn for phrase 2. Using the song "Rocky Mountain," students can draw a picture of a "mountain" in the air for each phrase of the song.

ROCKY MOUNTAIN

Southern Folk Song

Rock - y Moun - tain, Rock - y Moun - tain, Rock - y Moun - tain high,

When you're on that Rock - y Moun - tain, Hang your head and cry.

Do, do, do, do, Do re - mem - ber me.

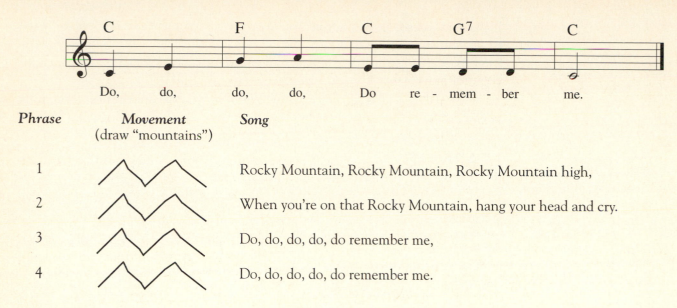

Do, do, do, do, Do re - mem - ber me.

Phrase	Movement (draw "mountains")	Song
1		Rocky Mountain, Rocky Mountain, Rocky Mountain high,
2		When you're on that Rocky Mountain, hang your head and cry.
3		Do, do, do, do, do remember me,
4		Do, do, do, do, do remember me.

Help students understand that musical phrases are similar to sentences in language; therefore we usually breathe between phrases as we would breathe between sentences.

LEARNING   In a musical composition, all phrases may be the same.

Strategies

Once students can discover where phrases begin and end, they can begin identifying same and different phrases. Sing a short song containing two phrases that are the same, such as "Marching." Have students discover where the two phrases begin and end.

MARCHING

Hungary

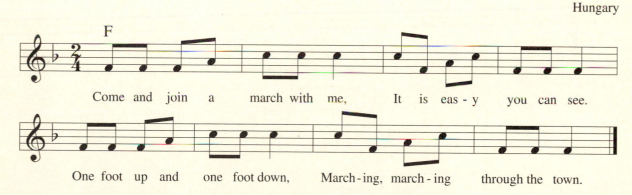

Come and join a march with me, It is eas-y you can see.

One foot up and one foot down, March-ing, march-ing through the town.

Draw the melodic contour of each phrase on the chalkboard, as in **Visual F1.**

VISUAL F1

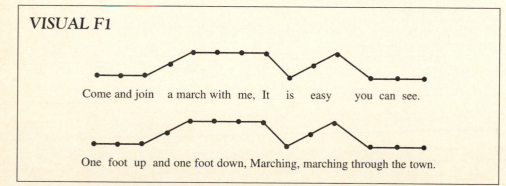

Come and join a march with me, It is easy you can see.

One foot up and one foot down, Marching, marching through the town.

Have students study the contour and discover whether the two phrases in Visual F1 are the same or different.

Sing the song again while students move to the contour of each phrase with locomotor movements.

To reinforce the learning, provide students with additional songs containing phrases that are the same.

LEARNING   In a musical composition, all phrases may be different from each other.

Strategies

Sing a song containing two phrases that are different, as in "Bow Wow Wow." Have students discover where each phrase begins and ends.

BOW WOW WOW

Game Song

Bow-wow-wow!   Whose dog art thou?   Lit-tle Tom-my Tuck-er's dog! Bow-wow-wow!

Draw the contour of each phrase on the chalkboard, as in **Visual F2.**

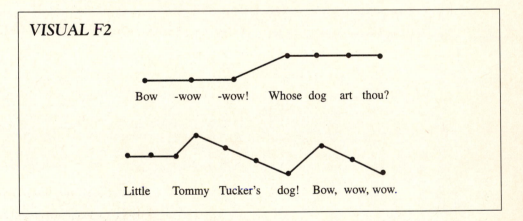

VISUAL F2

Bow   -wow   -wow!   Whose   dog   art   thou?

Little   Tommy   Tucker's   dog!   Bow,   wow,   wow.

Have students study the contour of Visual F2 to determine whether the two phrases are the same or different.

Sing the song again while students move to the contour of each phrase with locomotor movements.

Sing other songs with phrases that are different from each other.

LEARNING   In a musical composition, some phrases may be the same and others may be different.

Strategies

Sing a song containing both like and unlike phrases, such as "The Jolly Miller." Have students identify each of the four phrases in the song.

THE JOLLY MILLER

New England Song

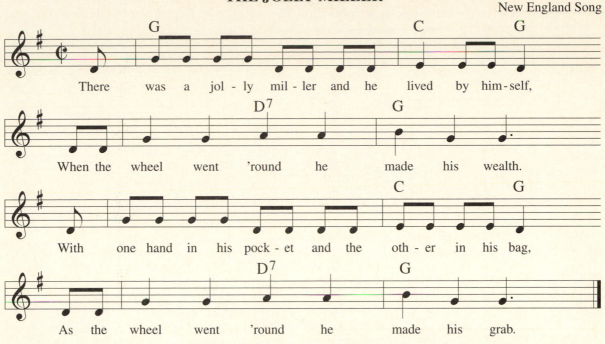

Draw the contour of each phrase on the chalkboard, as in **Visual F3.**

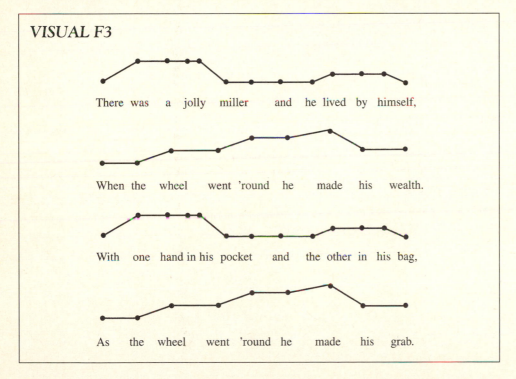

VISUAL F3

Students should study the contours and identify those that are the same and those that are different.

Sing the song while students use locomotor movements to portray the contour of each phrase in Visual F3.

Discover other songs that combine same and different phrases. Sing them, draw their contours, and move to them.

Have students create their own songs with same or different phrases. When this exercise is first assigned, the teacher will need to give some parameters to help ensure success. The number of phrases and measures to be used, the meter, and the starting and ending pitches might be given. The teacher might also limit students to a few pitches, such as C, D, E, and G, and provide words for the song being created. It may also be helpful to restrict the number of rhythmic symbols used; for example, allow the use of only quarter notes, eighth notes, and quarter rests. **Visual F4** shows how the restrictions can be presented.

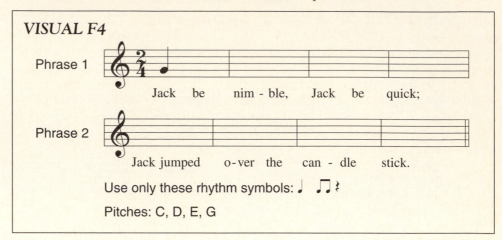

VISUAL F4

Phrase 1

Jack   be   nim - ble,   Jack   be   quick;

Phrase 2

Jack jumped   o - ver   the   can - dle   stick.

Use only these rhythm symbols:

Pitches: C, D, E, G

Using the format in Visual F4, students can compose two phrases that are the same or two that are different from each other. Have students play their compositions on melody instruments, making changes until they are satisfied. While part of the class performs the composition on instruments, the remainder of the class can move to each phrase in some creative way.

LEARNING

Some phrases in a musical composition are similar but not exactly the same.

Strategies

Sing a familiar song containing phrases that are similar, but not exactly the same, as in "Poor Little Kitty Cat."

POOR LITTLE KITTY CAT

American Folk Song

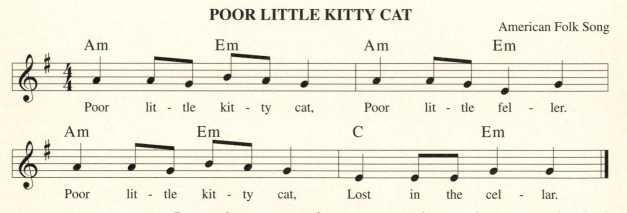

Am   Em   Am   Em

Poor   lit - tle   kit - ty   cat,   Poor   lit - tle   fel - ler.

Am   Em   C   Em

Poor   lit - tle   kit - ty   cat,   Lost   in   the   cel - lar.

Repeat the song, one phrase at a time, drawing the contour of each phrase on the chalkboard, as in **Visual F5.**

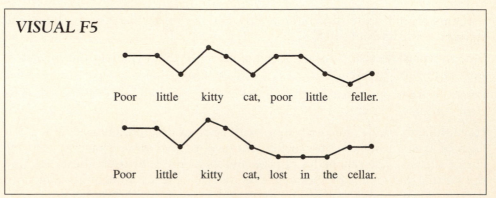

VISUAL F5

Poor   little   kitty   cat, poor   little   feller.

Poor   little   kitty   cat, lost   in   the   cellar.

Help students discover that both phrases begin the same but end differently. While singing the song again, students can draw the contour of each phrase in the air or move to each phrase with locomotor movements.

Find and compose other songs having similar phrases.

Instruments can be added to reinforce students' awareness of same and different phrases at all stages of the above learnings. For example, instruments can be played when singing the song "The Jolly Miller," outlined in Visual F3. Since phrases 1 and 3 are the same, students can play the claves or other appropriate instrument when singing these two phrases. Likewise, phrases 2 and 4 are the same, but are different from phrases 1 and 3. Therefore, a different instrument should be played for phrases 2 and 4, such as a triangle. The chart that follows clarifies this strategy:

Phrase 1	"There was a jolly miller . . ."	claves
Phrase 2	"When the wheel went 'round . . ."	triangle
Phrase 3	"With one hand in his pocket . . ."	claves
Phrase 4	"As the wheel went 'round . . ."	triangle

Visuals can be used to reinforce an understanding of same and different. Two pictures of the same dog or the same cat can represent two phrases that are the same; a picture of a helicopter and one of a rocket can designate two phrases that are different; two pictures of the same balloon, one colored red and one colored blue, can be used to represent two phrases that are similar but not exactly the same. Provide a variety of pictures for students to arrange that will match the phrases of any particular song. For example, the teacher could place six pictures in the front of the room: three pictures of a man and three of a wheel. To show the form of the song "The Jolly Miller," students would select appropriate pictures for each phrase, as designated in this:

Phrase	*Words*	*Picture Card*
1	"There was a jolly miller . . ."	man
2	"When the wheel went 'round . . ."	wheel
3	"With one hand in his pocket . . ."	man
4	"As the wheel went 'round . . ."	wheel

In arranging the picture cards, the following progression would show the form of "The Jolly Miller":

Geometrical shapes, such as □ ○ △, can also be arranged to show *same:* □ □ or *different:* ○ △ or *similar:* □ ■ phrases.

Once students are reading and printing, cards containing lowercase letters can be constructed to designate same, different, and similar phrases:

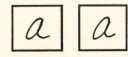
same

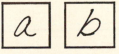
different

similar

Notice that numbers or other symbols may be used to designate a succession of phrases that are similar but not exactly the same, such as:

a a¹ a² or a a' a''

When students are able to use picture cards to show form, as in the example of the song "The Jolly Miller," it is a short step to replace the pictures with cards containing geometrical shapes or letters, as shown here:

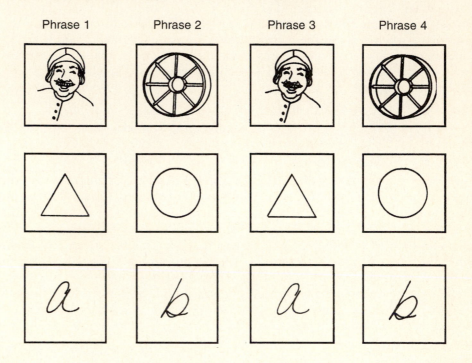

Students can apply the above strategies to recorded music as well. After listening to short examples of recorded music several times, students can draw the contour of each phrase and then arrange, in their proper sequence, cards having lower-case letters, as shown above. Let students decide what locomotor movements to use for each phrase. After performing these movements, students can discuss whether the movements matched what they heard in the music. If not, choose a different movement until students are satisfied with their choreographed interpretation of the music on the recording.

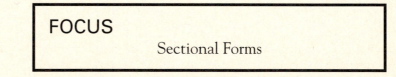

LEARNING Musical phrases can be combined to form larger units called *sections*. Sections can be relatively short or hundreds of measures in length. A *double bar* often separates one section from another. Just as the terms of same, different, or similar characterize phrases, so, too, are sections identified as being same, different, or similar. Common sectional forms are binary (AB), ternary (ABA), strophic (AAA), theme and variations (A A¹ A² A³ A⁴ etc.), and rondo (ABACA or ABACABA). Capital letters are generally used to designate each section in a composition.

Strategies

Sing through the song "Shoo, Fly" until students know it well.

SHOO, FLY

Billy Reeves

Frank Campbell

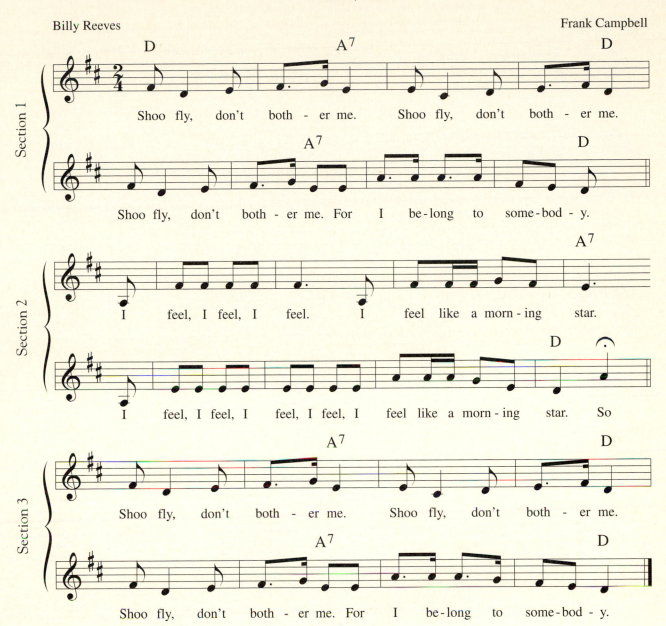

Have students analyze "Shoo, Fly" to discover its three distinct sections, the first and last sections being the same. Notice the double bar dividing each section. Label each section: 1=A; 2= B, 3=A.

Have students look through their music textbook to discover other sectional songs.

LEARNING
Some compositions are divided into two sections, the second being different from the first. The form of this two-part composition is known as *binary* or AB.

Strategies

Sing a common two-section song, such as "Riding in the Buggy." Have students notice the double bar between the two sections. Because the two sections are different one from the other, their design can be indicated as AB. In binary form, either the A or the B may be repeated: AAB, ABB, or AABB.

RIDING IN THE BUGGY

Play-Party Song

Rid-ing in the bug-gy Miss Mar-y Jane, Miss Mar-y Jane, Miss Mar-y Jane,

Rid-ing in the bug-gy Miss Mar-y Jane, I'm a long way from home.

Who mourns for me, Who mourns for me,

Who mourns for me, my dar-ling, Who mourns for me?

Place on the overhead projector a diagram showing the design of both the phrases and the sections of a two-part song, such as "Riding in the Buggy." See **Visual F6.** Sing the song while following its design on the diagram.

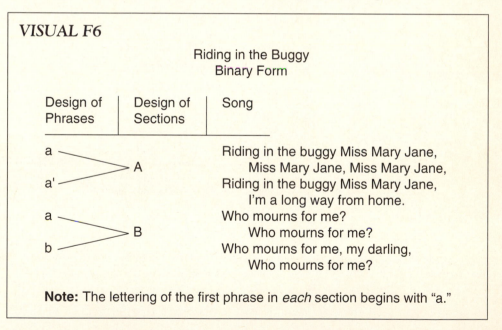

Diagram other familiar, binary form songs.

Have students listen to recordings of music in binary form, such as those listed here. Discover where the "B" section begins, and if either the A or the B section repeats. Write the sectional design on the chalkboard.

a. "Copacabana" from *Saudades do Brazil* by Milhaud
Form: AB interlude AB

b. "Sarabande" from *Suite for Strings* by Corelli-Pinelli
Form: Introduction AABB Coda
Note: "Introduction," "Interlude," and "Coda" are discussed in the *Focus* following "strophic form."

c. "Gigue" from *French Suite No. 4* in E-flat by Bach
Form: AABB

LEARNING Some compositions are divided into three sections. The second section is different from the first, but the third section is the same as or similar to the first section. Three-part compositions are called *ternary* or ABA.

Strategies

Sing a familiar three-section song such as "Nobody Knows the Trouble I've Seen." Notice the use of *refrain* (same melody, same words) and *verse* (different words, and sometimes a different melody).

NOBODY KNOWS THE TROUBLE I'VE SEEN

Spiritual

Notice the two sets of double bars that divide the song into three sections of which the first and last are the same. This design can be indicated as ABA, otherwise known as *ternary form*. Although any part in ternary form may be repeated, repetition of the first section is the most common: AABA.

Place on the overhead projector a diagram showing the design of both the phrases and the sections of "Nobody Knows the Trouble I've Seen." See **Visual F7.** Sing the song while following its design on the diagram.

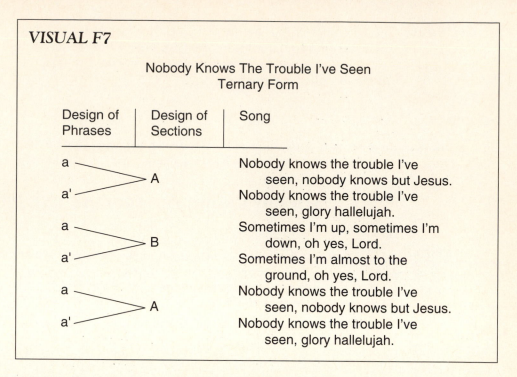

VISUAL F7

Nobody Knows The Trouble I've Seen
Ternary Form

Design of Phrases	Design of Sections	Song
a a'	A	Nobody knows the trouble I've seen, nobody knows but Jesus. Nobody knows the trouble I've seen, glory hallelujah.
a a'	B	Sometimes I'm up, sometimes I'm down, oh yes, Lord. Sometimes I'm almost to the ground, oh yes, Lord.
a a'	A	Nobody knows the trouble I've seen, nobody knows but Jesus. Nobody knows the trouble I've seen, glory hallelujah.

Diagram other familiar, ternary form songs.

Play recordings of music in ternary form, such as the ones listed here. Again, discover where the "B" section begins and if either the A or the B section repeats. Place the sectional design on the chalkboard.

a. *Mazurka No. 24* by Chopin
Form: ABA
b. "Träumerei" from *Scenes from Childhood* by Schumann
Form: AABA[1]
c. "Hoe-Down" from *Rodeo—Ballet Suite* by Copland
Form: Introduction A Interlude B Interlude A Coda

LEARNING   In some musical compositions the original theme always returns after each digression or contrasting theme. This form is known as *rondo*, and is usually symbolized by ABACA or ABACABA.

Strategies

Divide the class into five groups. Let each group know that they are responsible for one section of a five-part composition they will be creating. Have each group work on the following assignments:

Group 1: Sing a familiar song.
Group 2: Do an eight-measure rhythmic composition, using only body sounds.
Group 3: Sing again the familiar song with accompaniment on a xylophone or other melody instrument.
Group 4: Perform an eight-measure rhythmic composition using rhythm instruments.
Group 5: Sing the familiar song again.

When they are ready, have each group present its section, one after another, without breaks, so that the five sections are perceived as parts of a whole. After students have presented their five-part composition, have them analyze it to discover the overall form of their piece. Their analysis should give the following formal design.

A Sing a familiar song.

B Do an eight-measure rhythmic composition, using only body sounds.

A¹ Sing again the familiar song with accompaniment on a xylophone or other melody instrument.

C Perform an eight-measure rhythmic composition using rhythm instruments.

A Sing the familiar song again.

Point out that the design ABA¹CA is known as rondo form because the theme always returns after a contrasting theme is presented.

Play the opening measures of a composition set in *rondo form,* such as "Waltz" from *Masquerade Suite* by Khachaturian. Being familiar with the beginning of the "A" section, as given in **Visual F8,** will enable students to hear the return of A each time it occurs.

VISUAL F8

Opening Measures of "Waltz"

Theme 1:
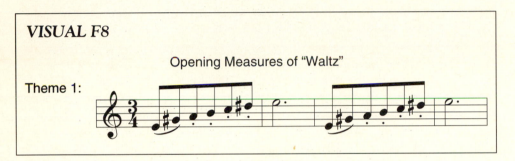

After students are familiar with the beginning of the A section, play the recording of "Waltz," having students raise their hands each time A returns.

Place a diagram of "Waltz" on the overhead projector, as in **Visual F9.**

VISUAL F9

Overall Design of "Waltz"

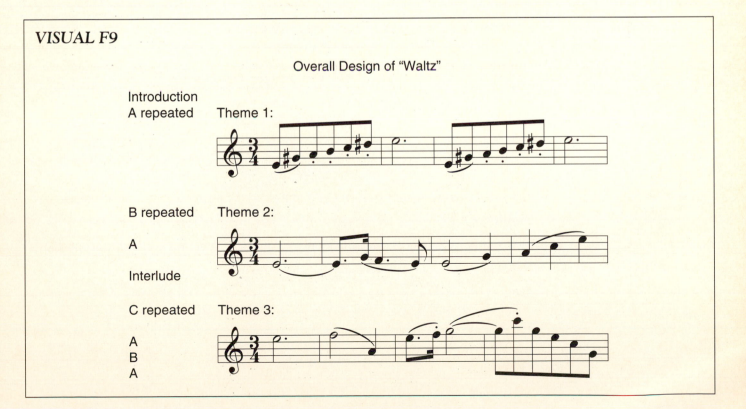

Introduction
A repeated   Theme 1:

B repeated   Theme 2:

A

Interlude

C repeated   Theme 3:

A
B
A

On a melodic instrument, play the opening measures to sections B and C to familiarize students with these contrasting themes.

Play the recording of "Waltz" again, pointing to each section on the diagram as it occurs in the music.

Provide additional experiences with rondo form. The following recordings may be helpful:

a. "Dance of the Comedians" from *The Bartered Bride* by Smetana
b. *Gypsy Rondo* by Haydn
c. "The March of the Siamese Children" from *The King and I* by Rodgers

LEARNING

The theme of some compositions is sometimes repeated again and again, but is altered in different ways for each succeeding repetition. The resulting form is known as *theme and variations* or $A\ A^1\ A^2\ A^3\ A^4$.

Strategies

Prepare students to hear music set in theme and variations form by placing on the board the common design used for music having this structure: $A\ A^1\ A^2\ A^3\ A^4\ A^5$, and so on.

Point out that the original theme is performed again and again but is altered in some way for each succeeding repetition. Repetition could have changes in tempo, dynamics, key, *mode* (major or minor), instrumentation, accompaniment, harmony, rhythm, or even melody.

Have students notice that, although rondo form had contrasting sections based on new themes, theme and variation form uses only one theme throughout.

Provide a diagram of a composition using theme and variations form, such as *Variations on the Theme "Pop! Goes the Weasel"* by Cailliet. See **Visual F10.**

VISUAL F10

Variations on the Theme "Pop! Goes The Weasel"
Theme and Variations Form

Sections	Tempo	Dynamics			Other Characteristics
Introduction	fast	loud			fragments of the theme
Theme	fast	loud			full orchestra
Variation I	fast		p	f	different instruments playing different parts of the theme
Variation II	slow		p	mf	dance (minuet) style
Variation III	very slow	very soft			gypsy violin
Variation IV	fast	medium loud			music box (waltz style)
Variation V	very fast	very loud			jazz style
Coda	fast		p	ff	fragments of the theme

Play or sing "Pop! Goes the Weasel." Explain to the students that this is the theme in the new form they are about to study. In theme and variations form, the theme may be original or may be a tune borrowed from another composer. In either case it is usually very simple in style, lending itself easily to many variations. The composer, after stating the theme, will present it in different disguises, or variations, one after the other. The overall design for the Cailliet composition should be identified as:

Introduction   A A^1 A^2 A^3 A^4 A^5 Coda

Play the recording of *Theme and Variations on "Pop! Goes the Weasel."* Using the diagram in Visual F10, point to each variation as it occurs in the music. After several hearings, the students should be able to recognize each section without the diagram in front of them.

Provide additional listening experiences to reinforce students' understanding of theme and variations form. The following examples may be used:

a. *Ah! Vous Dirai-je Maman* by Mozart
   Theme: "Twinkle, Twinkle Little Star," originally a French folk song
b. *Bolero* by Ravel
c. *American Salute* by Gould
   Theme: "When Johnny Comes Marching Home"

Have students discover the overall design for each theme and variations recording. Discuss the different techniques the composer uses in each variation to make it different from the theme.

Provide opportunities for students to create their own theme and variations form. The following design could be used:

A   Sing a familiar song.
A^1 Sing the same song half as fast.
A^2 Sing the song in its original tempo with rhythmic accompaniment.
A^3 Sing the song in a new key.
A^4 Repeat the song in the new key with autoharp accompaniment.
A^5 Sing the song in its original key with rhythmic and autoharp accompaniment. Add a simple melodic ostinato.

LEARNING

When all the stanzas of a poem are set to the same music, the resulting form is called *strophic* or AAA. Strophic form may have any number of "A's," depending on the number of stanzas in the poem.

Strategies

Sing a strophic-form song, such as "America the Beautiful." Notice that this song has a number of stanzas set to the same music.

AMERICA THE BEAUTIFUL

Katherine Lee Bates

Samuel A. Ward

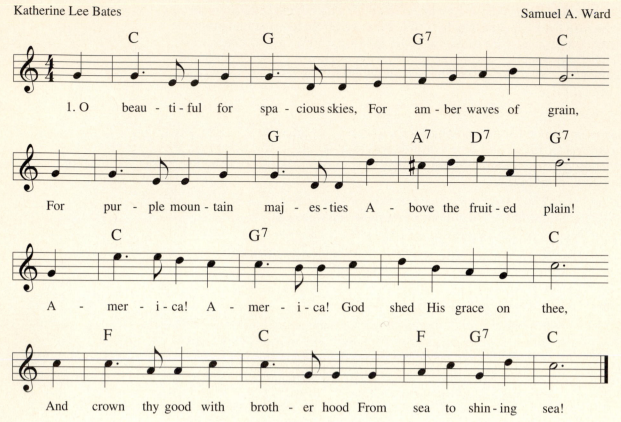

1. O beau - ti - ful for spa - cious skies, For am - ber waves of grain,

For pur - ple moun - tain maj - es - ties A - bove the fruit - ed plain!

A - mer - i - ca! A - mer - i - ca! God shed His grace on thee,

And crown thy good with broth - er hood From sea to shin - ing sea!

2. O beautiful for Pilgrim feet,
   Whose stern impassioned stress
   A thoroughfare for freedom beat
   Across the wilderness.
   America! America! God mend thine every flaw,
   Confirm thy soul in self-control,
   Thy liberty in law.

3. O beautiful for heroes proved
   In liberating strife,
   Who more than self their country loved,
   And mercy more than life.
   America! America! May God thy gold refine
   Till all success be nobleness
   And every gain divine.

4. O beautiful for patriot dream
   That sees beyond the years,
   Thine alabaster cities gleam
   Undimmed by human tears.
   America! America! God shed His grace on thee,
   And crown thy good with brotherhood
   From sea to shining sea.

To show the repetition of the "A" section, place a diagram of "America the Beautiful" on the overhead projector. See **Visual F11.** Outline both the phrases and the sections of this strophic song. Sing the song while following its design on the diagram.

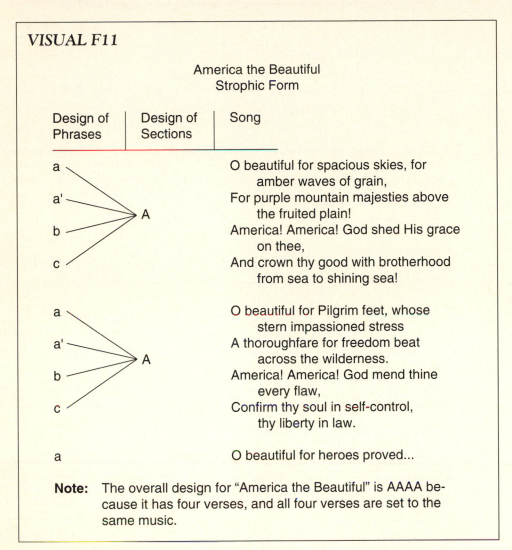

VISUAL F11

America the Beautiful
Strophic Form

Design of Phrases	Design of Sections	Song
a		O beautiful for spacious skies, for amber waves of grain,
a'		For purple mountain majesties above the fruited plain!
b	A	America! America! God shed His grace on thee,
c		And crown thy good with brotherhood from sea to shining sea!
a		O beautiful for Pilgrim feet, whose stern impassioned stress
a'		A thoroughfare for freedom beat across the wilderness.
b	A	America! America! God mend thine every flaw,
c		Confirm thy soul in self-control, thy liberty in law.
a		O beautiful for heroes proved...

Note: The overall design for "America the Beautiful" is AAAA because it has four verses, and all four verses are set to the same music.

Diagram other familiar strophic songs. Many of the hymns sung in church and many folk songs are in strophic design.

Play recordings of songs in strophic form, listening for the repetition of each new stanza. "Who Is Sylvia" and "Heiden Röslein" by Schubert are good examples of songs using strophic form.

LEARNING

An *introduction* is a passage occurring before the major sections of a form. Its function is varied but many be used to set the tempo, the mood, or the key of the musical work; or it may be used to prepare the listener for the first thematic idea.

A *coda* is a passage added to the last major section of a form. A coda's function may also be varied but usually serves to bring the music to a more satisfactory close.

An *interlude* is a passage added to the interior of a composition; it connects one section to another more smoothly than would occur if it were absent.

Strategies

Sing a familiar song. Ask students to devise a rhythmic introduction and coda for the song. One solution can be found in **Visual F12.**

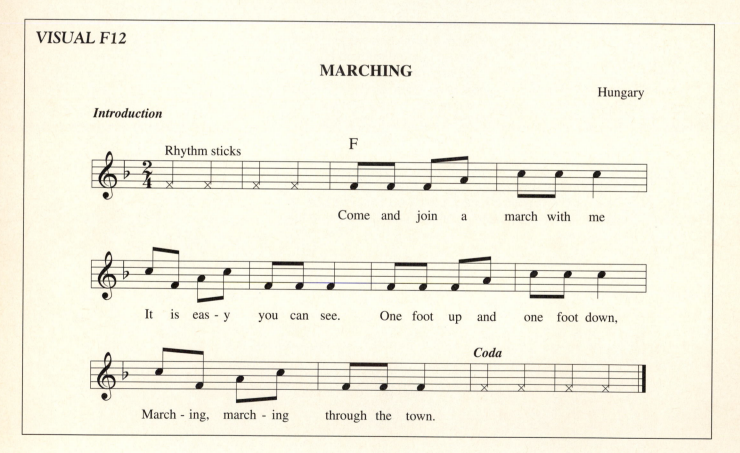

VISUAL F12

MARCHING

Hungary

Introduction

Rhythm sticks

Come and join a march with me

It is eas - y you can see. One foot up and one foot down,

Coda

March - ing, march - ing through the town.

Have students create additional, more difficult rhythmic introductions and codas for "Marching" and for other familiar songs.

Create a melodic introduction and coda for a familar song. The introduction can be extended into the song as an ostinato figure, as in **Visual F13.**

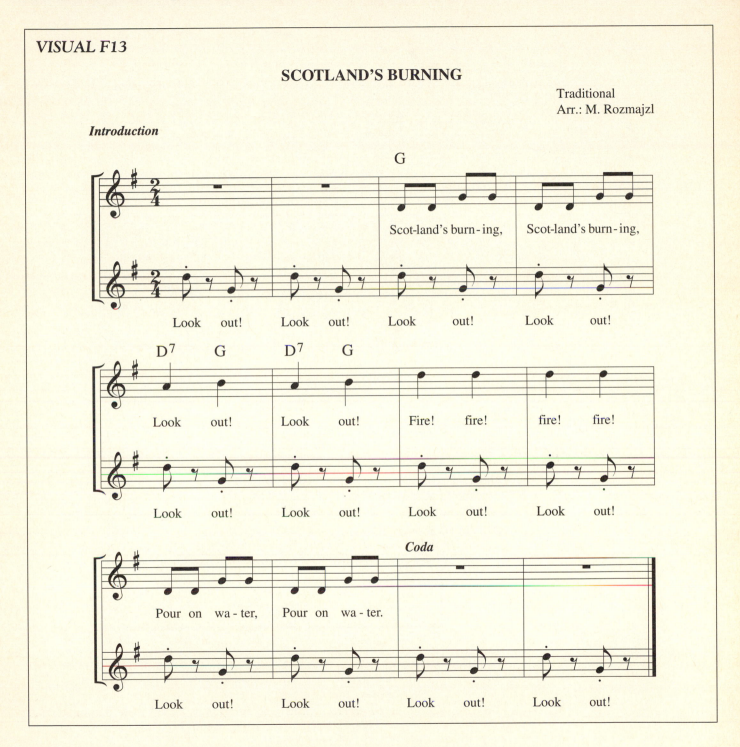

VISUAL F13

SCOTLAND'S BURNING

Traditional
Arr.: M. Rozmajzl

Introduction

Have students create additional melodic introductions and codas for other familiar songs.

Choose a familiar song with more than one verse. Create an interlude to be sung between verses, as in **Visual F14.**

LONDON BRIDGE

England
Arr.: M. Rozmajzl

Lon - don bridge is fall - ing down, fall - ing down, fall - ing down.

Lon - don bridge is fall - ing down, my fair la - dy.

Interlude

Bridge is down, fall - ing down. Bridge is down, fall - ing down.

Verse 2

Shake him up with pep-per and salt, pep-per and salt, pep-per and salt,

Shake him up with pep - per and salt, my fair la - dy.

Study introductions, interludes, and codas in larger forms. This can be done by replaying appropriate recordings used with the previous learnings on sectional forms. A number of suggested recordings included introductions, interludes, and codas in their overall design.

FOCUS

Repeat Signs

LEARNING   A variety of symbols are used by composers to denote what material in a musical composition should be repeated. The most common symbols are, ‖, ‖   ‖, *Da capo al fine* and *Dal segno al fine*. Composers use repeat signs within a composition to save space on the manuscript and to save the time it would take to write it all out.

Strategies

Place on the chalkboard the repeat sign ‖. Explain that this symbol—two dots to the left of double bar lines—is used when the composer wants the performer to repeat the music from the beginning of the piece. Have students find the repeat sign in "Bluebird." Explain that when repeating from the beginning of this piece, the second verse is sung. Sing the song, using the repeat sign.

BLUEBIRD

Game Song

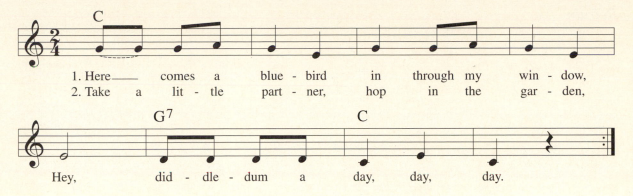

1. Here—— comes a blue - bird in through my win - dow,
2. Take a lit - tle part - ner, hop in the gar - den,

Hey, did - dle - dum a day, day, day.

The repeat signs ‖: :‖ are used when the composer wants repeated only mate-rial enclosed by the signs. Have students find these signs in the song "Hansel and Gretal Dance." Explain that when repeating lines 3 and 4, the second verse should be sung. Sing the song; repeat lines 3 and 4 as indicated by the repeat signs.

HANSEL AND GRETEL DANCE

Adelheid Wette
Translated by Constance Bache

E. Humperdinck

Part - ner come and dance with me, Both my hands I give to thee.

Right foot first, Left foot then, Round a-bout and back a - gain.

1. With your foot you tap, tap, tap, With your hands you clap, clap, clap.
2. With your head you nick, nick, nick. With your fin - gers click, click, click.

Right foot first, Left foot then, Round a-bout and back a - gain.

Again, the overall structure of the piece incorporates the material within the re-peat signs, resulting in an ABB sectional form.

Examine the song "Nobody Knows the Trouble I've Seen." Notice the abbrevia-tion D.C. at the end of the piece. This abbreviation stands for *Da capo al fine*, literally meaning "from the head or beginning to the word *fine* or end." Com-posers use D.C. al fine or just D.C. when they want performers to repeat a song from the beginning, but not to sing any farther than where *fine* is indicated.

NOBODY KNOWS THE TROUBLE I'VE SEEN

Spiritual

Point out that the song "Nobody Knows the Trouble I've Seen" was used earlier under "Ternary Form," but the first two lines were written out at the end of the verse. To save space and time, the repeat abbreviation D.C. replaces the rewriting of the first two lines. Sing the song, repeating the first two lines until you reach the word *fine*.

"Hop Old Squirrel" provides an example of music containing first and second endings. Place a copy of "Hop Old Squirrel" on the overhead projector. Verbalize how this song should be performed. Have students notice the first and second endings in line 2. Explain that this song is sung to the repeat sign (:||); then repeat the song from the beginning, but skip the first ending and sing the last two measures (second ending) the second time through.

HOP OLD SQUIRREL

African American

Have students study the song "Turn! Turn! Turn!" to discover where a new type of repeat sign is used. They will soon discover D.S. al fine above the last measure of the song, and will probably have several suggestions as to how this phrase relates to the symbol 𝄋 at the beginning of the piece. Explain that the phrase stands for *Dal segno al fine*, meaning to repeat from the sign 𝄋 and to continue until the word *fine*. Perform the song and include the repetition indicated.

TURN! TURN! TURN!

Text adapted from *Ecclesiastes*
by Pete Seeger

Pete Seeger

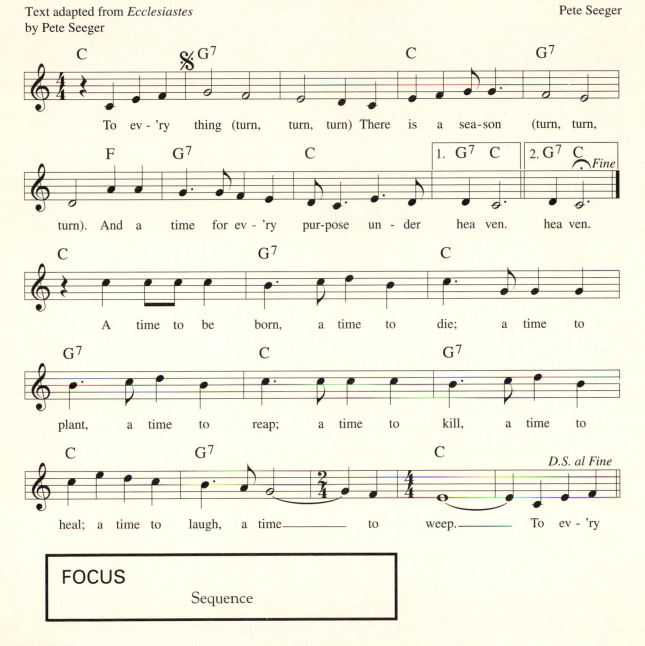

```
FOCUS

          Sequence
```

LEARNING A *sequence* results when a fragment of a melody is repeated immediately at a different pitch level.

Strategies

Place on the chalkboard several examples of sequence, as in **Visual F15.** In example 1, point out the pattern beginning on F. Have students notice that the repetitions begin on different pitch levels—E and D—but maintain the same rhythm (quarter notes) and the same intervals between notes (seconds and thirds). Analyze the interval content in example 2.

VISUAL F15

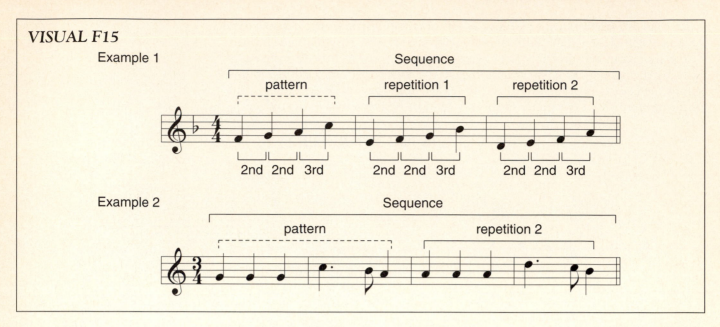

Play and sing each pattern and repetition in Visual F15. Sing "Lightly Row." Discover the sequences in this song, as in **Visual F16.** Stress to students that repetitions of a pattern must follow immediately after the pattern.

VISUAL F16

Study other songs to find if sequential patterns have been used. The following songs contain good examples of sequence:

a. "Bingo"
b. "O Christmas Tree"

INTRODUCING THE STRUCTURAL
COMPONENTS OF FORM
Suggested Sequencing by Grade Level

Kindergarten

1. Same/different (environmental)
2. Phrase-by-phrase questions and answers

Grade One

1. Same and different phrases using pictures, icons, letters
2. Introduction
3. Repeat sign: :‖

Grade Two

1. Coda
2. First and second endings
3. Sectional forms: AB, ABA, Rondo

Grade Three

1. Sectional form: Theme and Variations
2. Interlude
3. Repeat signs: ‖:   :‖

Grade Four

1. Sequence
2. Repeat signs: D.C. and D.S. al fine
3. Sectional form: Strophic

Grades Five and Six

Reinforce previous learnings with more difficult examples

WRITTEN AND PERFORMANCE-RELATED ASSESSMENTS THROUGH COOPERATIVE LEARNING ACTIVITIES: FORM

1. Give each group a melody instrument. Each group member should be able to improvise two phrases, four to eight measures in length, that are the same (aa) and two phrases that are different (ab). While each student plays his/her phrase, the other students demonstrate each phrase by drawing an arch in the air. When finished, students should perform their phrases for the teacher.

2. Provide each group with staff paper containing the words of a nursery rhyme divided among eight measures, similar to Visual F4. Rhythm, melody, and meter parameters are indicated on the paper. Using the words of the rhyme, students should create a song of two phrases, either the same or different (aa or ab), and notate it on the staff provided. They should be able to play and sing their song for the class.

3. Give each of four groups an opportunity to create one of the sections of a rondo in A B A^1 C A^2 form. Choose a short, familiar song for A. Assign to each of the four groups one of the remaining sections of the rondo: B A^1, C, and A^2. Sections B and C could each be an eight-measure rhythmic composition using mouth sounds, other body sounds, or rhythm instruments. Sections A^1 and A^2 would include the familiar song. Some accompaniment, however, must be added by the group. For example, a rhythmic ostinato, a melodic ostinato, a choreography, or a mime might be added to the song. Set a time limit for the completion of each group's task. Put the sections together and perform the rondo in its entirety.

4. Provide each group with a different short, familiar song, a melodic instrument, and several rhythm instruments. Each group's task is to create an introduction, an interlude, and a coda for its song. When completed, the extended compositions can be performed for the class.

5. Give each group one or two songs, each containing a different type of repeat sign. Each student also has an autoharp, if possible. Chords are marked for each song. Each group must be able to sing and play its song correctly, including the indicated repeat signs. When ready, the group should perform for the teacher. After two groups have completed their tasks, they can exchange songs and try again.

6. Create dance steps to accompany, "Hansel and Gretal Dance." The dance steps should be designed to visually show the form of the piece. Create dances or put movement to other pieces already experienced in this book. Again, the movement should show the form of the piece of music.

INTRODUCTION

Much like the threads that flow through a piece of fabric, the *texture* of music consists of horizontal and vertical elements which come together to add depth or substance to a musical composition. The texture of a musical work can be determined by how many or how few instruments or voices are being heard or sounded at the same time. It is obvious that, when singing an unaccompanied solo, the texture of that solo piece would be described as thin. However, if a choir of sixty-five is singing, accompanied by a one-hundred-piece orchestra, the texture would certainly be described as thick.

As early as 600 A.D., song literature consisted primarily of a single, unaccompanied melodic line known as *chant*. Today, these pieces represent some of the clearest examples of music that emphasize the sounding of a single, unaccompanied melody. By the twelfth century, composers were writing music that combined melody with other similar or contrasting melodies to produce harmony. This style of writing greatly dominated the works of many of the major composers and church musicians through the mid-nineteenth century. Concurrently, musicians began to take the horizontal threads of melody and combine them with the vertical threads of harmony, thus producing texture of an even greater thickness in contrast to the single-line compositions of early centuries. Today, musicians are involved in the exploration of all types of electronic and computerized materials that can affect the texture of a composition.

The student's comprehension of texture in music will add a new dimension of understanding and appreciation for the composer's skillful techniques used to create the musical "whole."

Counterpoint is just as much subject to constant evolution and flux as are melody and harmony, with which it is indissolubly interwoven.
—Ernest Toch

FOCUS

Monophonic Texture

LEARNING Music that consists of a single, unaccompanied, melodic line is monophonic in texture. The word *monophonic* originates from a Greek word meaning "one voice."

Strategies

Have students listen to a recording of Gregorian chant. Examples might include:

a. "Alleluia," from *Masterpieces of Music Before 1750*, The Haydn Society, HSE 9038.

b. "Lament for the Dead," from *Ethnic Folkways Library, No. 13*, FE 4504D

Play the recording and lead students to discover the basic characteristics of chant. Comments might include:

a. Men's or boys' voices were singing.
b. The chant was unaccompanied.
c. There was a lack of strong accents that marked off groups of beats, thus making it unmetered.
d. The range of voices was limited.
e. There was no harmony among the voices, only unison singing.
f. There were essentially no extremes in dynamics.

Have students examine "Psalm 22." Point out that this psalm represents a clear example of Gregorian chant, as did the previous examples they heard. Gregorian chant represents one of the earliest musical styles that focuses primarily on the melodic element of music. Because Gregorian chant is a single, unaccompanied line, it is monophonic in texture.

PSALM 22

Dó-mi-nus ré-git me, et ni-hil mí-hi dé-e-rit: * in ló-co pá-scu-ae i - bi me *col-lo*-cá - vit.

Note: The type of notation used in "Psalm 22" is called *neumatic notation*. Each individual note is called a *neume*.

Provide a copy of "Psalm 22" using standard notation. Have students draw the contour of the example, similar to that in **Visual T1.**

PSALM 22

Standard Notation

Do-mi-nus re-git me, et ni-hil mi-hi de-e-rit: in lo-co pa-scu-ae i - bi me col-lo-ca - vit.

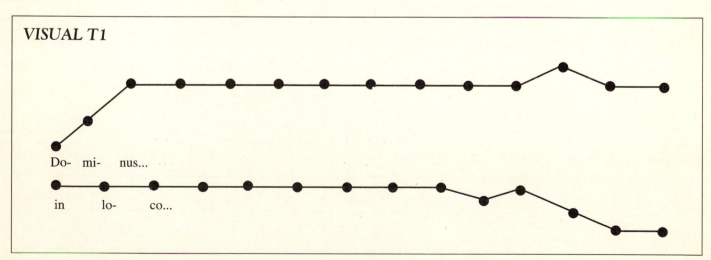

VISUAL T1

Do- mi- nus...

in lo- co...

Folk songs of some cultures are also monophonic in texture. Much of the music of the Asian world, such as China and Japan, and the music of the Arab nations is largely monophonic.

Using examples of songs and other pieces already performed or heard in class, talk about ways to create monophonic texture. Two basic suggestions might include:

1. No accompaniment can be added to the song or piece being sung or performed.
2. Unison singing or playing must take place throughout the composition. This does not mean that more than one instrument or singer cannot perform the same part at the same time.

Have students create, either individually or in small groups, examples of monophonic music.

Provide students with other examples of chant that demonstrate monophonic texture, such as:

a. any "Kyrie Eleison," "Sanctus," or "Agnus Dei"
b. the antiphon "Salve Regina"
c. the canticle of Simeon "Nunc dimittis servum tuum"

FOCUS
Polyphonic Texture

LEARNING *Polyphonic texture* occurs when two or more independent melodic lines sound simultaneously, causing harmony to result between the horizontal lines. The term *polyphony* means "many voices." The melodic lines may contain the same melody or may be different melodies.

Strategies

Have students sing a familiar round, such as "Are You Sleeping," in two parts. Divide the class into two groups; group 2 begins singing when group 1 reaches the third measure in the song.

FRÈRE JACQUES

French Round

Are you sleep-ing, Are you sleep-ing, Broth-er John, Broth-er John?
Frè - re Jac - ques, Frè - re Jac - ques, Dor - mez vous, Dor - mez vous?

Morn-ing bells are ring-ing, Morn-ing bells are ring-ing, Ding ding dong, Ding ding dong.
Son - nez les ma - ti - nes, Son - nez les ma - ti - nes, Din din don, Din din don.

Provide a visual, similar to that in **Visual T2,** which demonstrates the interweaving of the two melodic lines in the opening measures of "Are You Sleeping." Identify this texture as polyphonic. Notice that both melodic lines contain the same melody.

ARE YOU SLEEPING?

French Round

Explain that polyphonic texture can be created in the classroom through the singing and playing of rounds and canons. A *canon* is a device whereby the melody of one part is strictly imitated from beginning to end in a second voice, or even in a third or fourth voice. The beginning voice in a canon is known as the *leader*; all other voices are *followers*.

A *round* is simply a canon in which each performer returns to the beginning of the song after its conclusion. "Are You Sleeping?" is a round. When singing a round, the performers may repeat it as many times as they wish.

Provide students with other examples of songs and instrumental pieces that are usually performed in canon or in round, such as the examples provided here.

DONA NOBIS PACEM
(Give To Us Peace)

Latin Hymn

1 Do - na no - bis pa - cem, pa-cem, do - na___ no - bis pa - cem.

2 Do - na no - bis pa-cem, do - na no - bis pa - cem.

3 Do - na no - bis___ pa-cem; do - na no - bis pa - cem.

MAKE NEW FRIENDS

Round

Make new friends but keep— the— old;— One is sil-ver and the oth-er gold.

HEY, HO! NOBODY HOME

English Round

Hey, ho! No-bod-y home, Meat nor drink nor mon-ey have I none,

Yet will I be mer — ry,— Hey, ho! No-bod-y home.

The following recordings contain other examples that will further reinforce an understanding of polyphonic texture:

a. "Menuetto" from *String Quartet*, Op. 76, No. 2 by Haydn. The minuet (not the trio section) is an example of a canon that is in two parts throughout.

b. "Sumer Is Icumen In," composer unknown. This piece is in four-part canon, accompanied by two additional voices.

c. "Little Dance in Canon Form," "Canon at the Fifth," and "Canon at the Octave" from *Mikrokosmos I* by Bartok.

LEARNING Although some polyphonic compositions contain only one melody sung by different groups, as in rounds and canons, other polyphonic music may contain two or more *different* songs that share an identical harmonic structure and are performed at the same time. These are known as *partner songs*.

Strategies

Have half the class sing "Skip to My Lou" while the other half sings "Mulberry Bush." Explain that the simultaneous performance of two or more different, independent melodies also results in polyphonic texture.

SKIP TO MY LOU

American Singing Game

Skip, skip, skip to my Lou! Skip, skip, skip to my Lou!

Skip, skip, skip to my Lou! Skip to my Lou, my dar - ling.

MULBERRY BUSH

English Game Song

Here we go 'round the mul-ber-ry bush, the mul-ber-ry bush, the mul-ber-ry bush.

Here we go 'round the mul-ber-ry bush, so ear - ly in the morn - ing.

Sing additional partner songs as examples of polyphonic texture, such as "This Old Man" and "Skip to My Lou" or "This Old Man" and "Mulberry Bush." Other usable combinations include:

a. "Home on the Range" and "My Home's in Montana"
b. "Frère Jacques" and "Farmer in the Dell"
c. "Go Tell Aunt Rhody" and "London Bridge"

THIS OLD MAN

England

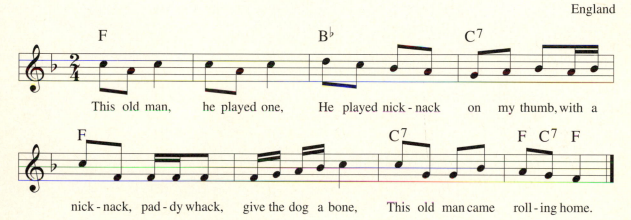

This old man, he played one, He played nick - nack on my thumb, with a

nick - nack, pad - dy whack, give the dog a bone, This old man came roll - ing home.

LEARNING A *descant* is a countermelody, or second melody, that is sung higher than the original melody. Songs having descants are polyphonic in texture.

Strategies

Teach "Music Alone Shall Live." After students are comfortable with the song, have them sing it while listening carefully to the upper melody or descant that the teacher will add. Discuss with the students what has taken place. Students may notice that harmony results when both melodies are sung together. Have students transfer the descant to melody instruments. Students can practice both parts until they play and sing them well enough to switch parts.

MUSIC ALONE SHALL LIVE

German Round

All things shall per - ish un - der the sky.
Him - mel und Er - de müs - sen ver - gehn.

Mu - sic a - lone shall live, mu - sic a - lone shall live,
A - ber die Mus - i - ci a - ber die Mus - i - ci,

Mu - sic a - lone shall live, nev - er to die.
a - ber die Mus - i - ci, blei - ben be - stehn.

Descant

All things per - ish un - der the sky.___ Mu - sic nev-er to die.

LEARNING One of the most complex examples of polyphonic texture can be found in the fugue. A *fugue* is a polyphonic composition based on a theme, called the *subject*, which is stated at the beginning of the piece and then is taken up imitatively in other voices, called the *answers*, in close succession. The subject and its answers are restated at different points in the composition.

Strategies

Play an example of a fugue, such as "Little Fugue in G Minor" by Bach. Ask students how this recording is both similar to and different from the recordings of canon heard earlier. Responses will most likely include references to imitation of theme, but not so strictly as in a canon.

Play the opening theme of "Little Fugue in G Minor" on a melodic instrument. See **Visual T3.**

VISUAL T3

LITTLE FUGUE IN G MINOR

J. S. Bach

Theme 1: Subject

Have students hum along until they are very familiar with the theme. Replay the fugue recording and have students raise their hands each time the subject is repeated.

Explain that fugues contain a *countersubject*, or second theme, that follows the statement of the first theme. When voice 2 enters to sound the main theme, it does so against the countersubject in voice 1. Place a copy of **Visual T4** on an overhead projector so that students can see the interweaving of the melody with the countersubject in this polyphonic example.

VISUAL T4

LITTLE FUGUE IN G MINOR

Theme 2: Countersubject

Theme 1: Answer

Provide opportunities for additional listening to compositions using the fugue form, such as:

a. *The Cat's Fugue* by Scarlatti
b. Any of the fugues in *The Well-Tempered Clavier* by Bach

FOCUS
Homophonic Texture

LEARNING In much accompanied music, the texture consists of a succession of chords that support a melody. This texture is called *chordal* or *homophonic*.

Strategies

Have the class sing "Jolly Old St. Nicholas" while someone plays its accompaniment on the piano. Explain that a single melody with a chordal accompaniment is an example of homophonic texture. Identify the melody and the chordal accompaniment in the song.

JOLLY OLD ST. NICHOLAS

Traditional Carol

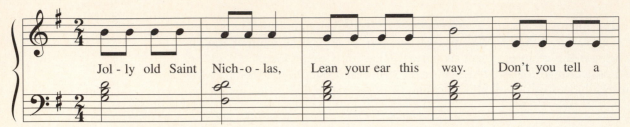
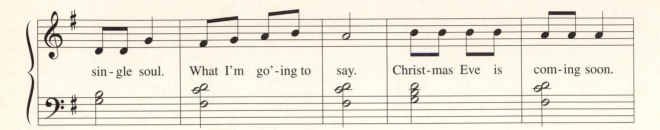

Compare the vertical harmony of "Jolly Old St. Nicholas" to the horizontal harmony of the rounds sung previously.

Explain that most harmonizations found in songbooks or hymnals are homophonic in texture, as are the harmonies of most popular songs. Provide students with other examples of homophonic music, such as the excerpts that follow. Have students identify the melody and the chordal support found in each example.

BACH CHORALE: "ERMUNTRE DICH, MEIN SCHWACHER GEIST"

J. S. Bach

OH, ROCKA MY SOUL

Arr.: Jester Hairston

INTRODUCING THE STRUCTURAL COMPONENTS OF TEXTURE
Suggested Sequencing by Grade Level

Kindergarten, Grade One

1. Unaccompanied and accompanied singing
2. Unison singing

Grade Two

1. Monophony: unaccompanied melody
2. Homophony: melody with harmony
3. Polyphony: rounds

Grades Three and Four

Polyphony: partner songs and descants

Grades Five and Six

1. Polyphony: fugue
2. Reinforce monophony, homophony, polyphony with a variety of experiences that increase in difficulty

WRITTEN AND PERFORMANCE-RELATED ASSESSMENTS THROUGH COOPERATIVE LEARNING ACTIVITIES: TEXTURE

1. Invite each group to experiment with changing the texture of a known song through the layering of instruments. Elicit from the students a number of ways to accomplish this task. Their suggestions might include:
   a. begin by singing the song unaccompanied;
   b. add a single rhythmic timbre as accompaniment—play a rhythmic ostinato on the claves or cabasa—while singing the song;
   c. accompany the song with different wood, metal, or skinned instruments; or
   d. mix woods, metals, and skins to accompany the song.
   Students should perform for the teacher when they are ready.

2. Choose a simple, short canon for each group. Ask group members to perform their song on bells to demonstrate monophonic, polyphonic, and homophonic textures. To accomplish their task, groups might
   a. first play the song unaccompanied (monophony);
   b. play the song in two-part canon (polyphony);
   c. perform the song with a bordun or melodic ostinato (homophony).
   Group members may choose to sing along with the melody as they perform each of the song's textures. When the task is completed, they should perform for the teacher.

3. Give each group several autoharps and a musical selection. "O Susanna," "Home on the Range," "When the Saints Go Marching In," and "This Land Is Your Land" are good beginning songs. Group members should experiment with chords until they can play the song with a workable chordal (homophonic) accompaniment. Students should sing while playing the chords. Students can perform their accompanied songs for the class.

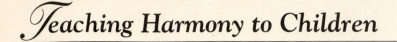

Chapter 8

INTRODUCTION

Most of the music we hear today consists of a melody that is sung or played and supported by other sounds. Whenever this type of simultaneous interaction occurs between the pitches in the melody and the melodic sounds in one or more accompanying voices, *harmony* results. These accompanying sounds may include a few pitches or many tones, as in supportive chords, or could even be one or more melodies, either the same or different from the original melody. The accompanying or supportive sounds, whether produced by voices or instruments, enrich the beauty of the melody.

When harmony is added to a melody, the resulting texture is either homophonic or polyphonic, as studied in Chapter 7. Some of the techniques used to introduce harmonic structures to children have already been studied in relation to these two textures. Even so, these techniques are repeated here, within the new context of harmony, so that a complete overview of the teaching of harmony is presented.

> *In music it is as with chess-playing—*
> *the Queen, melody, possesses supreme*
> *power; but it is the King, harmony,*
> *who ultimately decides.*
> *—Schumann*

FOCUS
Aural Harmonic Awareness

LEARNING *Harmony* results when a melody is accompanied with a pitched instrument, such as an Orff instrument, an autoharp, a guitar or dulcimer, or the piano.

Strategies

Students should have many experiences listening to the teacher sing a short melody while playing a simple accompaniment on a pitched instrument. Students should be carefully prepared for these experiences by being invited to sit in a comfortable position with quiet attention. Recordings containing a simple, uncomplicated accompaniment to a melody may also be used for this experience.

FOCUS
Preparation for Harmony

LEARNING The simultaneous performance of two different musical activities, one melodic and one rhythmic, or both rhythmic, builds a foundation for some of the skills that will be needed later when playing or singing in harmony.

Strategies

Have students chant rhymes or sing songs while performing accompanying actions. Actions might be suggested by the words of the rhyme or can be newly created, as in **Visual H1.**

VISUAL H1

Teddy Bear

Actions	Rhyme
Turn Around	Teddy Bear, teddy bear, turn around.
Touch ground	Teddy Bear, teddy bear, touch the ground.
Show shoe	Teddy Bear, teddy bear, show your shoe.
Shake finger	Teddy Bear, teddy bear, that will do.

DOWN BY THE STATION

Southern Folk Song

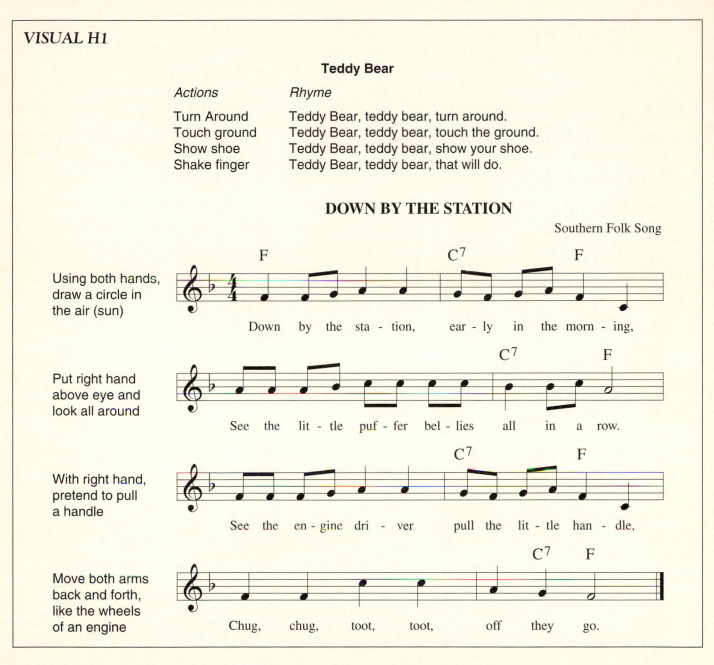

Using both hands, draw a circle in the air (sun) — Down by the sta-tion, ear-ly in the morn-ing,

Put right hand above eye and look all around — See the lit-tle puf-fer bel-lies all in a row.

With right hand, pretend to pull a handle — See the en-gine dri-ver pull the lit-tle han-dle,

Move both arms back and forth, like the wheels of an engine — Chug, chug, toot, toot, off they go.

Have students patsch, clap, or walk to the beat while saying a rhyme or singing a song.

Have students clap the rhythm of a rhyme or song while saying or singing it.

Have students patsch the beat of the first phrase of a song or rhyme, then clap the rhythm of the second phrase. Continue rotating the performance of beat and rhythm to the end of the song or rhyme.

While students chant a rhyme or sing a song, such as "Bounce High, Bounce Low," have them perform a rhythmic ostinato. Begin with the two-beat pattern ‖: ♩ 𝄽 :‖ ; later, progress to ‖: ♫ ♩ :‖ ; and finally, have them perform a four-beat rhythmic ostinato ‖: ♩ ♩ ♫ ♩ :‖ . More difficult patterns should follow over a period of time. See **Visual H2.**

BOUNCE HIGH, BOUNCE LOW

Traditional

Bounce high, bounce low, bounce the ball to Shi - loh.

To challenge the older student, place on the chalkboard a series of rhythms from a given song, such as "Arirang," as in **Visual H3.** As students sing the song, point to different rhythms in turn for them to clap as an ostinato to the song.

VISUAL H3

ARIRANG

Korean Folk Song

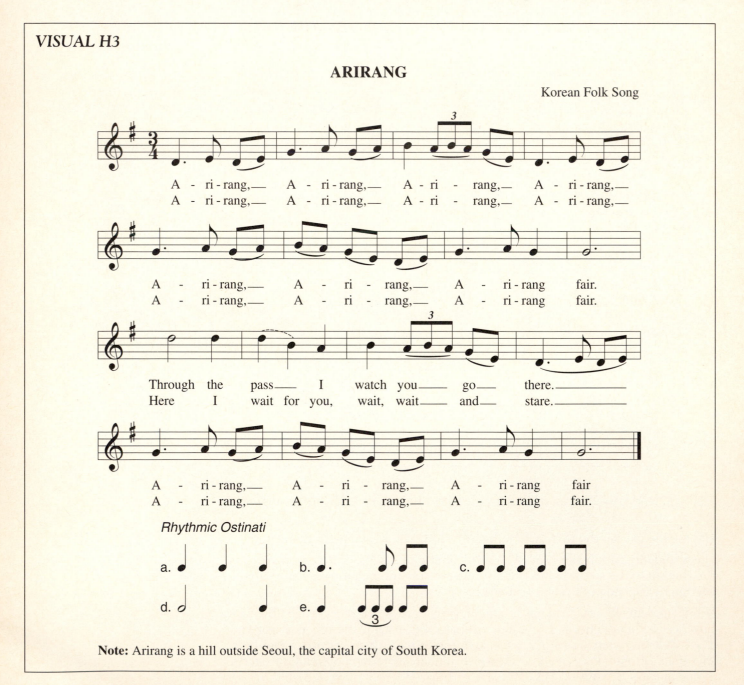

A - ri - rang,— A - ri - rang,— A - ri - rang,— A - ri - rang,—
A - ri - rang,— A - ri - rang,— A - ri - rang,— A - ri - rang,—

A - ri - rang,— A - ri - rang,— A - ri - rang fair.
A - ri - rang,— A - ri - rang,— A - ri - rang fair.

Through the pass— I watch you go— there.—
Here I wait for you, wait, wait— and— stare.—

A - ri - rang,— A - ri - rang,— A - ri - rang fair
A - ri - rang,— A - ri - rang,— A - ri - rang fair.

Rhythmic Ostinati

a.   b.   c.

d.   e.

Note: Arirang is a hill outside Seoul, the capital city of South Korea.

After students can perform well a rhyme that has actions, ask them to do the rhyme and actions as a round. Divide the class into two separate circles. Using the rhyme "Teddy Bear," have one group chant the first phrase while performing the appropriate actions. As group one begins the second phrase, group 2 starts phrase one, as in **Visual H4.** Continue through the rhyme and its actions until both groups are finished.

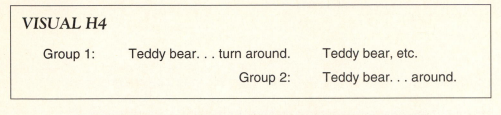

VISUAL H4

 Group 1: Teddy bear. . . turn around. Teddy bear, etc.

           Group 2: Teddy bear. . . around.

FOCUS

    Singing Rounds

LEARNING Singing in round is an effective way to produce harmony.

Strategies

After students have had a number of experiences performing rhymes in round, they will be ready to sing in round. Pentatonic songs can usually be sung successfully as rounds. Students should know well the song and its actions before the teacher divides the group into two circles for performing the round. "Bow Wow Wow" is a good starting song for round singing in two parts. See **Visual H5.**

VISUAL H5

BOW WOW WOW

Pat thighs to the rhythm — Bow - wow - wow!

Clap hands to the rhythm — Whose dog art thou?

Turn around in a complete circle — Lit - tle Tom - my Tuck - er's dog!

Pat thighs to the rhythm — Bow - wow - wow.

As students develop musically, rounds in three and four parts can be added and actions can be omitted. However, students enjoy adding actions to their rounds. Periodically, have them create their own movements to a round and perform them in groups of two, three, or four, depending on their performance abilities.

```
┌─────────────────────────────────────────────────┐
│                    FOCUS                          │
│                Melodic Ostinato                   │
└─────────────────────────────────────────────────┘
```

LEARNING   Adding melodic ostinati to a melody is another way to create harmony.

Strategies

A single-note drone that is played or sung is a good beginning experience for performing melodic ostinati with well-known songs. Later, students can sing or play two, more interesting beats, and then four repeated beats, with the patterns becoming increasingly difficult. See **Visual H6.**

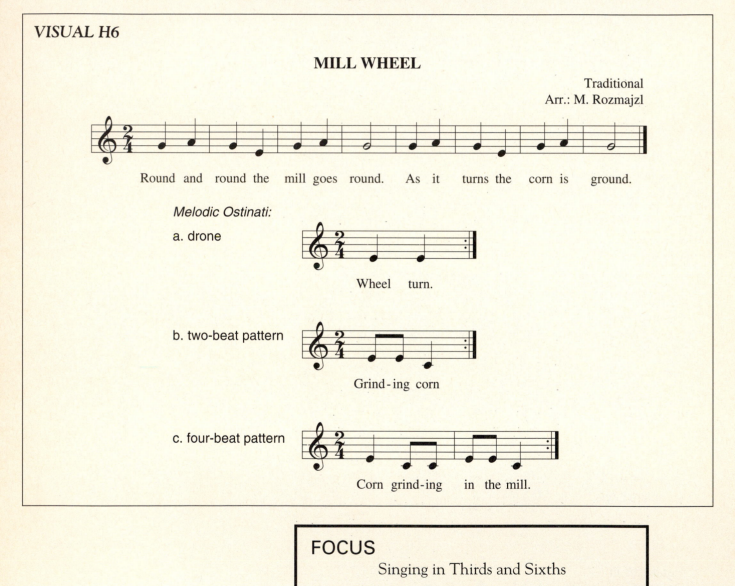

```
┌─────────────────────────────────────────────────┐
│                    FOCUS                          │
│            Singing in Thirds and Sixths           │
└─────────────────────────────────────────────────┘
```

LEARNING   Harmony in thirds and sixths can add to the interest of a melody.

Strategies

Add a simple harmony in thirds or sixths at the end of phrases in a song, as in **Visual H7.**

SAN SERENI

Hispanic Children's Song
Puerto Rican Variant

San Se - re - ní de la bue - na, bue - na vi - da,

Ha - cen a - sí, a - sí___ los doc - to - res

A - sí, a - sí, a - sí, a - sí me gus - ta mi.

Note: Translation: In San Sereni, everyone lives the good life.

Later, add harmony in thirds and sixths to larger portions of a song, as in **Visual H8.**

VISUAL H8

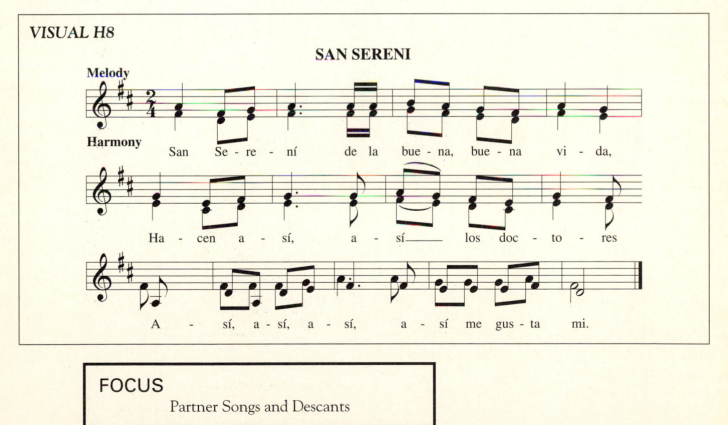

SAN SERENI

Melody

Harmony

San Se - re - ní de la bue - na, bue - na vi - da,

Ha - cen a - sí, a - sí___ los doc - to - res

A - sí, a - sí, a - sí, a - sí me gus - ta mi.

FOCUS

Partner Songs and Descants

LEARNING The simultaneous singing of two or more different melodies that use the same harmonic structure will result in harmony. Different melodies that can be sung together are known as *partner songs*.

Strategies

A number of familiar songs can be sung together as partner songs to create harmony. Be sure each song is well learned before asking students to sing both of them at the same time. "Paw Paw Patch" and "Skip to My Lou" are harmonically satisfying when sung together, as are the following songs:

"Skip to My Lou" and "Mulberry Bush"
"This Old Man" and "Skip to My Lou"
"This Old Man" and "Paw Paw Patch"
"Paw Paw Patch" and "Mulberry Bush"
"Row, Row, Row Your Boat" and "Three Blind Mice"
"The Farmer in the Dell" and "Three Blind Mice"
"Home on the Range" and "My Home's in Montana"

Simple, newly composed melodies can also be played or sung, either above or below a melody, to add harmony to a song, as in **Visual H9.** These simple melodies are known as *descants.*

VISUAL H9

LAVENDER'S BLUE

England
Arr.: M. Rozmajzl

Have students sing, "Oh When the Saints," "Swing Low,' and "This Train" by
themselves and then together as partner songs.

THIS TRAIN, OH WHEN THE SAINTS, SWING LOW

Spiritual
Arr.: René Boyer-Alexander

To be sung as partner songs

This train is bound for glo - ry, this train.

Oh when the Saints_____ go march-ing in.____ Oh when the

Swing low. Sweet char - i - ot____

This train is bound for glo-ry, This train.____ This train is bound for glo-ry

Saints go march - ing in. Oh Lord I want to be in that

com-in' for to car - ry me home. Swing__ low. Sweet

If you ride it you must be ho - ly This train is bound for glo - ry this train.

num-ber____ When the Saints go march - ing in.

cha - ri - ot____ Com-in' for to car - ry me home.

LEARNING A melody can be accompanied by playing one or more *bordun*, which is a repeated pattern, usually consisting of two pitches: the first and fifth tones of the scale.

Strategies

Place on the chalkboard the bordun C to G. Using Orff instruments, have students sound the C bordun on the downbeat of each measure of "Row, Row, Row Your Boat" while singing the song. Show students the bordun as it appears on the staff:

ROW, ROW, ROW YOUR BOAT

American Round

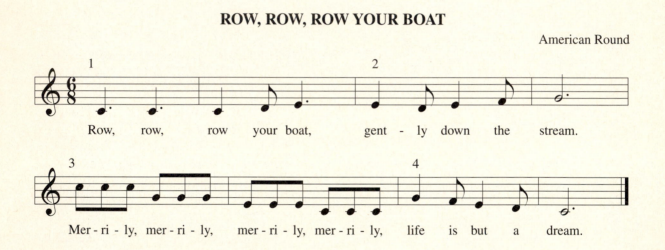

Row, row, row your boat, gent - ly down the stream.

Mer - ri - ly, mer - ri - ly, mer - ri - ly, mer - ri - ly, life is but a dream.

Students should have repeated experiences using a bordun to add harmony to a song. When they are ready, students can use two different bordun in a song to provide harmony for the melody. For the song "Clementine," G to D and D to A can be used as bordun. At first, one group of students can play the G-D bordun when it occurs; a second group can play D-A. Later, the same students can play both bordun. See **Visual H10.**

CLEMENTINE

American Folk Song

In a cav-ern, in a can-yon, Ex-ca-vat-ing for a mine,

Dwelt a min-er, for-ty-nin-er, And his daugh-ter Clem-en-tine.

Oh, my dar-ling, oh, my dar-ling, Oh, my dar-ling Clem-en-tine!

You are lost and gone for-ev-er, Dread-ful sor-ry, Clem-en-tine!

FOCUS

Chordal Accompaniment

LEARNING A *chord* is the simultaneous sounding of three or more different pitches, as distinguished from a *harmonic interval* in which two pitches are sounded together.

Strategies

Place on the chalkboard a C major chord consisting of the pitches C, E, and G. Give a resonator bell with these pitches to each of three students. A *resonator bell* is a barred instrument that plays only one pitch and can be held comfortably in the hand. Have students practice playing their pitches simultaneously, to produce a chord. When they are ready, have them play the C chord on the downbeat of each measure of "Row, Row, Row Your Boat" as the class sings the song. When they are physically mature enough to handle three mallets in two hands, students can play all three notes by themselves on Orff instruments. See **Visual H11.**

VISUAL H11

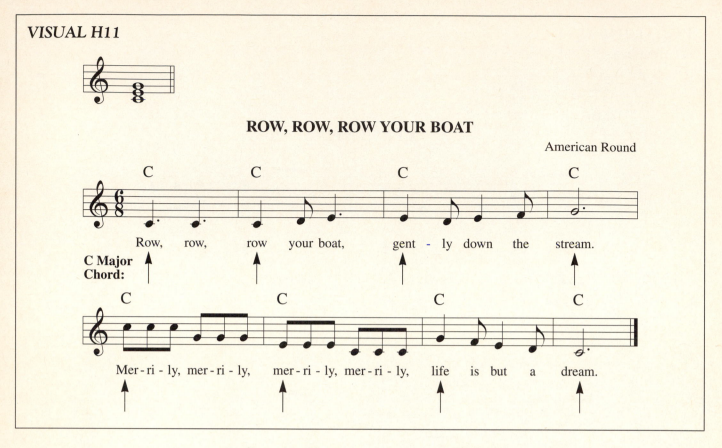

ROW, ROW, ROW YOUR BOAT

American Round

Row, row, row your boat, gent - ly down the stream.

C Major Chord:

C

Mer - ri - ly, mer - ri - ly, mer - ri - ly, mer - ri - ly, life is but a dream.

Students should practice playing a simple chord to a number of one-chord songs, such as "Are You Sleeping," which can be accompanied with the F major chord. Place on the chalkboard an F major chord:

While singing "Are You Sleeping," have students play the F chord on the downbeat of each measure.

Then ask students to sing the song again in the key of C major, and accompany it using only the C major chord. See **Visual H12.**

VISUAL H12

ARE YOU SLEEPING
in F Major

French Round

Are you sleep-ing, Are you sleep-ing, Broth-er John, Broth-er John?

Morn-ing bells are ring - ing, Morn-ing bells are ring - ing. Ding ding dong.

Have students accompany "Candles of Hanukkah" playing the D minor chord on the downbeat of each measure:

CANDLES OF HANUKKAH

Adapted by
Roberta McLaughlin and Lucille Wood

Jewish Folk Song

Burn, lit-tle can-dle, burn, burn, burn. Ha-nuk-kah is here.

Burn, lit-tle can-dle, burn, burn, burn. Burn-ing bright and clear.

LEARNING
A chord containing three notes, including a root, a third, and a fifth, is called a *triad*.

Strategies

Explain that a chord can be built on any pitch of a scale. Draw a C major scale on the chalkboard. Build a three-note chord on each tone of the scale as in **Visual H13.** Tell students that a chord having three different pitches is called a triad. Emphasize that the notes within a triad are placed in a line-line-line or space-space-space position.

VISUAL H13

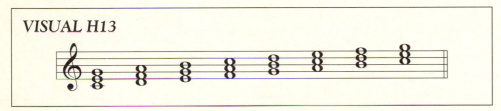

Give students practice in building triads by providing them with a beginning tone and having them spell triads aloud. See **Visual H14.**

VISUAL H14

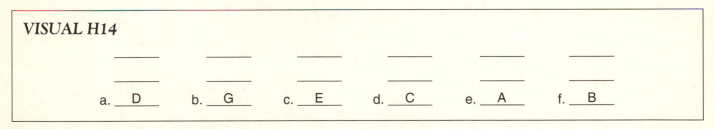

a. D   b. G   c. E   d. C   e. A   f. B

Identify the bottom tone of a chord as the *root,* the middle tone as the *third,* and the upper tone as the *fifth,* as in **Visual H15.**

VISUAL H15

← fifth
← third
← root

F Chord

LEARNING

The *primary chords* in any key are the most important chords, because they determine in what key a song is written. In any key, major or minor, the primary chords are those built on the first, fourth, and fifth tones of the scale. These chords are called the *tonic* or I chord, the *subdominant* or IV chord, and the *dominant* or V chord, respectively. All the remaining chords are called *secondary chords*. Secondary chords are used to add color and interest to a song.

Strategies

When students are able to perform a one-chord song using only the tonic chord, introduce the dominant chord built on the fifth tone of the scale. Place on the chalkboard the tonic and dominant chords for "Clementine," as in **Visual H16.** After practicing the chords on resonator bells or Orff instruments, have the students play them as indicated in the song, while singing the words of the song.

VISUAL H16

Tonic Chord:

I

Dominant Chord:

V

CLEMENTINE

American Folk Song

Verse

In a cav-ern, in a can-yon, Ex-ca-vat-ing for a mine,

Dwelt a min-er, for-ty-nin-er, And his daugh-ter Clem-en-tine.

Refrain

Oh, my dar-ling, oh, my dar-ling, Oh, my dar-ling Clem-en-tine!

You are lost and gone for-ev-er, Dread-ful sor-ry, Clem-en-tine!

Have students perform additional songs that can be accompanied with the tonic and dominant chords, such as "Mein Hut."

MEIN HUT

German Folk Song

Mein Hut er hat drei Eck-en,_____ Drei Eck-en hat mein Hut;_____
My hat it has three cor-ners,_____ Three cor-ners has my hat;_____

Und hat er nicht drei Eck-en,_____ Denn das is nicht mein Hut._____
And had it not three cor-ners,_____ Then it is not my hat._____

After students have had sufficient practice with two-chord songs, introduce the subdominant chord, built on the fourth tone of the scale. Place on the chalkboard the primary chords for "Tinga Layo," as in **Visual H17.** After students have practiced these chords, use them to accompany the song while singing its words.

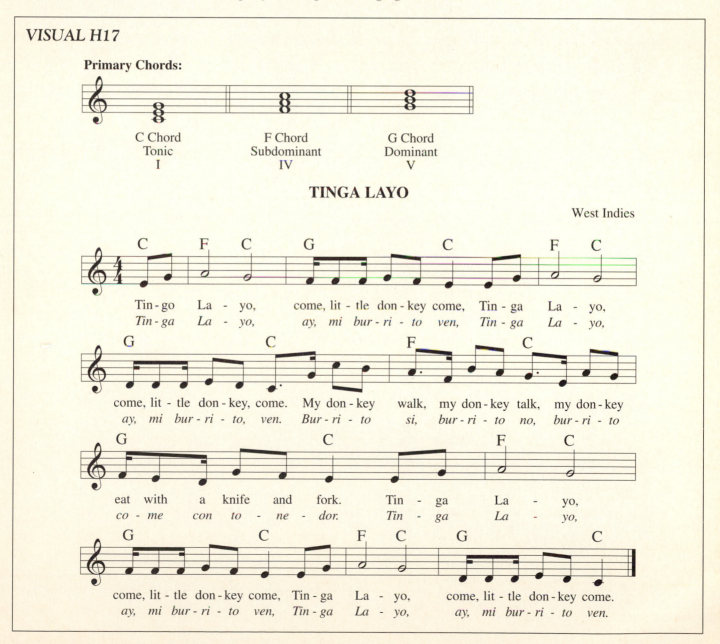

VISUAL H17

Primary Chords:

C Chord   F Chord   G Chord
Tonic   Subdominant   Dominant
I   IV   V

TINGA LAYO

West Indies

Tin-go La - yo,   come, lit-tle don-key come, Tin-ga La - yo,
Tin-ga La - yo,   ay, mi bur-ri-to ven, Tin-ga La - yo,

come, lit-tle don-key, come. My don-key   walk, my don-key talk, my don-key
ay, mi bur-ri-to, ven. Bur-ri-to   si, bur-ri-to no, bur-ri-to

eat with a knife and fork.   Tin-ga La - yo,
co-me con to-ne-dor.   Tin-ga La - yo,

come, lit-tle don-key come, Tin-ga La - yo,   come, lit-tle don-key come.
ay, mi bur-ri-to ven, Tin-ga La - yo,   ay, mi bur-ri-to ven.

Find other songs that use the I, IV, and V chords for accompaniment; have students identify the chords, place them on the chalkboard, and play them while singing the song. "Au Clair de la Lune" can be used to reinforce the playing of primary chords.

AU CLAIR DE LA LUNE

French Folk Song

In the shin - ing moon - light, My dear friend Pier - rot,
Au clair de la lu - ne, Mon a - mi Pier - rot,

Came to ask a fav - or But I told him no.
Prê - te - moi ta plu - me, Pour é - crire un mot.

He came far too late and I had gone to bed.
Ma chan - delle est mor - te, Je n'ai plus de feu,

"Come a - gain to - mor - row. Ask me then in - stead."
Ou - vre - moi ta por - te, Pour l'a - mour de Dieu.

To ensure the understanding of primary chords, have students spell the tonic, the subdominant, and the dominant chords in various major keys. Using **Visual H18,** the following steps can be applied to facilitate this exercise:

Step 1: Draw a D major (or any major) scale; designate the tones on which the I, IV, and V chords will be built.

Step 2: Build a triad on each of these three scale degrees.

Step 3: Place accidentals where they belong, as indicated by the key signature.

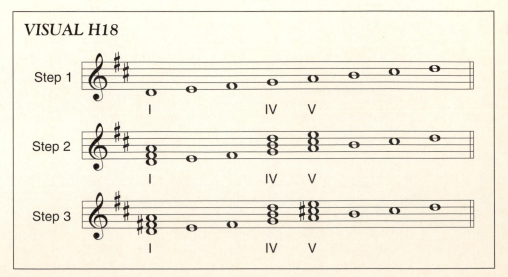

VISUAL H18

Building the dominant chord in a minor key is a bit more difficult than building it in a major key because it involves the use of the harmonic minor scale; that is, the seventh tone of the scale must be raised (see Chapter 3 on melody to review harmonic minor scale). The seventh tone of the scale is the same as the third of the dominant chord, as can be seen in **Visual H19.**

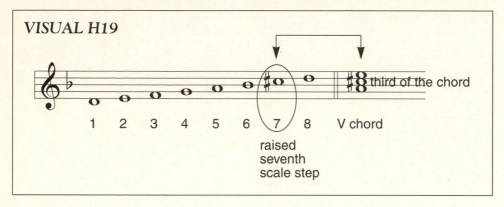

VISUAL H19

To accompany a song in a minor key, always remember to raise the third of the V chord. Practice doing this when accompanying "Joshua Fought the Battle of Jericho."

JOSHUA FOUGHT THE BATTLE OF JERICHO

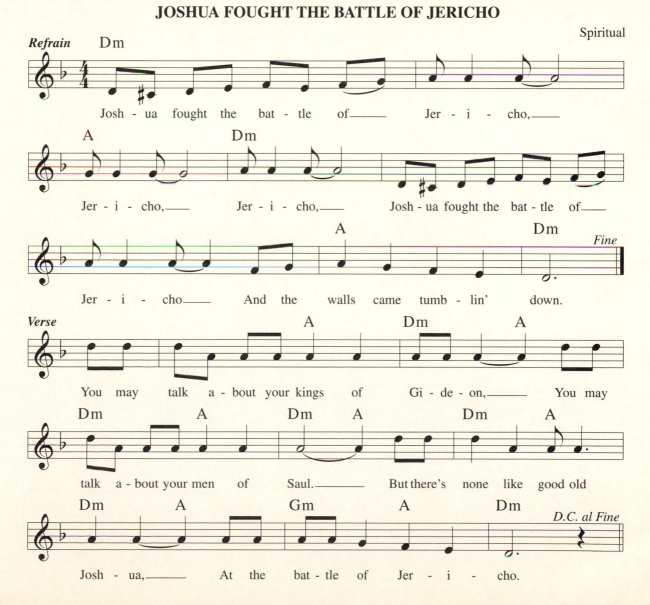

LEARNING A *seventh chord* is a chord containing four pitches.

Strategies

Place on the chalkboard a seventh chord built on G; play the chord. Identify this as a seventh chord because it has four different pitches, each an interval of a third apart. Tell students that this chord is called "seventh" because the top pitch (F) is a distance of seven tones from the bottom pitch (G). Explain that a seventh chord may occur on any pitch of the scale. One of the most important seventh chords, however, is the one that occurs on the dominant chord (V). A dominant seventh chord is indicated by the symbol V^7. See **Visual H20.**

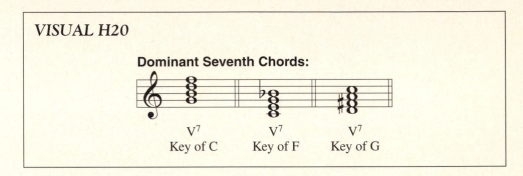

VISUAL H20

Dominant Seventh Chords:

V^7 V^7 V^7
Key of C   Key of F   Key of G

Practice playing a number of songs containing dominant seventh chords (V^7), such as "Tinga Layo."

TINGA LAYO

West Indies

Chord Inversions

LEARNING When the I, IV, and V⁷ chords are used to accompany songs on the piano or on Orff instruments, chord inversions are frequently used to allow for a smoother progression from one chord to the next. A *chord inversion* is a triad or seventh chord whose root is not at the bottom of the chord.

Strategies

Many teachers do not have enough time in the school year to master chord inversions with their students. The information given here, therefore, is primarily for the teacher's information, should these strategies be needed.

Construct a C major triad on the chalkboard. Rearrange the chord so that the third of the triad is the bottom tone. Now, rearrange the notes of the chord and let the first serve as the bottom tone. See **Visual H21.**

VISUAL H21

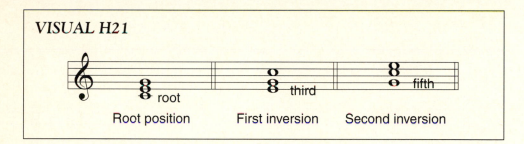

Root position   First inversion   Second inversion

Students should play on the piano the I, IV, and V⁷ chords in the key of C major. While the students are playing these progressions, discuss the awkwardness involved in having to lift the entire hand and arm to change from one chord to the next. Discuss ways that the same chord can be played but in a smoother manner. The following suggestions could be given:

1. Have students play the I chord in root position.
2. Then play the IV chord in second inversion.
3. Finally, play the V⁷ chord in first inversion, omitting the chord fifth.

See **Visual H22** for examples of these three chord progressions.

VISUAL H22

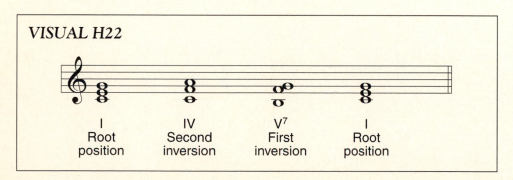

I	IV	V⁷	I
Root position	Second inversion	First inversion	Root position

Provide students with a chart, similar to **Visual H23,** of chordal progressions that are most often used when playing the piano. Have students practice them on individual keyboards and on the piano until they can change easily from one chord to another in each key. The numbers to the left of each chord are suggested fingerings for the right hand.

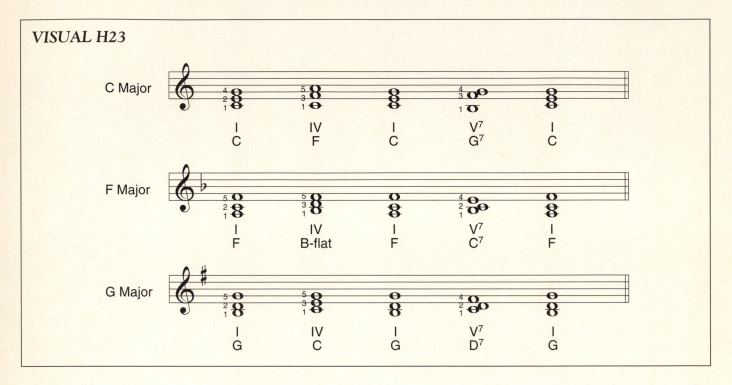

"Cockles and Mussels" provides an example of a song accompaniment that includes chords in root position as well as chords in their inversions.

COCKLES AND MUSSELS

Irish Folk Song

A - live, a - live, oh,— a - live, a - live, oh,—

Cry - ing coc - kles and mus - sels, a - live, a - live, oh!

The following examples are primarily for the teacher's use. They include more detailed information about chords and their structure. This information is included here to provide the teacher with a more complete background in this area. Whether or not to share any of this information with students during a music class must be decided by each individual teacher.

LEARNING Each triad contains two intervals consisting of a third each. These thirds may be either major or minor.

A *major third* consists of four half steps; a *minor third*, of three half steps. Triads are classified according to their major and minor interval combinations. These result in four types of triads: major, minor, diminished, and augmented.

A *major triad* consists of an interval of a major third on the bottom and a minor third on the top. A *minor triad* consists of just the reverse—an interval of a minor third on the bottom and a major third on the top. A *diminished triad* is composed of two minor thirds. An *augmented triad* contains two major thirds.

The diagram below shows how a chord can be built on each tone of the F major scale. Major (M) and minor (m) thirds are indicated, and each chord is classified as major, minor, or diminished.

Chord Structure

Triads: Major   Minor   Minor   Major   Major   Minor   Diminished   Major

The following exercises may help to reinforce a teacher's understanding of how to classify chords according to major, minor, augmented, or diminished.

LEARNING Each triad has a letter name, a number name, and a descriptive name. A triad takes its letter name (C, D, etc.) from its root. Its number name is designated by a Roman numeral. Capital Roman numerals (I, IV, V) are used to represent major triads. Lowercase Roman numerals (ii, iii, vi) are used to represent minor triads. mediant

The following diagram shows a triad built on each tone of the C major and A harmonic minor scales. Each triad is given its appropriate letter name, Roman numeral name, and descriptive name. Note the way diminished and augmented chords are symbolized:

vii° = diminished
III⁺ = augmented

Giving Chords a Name

C Major Scale

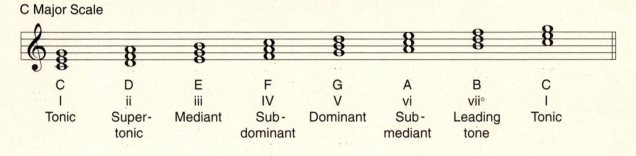

C	D	E	F	G	A	B	C
I	ii	iii	IV	V	vi	vii°	I
Tonic	Super-tonic	Mediant	Sub-dominant	Dominant	Sub-mediant	Leading tone	Tonic

A Harmonic Minor Scale

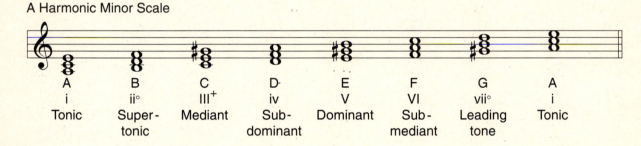

A	B	C	D	E	F	G	A
i	ii°	III⁺	iv	V	VI	vii°	i
Tonic	Super-tonic	Mediant	Sub-dominant	Dominant	Sub-mediant	Leading tone	Tonic

INTRODUCING THE STRUCTURAL COMPONENTS OF HARMONY
Suggested Sequencing by Grade Level

Kindergarten

1. Harmony preparation
   a. Aural awareness
   b. Doing two things at once: chant or sing while moving

Grade One

1. Simple rhythmic ostinati
2. One-note drone ostinato
3. Spoken round

Grade Two

1. Simple melodic ostinati
2. Bordun
3. Sung round

Grade Three

1. Countermelody
2. Singing in thirds or sixths
3. Partner songs

Grade Four

1. More difficult activities using Grade Three components
2. Descant
3. Simple two-part singing

Grades Five and Six

1. Harmonic intervals
2. Chords: I, IV, V
3. Two- and three-part singing
4. Seventh chords: V^7

WRITTEN AND PERFORMANCE-RELATED ASSESSMENTS THROUGH COOPERATIVE LEARNING ACTIVITIES: HARMONY

1. Give each group a short song that can be sung in canon. Many pentatonic songs work well in two-part canon. Students must create movements to each phrase of the song. When ready, students sing and perform the song for the class. Later, the songs with their actions can be performed by the entire class in two- three- or four-part canon (depending on the song and the students maturity).

2. Give each group several barred instruments and a song with two or three different ostinati indicated on the score. The group's task is to perform the song on barred instruments, together with at least one of the ostinati of their choice.

3. Distribute a known song, staff paper, and several barred instruments to each group. Group members must create a melodic ostinato for their song, notate it, and perform it on the barred instruments, while simultaneously singing their song. Each group can then perform its accompanied selection for the class.

4. Each group has autoharps and a different song with chords indicated. Included on the song manuscript is a single staff containing the eight tones of the song's scale. Roman numerals I, IV, and V (or I and V) are placed under the first, fourth, and fifth tones of the scale. Group members must notate the three triads indicated, practice them on their autoharps, and then sing the song while accompanying themselves with those three chords. Each group can perform for the class when ready.

5. Divide the class into groups of eight. Seven of the eight group members should have one of the resonator bells for a given scale—C, G, or F—and a piece of manuscript paper with the scale on it. The group member without a resonator bell is the scribe. Students must first complete the triads above every scale step. The scribe writes the notes on the staff. Then they must be able to play each triad using their resonator bells. The scribe spells out the tones of each triad before they are played. When students run out of resonator bells for scale tones beyond the seventh bell, they play the tone an octave lower, creating a chord inversion. For example, when students come to the F triad in C, they do not have a high C. Whoever has middle C plays that tone instead, creating an inverted F chord. The teacher hears their completed assignment.

6. Each group has a copy of a well-known song. No chords are marked. Students must experiment and discover what chords to use to accompany the song. They should write the chord letter names onto the manuscript. Class performance ends the activity.

7. Using the chord inversions as outlined in **Visual H23,** create an accompaniment to "There's a Brown Girl in the Ring." Try adding a calypso rhythm to the accompaniment by following this rhythmic pattern as you continue to change the chords:(♩ ♫ ♩ ♩)

THERE'S A BROWN GIRL IN THE RING

Jamaican Folk Song
Arr.: René Boyer-Alexander

There's a brown girl in the ring. Tra - la-la-la-la; A brown girl in the ring. Tra-la-la-la-la

There's a brown girl in the ring. Tra - la - la - la - la I won-der what she can do.

Chords:

There's a brown girl in the ring. Tra - la-la-la - la-

SECTION II
Developing Musical Skills

The Singing Voice

Chapter 9

Singing is one of the most important of all musical experiences. In fact, it could be considered the heartbeat of the music program in the primary years. The human voice is the one instrument that most individuals possess, making singing the one musical skill that many elementary teachers can afford to develop. Unless there is a physical defect in the vocal mechanism, almost every child can learn to sing. Many of the basic musical learnings presented throughout this book can be realized through singing experiences.

Content Standard #1 as outlined in the National Standards for Arts Education emphasizes students' ability to "sing, alone and with others, a varied repertoire of music." It is highly recommended that students:

a. sing independently, on pitch and in rhythm, with appropriate timbre, diction, and posture, and maintain a steady tempo
b. sing expressively, with appropriate dynamics, phrasing, and interpretation
c. sing from memory a varied repertoire of songs representing genres and styles from diverse cultures
d. sing ostinati, partner songs, and rounds
e. sing in groups, blending vocal timbres, matching dymanic levels, and responding to the cues of a conductor

It is important, therefore, for classroom teachers to become vocally competent, so that they can guide their students in experiencing the joy, excitement, and understanding that comes from singing.

Many beginning teachers feel insecure and uncomfortable when using their singing voice. Nevertheless, if a teacher possesses an open mind and willingness to try, regardless of preconceived fears, it is possible to develop the vocal mechanism to a respectable level of performance.

ADULT VOICE

In the typical music methods course for classroom teachers, there are many levels of vocal competency from one student to the next. For example, there are adults who:

1. have much difficulty in matching pitch
2. match pitch but have difficulty in sustaining correct pitches throughout a song
3. have been influenced by others in their environment and, as a result, misuse the entire vocal mechanism
4. sing acceptably with good tone quality and have varying degrees of music reading experience

Regardless of how competent or incompetent a singer may be, all prospective teachers can develop their vocal abilities. A brief explanation of the singer's vocal mechanism is helpful in understanding how musical sounds are produced.

VOCAL MECHANISM

The entire body, as well as an individual's psychological state, contributes to the production of good tone. There are several stages involved in this process:

1. The brain begins the activity. It is the brain that sets into motion the concepts that will be formulated and gives the signal, through the central nervous system, to the participating muscles, organs, and limbs, to begin tone production.
2. The breathing system goes into action, relying heavily on the strength and support of major muscles used in singing. The diaphragm is the most important of these muscles. The *diaphragm* is a large muscle that lies across the body under the lungs. Its up-and-down motion supplies the impetus that becomes the foundation of the entire breathing system. The sides, ribs, and lower back muscles of the body work with the diaphragm to control intake and outflow of air in the lungs.
3. The production of sound follows. The process of *phonation*, or making sound with the voice, takes place when vocal bands in the larynx vibrate. The vibration is a direct result of breath pressure supported by the diaphragm.
4. The resonating chambers of the chest and the head (mouth and nasal cavities) work to amplify, shape, and project the tone produced. The art of placement allows the performer to sing a sequence of correctly shaped sounds, resulting in a continuous, well-pitched vocal line.
5. The tongue, palate, lips, teeth, and jaw work to articulate vowels and consonants.

The following diagram points out the different parts of the vocal mechanism used to produce a musical sound.

Vocal Mechanism

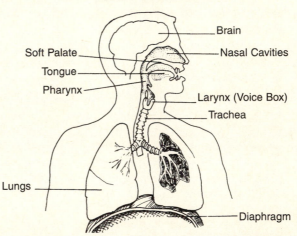

- Brain
- Soft Palate
- Nasal Cavities
- Tongue
- Pharynx
- Larynx (Voice Box)
- Trachea
- Lungs
- Diaphragm

ADULT VOICE CLASSIFICATIONS

Male and female voices are usually classified according to the timbre or quality of tone produced by the voice, as well as its range. There are four basic classifications of voices: soprano, alto, tenor, and bass. The female *soprano* usually sings the highest pitches represented on the treble staff, while the female *alto* sings the lowest pitches on the treble staff. The *tenor* is the highest male classification, and the *bass* voice is the lowest classification for male singers. Each of these four categories can be subdivided into more specialized categories. For example, a soprano who is incapable of performing the extreme high pitches of the treble staff and possesses a fuller or richer quality of tone may be classified as a *mezzo-soprano* or medium soprano. Female voices capable of singing extremely low pitches and possessing a much deeper tone quality than the average alto are classified as *contralto*. Likewise, the tenor voice may be divided into a *first* (extremely high) and *second* (medium-voiced) tenor. Many male voices fall comfortably into a range that lies between that of a bass and a second tenor. These voices are usually classified as *baritones*. The following diagram provides ranges for each of these major classifications.

Note: Tenor voices are written one octave higher than they sound.

VOCAL REGISTERS

When singing, the human voice moves through different positions of the vocal range, known as *registers*. At the top and bottom of the vocal register, differences in vibration rate occur. There is a faster vibration rate the higher one sings, and a slower vibration rate the lower one sings. The changes in vibration rates make it necessary for a person's voice to adjust or change to a different position, similar to a car having to change gears to accelerate in speed. Since registers are an integral part of the voice, prospective singers must be able to recognize them aurally and use them effectively.

There are many theories regarding the number of vocal registers within the human voice. One of the most commonly accepted is that the human voice has two registers, the head and the chest. The *head register*, or lighter vocal register, is governed by a set of throat muscles that control the vocal mechanism for upper register singing. Head cavities are used, for the most part, to resonate the tone. The *chest register*, or heavier vocal register, is governed by a different set of throat muscles that control lower register singing. When sounds are produced in the chest register, the chest cavities act as the primary resonators. Tones produced in the chest register are usually thick and heavy and possess great power and depth. Tones produced in the head register are generally lighter and thinner in texture. Lower pitches are often sung using the chest register, and higher pitches are more easily performed in the head register.

Professional singers practice for years to "bridge" the two registers so that the "break" between them is not noticeable to listeners. The beginning adult singer may find it helpful to identify the break that occurs in the voice where the high and low registers overlap. Analyze what happens at this break point: How does the voice change? Is there any straining or tenseness occurring? Does a breathy quality appear in the voice? Does the change of register affect the projection capabilities of the voice?

Registers

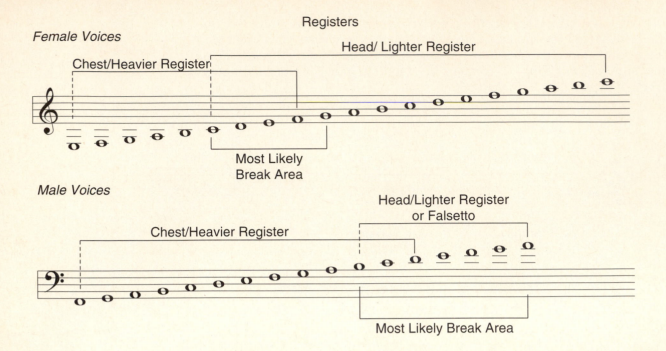

Female Voices

Chest/Heavier Register

Head/ Lighter Register

Most Likely
Break Area

Male Voices

Chest/Heavier Register

Head/Lighter Register
or Falsetto

Most Likely Break Area

Women generally sing in the head register, and men's voices lie, for the most part, in the chest register. All voices, however, use both registers, and the best adult singing draws from the benefits of both the head and the chest registers.

Adult students can practice simple exercises in preparation for teaching children to sing correctly. The following exercises have been sequenced according to skill level. These exercises should be performed over the complete vocal range; repeat each exercise a number of times, each time beginning a half step higher or lower. Care should be taken not to strain the voice by forcing it to sing too high, too low, or too loudly. The exercises should be repeated often, so that the adult student learns to control the singing voice. Special attention should be given to the production of good tone quality. Students should strive for clear, resonant, and well-supported tones without strain or tenseness. Exercises should be played and sung one octave lower for male voices.

Exercises

Hum_____

Mah_____
Moh_____
Mee_____

Oo_____

Mah_____
Moh_____
Mee_____
Moo_____

Yoh_____

Fah_____

Ha_____
Heh_____
Hee_____
Hoh_____
Hoo_____

Vah - ha - ha - ha_____ ah_____

Oh_____
Ah_____
Ee_____

CHARACTERISTICS OF THE CHILD'S VOICE
AT THE PRIMARY LEVEL

The quality, range, volume, and flexibility of children's singing voices differ from those of adult voices. A child's singing voice is light and clear in tone. The volume of correctly produced tones is usually soft, not exceeding mezzo-forte in its dynamic volume. In fact, it is almost impossible for children to perform songs at a fortissimo level or louder without straining and possibly damaging the vocal mechanism. The most comfortable singing range, or tessitura, of children's voices during primary years is usually limited to an interval of a sixth. Because of the high, flutelike quality of the child's voice, the use of the head register or head voice is desired.

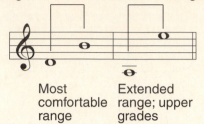

Diagram of Children's Vocal Ranges

Most comfortable range

Extended range; upper grades

CHARACTERISTICS OF THE CHILD'S VOICE AT THE UPPER ELEMENTARY LEVEL

Although the soprano-like tone color of girls' and boys' singing voices is similar during the primary years, some boys' voices begin to develop a deeper, more resonant sound starting as early as fourth or fifth grade. Gradually, the boy's changing voice drops into the alto register, and often has a very limited, unstable range for a few months.

Boys need to know what to expect when their voices start to change. Their voices may "crack" or change register suddenly when they are speaking or singing. Temporarily, their voices may not be as flexible or manageable. Boys may have trouble matching pitches until they have become accustomed to the sound of their new voices. These are all natural signs of physical growth and maturation.

Many girls' voices continue to retain their light and clear texture throughout the elementary years, while a few girls will develop a heavier tone quality. During adolescence, however, both groups of female voices may take on a breathy quality. With proper vocal guidance and physical maturity, this breathiness will usually disappear.

SOLVING VOCAL PROBLEMS IN THE OLDER STUDENT

Teachers should strive to help their students understand the physical and psychological phenomena that affect their singing voices. Skilled teachers who explain the problems that their singers may be encountering, and treat these problems in a positive way, will have a great impact on their students' future attitudes toward singing.

Teachers can take immediate steps to help remedy many of the problems that arise among singers whose voices are beginning to change. The following suggestions might solve some of these problems:

1. Lower the key of the song being sung. Often, songs are pitched too high, and students become self-conscious in their singing.
2. Select song literature that appeals to the fifth- and sixth-grade singer. It is important to win the confidence and spark the enthusiasm of singers by selecting songs from a variety of styles and cultures. Contemporary melodies and harmonies, both popular and classical, should be included in students' repertoire.
3. Avoid songs that have words that, though acceptable at the time the song was written, contain double meanings that would be embarrassing for a young adult to sing today.
4. Write out special parts for boys' changing voices. Range and technical passages must be appropriate to the limitations of these voices. "Rock-a My Soul" is an example of a song designed for the changing voice. Note that there are three independent parts. All parts should be taught separately and eventually sung simultaneously.

ROCK-A MY SOUL

Spiritual
Arr.: René Boyer-Alexander

Part I

Rock - a my soul in the bos - om of A - bra - ham,

Rock - a my soul in the bos - om of A - bra - ham, Rock - a my soul in the

bos - om of A - bra - ham, Oh, Rock - a my soul.

Part II

Rock - a my soul,_____ Oh yes, Rock - a my

soul, Oh, Lord - y Rock - a my soul_____ in the

bos - om of A - bra - ham, Hal - le - lu - jah, Oh, a

Part III

Rock, Rock, Rock - a my soul in the

bos - bos - bos - om of A - bra - ham, Rock, Rock, Rock -

a my soul in the bos - om of A - bra - ham.

HELPING CHILDREN FIND THEIR SINGING VOICE

For years teachers have experienced problems in helping first graders learn to sing. Some first graders still do not know that there is a difference between the speaking and the singing voice and that in singing, speech is sustained and lengthened to produce a tune. These students attempt to sing on what can be described as a *speech drone:* they sing only on one pitch, much lower than the rest of the class. Teachers can begin work to correct this problem in young singers by helping them focus on differences between speech and singing.

By having students echo melodic fragments as well as spoken fragments, teachers can help children differentiate aurally and vocally between the two. For example, a teacher might ask students to echo the following:

This   is   my speak-ing voice,   This   is   my sing-ing voice.

"Little Bunny Foo Foo" provides an example of a child's play song designed to assist children in distinguishing between speaking and singing voices. Appropriate physical actions can be used throughout the song to enhance children's interest. For example, students can make a bunny with their fist and two fingers (for ears). "The rabbit" should hop from one side of the body to the other to demonstrate how a rabbit would hop through a forest. The entire hand should move in a scooping position, followed by a gentle tap on the top of the head. Students will enjoy creating their own movements for the play song that follows.

Children can use a variety of means to explore their vocal range, such as children's stories, singing games, and vocal improvisations. "Between the Valleys" is an example of one story that is designed to help children experiment with the upper and lower range of the voice. Each time the teacher comes to "up the hill and down the hill" in the story, children should join in. At this point the voice should travel up and down with the words. In this way children who normally use a speech drone will be encouraged to experiment with other parts of their vocal range.

LITTLE BUNNY FOO FOO

Traditional

Lit - tle Bun - ny Foo - Foo, Hop - ping through the for - est,

Scoop - ing up the field mice and bop-pin' 'em on the head.

(spoken)

Down came the good fairy—And she said:

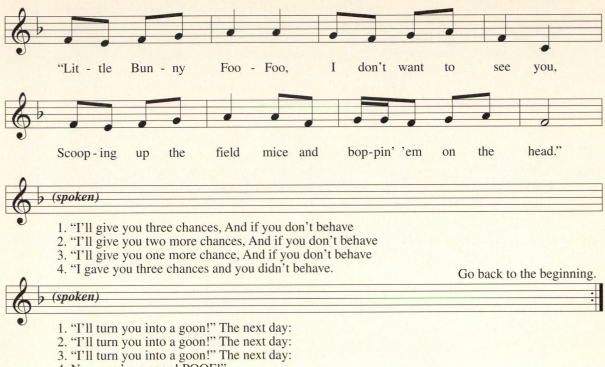

"Lit - tle Bun - ny Foo - Foo, I don't want to see you,

Scoop - ing up the field mice and bop-pin' 'em on the head."

(spoken)

1. "I'll give you three chances, And if you don't behave
2. "I'll give you two more chances, And if you don't behave
3. "I'll give you one more chance, And if you don't behave
4. "I gave you three chances and you didn't behave.

Go back to the beginning.

(spoken)

1. "I'll turn you into a goon!" The next day:
2. "I'll turn you into a goon!" The next day:
3. "I'll turn you into a goon!" The next day:
4. Now you're a goon! POOF!"

And the moral of the story is: "Hare today; goon tomorrow."

Between the Valleys

This is Roscoe the Rabbit. (Form a fist with the right hand and raise fingers 1 and 2 for rabbit ears.) Roscoe is a very happy fellow who lives at the top of a grassy hill. Roscoe has many friends who live with him in the Valley of the Twin Oaks and others who live even farther away in the Valley of the Big Rocks.

This is Guppy the Goose, Roscoe's best friend. (Have all the fingers on the left hand stick together while they move in contrary motion to the thumb.) Guppy the Goose lives in a pond in the Valley of the Big Rocks.

One day Roscoe the Rabbit decided to pay Guppy the Goose a visit in the Valley of the Big Rocks. So he opened his door, stepped outside, closed the door, and proceeded down the hill and up the hill and down the hill and up the hill and down the hill to Guppy's pond. (Encourage children to join in with the teacher on the last sentence, allowing their voices to go from high to low as they go "up and down" the hills.) When Roscoe arrived, Guppy the goose was nowhere in sight, so Roscoe the Rabbit had to turn around and go back home. Up the hill and down the hill and up the hill and down the hill and up the hill he traveled until he reached his own house. He went inside and decided to call it a day.

The next morning, Guppy the Goose wanted to visit Roscoe the Rabbit. So he opened his door, stepped outside, closed the door, and went up the hill and down the hill and up the hill and down the hill and up the hill to Roscoe's house. When Guppy the Goose arrived, Roscoe the Rabbit was nowhere to be found, so poor Guppy the Goose had to return home. Down the hill and up the hill and down the hill and up the hill and down the hill he waddled until he reached his pond in the Valley of the Big Rocks.

On the third day, Roscoe the Rabbit decided to try it again, and Guppy the Goose made a similar decision. So they began their journey. One went down the hill, and the other went up the hill until . . . they met at the very top. Roscoe the Rabbit said in a very high voice, "How do you do, Guppy?" Guppy responded in a very low voice, "And how are you, Roscoe?" They talked. Finally, when the sun began to set, each returned home again, going down the hill and up the hill and down the hill and up the hill—Roscoe the Rabbit to the Valley of the Twin Oaks and Guppy the Goose to the pond in the Valley of the Big Rocks.

Other activities that can help students discover and explore their vocal ranges include the imitation of sirens and other environmental sounds. Students can produce siren sounds that move up or down the whole range of their imaginary "vocal paths." Teachers can help students become even more comfortable with their vocal range by having them move their hands up and down with the rise and fall of the melody they are singing. Students can also draw the contour of a melodic line in the air while singing.

Many vocal problems that are encountered by primary students often stem from poor exposure to music at home, at church, in preschool programs, and in their everyday environment. Children have a strong tendency to imitate what they hear around them. Unfortunately, what they hear is often not appropriate for imitation. For example, they hear pop and rock singers perform in keys that are totally unrealistic for children to even attempt; yet, the child tries to duplicate the songs of these popular artists as loudly and forcefully as possible. Sadly, the beginnings of vocal abuse are rampant at a very early stage in the child's vocal development. Much of this abuse can be attributed to the fact that children just don't know any better. They have never been informed about the physical dangers—such as the development of vocal nodes—that they may encounter if improper use of the voice continues. It becomes the teacher's job not only to inform students of such dangers, but also to help restore their damaged voices, if possible.

These suggestions can serve as guides to help students find and adjust to their appropriate vocal registers:

1. Insist that the child sings softly.
2. Explain that everyone has two voices within his or her body: a "lighter" voice or head voice and a "heavier" voice or chest voice. Each of these voices should be explored. Students should talk about and attempt to describe "how it feels to sing using a lighter and then a heavier voice." Talk about which is more comfortable. Create a dialogue that involves the use of both these registers. Practice to develop the lighter and the heavier registers by having students:
   a. Stretch and yawn: then sigh on a high-to-lower pitch, beginning on fourth line D. Using the vowel *oh*, sustain the first pitch; then make a *glissando* (rapidly sliding up or down with the voice) to a lower pitch.
   b. Remind students that they need to breathe deeply to support the tone and to sing the pitches that are low in their range and close to their speaking voices. Ask students to imagine they have an inner tube around their waists. Place their hands at the waist. Blow out the "old" air and deeply inhale the "new" air as the teacher counts to 3. Their hands should feel their waists expanding. As students let air escape, they should "sizzle" or make a "hissing" sound and move their hands to their sides. This activity should be repeated, inhaling to the count of 4 and exhaling to the count of 6.
   c. Have students hum the letter *n* on fourth line D, with lips and teeth slightly apart and the tip of the tongue resting lightly against the bottom teeth. Lower the jaw and change to an *oo* sound. Do this exercise by half steps down to G. Continued practice of this exercise will increase the vocal range and bridge the two singing registers.

3. Become knowledgeable about the background of the song. Try to be as culturally authentic as possible when performing and teaching the song. Many folk songs, depending on where they come from, are more accurately sung using the heavier register of the voice and not the lighter register. Help students understand this and encourage them to make necessary adjustments.
4. Choose songs that have a narrow range, comfortably located within the range of the child's voice.
5. If a student is not accurately matching pitch, toss a beanbag to him/her and make, in the lighter register, an *oo* sound that follows the arc of the bag's path. Have the student toss the bag back to the teacher or to another classmate and encourage him/her to use the head voice in imitating the rise and fall of the beanbag's arc.
6. Place uncertain singers between stronger and more confident singers. Suggest that the students adjust their volume so that they are always able to hear both singers on either side of them.
7. Before students begin singing, make sure they are together on the same starting pitch. Have them hum and sustain the beginning pitch of the song until everyone has it.
8. Provide assistance on a daily basis, if possible. It only takes a few minutes to involve each student in musical conversations similar to those below. Exercises of this type will be helpful in developing the child's listening and vocal performance skills.

PHYSICAL CHARACTERISTICS OF GOOD SINGING

One of the first and most basic requirements for good tone production is correct posture. Just as athletes ready themselves physically and mentally before engaging in a physical activity, so must singers prepare themselves to produce good tone. As early as first grade, students are presented with series books that contain colorful pictures, music, and diagrams. When concentrating on producing good tone, however, students should give full attention to the teacher. Having books in their hands may distract them.

Because oversized and undersized chairs continue to present a physical problem for children on the elementary level, it is sometimes best to have young students sit as erectly as possible on the floor with their feet crossed and tucked close to the body. This does not take precedence, however, over properly sized chairs or stools which allow students to establish good posture, thus making it possible for the vocal instrument to function as it should. When seated, students should come forward in their chairs as though they are about to stand. They should sit tall with their shoulders relaxed and down. Students should automatically return to this "singing" position when requested to do so by the teacher. If children must sit on the floor, the teacher should make sure that students alternate between this position and standing. This will help to avoid unnecessary slumping, cramping, and restlessness that result from children being in the same position too long. When standing, children should stand up straight and tall with their feet firmly grounded on the floor, one foot slightly in front of the other. Correct posture will allow the vocal mechanism to do its job without being hampered in any way.

After the procedures involved in acquiring good posture have been set in place, teachers should focus on correct breathing techniques. Children should work on being able to produce a steady stream of air with the proper amount of support from the diaphragm. They should understand that proper breath control and support are crucial to the development of good vocal tone, just as a bow is important to a violin's sound. If the bow stops, the violin will no longer speak. If the air pressure stops, vocal tone can no longer be projected. As the air pressure disappears, the lack of support will cause the tone to flatten in pitch. Therefore, the ability to control the flow of air is especially important in maintaining a smooth, legato-like style of singing.

The following two exercises should help students grasp the concept of diaphragmatic breathing:

1. Have students place one hand on their chests and the other on the abdomen, below the waist. Next, have students pretend to put an imaginary drinking straw to their lips and slowly "sip" a glass of juice to the count of 3. Exhale on s-s-s to the count of 5. Students should feel their abdominal muscles expand but should not feel movement of the hand on the chest. If this procedure is followed, students should be breathing correctly. Repeat this process, but this time have students "sip" to the count of 4 and exhale to the count of 6.
2. Have students place their hands on their abdomens and pretend that they are a locomotive chugging to pull a heavy load. They should feel the abdominal muscles at work as they make the sounds ch, ch, ch, ch.

Children often forget to sing the texts of songs so that they can be understood by a listener. Not only is the pronunciation of words not recognizable at times, but the enunciation of vowels and consonants needs serious attention. Teachers should have students exaggerate by overenunciating if positive results are to occur. This will force children to open their mouths and produce clearly articulated tones.

OBJECTIVES AND GUIDELINES FOR SINGING AT THE ELEMENTARY LEVEL

The following objectives will give direction to the development and use of the singing voice at the primary level. Young students should be able to:

1. hear and repeat a short melody accurately and expressively
2. develop some control in the quality of sound used when singing
3. sing a wide variety of songs, in many styles
4. demonstrate knowledge of rhythm, melody, form, harmony, dynamics, tempo, and tone color through singing
5. demonstrate the ability to sing accurately a variety of melodic intervals, using their accompanying hand signs (see p. 215 for hand signs)
6. sight read the notation of simple songs

As students mature in their abilities to use their voice, more difficult vocal challenges can be presented. The older student should be able to:

1. hear and reproduce from memory more complex melodic patterns both in singing songs and in echo singing.
2. sing more difficult literature with better tone quality, pitch accuracy, and expressiveness
3. recognize and respond to more difficult interval relationships with syllables, hand signs, and number and/or letter names
4. read and perform more difficult pieces of music
5. demonstrate greater vocal independence. They should feel comfortable in performing echo songs, descants, rounds, and melodic ostinati.
6. improvise, using the singing voice.
7. harmonize by "ear"
8. use concepts previously learned to help facilitate learning new songs

TEACHING A SONG BY ROTE

In the initial stages of musical development, children learn songs best through an imitative process called *rote learning*. Rote learning takes place when a teacher speaks, sings, or moves and students imitate. The process is repeated until the song is learned well. Learning a song by rote allows children to focus their attention on the beauty of the sound being imitated, the production of correct interval relationships, the expressive interpretation of the music, and the clear enunciation of vowels and consonants. The most common approaches used to teach songs by rote are the part or phrase method and the whole song method. The teacher's choice of method is determined by the length and difficulty of the song material, the children's previous musical background and experience, basic mental and musical aptitudes, and the motivation and interest children possess in regard to the song.

The *whole song method* can be applied to the learning of a song in two different ways. The first approach is used to teach songs that can usually be imitated by students after one or two hearings. Songs that are short and have much repetition in text and melody are usually taught using the whole song approach. The following steps can assist the teacher in using this approach:

1. Motivate interest in the song through the use of appropriate pictures, stories, or questions.
2. Ask children to listen for something specific in the song prior to its actual presentation.
3. Present the whole song to the class.
4. Ask questions about the children's understanding or enjoyment of the song.
5. Sing the song one or more additional times, depending on the children's readiness to participate.
6. Have the class join in.

"I'm Gonna Sing" is an example of a song that can be taught to children by rote, using the whole song approach. The song is short and very repetitive. It also allows room for creative movement and playing activities. The song needs little discussion to attract students' attention. The tempo and bouncing rhythms throughout the song provide adequate attention getters. After learning the song, children can be invited to create movements other than those suggested by the song. Students might substitute actions such as: "I'm gonna walk, skip, slide, or turn when the spirit says _____." Students can also replace the movement actions with the sounds of different rhythmic instruments, which can be performed in various ways. "I'm gonna hit, rub, shake, or scrape when the spirit says _____," are some examples. Discussion should follow regarding the overall meaning and style of the song.

I'M GONNA SING

Spiritual

The second approach to using the whole song method is useful with songs containing many verses, each verse having areas of repetition. This type of song is more challenging for children to learn because it is difficult for them to remember the order of the verses. "Ida Red," found in Chapter 10, has several verses, each one ending differently:

. . . Ida Red, Ida *Blue*, I got stuck on Ida too.
. . . Ida Red, Ida *Gold*, She is something to behold. Etc.

To facilitate the learning of this song, the teacher can make a set of flash cards, each one containing a little girl dressed in a different color—in blue, in gold, and in the other colors found in subsequent verses. The teacher should sing through the entire song, holding up the appropriate card for each verse. The second time through the song, the teacher should invite the students to join in wherever possible. By the completion of the third singing, the children will know the song quite well, if they can refer to the flash cards to help them in singing the verses in the correct order.

The *part* or *phrase method* is used to teach a song that is longer, more complex, and cannot be easily learned after just one or two hearings. This method also has two different approaches. The steps used in teaching a song using the phrase method are similar to steps 1 through 4 of the whole song approach. The change occurs when children are ready to join in, at step 5. When using the first approach to the phrase method, the following steps can be used:

5. The teacher sings phrase 1 and the children repeat it.
6. The teacher sings phrase 2 and the children repeat it.
7. The teacher sings phrases 1 and 2 and the children repeat them.
8. The teacher continues throughout the song in a like manner.
9. When the song is completed, the teacher returns to the beginning and sings through the song again, two phrases at a time, and the children repeat. Any

step in the above process can be repeated if children need additional hearing or singing of a phrase.

10. When all phrases have been sung, the teacher invites the children to sing the song through from beginning to end. If there are still a few problems, the teacher addresses them at this time.

"The Magic Penny" is a more complex song that can be taught best by using the first approach to the phrase method. Because of the overall length of the piece and lack of constant repetition, it is more practical for students to learn one phrase at a time.

THE MAGIC PENNY

Malvina Reynolds

Love is some - thing if you give it a-way, Give it a-way, give it a-way,

Love is some - thing if you give it a-way, You end up hav-ing more.

It's just like a mag-ic pen-ny, hold it tight and you won't have an-y;

Lend it; spend it and you'll have so man-y they'll roll all o - ver the floor, for

The second approach to the phrase method of learning a new song consists of the teacher singing the first part of a phrase and the children completing it. A song such as "Bow Wow Wow," found in Chapter 6, lends itself well to this approach:

Beat:	1	2	3	4
	Bow	wow	wow	
	Whose	dog art	thou	
	Lit-tle	Tom-my	Tuck-er's	dog
	Bow	wow	wow	

Once again, the teacher can begin the lesson using steps 1 through 4 of the whole song method. Then the following steps can continue:

5. The teacher asks the children to listen very carefully as the song is sung a second time.
6. Children are invited to sing the "mystery words" whenever the teacher stops singing. Using the following order:
   a. the teacher sings the first three beats of each phrase, and the children sing only the last beat—in this song, beat 4 in phrase 3;
   b. the teacher sings the first two beats of each phrase; the children complete the last two beats;
   c. the teacher sings the first beat of every phrase; the children sing the last three beats;
   d. the children sing the song through from beginning to end. Any of the steps may be repeated along the way if there is a problem.

The teacher should always sing or play a recording of the entire song first, so that children become acquainted with it before it is presented in shorter segments. Sometimes a discussion of the text is needed if it contains unfamiliar words or words used in any unusual manner.

When teaching songs, remember to give students the starting pitch of the song or of each phrase. A piano, pitch pipe, resonator bell, or soprano recorder may be used. The teacher should sound the pitch and then sing the pitch on a syllable such as "loo." When needed, students can imitate the teacher's pitch and then transfer it to the beginning text of the song. Regardless of which method is used to teach a new song, the teacher must be an active listener, isolating rhythmic and melodic problems and clarifying their correct production throughout the learning process.

TEACHING A SONG BY NOTE

Although teaching songs by rote during the early years has its advantages, continued dependence on this type of teaching and learning process will eventually become a hindrance to the musical development of the student. Students cannot develop to their fullest potential using this process alone, because it keeps students dependent on the teacher. Teachers must also provide students with the basic knowledge and skills needed to read music by note, so that students can learn a musical work independently of the teacher. Learning music *by note* implies that students have a working knowledge of staff notation and interval relationships, which will enable them to sing or play a melody without anyone's assistance.

It is recommended in Content Standard #5 of the National Standards for Arts Education that all students:

a. read whole, half, dotted half, quarter, and eighth notes and rests in 2/4, 3/4, and 4/4 meter signatures
b. use a system (that is, syllables, numbers, or letters) to read simple pitch notation in the treble clef in major keys
c. identify symbols and traditional terms referring to dynamics, tempo, and articulation and interpret them correctly when performing
d. use standard symbols to notate meter, rhythm, pitch, and dynamics in simple patterns presented by the teacher

Zoltán Kodály. It was the Hungarian composer and music educator, Zoltán Kodály, who developed a philosophy based on the belief that young children should learn to read and write music just as they learn to read and write the language of their mother tongue. He strongly believed that the development and use of the singing voice should be at the core of a school's approach to music literacy for every child.

Kodály emphasized the use of solmization and the movable "do" system as major vehicles through which musical literacy could be achieved. *Solmization* is a technique that involves assigning syllables to pitches to facilitate the hearing and reproduction of melodic intervals. *Solfège syllables*—do (doh), re (ray), mi (me), fa (fah), so (soh), la (lah), ti (te)—represent each of the tones of the diatonic scale. Kodály believed that successions of these solfège syllables are easier and more reliably memorized than letters; in addition, the syllables indicate clearly the tonal function of pitches, and by memorizing pitches within an interval, children can develop their sense of tonal function. *Hand signs* can be used as tools to reinforce the inner hearing of the intervals; they provide a visualization in space of the tonal relationships being sung. Hand signs usually accompany the singing of solfège syllables. They were developed in England around 1870 by John Cürwen. Since then, the signs have been revised and are presented here in their revised form.

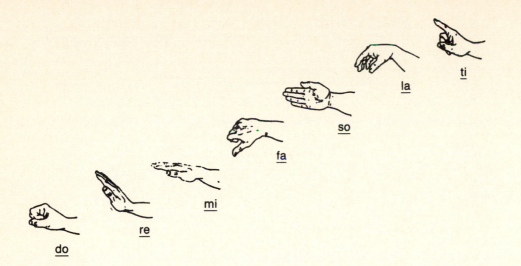

Kodály observed that, during childhood, children in Hungary naturally express themselves through singing games and other singing experiences. Many of these singing experiences consist of tonal patterns that are particularly easy for children to sing and read. The interval of the descending minor third, so-mi, or the "call" as it is often named, appeared to be one of the most common intervals used among young children. Further research affirmed that an extension of the minor third, so-mi-la, was heard in children's natural and undirected play all over the world. This pattern has since become known as the "chant." The process of music literacy that was proposed by Kodály suggested that, if teachers include song literature that contains these easy-to-sing-and-read tonal patterns, they should be able to accelerate the vocal progress of children.

Pentatonic Scales. Kodály found the pentatonic scale to be most valuable in teaching musical literacy because this scale has certain properties that make it significant for first experiences in singing and reading music. First, the pentatonic scale does not contain half steps, which are difficult to sing in tune. Second, only five different sounds are used in the pentatonic scale as compared to seven for the major and minor scales. This more limited range of tones can be easily manipulated by children with limited ability, as well as by those with more advanced skills. Third, the choice of pitches used in composing melodies is much freer, because the more dissonant half step is not used. Fourth, a short melodic phrase can easily be joined to other phrases to form longer and more varied musical selections.

During the elementary years, sequencing the teaching of musical structures and skills must be organized to correspond with the developmental level of children. This means that children should begin with the simplest two- and three-note melodies as well as the simplest rhythms and gradually progress to more complex structures.

The following songs and strategies demonstrate a step-by-step procedure that can be used, not only to help children develop in their abilities to hear and produce good tone, but to serve as guidelines that will assist them on the road toward reading music by note.

Solmization. Begin students' introduction to solmization by singing songs containing the interval most often chanted by small children at play: so-mi. The songs below can be used to teach this interval.

STAR LIGHT

American Folk Song

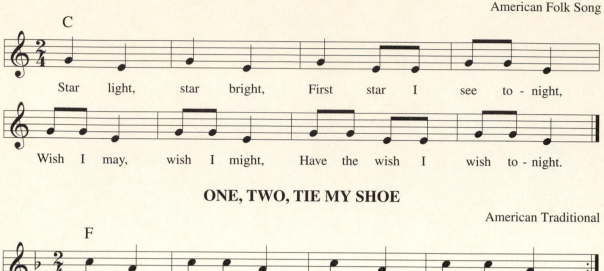

Star light, star bright, First star I see to-night,

Wish I may, wish I might, Have the wish I wish to-night.

ONE, TWO, TIE MY SHOE

American Traditional

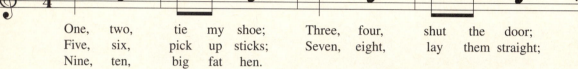

One, two, tie my shoe; Three, four, shut the door;
Five, six, pick up sticks; Seven, eight, lay them straight;
Nine, ten, big fat hen.

Once children are familiar with the songs, the names of the corresponding solmization syllables can be sung. **Visual S1** shows the solmization syllables for "Star Light."

VISUAL S1

so mi so mi so mi mi so so mi

Hand signs are often used to reinforce the inner hearing of melodic or harmonic intervals; they accompany the singing of solmization syllables. **Visual S2** shows the hand signs for "Star Light." Students should sing the song and use the appropriate hand signs.

VISUAL S2

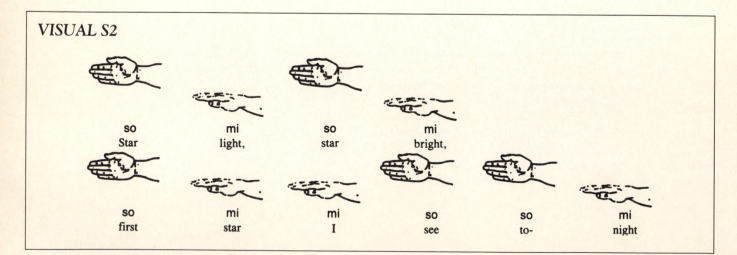

so   mi   so   mi
Star   light,   star   bright,

so   mi   mi   so   so   mi
first   star   I   see   to-   night

The so-mi, mi-so interval should be placed on the staff so that children understand that there is always a line or space between the two tones of the interval, as in **Visual S3.**

VISUAL S3

To further reinforce the minor third interval, place either mi or so on the staff and have the children complete the interval as in **Visual S4.**

VISUAL S4

When students are comfortable with the minor third and can sing it on pitch in a variety of songs, a new solmization syllable can be introduced. A suggested sequence for introducing the syllables is given in **Visual S5.** Remember to reverse the order of each interval presented, besides singing it in its original form. For example, the interval do-so should also be sung as so-do.

VISUAL S5

Suggested Sequence for Introducing Intervals

so-mi:	so-mi **(reverse** = mi-so)					
la:	la-so	la-mi				
do:	do-so	do-mi	do-la			
re:	re-so	re-mi	re-la	re-do		
la,:	la,-so	la,-mi	la,-la	la,-re		
so,:	so,-so	so,-mi	so,-la	so,-do	so,-re	so,-la,
do':	do'-so	do'-mi	do'-la	do'-do	do'-re	do'-la,	do'-so,
fa and ti	all combinations					

Notice the way pitches are symbolized when written below and above the primary scale being sung: below = la,; above = do'.

la, ti, do re mi fa so la ti do' re'

primary scale

The following songs can be used to reinforce the singing of intervals through solmization:

LUCY LOCKET

mi-so-la
do: C

American Game Song

Luc - y Lock - et   lost   her   pock - et,   Kit - ty   Fish - er   found   it,
Not   a   pen - ny   was   there   in   it,   on - ly   rib - bon   round   it.

RING AROUND THE ROSY

do-mi-so-la
do: C

American Game Song

Ring   a - round   the   ros - y,   Pock - et   full   of   pos - y,

Ash - es,   ash - es,   All   fall   down.

BUTTON

do-re-mi-so-la
do: F

American Game Song

But - ton,   you   must   wan - der,   wan - der,   wan - der,

But - ton   you   must   wan - der   ev - 'ry - where,

Bright   eyes   will   find   you,   sharp   eyes   will   find   you,

But - ton,   you   must   wan - der   ev - 'ry - where.

LAND OF THE SILVER BIRCH

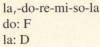

la,-do-re-mi-so-la
do: F
la: D

Canadian Folk Song

Land of the sil - ver birch, home of the bea - ver,

Where still the might - y moose wan - ders at will,

Blue lake and rock - y shore, I will re - turn once more,

Boom de de boom boom, boom de de boom boom boom.

NOW LET ME FLY

so,-la,-do-re-mi-so-la
do: G

Spiritual

Way down yon - der in the mid - dle of the field,

See me work - ing at the char - iot wheel.

Not so par - tic - 'lar 'bout work - ing at the wheel, but I

just went to see how the char - iot feels.

WHEN THE TRAIN COMES ALONG

do-re-mi-so-la-do'
do: C

American Folk Song

When the train comes a-long—— when the train comes a-long——

I'll meet you at the sta-tion when the train comes a-long.

It may be ear-ly, it may be late,

But I'll meet you at the sta-tion when the train comes a-long.

ORANGES AND LEMONS

do-re-mi-fa-so
do: C

English Folk Song

Oran-ges and lem-ons say the bells of Saint Clem-ent's, You

owe me five farth-ings, say the bells of Saint Mar-tin's.

LAUGHING SONG

so-la-ti-do′
do: C

Sweden

Ha ha ha! Hee hee hee! An - der - son and Pe - ter - son and Jen - son and me. Ha ha ha! Hee hee hee! Sing - ing all to - geth - er, sing - ing mer - ri - ly.

Once children are familiar with the syllable do, the movable *do clef* (𝄢) can be placed on the staff. Intervals can then be related to the position of do. For example, when do is on a line, so and mi are on lines. When do is in a space, so and mi are in spaces, as in **Visual S6.**

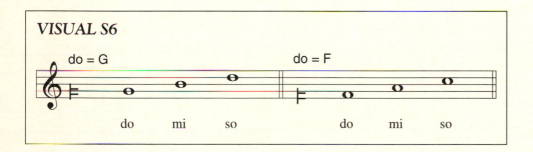

VISUAL S6

do = G   do = F

do mi so   do mi so

WRITTEN AND PERFORMANCE-RELATED ASSESSMENTS THROUGH COOPERATIVE LEARNING ACTIVITIES: SINGING VOICE

1. Assign to each group the same taped song performed by a children's choir. Ask students to listen to the tape and list all the things they liked about the way the song was performed. Then ask them to list what they would change if they were to perform the song as a group.

2. Give each group a different, known folk song compatible with the class's level of music skill development. The starting solfège syllable should be indicated on each song. Ask each group to mark the solfège first and work out the hand signs. Then the group should practice singing and signing the song until the students can perform it smoothly for the class.

3. Give a simple, unknown song and a resonator bell to each group. Have students clap the rhythms of the song and speak the rhythm syllables first. Then have them mark the solfège syllables and work out the hand signs. After sounding the resonator bell for their starting pitch, students should pratice the song using the solfège syllables and hand signs. When the song is learned well, they should sing it with words. When they are ready, students should be able to sing and sign the song individually for the teacher.

Playing Musical Instruments *Chapter*

10

PLAYING CLASSROOM INSTRUMENTS

From their earliest years, children have sought creative ways to produce sound by shaking, striking, or scraping whatever could be found in their environment. It is natural, therefore, for children to want to continue their exploration of sound by experimenting with a variety of musical instruments found in the classroom. In addition, the playing of musical instruments contributes to the development of the child's kinesthetic abilities, which are vital to his or her total musical growth. Simple classroom instruments can also be important pedagogical tools for teaching and reinforcing the elements of music and their structural components.

Content Standard #2 outlined in the National Standards for Arts Education states that children must "perform on instruments, alone and with others, a varied repertoire of music." To achieve this standard, teachers should have students:

a. play instruments on pitch, in rhythm, with appropriate dynamics and timbre, and maintain a steady tempo;
b. perform easy rhythmic, melodic, and chordal patterns accurately and independently on rythmic, melodic, and harmonic classroom instruments;
c. perform expressively a varied repertoire of music representing diverse genres and styles;
d. echo short rhythms and melodic patterns;
e. perform in groups, blending instrumental timbres, matching dynamic levels, and responding to the cues of a conductor;
f. perform independent instrumental parts while other students sing or play contrasting parts

Classroom instruments can be divided into two groups: rhythm instruments and melody instruments.

Rhythm Instruments

A varied assortment of rhythm instruments is available for classroom use. The following are among the most useful and interesting.

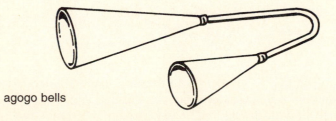

agogo bells

Agogo bells are two conical metal bells, each having a different pitch. They may be struck with a small metal rod to produce a ringing sound.

bongo drums

These two small, connected drums are usually played by placing them between the knees with the larger drum to the right. *Bongos* may be hit with the palm of the hand or with the first two fingers to produce a two-pitched percussive sound.

cabasa

The *cabasa* consists of metal beads encircling a large wooden spool. The handle attached to the spool can be turned or shaken, producing an unusual, raspy sound.

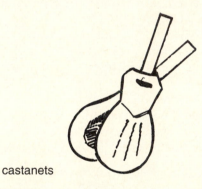

castanets

Castanets are two semi-hollow disks of wood attached to a stick by a cord. When shaken or hit against the palm of the hand, castanets produce a strong, staccato, tapping sound.

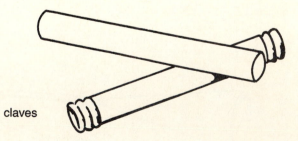

claves

Claves are two wooden cylinders containing hollowed spaces that provide resonating chambers. One cylinder is cupped in one hand while the other cylinder is used to strike it with the opposite hand.

conga drum

The *conga drum* is a long cylindrical drum that is open at the bottom. It may be played by striking the head with the palms of the hands, the fists, or the fingers.

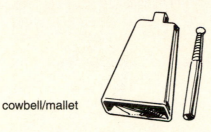

cowbell/mallet

The *cowbell* is a metal instrument that is struck with a mallet or a metal bar. It produces a ringing timbre.

cymbals

Cymbals are two metal disks. One is held in each hand. To produce a sound, they are struck together using a vertical movement. One disk continues upward; the other, downward, after being struck. Pairs of cymbals come in various sizes.

finger cymbals

Finger cymbals are small, two-inch metal plates that are attached to the thumb and a finger of one hand. When struck together, they produce a very high-pitched, delicate sound.

gong

The *gong*, a disk-shaped metal instrument, is struck with a soft-head mallet. Its sound may be sustained for a long period of time, depending on the gong's size.

guiro

The *guiro* is a hollow gourd with horizontal grooves cut across its surface. It is scraped or hit with a small wooden stick. This instrument is often referred to as "the fish" because of its fishlike shape.

hand drum

A *hand drum* is a cylindrical drum head. The drum is held by the rim while being struck with the opposite hand. Various timbres are produced, depending on where the drum head is struck and the amount of power used to hit it. Hand drums come in various sizes.

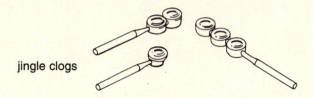
jingle clogs

Jingle clogs or *jingle taps* are instruments that have one or more pairs of metal disks loosely attached to a handle. When shaken or hit against the palm of the hand, they produce a jingle-like sound.

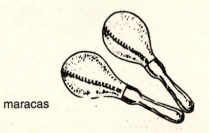
maracas

Maracas are gourds that contain dried seeds. The gourds produce a rattling sound when shook. Maracas are usually played in pairs, one in each hand.

ratchet

The *ratchet* is a miniature, machine-like instrument that produces an extremely raspy, grinding sound. A handle, which is turned in a circular manner, allows the player to determine the duration of the ratchet's sound.

rhythm sticks

Rhythm sticks are long, narrow, cylindrical pieces of wood that are hit together to produce sound. Their surfaces are either smooth or ridged. Ridged rhythm sticks can be scraped together like a guiro.

sand blocks

Sand blocks are blocks of wood covered with sand paper, ranging from fine to course texture. A small handle on each block allows the player to hold the instruments while rubbing one against the other.

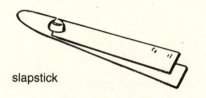

slapstick

The *slapstick* is a paddle-like instrument made of two pieces of wood hinged together to make one piece flexible. When controlled by a quick, short wrist movement, one side of the instrument slaps against the other, making a sound similar to that produced by a whip.

sleigh bells

Sleigh bells are bells that are attached to a handle or a piece of material. When shaken, they produce a jingling sound. Sleigh bells may be held in the hand or worn around the wrist or the ankle.

tambourine

The *tambourine* is a round rim of wood with several pairs of metal disks attached to it. It can be shaken or hit against the body.

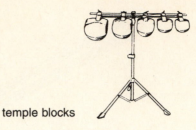

temple blocks

Temple blocks are hollowed gourds of varying sizes that are attached to a frame. Different sized gourds produce different pitches. Temple blocks are struck with a mallet.

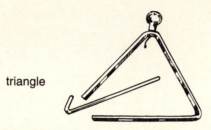

triangle

The *triangle* is a triangular piece of metal suspended from a cord. It is struck by a metal stick to produce a high-pitched, ringing sound.

vibra-slap

The *vibra-slap* is an instrument that vibrates when slapped by the hand or hit against the body. Its ability to vibrate for a long period of time and its unusual timbre make the vibra-slap a popular instrument for producing sound effects.

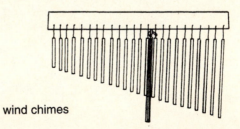

wind chimes

Tubular pieces of metal of different lengths are attached to a bar to produce *wind chimes*. When gently swept with the hand, this instrument produces a gentle, ethereal sound.

wood block

The *wood block* is a semi-hollow, rectangular-shaped piece of wood. It is either cupped in the hand or suspended from a cord to allow for its full resonating potential. It is struck with a wooden mallet.

Several examples for incorporating rhythm instruments into the music class follow. Other suggestions have been included in the chapters on rhythm and timbre.

The song "Hey, Betty Martin" can be used with rhythm instruments to explore their sounds. The original words of the song are:

Hey, Betty Martin, Tiptoe, tiptoe,
  Hey, Betty Martin, Tiptoe fine;
Hey, Betty Martin, Tiptoe, tiptoe,
  Hey, Betty Martin, Tiptoe fine.

The words in the second measure of each phrase can be replaced to designate a specific instrument to be played, as is shown here.

HEY, BETTY MARTIN

American Folk Song

Hey, Bet-ty Mar - tin *(Play the bon-go)* Hey, Bet-ty Mar - tin *(Play it fine)*

Hey, Bet-ty Mar - tin *(Play the bon-go)* Hey, Bet-ty Mar - tin *(Play it fine)*

Numerous songs and speech activities can be performed in a more interesting way by simply adding a rhythm accompaniment. In "Chumbara, Chumbara," for example, instruments are played on specific beats—beats 1 and 3. If repeated throughout, a simple ostinato accompaniment is created. More difficult ostinati patterns can be used with songs such as "Mary Ann." Sing "Chumbara, Chumbara" and accompany it with the following pattern:

Ostinato pattern:

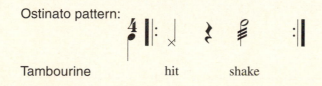

Tambourine   hit   shake

CHUMBARA, CHUMBARA

Canadian Folk Song

Chum - ba - ra,_____ Chum - ba - ra, Chum - ba - ra,_____ Chum - ba - ra,

Chum-ba - ra,_____ Chum-ba - ra, Chum, chum, chum, chum, chum, chum, chum, chum,

Chum - ba - ra,_____ chum - ba - ra, Chum - ba - ra,_____ Chum - ba - ra,

Chum - ba - ra,_____ Chum - ba - ra, Chum, chum, chum.

Note: *Chumbara* is a nonsense word.

Sing "Mary Ann" and provide the percussion parts notated here:

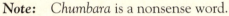

Ostinato Accompaniment

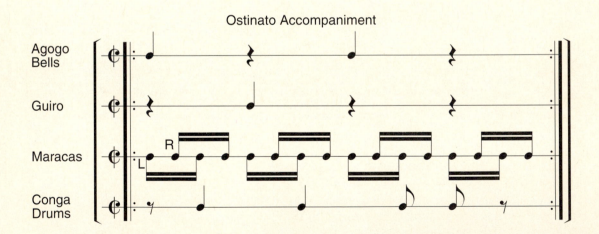

MARY ANN

Calypso

All day,___ all night,___ Miss Mar - y Ann,___

Down by___ the sea - shore___ sift - ing sand.___

All the lit - tle chil - dren___ love Mar - y Ann,___

She sings___ ca - lyp - so,___ Mar - y Ann.___

Classroom percussion instruments can also be added to recordings of popular music, especially those with a strong, regular pulse.

Students can create their own rhythmic compositions. The rondo below is an example that incorporates both predetermined rhythms and improvisation performed on rhythm instruments. Each student should choose a different rhythm instrument to play the B and the C themes.

RONDO

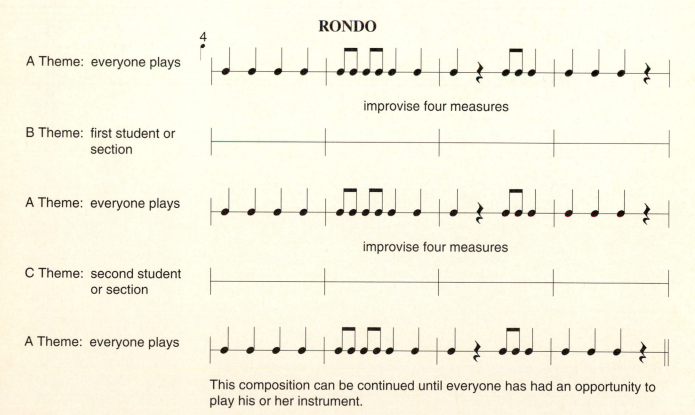

A Theme: everyone plays

improvise four measures

B Theme: first student or section

A Theme: everyone plays

improvise four measures

C Theme: second student or section

A Theme: everyone plays

This composition can be continued until everyone has had an opportunity to play his or her instrument.

"Stanpipes" is a thirteenth-century instrumental piece. The class can be divided into five groups to perform this work. When the class knows the piece well, it can be performed with one or two students to a part, as an added challenge.

STANPIPES

13th Century

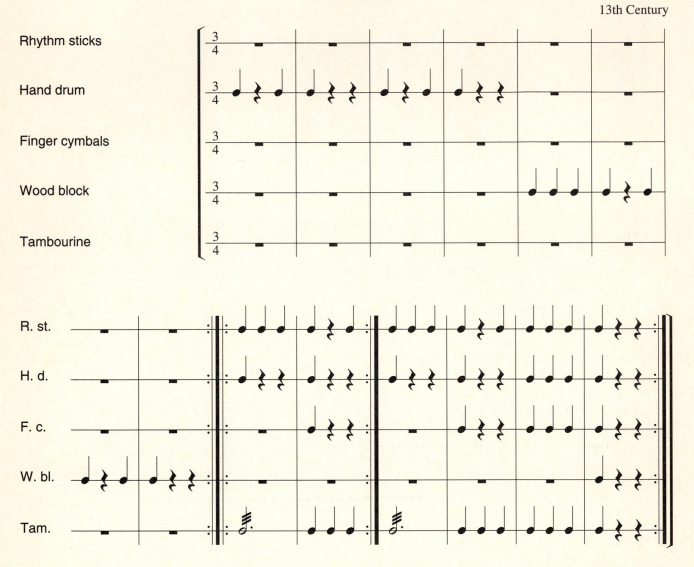

Melody Instruments

Resonator bells are individual metal bars tuned to each tone of the chromatic scale. Each bar is mounted on a block of wood containing a resonator. A set of resonator bells usually includes one to two octaves of bars. Small rubber mallets are provided for each bar. Resonator bells are easily manipulated; therefore, they can be used to teach each structural components as high and low pitch, intervals, scales, and chords. Because they can be easily distributed and used by more than one child at a time, resonator bells have earned a permanent place in music instruction at the elementary level.

resonator bells

One or more resonator bells can be added to a song to reinforce the melody or to create harmony. For example, in "St. Paul's Steeple," students can reinforce the C major scale by playing a resonator bell on each scale tone as they sing the melody.

ST. PAUL'S STEEPLE

English Folk Song

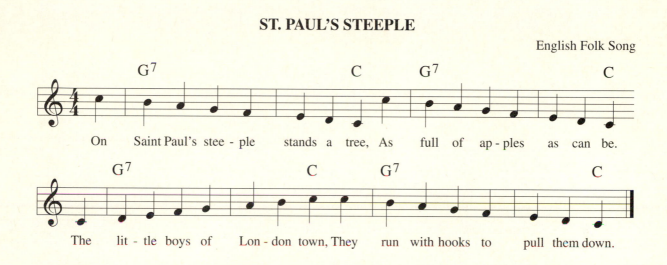

On   Saint Paul's stee - ple   stands a tree, As   full   of   ap - ples   as   can   be.

The   lit - tle boys of   Lon - don town, They   run   with hooks   to   pull them down.

Clusters of chords can be created with resonator bells to provide a harmonic accompaniment. The song "The Hummingbird" contains three chords: I (D), IV (G), and V^7 (A^7). Resonator bells having the tones of the tonic chord (D, F-sharp, A) can be given to three students. Likewise, resonator bells can be distributed for the subdominant and dominant seventh chords. Students should play their chord when it corresponds to the harmonic changes taking place in the song.

THE HUMMINGBIRD

Austrian Folk Melody

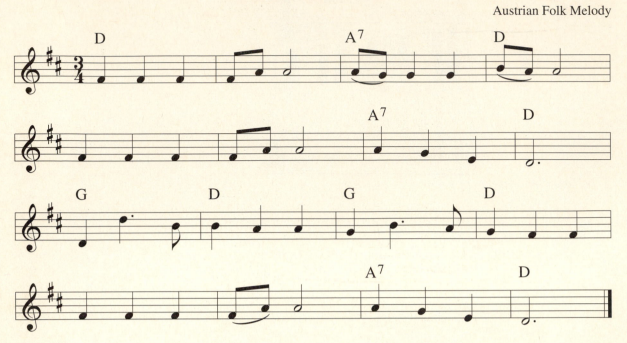

Carl Orff.   Carl Orff (1895–1982) was a German educator and composer. Orff believed that speech, music, and movement were inseparable. His understanding of elemental music included the belief that children must relive the early stages of historical development in music if they are to develop musically; early involvement with music must center around active participation that is untrained, unsophisticated, and inseparable from speech and movement. Orff teachers provide experiences for students to develop their creative potential, which manifests itself in a child's ability to improvise. Opportunities for improvisation are continually provided as children are encouraged to explore space, sound, and form. Special instruments are a distinctive feature of Orff's approach to teaching. These instruments, called the instrumentarium, include barred instruments—xylophones, metallophones, and glockenspiels; recorders; drums; woods, such as claves and maracas; metals, including cymbals and cowbells; and strings, such as guitars and cellos.

Primary among the melody instruments devised by Carl Orff as part of his instrumentarium are glockenspiels, metallophones, and xylophones—known collectively as Orff instruments.

Glockenspiels

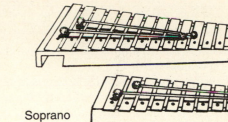

Alto

Soprano

Metallophones

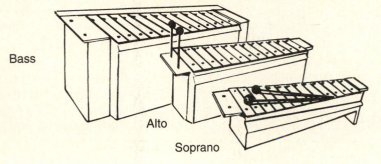

Bass

Alto

Soprano

Xylophones

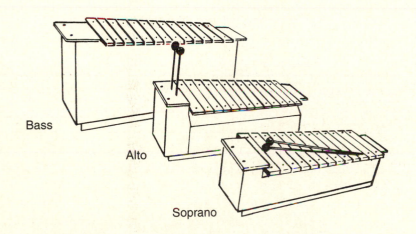

Bass

Alto

Soprano

Range	Glockenspiel	Metallophone	Xylophone
Soprano	Sounds two octaves higher than written	Sounds one octave higher than written	Sounds one octave higher than written
Alto	Sounds one octave higher than written	Sounds as written	Sounds as written
Bass		Sounds one octave lower than written	Sounds one octave lower than written

Playing the Orff Barred Instruments

The Orff melody instruments were specifically designed to meet the needs of children. Each instrument contains bars that can be easily removed so that only pitches needed in a particular melody or pattern are present. This helps ensure successful and satisfying musical experiences.

Because of the cost of these instruments, few schools provide instruments for every child in the classroom. Therefore, children should be prepared to take turns playing an instrument. Each child who is selected to play should sit on a carpeted floor with his or her legs crossed behind the instrument. The lower pitched bars, which are the larger bars, should be to the player's left. Teachers should make every effort to purchase stands or small tables for each of the instruments so that students may stand comfortably and develop the best possible hand position in relation to the instrument. If stands or tables are used, the teacher should be sure that the playing surface is at the player's waist level.

Barred instruments are played with two or more mallets or beaters. A pair of beaters that is appropriate for the instrument will be included with the purchase of that instrument. Teachers should be careful not to allow students to play the metal barred instruments with metal or wooden mallets. A yarn- or felt-covered mallet should be used instead. Correct mallet selection will ensure against ear damage.

Teachers should ask students to grip the mallets as though they were getting ready to ride on a bicycle or motor cycle. The backs of the hands should be in an upward position. The mallets should be held with the thumb and index and middle fingers. Holding the mallets with the fingertips or entire hand is not recommended. The fourth and fifth fingers should be curved around the end of the stick.

A quick wrist action should be used to hit the mallet against the center of each bar. It is important to quickly bounce the mallet because this will ensure the proper vibration between the mallet and the bar. Deadening the sound by leaving the mallet on the bar should be avoided.

Last, students should be encouraged to use both hands and to alternate their mallets when playing.

Speech Activities

Speech is one of the most basic elements of the Orff-Schulwerk or "school work" process. Orff believed that speech, or the spoken word, should be used to reinforce the inner feelings of rhythm. Once a rhythmic pattern is internalized through the use of language, it is then transferred to a rhythmic or barred instrument. Enunciation, tone quality, and rhythmic accuracy are of great importance if speech is to be a valuable tool in the Orff process. The lesson plan that follows demonstrates how the use of speech can be transferred to the body and then to rhythmic instruments.

PITO, PITO

ORFF LESSON 1*

Behavioral Objectives

Students will become familiar with a Spanish game song entitled, "Pito, Pito."
Students will perform an ostinato accompaniment using rhythmic instruments.

Materials

A copy of the folk song, "Pito, Pito" (see page 238).
Rhythm instruments: agogo bell, guiro, vibra-slap, small drum

*Lesson plans, pages 236–240, created by René Boyer-Alexander.

Procedure

1. Have students speak the words to "Pito, Pito" while playing the basic beat on their laps.
2. Speak the rhyme again and clap the rhythm of the words.
3. Divide the class into two groups. Direct group 1 to clap the rhythm of the words while group 2 pats the beat. Switch parts.
4. Ask the children to look and listen to the last line as the teacher recites it.

5. Ask students to suggest ways in which the words in the last line can be placed on different parts of the body. One suggestion might be:

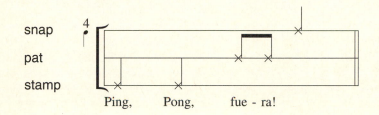

   Practice this with the students until they are comfortable with the pattern and its corresponding movement.
6. Tell the class that the pattern they just learned can be used as a *rhythmic ostinato*. A rhythmic ostinato consists of a rhythmic pattern that is repeated again and again and used as an accompaniment.
7. Divide the class again into two groups. Have group 1 say the speech and group 2 perform the ostinato. Switch parts.
8. Ask students to suggest an instrument that can play the rhythm that is in the feet. Suggest another that can play the rhythm on the thighs and another that can take the place of the finger snap. A final transfer from the body to instruments may look like this.

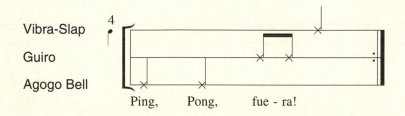

9. Assign students to each of the accompanying instruments and have them play while the rest of the class performs the speech activity.

Summary/Evaluation

The teacher could ask the students the following:

a. What do we call the steady, continuous pattern that we played on our laps? (beat/pulse)
b. What do we call the varied lengths of sounds and silences as demonstrated through the speech or the words of "Pito, Pito"? (rhythm)
c. What do we call a pattern that repeats and is used as an accompaniment? (ostinato)
d. Name the instruments we used in the ostinato pattern. (agogo bell, guiro, vibra-slap)

PITO, PITO

Spanish Game Song
Collected by René Boyer-Alexander

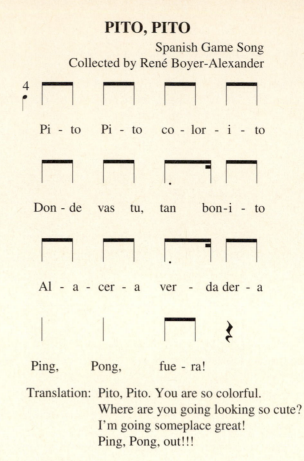

Pi - to Pi - to co - lor - i - to

Don - de vas tu, tan bon - i - to

Al - a - cer - a ver - da der - a

Ping, Pong, fue - ra!

Translation: Pito, Pito. You are so colorful.
Where are you going looking so cute?
I'm going someplace great!
Ping, Pong, out!!!

Singing and Playing Activities

Orff-Schulwerk is a creative process. Therefore, it is recommended that children be allowed to actively participate in the creation of their first musical pieces. The use of the pentatonic scale as a beginning stepping stone to tonal understanding is recommended because, as discussed in Chapter 9, this scale enables them to sing, play, or create a melody without anyone's assistance. Central to the pentatonic scale is the minor third interval (so-mi), which is known as the "call" by Orff specialists.

The addition of "la" to the so-mi creates a universal "chant" sung by most children. The chant tones are then extended by adding mi, re, do, thus creating the pentatonic scale or five-tone scale—the beginning of the tonal sequence in the Orff-Schulwerk process.

ORFF LESSON 2

Behavioral Objectives

Students will set "Pito, Pito" to a pentatonic melody.
Students will better understand the meaning of "tonal center."

Materials

Melody instruments; staff paper, pencil, chalkboard

Procedure

1. Have students take their places behind the Orff barred instruments.
2. Have students properly remove all Bs and Fs (burgers and fries) by placing their fingers on the top and the bottom of a bar and lifting it directly off. Tell the students that they are now set up to play in C pentatonic and that C is the tonal center.

3. Give students about three minutes to compose a tune to "Pito, Pito." Let them know that they must begin their tune on "so" and end the piece on "do" or "C." Also inform them that changing the rhythm in this activity is not allowed.
4. Have students who wish to do so perform their tunes for the class.
5. As a group, choose one of them.
6. Write out the tune together on the chalkboard, using a five-lined staff. The tune may look like the following:

7. Play the tune on the barred instruments.

Summary/Evaluation

Ask the students to describe the process they went through to compose a piece of music.

ORFF LESSON 3

Behavioral Objectives

Students will learn the function of a drone or bordun.
Students will create a variety of drone patterns that can accompany "Pito, Pito."
Students will layer three drones on top of one another to create a more complex harmonic structure.

Materials

Orff barred instruments

Procedure

1. Tell the students, "Every good melody deserves harmony." Orff introduces us to various drone or bordun patterns, which allow students to accompany themselves using pentatonic melodies in a non-threatening way.
2. Tell the students that drones or borduns are made up of the first and fifth degrees of the scale. See **Visual P1** for Barred Patterns for Simple Accompaniments.
3. Have students demonstrate how many combinations of notes C and G they can create. Encourage them to play the pitches together and apart.
4. The teacher should ask each student to mirror herself or himself as she or he pats a variety of drone patterns on her or his lap. This technique is called patching. *Patching* is a German word that means hitting the knees or thighs. Usually this procedure is used to physically prepare the student to play a specific pattern on the barred instruments.
5. Have students create a simple bordun accompaniment on the bass xylophone to the song, "Pito, Pito."
6. Have students then create a simple bordun that can be played on a metallophone. Metallophones have a more sustained tone, and therefore students should play longer notes on them.

7. Play the melody on a glockenspiel.
8. Starting with the lowest instrument, the bass xylophone, layer in all the parts to create an interesting accompaniment of which all the children can be proud.
9. Sing the song "Pito, Pito" while playing an accompaniment.

Summary/Evaluation

The children's ability to successfully put all this together should be praised. They are now ready to do it again.

VISUAL P1

BARRED PATTERNS FOR SIMPLE ACCOMPANIMENTS

Four melodic ostinati have been created to accompany the song "Dreams." Have students sing the melody while playing the ostinati on the designated Orff instruments.

DREAMS

Poem by Langston Hughes

Arr.: René Boyer-Alexander

Wind chimes can be added for special effects either throughout the piece or at the very end.

Rhythm and melody instruments can be combined to add to the interest of a musical composition. "Ida Red" provides opportunities for combining rhythmic and melodic timbres in a creative way.

IDA RED

Kentucky Folk Song
Arr.: M. Rozmajzl

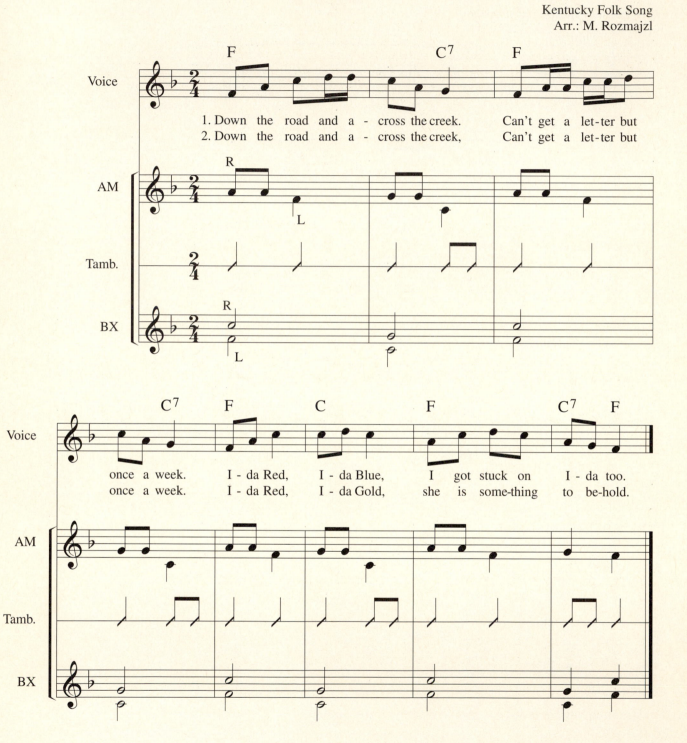

1. Down the road and a - cross the creek. Can't get a let-ter but
2. Down the road and a - cross the creek, Can't get a let-ter but

once a week. I - da Red, I - da Blue, I got stuck on I - da too.
once a week. I - da Red, I - da Gold, she is some-thing to be-hold.

PLAYING THE SOPRANO RECORDER

The twentieth century witnessed a revival of interest in recorder playing. The recorder emerged as a melody instrument in the fifteenth century and was popular until the eighteenth century, when it was replaced by the modern flute. It is usually made in six sizes: sopranino, soprano, alto, tenor, bass, and contrabass. The recorder can assist a student in learning to read music, in improvising, and in developing performance skills. The soprano recorder continues to be an integral part of elementary music education because it is easy to play, is inexpensive, and closely parallels the tone quality of the child's voice. In addition, it provides an opportunity for students to perform literature written by some of the greatest composers in our history. The study of the soprano recorder usually begins in third or fourth grade.

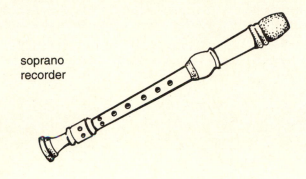

soprano recorder

Introducing the Recorder

The soprano recorder is a C instrument. This means that the lowest possible tone that can be produced is C. The range of the soprano recorder encompasses two octaves; therefore, it is capable of playing almost any melody. All pitches sound one octave higher than written.

The holes on the top and back of the recorder, when covered, change the length of the air column, producing variations in pitch.

Two standard types of recorders are commonly used in schools today: Baroque (English) and German. The fingerings are slightly different for each. The activities presented in this chapter are for that Baroque recorder.

Fingering the Recorder

The first three fingers of the left hand cover the top three holes on the recorder. The left-hand thumb is placed over the back hole. The bottom four holes are covered by the four fingers of the right hand, leaving the right-hand thumb free to support the instrument.

Care must be taken to ensure that the holes being used are completely covered. Escaping air will cause the instrument to squeak. To avoid this, the player should cover the holes with the fleshy pads of the fingers.

When playing the recorder, hold it with the bell pointed toward the floor, not straight out from the body.

Blowing into the Recorder

The mouthpiece of the recorder should be held firmly by the lips, not between the teeth. Blow gently and evenly into the recorder while articulating the syllables "doo" or "too" against the roof of the mouth, near the upper teeth. It is important to continue the airflow while articulating the syllables. This technique is called *tonguing*. Tonguing is used to sound each pitch unless otherwise indicated in the music.

When playing the recorder, be careful not to overblow. Squeaks will also result if too much air is forced into the pipe.

Because of the moisture buildup inside the recorder while playing, it is important to place the index finger over the tone hole and blow forcefully to clear the moisture from the tube when it becomes excessive.

Playing Music

Covering the holes for the thumb and the first finger on the left hand, improvise a variety of rhythmic patterns until you are comfortable blowing into the instrument. This pitch is B and will always correspond to the staff notation and the recorder fingering diagrams shown here.

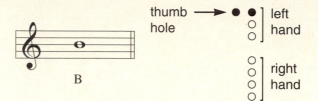

Practice playing the following exercises:

By simply adding the second finger of the left hand to the fingering for the pitch B, the new pitch A is produced.

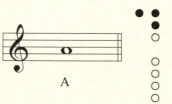

Practice the following exercises:

Note G is fingered by adding the covered third hole to the A fingering.

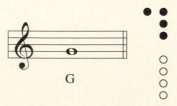

Note G should be practiced alone and with notes B and A until the students' fingerings become automatic. Playing the following songs will help reinforce the reading of B, A, and G.

HOT CROSS BUNS

England

Hot cross buns. Hot cross buns. One a pen-ny, two a pen-ny, Hot cross buns.

GOOD NEWS

Spiritual

Good news! Char-iot's com-ing! Good news! Char-iot's com-ing!

Good news! Char-iot's com-ing! Don't leave me be - hind.

THE BOATMAN

African American Song

Oh, the boat-man dance, the boat-man sing, The boat-man up to ev - 'ry thing.

When the boat-man comes on shore, He spend his mon-ey and he work for more.

As the student continues to learn new notes on the recorder, it may be helpful to use the following procedures:

a. Clap the rhythm of the song first.
b. Sing the melody using the letter name of each note.
c. Repeat item "b" and finger the notes on the recorder.
   Rest the recorder comfortably on the chin while doing this exercise.
d. Play the music on the recorder.
e. Sing the words to the song.

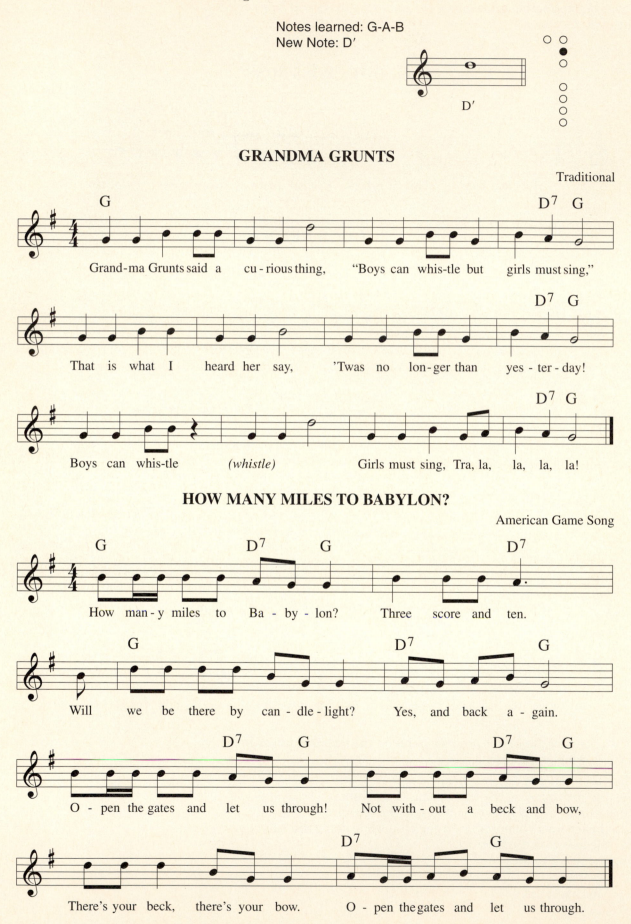

Practicing the Recorder

Notes learned: G-A-B
New Note: D′

D′

GRANDMA GRUNTS

Traditional

Grand-ma Grunts said a cu-rious thing, "Boys can whis-tle but girls must sing,"

That is what I heard her say, 'Twas no lon-ger than yes-ter-day!

Boys can whis-tle *(whistle)* Girls must sing, Tra, la, la, la, la!

HOW MANY MILES TO BABYLON?

American Game Song

How man-y miles to Ba-by-lon? Three score and ten.

Will we be there by can-dle-light? Yes, and back a-gain.

O-pen the gates and let us through! Not with-out a beck and bow,

There's your beck, there's your bow. O-pen the gates and let us through.

Notes learned: G-A-B-D′
New Note: C′

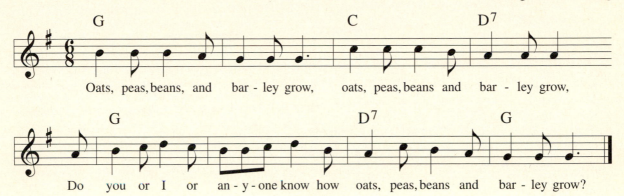

C′

OATS, PEAS, BEANS

English Game Song

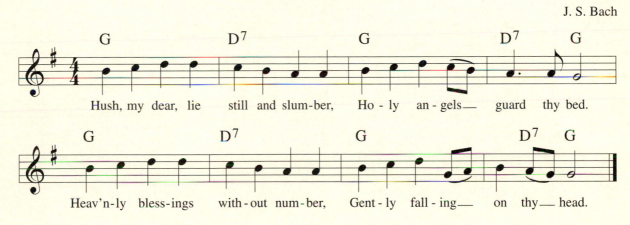

Oats, peas, beans, and bar - ley grow, oats, peas, beans and bar - ley grow,

Do you or I or an - y - one know how oats, peas, beans and bar - ley grow?

CRADLE HYMN

J. S. Bach

Hush, my dear, lie still and slum - ber, Ho - ly an - gels— guard thy bed.

Heav'n - ly bless - ings with - out num - ber, Gent - ly fall - ing— on thy— head.

Notes learned: G-A-B-C'-D'
New Note: E

JIM ALONG JOSIE

Oklahoma

G ... C

Hey, come a - long,_____ jim a - long Jo - sie,

G ... D⁷ G

Hey, come a - long,_____ jim a - long Joe. Hey, come a - long,_____

C ... G D⁷ G

jim a - long Jo - sie, Hey, come a - long,_____ jim a - long Joe.

POOR LITTLE KITTY CAT

American Folk Song

C G C G

Poor lit - tle kit - ty cat, Poor lit - tle fel - ler

C G C G

Poor lit - tle kit - ty cat, Lost in the cel - lar.

Notes learned: E-G-A-B-C'-D'
New Note: D

ACHSHAV

Israeli Folk Song

Ach - shav, ach shav, b' - E - mek Yis - r' - el.

Ach - shav, ach shav, b' - E - mek Yis - r' - el.

Tum - ba, tum - ba, tum - ba, b' - E - mek Yis - r' - el. Hey!

Tum - ba, tum - ba, tum - ba, b' - E - mek Yis - r' - el. el.

Pronunciation: äk-shäv, bē-mək, yis-ra-el   Translation: Now, in the valley of Israel. Tumba, tumba, tumba

Note: Movement to Achshav can be found on page 308.

THE YOUNG MAN WHO WOULDN'T HOE CORN

American Frontier Song

I'll sing you a song, and it's not ver - y long, It's a -

bout a young man who would - n't hoe corn, The rea - son

why, I can't tell, This young man was al - ways well.

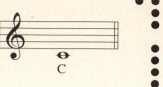

POURQUOI

American Folk Song

"Oh," said the Black - bird sit - ting on a tree,

"I had a wife as well as thee. But she flew a - way and

nev - er came back, And ev - er since then my head's been black."

RIDING IN THE BUGGY

Play-Party Song

Rid-ing in the bug-gy Miss Mar - y Jane, Miss Mar - y Jane, Miss Mar - y Jane,

Rid-ing - in the bug-gy Miss Mar - y Jane, I'm a long way from home.

Who mourns for me, Who mourns for me,

Who mourns for me, my dar - ling, Who mourns for me?

Notes learned: C-D-E-G-A-B-C′-D′
New Note: F

STARS SHININ'

Texas

By'n bye, by'n bye. Stars shin-ing num-ber, num-ber one, Num-ber

two, num-ber three, Good lawd, by'n bye, by'n bye, Good lawd, by'n bye.

THE LITTLE DAPPLED COW

Traditional

Once there was a lit-tle man, where the lit-tle riv-er ran,

And he had a lit-tle farm and lit-tle dai-ry-o,

And he had a lit-tle plow, and a lit-tle dap-pled cow,

Which he of-ten called his pret-ty lit-tle Mar-y-o.

Notes learned: C-D-E-F-G-A-B-C′-D′
New Note: F-sharp

F#

VIVA LA MUSICA

Michael Praetorius

Vi - va, vi - va la mu - si - ca!   Vi - va, vi - va la

mu - si - ca!   Vi - va   la mu - si - ca!

SIMPLE GIFTS

Shaker Tune

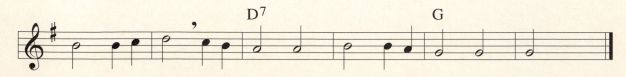

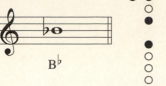

B♭

SCARBOROUGH FAIR

England

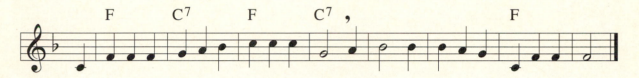

MANGO WALK

Jamaican Calypso

My moth-er deed-a tell me that you go man-go walk, you

go man-go walk, you go man-go walk.

My moth-er deed-a tell me that you go man-go walk, and

eat all the num-ber 'lev-en.

Unusual meanings:

    deed-a = did
    go mango walk = walk in the mango orchard
    eat all the number 'lev-en = eat the best mangos in the orchard

Playing Duets

In a duet two different lines of music are being played at the same time. Divide the class into two parts. Have half play the top line and the other half play the bottom line.

OVER MY HEAD
(A Duet for Two Recorders)

Spiritual
Arr.: René Boyer-Alexander

LA PIÑATA
(A Duet for Two Recorders)

Latin American Folk Song
Arr.: René Boyer-Alexander

Top Line

Da - le, da - le, da - le, no pier - das el ti - no;

Bottom Line

Top Line

mi - de la dis - tan - cia que hay en el ca - mi - no.

Bottom Line

Translation: This evening's piñata   Hit it, hit it, hit it,
Looks just like a star   Don't lose your good aim.
Hurry over for a taste   Measure out the distance,
Let's have fun with it tonight   From here to there.

Playing Trios

In a trio three lines of music are played at the same time in harmony. Some play the top line, some the middle line, and some the bottom line.

Divide the class into three sections. Assign each section a line and play "Chop Sticks."

CHOP STICKS

American Folk Tune
Arr.: René Boyer-Alexander

The tones above high D can be produced by adjusting the thumb so that a portion of the thumb hole is left uncovered. These fingerings are included in the fingering chart shown here.

FINGERING CHART FOR SOPRANO RECORDER
BAROQUE (ENGLISH) FINGERING

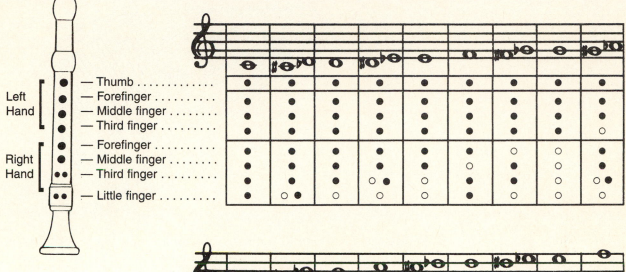

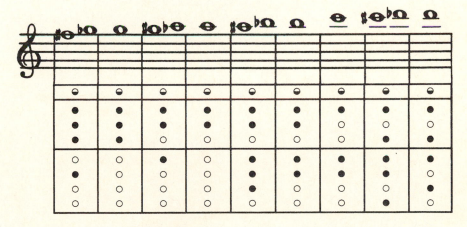

○ = open hole
● = covered hole
◐ = partially covered hole

PLAYING THE AUTOHARP

The *autoharp* is a strumming instrument that is used to accompany songs and other musical compositions. It is simple to play, making it an ideal instrument for the elementary classroom.

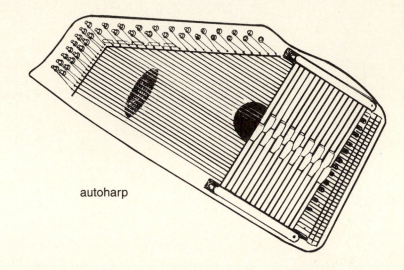

autoharp

To produce sound on the autoharp the player simply depresses a bar with the left hand and crosses over that hand to strum the strings with the right hand. Each bar is attached to felt pads that allow some strings to sound and others to be dampened. Strings are generally strummed with a pick, using an arm motion away from the body. The autoharp may be placed on the player's lap or may be held in an upright position against the body. The latter position is known as Appalachian style.

Notice the chord symbols indicated on each bar. These symbols represent the chords that can be played on the instrument. The number of chords included on an autoharp may vary from instrument to instrument. Usually, the tonic, subdominant, and dominant chords for each key will be grouped close to each other. This makes it easier for the player to move out more smoothly from one chord to another within a key. Most autoharps can be played in the keys of C, G, and F major and A and G minor.

To become comfortable with the autoharp, the player should practice strumming the strings with the G-bar depressed:

strum = G   G   G   G   G   G

When the player is comfortable strumming the instrument, familiar songs can be added to the strum, such as "Farmer in the Dell" and "Are You Sleeping."

FARMER IN THE DELL

English Game Song

The farm-er in the dell;___ the farm-er in the dell;___

Heigh, ho, the Der-ry O, the farm-er in the dell.___

Change the chord to C and sing "Row, Row, Row Your Boat" while adding an accompaniment on the autoharp. Other songs in this book that can be accompanied by using a single chord include:

Song	Chapter	Key	Song	Chapter	Key
Above the Plain	14	F	Ring Around the Rosy	9	C
Marching	6	F	Star Light	9	C
One, Two, Tie My Shoe	9	F	Frère Jacques	7	G
Lucy Locket	9	C	Wind the Bobbin	5	G

Because children's song literature has as its basic harmonic structure some combination of the I, IV, and V^7 chords, students should develop facility in playing these chords in several keys. The following songs include combinations of these three chords in the keys of F, G, and C:

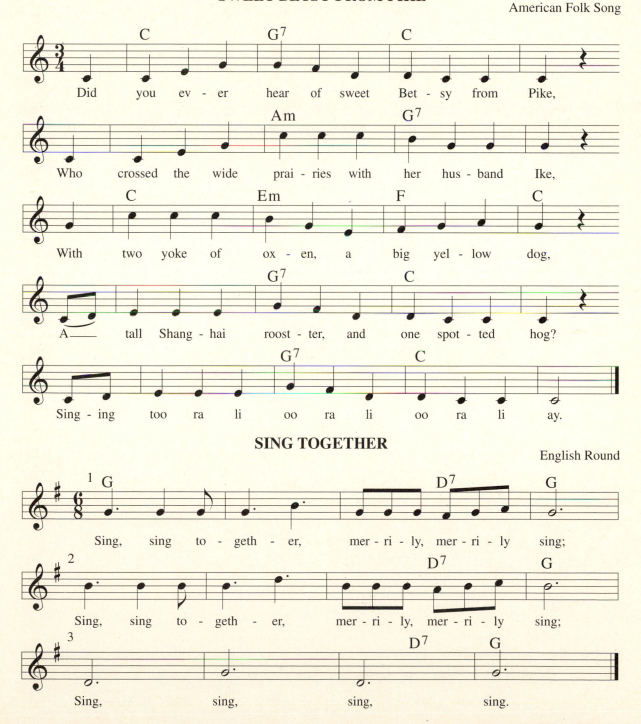

SWEET BETSY FROM PIKE

American Folk Song

SING TOGETHER

English Round

LOVE SOMEBODY

American Folk Song

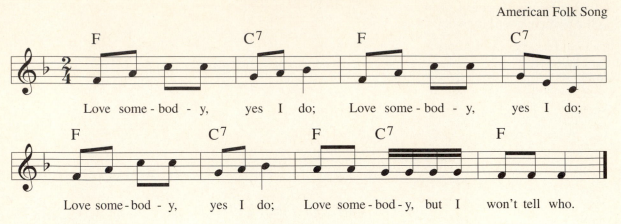

Love some-bod-y, yes I do; Love some-bod-y, yes I do;

Love some-bod-y, yes I do; Love some-bod-y, but I won't tell who.

OH, SUSANNA

Stephen Foster

I— came from Al - a - bam - a with my ban - jo on my knee,

I'm— going to Loui - si - an - a my— true love for to see;

It— rained all night the day I left, the weath - er it was dry;

The— sun so hot I froze to death; Su - san - na, don't you cry.

Refrain

Oh, Su - san - na, oh, don't you cry for me,

I've— come from Al - a - bam - a with my ban - jo on my knee.

Other songs using the primary chords in the keys of C, F, and G include:

Song	Chords	Chapter
Mein Hut	C G^7	8
My Home's in Montana	C F G^7	10
Riding in the Buggy	C F G^7	10
Silent Night	C F G^7	3
London Bridge	F C^7	5
Love Somebody	F C^7	10
Mary Ann	F C^7	10
Oh, Susanna	F Bb C^7	10
Twelve Days of Christmas	F Bb C^7	3
Grandma Grunts	G D^7	10
Hoo Hoo	G D^7	5
Sing Together	G D^7	10
Viva La Musica	G D7	10
America	G C D^7	3
Away in a Manger	G C D^7	3
Oats, Peas, Beans	G C D^7	10

PLAYING THE GUITAR

Because of its wide acceptance by folk artists and popular musicians, the guitar has become a widely used instrument in elementary music education. However, young children are limited in their abilities to play this instrument because their hands are so small. Children in upper elementary grades will have greater success in playing the guitar.

There are many types of guitars. The guitar most commonly used in the classroom is the acoustic, classical guitar with nylon strings. Although the guitar can be used to play melodies, its function in the elementary classroom is to provide accompaniments to songs and other musical compositions. The most important parts of the guitar are shown here:

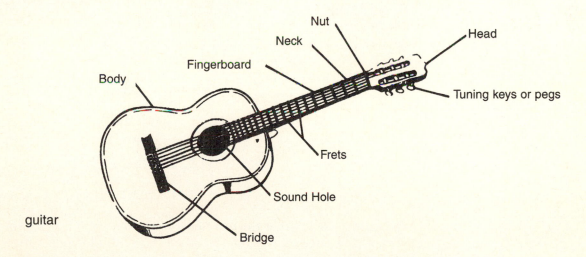

The acoustic, classical guitar usually has six strings of differing thickness and tension. The common tuning of the strings is E, A, D, G, B, and E′. Although there are several ways to tune the guitar, the easiest and most accurate for beginning players is to tune the strings to the piano. A pitch can be raised or lowered by turning the tuning pegs.

The diagram shows the relationship of each of the six guitar strings to its corresponding pitch on the staff and on the piano keyboard. (Guitar music is notated an octave higher than it sounds.)

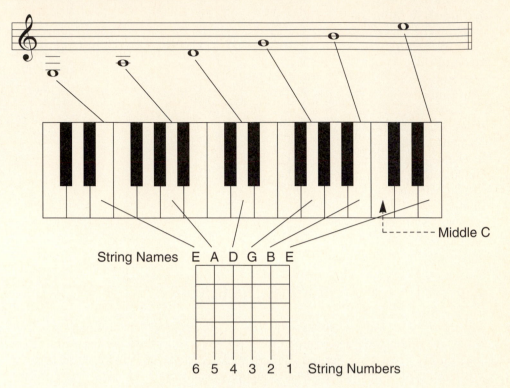

When playing the guitar in a seated position, rest it comfortably on the right thigh with the neck of the guitar slanted upward. The left-hand thumb should rest on the backside of the guitar neck close to the nut. Curve the left hand around the guitar neck and arch the fingers over the strings. The fingers of the left hand are numbered from 1 to 4; the index finger is number 1. The right hand can either strum or finger pick the strings over the sound hole.

To learn fingerings for a chord, guitar players refer to fingering charts. The charts correspond to the guitar strings on the fretted fingerboard. Look at the finger chart for the D major chord:

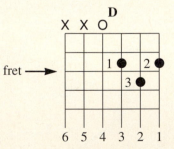

The chart indicates that the first finger of the left hand is placed on the second fret of the third string; finger 3 is placed on the third fret of string 2; and the second finger is placed on the second fret of string 1. String 4 is open, as indicated by the "O," and must be strummed with the first three strings. When playing this chord, strings 5 and 6 are not played, as indicated by the "X."

One of the most important aspects of learning to play the guitar is acquiring strumming techniques. A variety of strums can be learned. The most basic, however, are the sweep strum and the brush strum. The sweep strum involves a downward movement of the right-hand thumb across the strings. For the brush strum, the backs of the fingernails brush downward across the strings. The two strums are often used in combination; the sweep strum is used on accented beats, but either the sweep or the brush strum can be used on unaccented beats.

Practice strumming the D major chord with the sweep strum:

D D D D D D

Continue strumming the D chord while singing "Make New Friends."

MAKE NEW FRIENDS

Round

Make new friends but keep— the— old:— One is sil-ver and the oth-er gold.

Learn the fingering for the A⁷ chord and practice strumming it. Then combine it with the D major chord and play "Tom Dooley" and "Merrily We Roll Along."

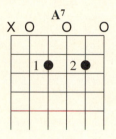

TOM DOOLEY

American Ballad

Hang down your head, Tom Doo-ley, Hang down your head and cry.

Hang down your head, Tom Doo-ley, Poor boy, you're bound to— die.

MERRILY WE ROLL ALONG

Traditional

Mer - ri - ly we roll a - long, Roll a - long, Roll a - long.

Mer - ri - ly we roll a - long, o'er the deep blue sea.

After learning the G chord, the player will be able to strum a variety of songs in the key of D. The player should practice "On Top of Old Smoky" and "Hawaiian Rainbows" until he or she can move smoothly from one chord to the next. Students should experiment with both the sweep and the brush strums.

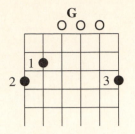

ON TOP OF OLD SMOKEY

American Folk Song

HAWAIIAN RAINBOWS

Hawaiian Folk Song

Other songs in the key of D, found in this book, include:

Song	Chapter
This Old Man	7
The Clown	5
Shoo Fly	6
Circle Round the Zero	12

In the key of C, the three primary chords are C (I), F (IV), and G^7 (V^7). Practice these chords. Now play "My Home's in Montana" until the chord changes are smooth.

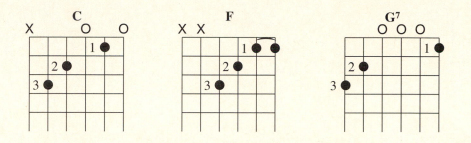

MY HOME'S IN MONTANA

Cowboy Song

My home's in Mon - tan - a, I wear a ban - dan - na,

My spurs are of sil - ver, My po - ny is gray.

When rid - ing the rang - es My luck nev - er chang - es:

With foot in the stir - rup I'll gal - lop a - way.

Other songs in the key of C, found in this book, are:

Song	Chapter
New River Train	3
Santa Lucia	3
America the Beautiful	6
Over the River and Through the Woods	3

A *capo* is a device that can be attached to the guitar neck. It is used to raise the pitch of the strings, making transposition to a higher key easier to achieve. For example, it is possible to play in the key of E-flat by placing the capo on the first fret and fingering the D chord at the third fret.

By referring to the following fingering charts, additional chords can be learned to accompany a variety of songs.

GUITAR CHORDS

Major Triads	*Dominant Sevenths*	*Minor Triads*
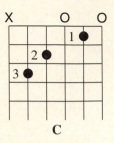C	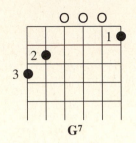G⁷	Am
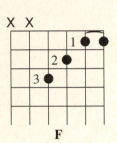F	C⁷	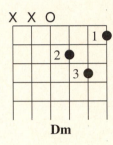Dm
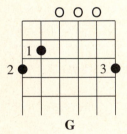G	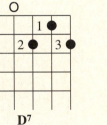D⁷	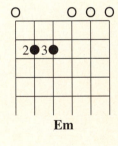Em
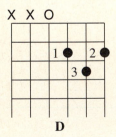D	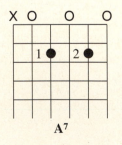A⁷	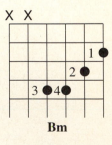Bm
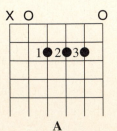A	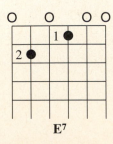E⁷	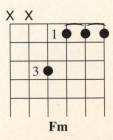Fm

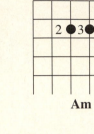
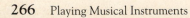

PLAYING KEYBOARD INSTRUMENTS

Keyboard instruments can be useful tools in providing children with enjoyable, creative experiences for melodic and harmonic growth. Primary among keyboard instruments is the piano, whose keyboard includes 88 keys, ranging from a low A to a high C. The piano has been the most popular professional and domestic keyboard instrument in Europe, Asia, and the United States since the late eighteenth century. It was originally called both *forte-piano* and *pianoforte* because of its greater capability in producing dynamic variations of soft and loud tones than was possible on its predecessors, the harpsichord and the clavichord. The terms *piano* and *forte* are Italian for *soft* and *loud*.

The piano was invented around 1709 by Bartolommeo Cristofori (1655–1730), an Italian from Florence. Its form has progressed through a number of sizes and shapes, but the most common forms today are the studio upright (46 inches high), the console (40 inches high), the spinet (36 inches high), and the grand, normally ranging from the nine-foot-long concert grand to the five-foot, two-inch baby grand.

Posture

Students should be seated in front of the middle of the keyboard, usually where the manufacturer's label is located. Attention should be given to a person's posture: (a) the back should be straight but not rigid; (b) the arms should be straight from the elbow to the hand, as the hand rests on the keyboard; and (c) the fingers should be close to the keys and curved slightly.

Keyboard

Notice that the black keys on the keyboard are grouped in twos and threes. The white keys are named for the musical alphabet, from A to G. Middle C is located to the left of the group of two black keys, near the center of the keyboard. Play middle C; then find and play other Cs on the keyboard. Find and play the remaining keys of the musical alphabet in the following order: D, B, A, E, F, and G. Notice their placement in relation to the black keys. The black keys are also named for the alphabet letters from A to G; however, because they are a half step higher or lower than the white key bearing the same name, they have a sharp or a flat placed to the right of their name, such as C♯ or B♭.

Fingering

Numbers corresponding to the fingers on the hand are often placed above or below the notes on the staff, indicating which fingers to use when playing those notes. Number 1 designates the thumb on each hand; index fingers are marked 2; 3 refers to the middle fingers; 4, the ring fingers; and the little fingers are 5.

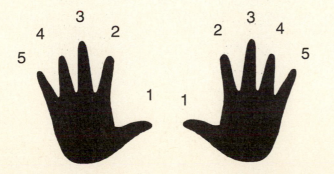

Playing Easy Melodies

The right hand usually plays notes written in the treble clef; the left hand plays bass-clef notes. Practice the following melodies with the right hand, until they become easy to play:

Repeat the melodic patterns above with the thumb placed on F (remember that the key of F has a B♭), and then on G. When finished, students will have played all the above melodies in the keys of C, F, and G. Experiment placing the thumb on some of the remaining keys of the musical alphabet, but be sure to play the sharps and flats needed for those keys. Reviewing Visual M50 may be helpful.

Now, practice these left-hand melodies:

Repeat these left-hand melodies with the fifth finger placed first on F and then on G. When students can play these melodies well in the keys of D, F, and G, let them experiment playing the melodies in some of the other keys.

Practice playing some of the songs in this book, first with the right hand, and then with the left. Some good beginning songs are:

Song	Chapter	Key
*Rocky Mountain	6	C
Hot Cross Buns	10	G
Good News	10	G
The Boatman	10	G
Grandma Grunts	10	G
How Many Miles to Babylon?	10	G
Oats, Peas, Beans	10	G
Cradle Hymn	10	G
*Poor Little Kitty Cat	10	G
Hop Old Squirrel	6	F
Marching	6	F
Lightly Row	6	F
Candles of Hanukkah	8	F
Merrily We Roll Along	10	D
Jim Along Josie	3	B♭
Skin and Bones	3	Em

*These songs extend slightly beyond the five-finger position. Students will need to decide on an appropriate fingering before practicing them.

Playing Chordal Accompaniments

Teachers can accompany the children's singing by playing the melody of the song with the right hand and appropriate chords with the left hand. Although there are a number of ways to play chord tones, the following are among the easiest:

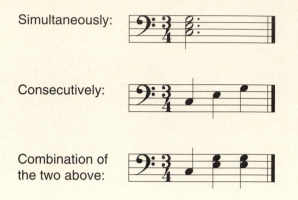

As discussed in Chapter 8, a chord can be built on any tone of the scale, but the most important are the primary chords, built on the first, fourth, and fifth scale tones. Use the left hand to practice the following chord progressions in the bass clef:

| I | IV | V⁷ | I | | I | IV | V⁷ | I | | I | IV | V⁷ | I |

I   IV   V⁷   I   I   IV   V⁷   I   I   IV   V⁷   I
C   F   G⁷   C   F   B♭   C⁷   F   G   C   D⁷   G

Now apply the the chords for the key of C, practiced above, to the playing of "Oranges and Lemons." Notice that appropriate chords (C and G⁷) are indicated on the musical score. Begin by playing the indicated chord on the first beat of each measure. Repeat the same chord in each measure until a new chord is designated.

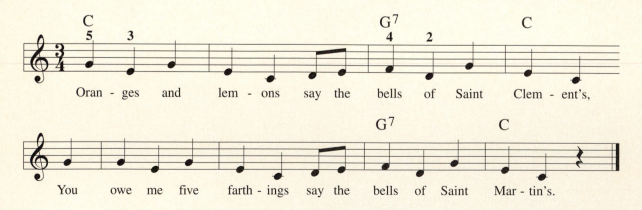

The preceding song, when placed on the grand staff with blocked chords notated, would be written in this manner:

Practice "Oranges and Lemons" until you can play it and sing the words simultaneously. Then practice some of the other songs in the list on page 258, using chords to accompany the melody.

Technology in the Classroom

Electronic keyboards and computers have become an integral part of most music classrooms across our nation. The combination of these two pieces of equipment, along with a sequencing program (which runs on the computer) and a sound module or tone generator (which is usually located within the keyboard), creates a musical system in which both children and adults can experience incredible music-making opportunities.

MIDI stands for Musical Instrument Digital Interface. It is a computer language that allows the computer, keyboard, sound module and sequencing program to communicate with one another. MIDI sequencing software can include a variety of tone colors and a collection of different sounds. This technology allows students to experiment freely with sound in a variety of ways. For example, if a student has a melody that is being played on a saxophone, a few simple mouse clicks will allow the student to hear the same melody played by a trumpet or violin.

Share the Music, a K–12 basil textbook series published by Macmillan McGraw-Hill, incorporates within its program a step-by-step process of how MIDI can be used to enhance musical learning and appreciation. (See the appendix for more information.)

Hearing combinations of chords in an accompaniment can be quite attractive to the ears of older students. Although it may appear to be difficult, it is really quite simple to provide these choral accompaniments. The song, "Martin Luther King" cries out for a more contemporary sound. As you look at the chords above the staff, you will find two that are different. They are C/E and B♭/G. The top letter tells us to play a chord, having that name in the treble clef, using the right hand. The bottom letter tells us to play just the note that bears that note name, in the bass clef, using the left hand.

MARTIN LUTHER KING

For my sixth graders at Taft Elementary School

Words and music by René Boyer Alexander

Verse

You gave your life to help free-dom ring. You

walked through-out this na-tion help-ing us to sing a-bout Ci - vil rights for both

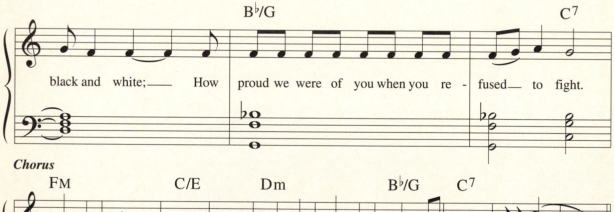

black and white; How proud we were of you when you re - fused to fight.

Chorus

Mar-tin Lu-ther King. Mar-tin Lu-ther King. ooh - ooh.

2. We won't forget how brave you were and how you died so young.
   We won't forget the life you led fighting freedom for everyone.

3. We call upon your wisdom. We call out your name so that
   we can sing about love and peace and the happiness that it brings.

4. Throughout our nation and abroad we'll do the best we can
   To walk together in peace and love, To help our fellow man.

WRITTEN AND PERFORMANCE-RELATED ASSESSMENTS THROUGH COOPERATIVE LEARNING ACTIVITIES: INSTRUMENTS

1. Assign to each group a different, known song. Each group's task is to write ostinati accompaniments for two to six rhythm instruments (depending on skill), similar to those that accompany the song "Mary Ann" in the text. The ostinati should be notated with specific instruments designated. Groups should practice singing their songs and playing the ostinati until they are ready to perform for the class.

2. Give a different song to each group. Groups should create melodic ostinati to accompany their songs. If possible, they should try to notate their ostinato patterns. Patterns should be practiced until groups can perform their songs for the class.

3. Have each group choose a song that it can play on the recorder. Create one rhythmic and one melodic ostinato to accompany the song. Groups members should decide on what instruments they will play the ostinati. Practice the song with recorders and ostinati until the group is ready to perform it for the class.

4. Give each group a song that has the chords marked. Group members should practice the song using guitar, autoharp, recorders, and/or barred instruments until they are ready to perform the melody with chordal accompaniment.

5. Assign to each group a song that does not have the chords marked. Group members should study their song and decide what chords they can use to accompany it. Chords should be tested on an autoharp, guitar, or piano. When the group is satisfied with its chord choices, it can practice singing the melody while playing the chords.

Listening to music is an integral part of everyone's life. No matter where we go we are exposed to music—in the car, at the supermarket, at a baseball game, in a restaurant, in the home, at church, and even while jogging. Listening occupies a large portion of our day; therefore, developing and refining listening skills are important activities in the elementary music program. Because of its importance, "Listening to, analyzing, and describing music" is listed as the sixth Content Standard proposed by National Standards for Arts Education.

In the music class children are continually involved in listening activities. They listen as they sing so that they produce a pleasant tone that is well pitched; they listen as they interpret music through creative movement; they listen while they improvise accompaniment patterns for a musical work. As children's listening skills develop, they progress from concentration on one or two simple concepts to the perception of a more complex musical structure.

GOALS FOR LISTENING ACTIVITIES

Well-designed listening experiences should provide the following outcomes:

1. help the child in developing an aural sensitivity to the works of many composers
2. assist the child in formulating specific music concepts
3. introduce the child to a variety of musical styles
4. acquaint the child with the music of many cultures, in addition to that of his or her own culture
5. help the child experience the satisfaction and joy that comes from actively listening to music

GUIDELINES FOR LISTENING

As teachers begin planning the listening lesson, it is helpful to keep the following guidelines in mind:

1. During listening activities, it is important for students to be listening for "something." To play a recording and ask the children simply to listen without any guidance usually invites boredom, inattention, and even discipline problems. If students are invited to listen for structural components that are already part of their conscious learning, the listening activity will prove to be a challenging learning tool rather than a frustrating activity.
2. The listening lesson is a portion of the daily music class and does not usually occupy the entire music period.
3. Musical selections used in listening activities should be short. It is not always necessary to play an entire composition; a short excerpt is often just as valuable.
4. It may be necessary to repeat a recording more than once during a lesson if the objectives for the listening activity are to be achieved.
5. If the teacher needs to guide students' attention through the listening process, then the visuals containing guides for listening should be at the front of the class.
6. When students become more independent in listening, individual call charts can be used. A *call chart* presents, in sequence, a visual representation of what is happening in the music. The sequence is usually numbered 1, 2, 3, and so forth.

The teacher calls out or points to each number or item as the musical event occurs. This limits verbal interruptions while the listening activity is taking place.

7. Printing and pictures used on visuals should be large enough to be seen by the entire class.
8. Visuals should be colorful so that they invite the students to look at them.

ORGANIZING LISTENING ACTIVITIES

Among the different kinds of call charts that can be used, three of the most popular types are: those using pictures, those using abstract representations, and those using the written word. Examples of these three types are presented here, along with strategies for their use.

Call Charts Using Pictures

Music: "Frightening" from *Scenes from Childhood Op. 15*, by Robert Schumann

Focus: Rondo Form (ABACABA)

Objective: By the end of the listening activity, students will be able to identify when the first section of "Frightening" reoccurs and when it is followed by a contrasting section.

The visuals presented below represent the form of this piece:

| Swan | Penguin | Swan | Seal | Swan | Penguin | Swan |

Have students listen to "Frightening" as the teacher posts each visual in the front of the room. Each visual should be displayed only when its corresponding section of music is heard. For example, the swan represents the A section of the rondo each time it occurs. Likewise, the B section of the rondo is represented by the penguin. The seal represents section C.

After all visuals have been posted, the teacher should discuss with the students what was happening in the music. Questions might include:

1. Did any part of our music happen over again?
2. Which parts repeated?
3. How could you tell?

After discussing the music, the teacher should be sure that students understand that some parts of the music are the same and some parts are different. This learning can be reinforced through movement. Play the music again and ask the children to improvise movement to each section of "Frightening." One group might move to the smooth, legato melody of section A by pretending to be swans. Another group would portray the short, brisk, stiff melodic line of section B much as a penguin might move. The playful, staccato melody of section C lends itself to the movements of a seal who is preparing to balance a ball on his nose and finally succeeds in doing it.

On another day, show students how sections that are the same can be given a letter name to represent them. Parts that are the same can be labeled with an "A"; contrasting sections are labeled with other letters in sequence, as needed. The form of "Frightening," then, would be ABACABA. This should be identified as rondo form.

Older students will find it a challenge to match the three themes found in "Frightening" with the music as it is heard. The themes presented below could be reproduced for each student to hold up as they occur in the music.

Theme A

Theme B

Theme C

An orchestral version of "Frightening" is available on the recording *The Small Listener*, part of The Small Musician Series published by Bowmar.

Music: "Baroque and Blue" from *Suite and Flute and Jazz Piano*, by Claude Bolling—opening measures only, ABAB
Focus: Baroque and blues styles
Objective: By the end of the listening activity, students will be able to identify simple differences between music in Baroque style and music in blues style.

Students should be asked to listen to an excerpt of "Baroque and Blue" while the teacher displays four visuals corresponding to the music: two visuals contain both a butterfly and a bird, and the other two visuals depict a "cool cat." The flute heard in the music is represented by the butterfly; the piano represents the bird; and the blues combo is characterized by the "cool cat."

A   B   A   B

Have students discuss what they heard in the four ABAB sections. Leading questions might include:

1. How many different parts to this music did you hear?
2. Which part did you prefer? Why?
3. How would you describe the part that you liked best?

After students have discussed the two intertwining melodies performed by the flute and the piano, the teacher should identify this style as Baroque. The blues style should be named after students have discussed the strong syncopated rhythm performed by the small combo of instruments.

Follow-up activities for a different day might include dividing the class into two groups. Have part of the first group move to the flute sounds while the other part moves to the sounds of the piano. The interaction of these two parts in group 1 represents the polyphonic texture of the Baroque period. Group 2 should be alley cats responding in a rhythmical manner to the syncopated rhythms of the blues style.

Music: Opening theme from *Also sprach Zarathustra* by Richard Strauss—theme used for the film *2001: A Space Odyssey*

Focus: Contrasts in timbre

Objective: By the end of the class students will be able to identify the changing timbres heard in the music: double bass, trumpet, timpani, trombone, organ, and full orchestra

Have students listen to the opening theme of *Also sprach Zarathustra*. Identify the instruments heard in the excerpt.

Distribute a copy of the call chart, shown here, to each student in the class. Replay the opening theme. Call the appropriate numbers on the chart as each instrument or full orchestra is heard on the recording.

Discussion how the contrasting timbres work together to produce the overall effect of the piece.

CALL CHART
Also sprach Zarathustra

1.

2.

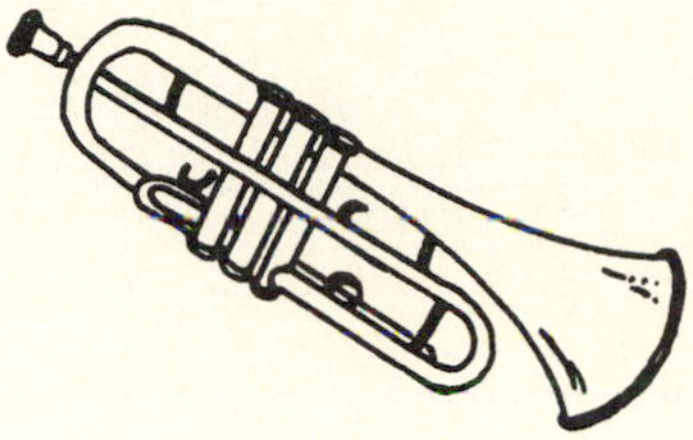

3. Orchestra

4.

5.

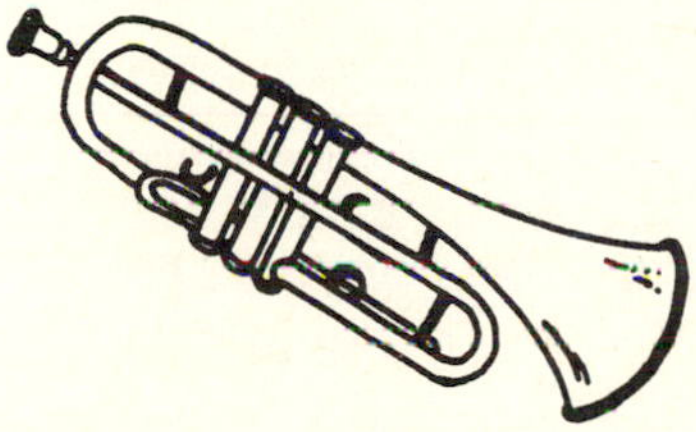

6. Orchestra

7.

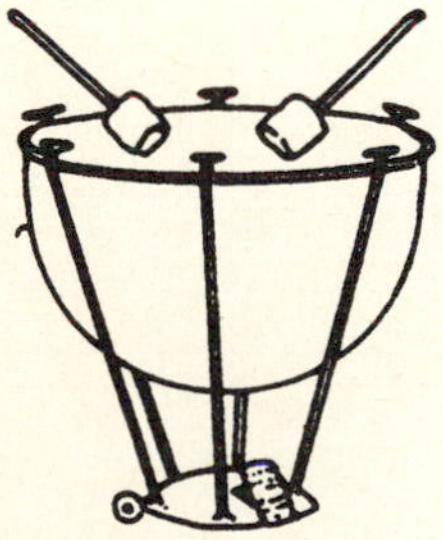

8.

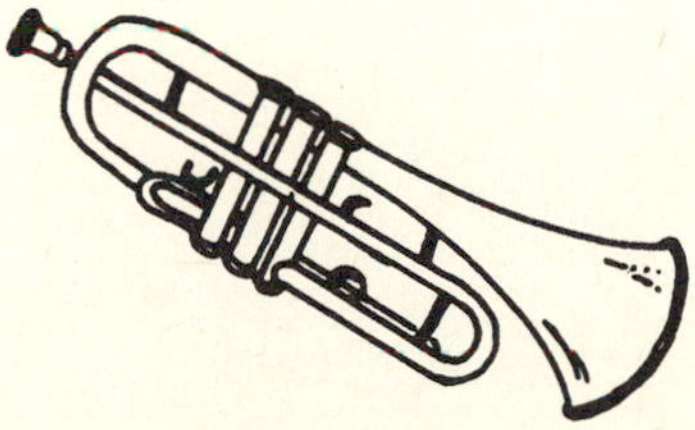

9. Orchestra

10.

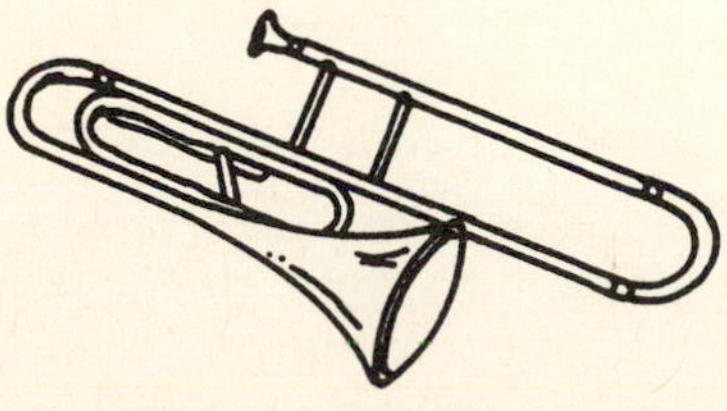

11. Orchestra

12.

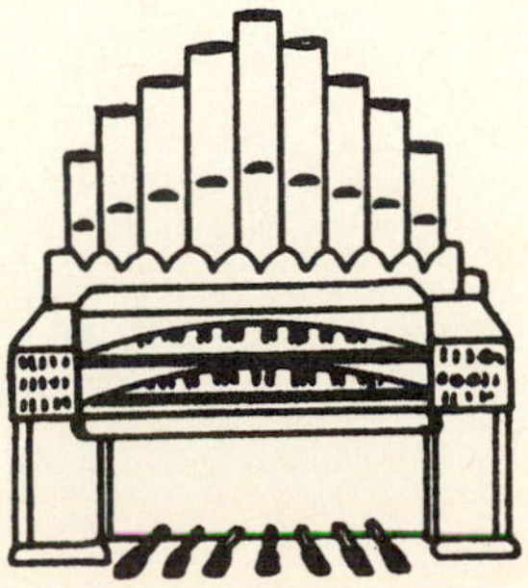

Call Charts Using Abstract Representations

Music: *Carmina Burana,* Part Five: "Ecce gratum," by Carl Orff
Focus: Staccato and legato articulation; repetition
Objectives: By the end of the listening activity students will be able to (a) recognize and move to staccato and legato passages in the excerpt and (b) respond through movement to the repetitions occurring in the music.

Because of the nature of the piece of music being heard, it is recommended that the aural experience and the visual experience occur simultaneously. The teacher should prepare abstract visuals, similar to those presented below, that correspond to the music being heard. The teacher should hold the charts in his or her lap so that proper sequencing takes place.

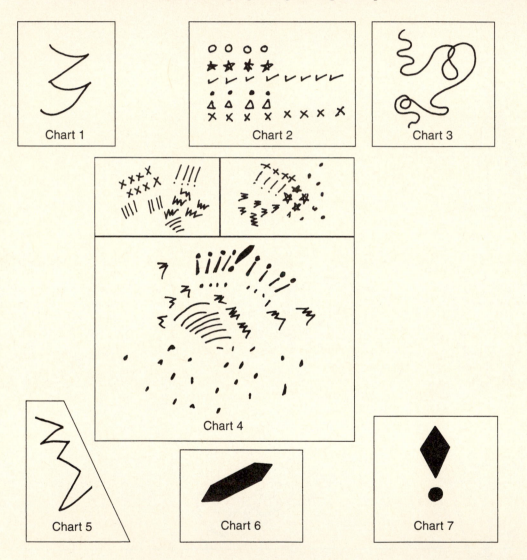

Play the excerpt of *Carmina Burana* while showing the charts in sequence. Help students to verbalize what they heard by asking questions such as:

1. What adjectives might you use to best describe what was heard?
2. Did you notice any repetitions?
3. How many times did the music repeat itself?
4. How might the body express what was heard in the music?

Divide the class into seven groups. Have each group represent one of the seven charts. Give each group time to decide how it will interpret the music represented by its abstract. Play the music while each group, in turn, recreates the music through bodily movement. Because the music is heard three times in succession, students should be instructed to "freeze" after they have performed their part until it is time for them to perform again.

As a culminating activity, review with the students the learnings that were being reinforced during their listening activity: staccato and legato articulation and repetition.

Music: *Poème Electronique* by Edgar Varèse
Focus: When a composer records natural sounds and then alters them electronically, the resulting music is known as *musique concrète*.
Objective: By the end of class, students will be able to identify the sound of bells and the human voice in the Varèse composition. Adjusting these sounds electronically will be recognized as a technique used in musique concrète.

Explain *musique concrète* to the class; that is, the recording of natural sounds altered electronically. Note that, in the Varèse composition, a musical instrument and the human voice occur at places marked with a question mark on the call chart. Ask students to listen to the recording while following the call chart. Play *Poème Electronique* and call the number for each frame as it appears. Discuss the use of the bell and the human voice in this composition. Replay the record as needed.

On another day, let students experiment with the taping of a variety of natural sounds; by adjusting these sounds on a reel-to-reel tape recorder, students can create their own musique concrète. Have students "notate" their composition using abstract representations.

CALL CHART
Poème Electronique

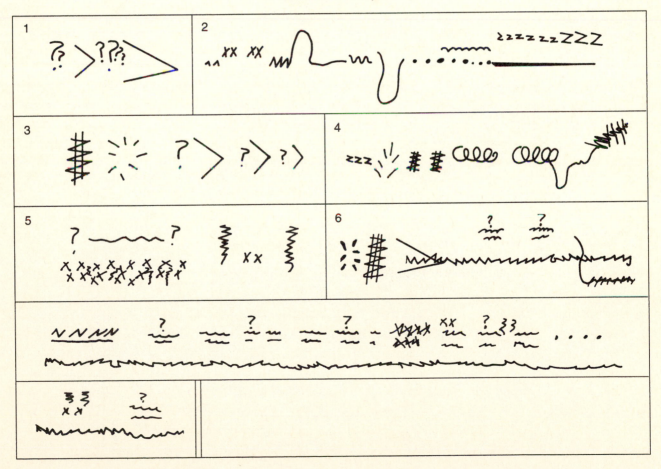

Music: "The Little Train of the Caipira," from *Bachianas Brasileiras No. 2* by Hector Villa-Lobos

Focus: crescendo and decrescendo; accelerando and ritardando

Objective: By the end of the listening activity, students will be able to recognize when music begins getting louder or softer, faster or slower.

Prepare a large call chart similar to the one below. This chart combines words with abstract representations. Play the recording and call out each number as it occurs in the music; point to the representations as they occur in the music. After the first hearing, have students express what was happening in each part of the music. The following questions may be helpful in eliciting from the students an analysis of this composition.

1. Did the music make you think about a train as you listened?
2. What did you hear in no. 1 that sounded like the train might be far away?
3. How did the composer imply in no. 2 that the train was moving along peacefully and steadily?
4. Similar questions can be asked through no. 8.

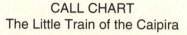

CALL CHART
The Little Train of the Caipira

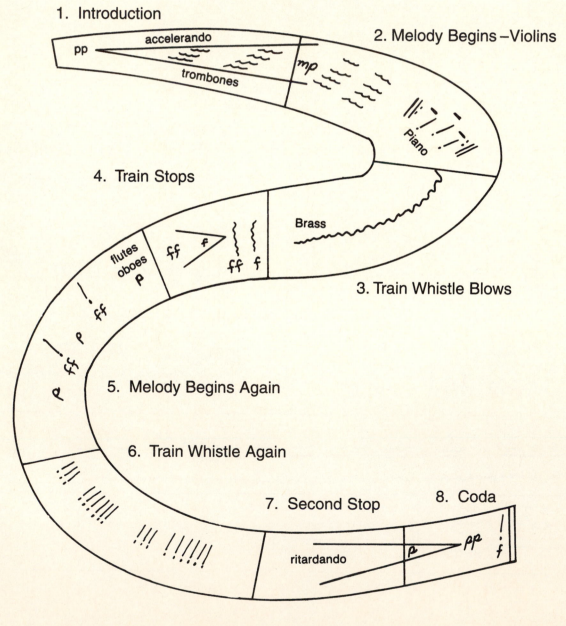

Replay the recording so that students have an opportunity to hear what they may have missed during the first hearing.

On another day, give wooden rhythm instruments to students and practice a simple sixteenth-note ostinato: ♩♬ . Play the recording while students perform the ostinato beginning slowly and softly. As the music progresses, let the students increase the tempo and dynamic level of their ostinato to match the changes in the score. Repeat several times until the students feel secure in performing the accelerando and crescendo at the beginning of the piece and the ritardando and decrescendo at the end of the piece.

Call Charts Using Words

Music: "In the Hall of the Mountain King," from *Peer Gynt Suite No. 1* by Edvard Grieg

Focus: In a musical composition, some elements may remain constant, providing unity through repetition; other elements often change, providing variety in the composition.

Objective: By the end of the listening activity, students will be aware of elements that repeat—theme—and those that change—tempo, timbre, dynamics, range—in the Grieg composition.

Discuss with the students the many ways in which a composer can create both unity and variety within a musical work. Demonstrate these principles through the use of a simple tune. Have students decide how to vary the tune to provide variety as the tune is performed over and over. For example, as the tune is repeated (unity), the class may choose to change its tempo, dynamics, range, key, or instrumentation (variety). Have the class perform its composition.

Give each student a copy of the handout provided on page 282 for "In the Hall of the Mountain King." Ask students to circle the correct responses as the composition progresses. Notice that, for this particular handout, it isn't necessary for the teacher to "call" any numbers. The students may need to hear the recording several times before completing the handout.

Discuss the responses on the handout. Have students verbalize how Grieg incorporated both unity and variety into his composition.

CALL CHART

In the Hall of the Mountain King

Directions: Circle the correct responses.

Introduction: yes   no

Melody/theme: keeps changing   always the same
one theme keeps returning after a different theme is played

Tempo: always fast   always slow   increasingly faster
usually fast with some slower parts

Timbre: progression from a few to many instruments
always full orchestra
different solo instruments keep alternating

Dynamics: increases from soft to loud
always soft   always loud

Melody/range of the theme: progresses from low to high
mostly low   mostly high

Coda: yes   no

Music: *Toccata for Percussion*, Mvt. 3, by Carlos Chávez
Focus: Every musical instrument has its own distinctive quality or color by which it can be identified. This quality of sound is called *timbre*.
Objective: By the end of the listening activity, students will be able to characterize, through the use of adjectives, the distinctive quality of each instrument heard on the Chávez recording.

Before music class, tape record the voices of several students. During music class, play the tape and ask students to identify each person speaking. Have students explain how they knew who was speaking on the tape by describing the "color" or "quality" of each voice heard. Identify the color or quality of a sound as *timbre*.

Review the four families of orchestral instruments: strings, brass, woodwinds, and percussion. Explain that each family has its own distinctive quality or color and that within each family, the individual instruments can also be distinguished one from another because each has its own distinctive quality or timbre.

Ask students to close their eyes. Compare instrumental timbres by playing a variety of percussion instruments—drum, claves, maracas, triangle—and asking students to identify each by the quality of its sound.

Give each student a call chart for *Toccata for Percussion*, shown on page 284. Play the recording and call each number as its contents occur in the music. Provide pictures of any unknown instruments heard on the recording. Elicit adjectives from the students that will characterize the quality of each instrument heard. Play the recording again.

On another day, students can study the overall form of the composition, comparing the beginning and ending (nos. 1–6 and 12–16) and describing the middle section.

CALL CHART

Toccata for Percussion, Mvt. 3

1. Timpani alone
2. Snare drum added to timpani
3. Tom-toms enter
4. Claves added
5. Claves and timpani together
6. Timpani alone
7. Snare drum added with tom-toms and chimes
8. Maracas lead, with timpani and snare drum; timpani drops out
9. Chimes, with maracas, timpani, and snare drum
10. Timpani leads, with tom-toms, snare drum, and claves
11. Timpani, with cymbals, tom-toms, and snare drum
12. Timpani alone
13. Snare drum added to timpani
14. Tom-toms enter
15. Claves added
16. Timpani alone to end

Music: "Danse Macabre" by Camille Saint-Saëns

Focus: Sometimes the composer will provide a story or "program" to use in interpreting his music. When this occurs, the composition is called *program music*.

Objective: By the end of the listening activity students will be able to follow the call chart and hear each event occurring in "Danse Macabre" as the composers portrays it in his "program."

Provide an explanation of program music as a creation of nineteenth-century composers. Prepare for the hearing of "Danse Macabre" by discussing the images associated with Halloween, such as skeletons dancing and tombstones in graveyards. Have students decide what instruments might be used to play themes associated with "death" and "skeletons dancing."

Distribute a copy of the "Danse Macabre" call chart shown on page 286 to each student. Play the themes and have students sing them on a neutral tone until they become familiar with them. Play the recording and ask students to follow each event as the teacher calls the numbers on the chart.

When the recording is finished, talk about what was heard in relation to the discussion preceding the use of the call chart. Were students' choices of instruments realized in the composition? Replay the recording and follow the call chart a second time.

On another day, ask students to listen to "Danse Macabre" without following the program. Discuss the possibility of the music being heard "for itself," apart from any program added to it.

Other examples of program music that can be incorporated into listening activities include:

Program Music	Composer
1. Sorcerer's Apprentice	Dukas
2. Till Eulenspiegel	Richard Strauss
3. Don Juan	Richard Strauss
4. Peter and the Wolf	Prokofiev
5. Billy the Kid	Copland
6. Peer Gynt suites	Grieg
7. An American in Paris	Gershwin
8. The Moldau	Smetana
9. Les Préludes	Liszt
10. Arlésienne suites	Bizet
11. Pelléas et Mélisande	Debussy
12. Symphonie Fantastique	Berlioz

CALL CHART

Danse Macabre

1. Harp begins the compositions by striking the "bewitching" hour of midnight.

2. Death tunes his fiddle.

3. Skeletons begin to dance.

4. Their dance theme is played first by the flute,

Theme 1:

5. Then by the violins.

6. Solo violin (DEATH!) plays a lyrical theme as more skeleton dancers join in the midnight revel.

Theme 2:

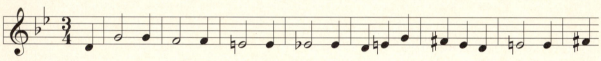

7. Dancing becomes wilder as these two themes are thrown about in the orchestra.

8. Building to a loud peak, the sound suddenly softens as the woodwinds and harp play the "Dies Irae," a Latin hymn for the dead. The rhythm of this hymn has been changed by the insertion of quarter rests and the shifting of the accent from where it originally occurred in the hymn.

Theme 3:

9. The third theme is played again by the trumpet and pizzicato violins.

10. A new setting of the second theme is played by solo violin and harp.

11. Rapid chromatic scale passages in the strings represent the wind blowing through the trees.

12. Different themes, including the three above, intertwine in an increasingly agitated manner, building to a climax that is suddenly interrupted by the crowing of the cock, heard in the oboe.

13. The revel comes to an end with the dawn of a new day.

14. Death plays his final notes, and the spirits evaporate into the atmosphere.

In addition to the use of call charts, teachers can involve students in other activities to enhance their listening skills. These activities include (a) charting a composition using abstract symbols, (b) dramatizing program music using shadow boxes, (c) identifying a composition's musical characteristics from choices listed on a check sheet, and (d) charting the rhythms in a song. Active involvement should characterize each activity.

Charting with Abstract Symbols

Music: "Ballet of the Unhatched Chicks" from *Pictures at an Exhibition* by Modeste Moussorgsky

Focus: Duration, musical line, tempo, and dynamics can be indicated using means other than standard notation.

Objective: By the end of the activity, each student will have charted a musical composition using abstract symbols.

Review the processes used to chart the Orff, Varèse, or Villa-Lobos compositions. Discuss different, abstract ways to represent musical line, duration, and increases or decreases in tempi and dynamics. Play "Ballet of the Unhatched Chicks" and have students listen for the form of the piece (Introduction AABA). Once the form is identified, give students the handout shown on page 288 on which to place their abstract representations. Except for the short introduction, every line on the chart represents eight measures in 2/4 meter.

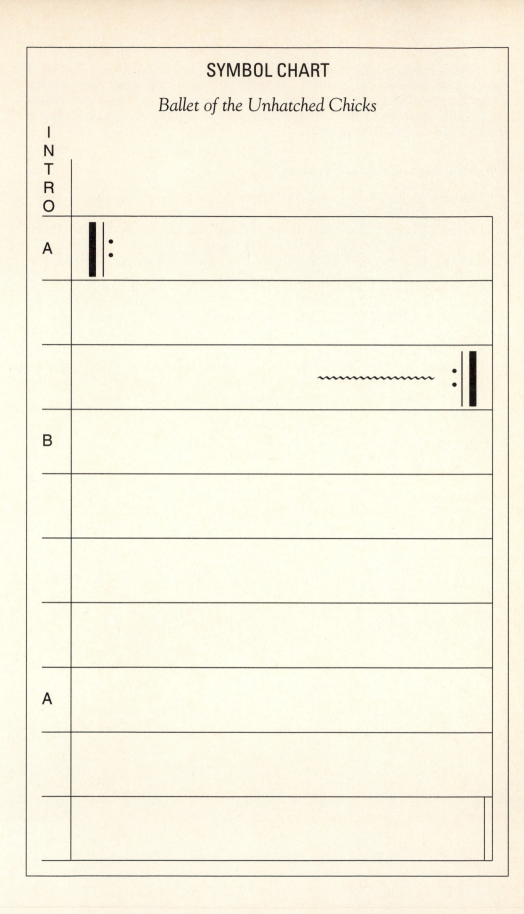

When students have finished charting the composition, they can review their charts with the teacher, choose the best one, or combine parts from different charts. The final choices of abstract representations should be drawn on a long piece of paper (brown packaging paper on rolls works well). The teacher can then attach the paper to the wall, at eye level for a small child, and use the chart with children in the lower grades. Kindergarten and first-grade children can watch the chart as they listen to the composition and simultaneously create movements to represent what is happening in the music.

Shadow Box Dramatizations

Music: *Peter and the Wolf* by Sergei Prokofiev
Focus: Different instruments playing designated melodies can represent a specific animal or person.
Objectives: By the end of the listening activity, students will be able to identify the sound of a flute, an oboe, a bass clarinet, a bassoon, a French horn, kettledrums, a bass drum, and strings within the context of program music.

Prepare students for their first listening of *Peter and the Wolf* by showing them a picture of each solo instrument in the music and identifying whom the instrument represents:

flute:	bird	French horn:	wolf
oboe:	duck	kettledrums:	hunters
bass clarinet:	cat	bass drum:	
bassoon:	grandfather	violins:	Peter

Give several students a puppet on a stick; these puppets represent each person and animal in the story. Play the recording, and as each character appears, have children hold up the appropriate puppet.

Make a simple shadow box; a taut bed sheet on a frame or fabric attached to a cardboard box works well. Place a light behind the sheet.

SHADOW BOXES AND PUPPETS
Peter and the Wolf

Scenery can be placed on the sheet if desired. Play the recording; as each character is heard, the child holding that puppet parades it behind the sheet.

Music: Maple Leaf Rag
Focus: Form of ragtime

Objectives:
1. By the end of this listening lesson, to have students able to identify the form of ragtime
2. To appreciate rag as an important musical form in American music history
3. To become acquainted with Scott Joplin

Procedure:
1. Tell the students that African Americans have contributed significantly to American music. One of the major styles of music that grew out of slavery was ragtime.
2. Explain to them that ragtime, or ragged time, is a style of music whose texture is created by continual syncopation against a regular beat. When played on the piano, the right hand typically does the ragged rhythm while the left hand does an oop-pah. Tell them that the form of ragtime can be clearly heard if they listen closely to the changing sections.
3. Tell the students that a Texas-born African American named Scott Joplin, who lived much of his life in Missouri, made ragtime famous. Famous rags such as "The Entertainer" have been included in soundtracks such as *The Sting* where Robert Newman and Robert Redford played major roles as con artists.
4. Let students know that the "Maple Leaf Rag" is one of the most famous of Scott Joplin's rags.
5. Have students listen to "Maple Leaf Rag" and, using pencil and paper, figure out its form.

   A A B B A C C D D

6. Share with the class.
7. Divide students into four sections. Assign each section a letter—A, B, C, or D. Have each section create a movement activity that can be performed when their section of music is heard.
8. Perform for the class.

Charting Rhythms

Music: "Over the River," a traditional folk song
"Who Will Buy," from *Oliver* by L. Bart
Focus: Rhythm can be broken down into a common unit (eighth notes) to reinforce each unit's relationship to the others.
Objective: By the end of the activity, students will improve their ability to notate the rhythm of songs containing quarter, eighth, dotted quarter, and sixteenth notes.

Some teachers have found it helpful to provide a grid for charting the rhythms of a given song. Each square in the grid represents an eighth note. After listening to the music, students place the rhythms of the song into the squares.

RHYTHM GRIDS

OVER THE RIVER

6/8 grid with rhythm notation (etc.)

WHO WILL BUY

3/4 grid with rhythm notation (etc.)

Music: Good Mornin', Blues by Huddie Ledbetter
Focus: The blues

Objectives:
1. To introduce the background of the blues
2. To introduce the significance of the lyrics in the blues
3. To introduce the harmonic progression of the 12-bar blues
4. To introduce the blues scale

Procedure:
1. Have the children realize that the blues is a style of African American music that developed after the Civil War
2. The words or lyrics of blues songs are often about sadness—poverty, lost love, or lonesomeness. However, they show hope and courage in the face of defeat and suffering.
3. Tell the students that the lyrics of the blues have a definite structure or form.
   A   My dog has not come home yet, I don't know what to **do.**
   A   My dog has not come home yet, I don't know what to **do.**
   B   It's beginning to get so dark, I'm goin' to find my **Blue.**
4. Have students create their own blues lyrics.
5. Blues songs began to be published and recorded in the early 1900s. Early blues are accompanied by guitar, piano, or a small instrumental combo.

6. The harmonic changes played by these instruments are predictable. Most blues pieces have a 12-bar harmonic structure that repeats again and again until the piece is over. After showing students the harmonic progression, have them listen to any blues piece to see if they can hear the harmonic changes.

I   I   I   I   IV   IV   I   I   V   V (or IV)   I   I

7. The blues style is more than just singing about hard times. The blues possesses a distinctive musical flavor that is created by singing or playing pitches that have been "bent." These are called blue notes. The lowered blue notes create the sound of the blues scale. This scale is somewhat like a major scale with two or three added notes. The lowered third, seventh, and sometimes fifth degrees of the scale are the most commonly used blue notes.

8. The blues influence has been extremely apparent in early rock and roll, jazz, and other popular music. Because the blues came out of each musician's own life, each blues performer has his or her own style. Some of the great blues musicians include Leadbelly (Ledbetter), Bessie Smith, W. C. Handy (knows as the Father of the Blues), Muddy Waters, Ma Rainey, Billie Holiday, and B. B. King.

9. Explain to the class that the piece that they will listen to today is one of the earliest of blues pieces performed by Huddie Ledbetter (1885–1949), or "Leadbelly." Tell them that the African American performer began singing and playing the guitar as a child. He played for dances and performed on the street. Later, he got into trouble and was sent to prison. While in prison, Leadbelly was able to share his music with two folklorists who had been commissioned by the Library of Congress to gether Southern folk song material. Leadbelly's cooperation in this project helped him obtain an early release from prison. In the 1930s and 40s he recorded hundreds of blues and other kinds of African American music, accompanying himself on the guitar.

10. Listen to Leadbelly sing, "Good Mornin', Blues." Listen for the harmonic progressions; the blues notes and the lyrics work together to form one of the most famous styles of music in the world.

GOOD MORNIN' BLUES

Arr.: René Boyer-Alexander

WRITTEN AND PERFORMANCE-RELATED ASSESSMENTS THROUGH COOPERATIVE LEARNING ACTIVITIES: LISTENING

1. Give students an opportunity to develop a call chart of their own. Have them bring to school what they consider a good piece of pop or rock music, with enough variety that it will lend itself to a call chart. After reviewing the possibilities, the teacher can choose one song for charting. Play the song so that the students become familiar with it. Have each group develop its own call chart, including items in specific categories, such as melody, rhythm, form, and dynamics.

2. Rather than having each student create an abstract symbol chart for a composition such as "Ballet of the Unhatched Chicks," let the members of groups work on the chart together.

3. Play a piece of program music, such as the *Sorcerer's Apprentice*, until students are familiar with it. Have each group work on a narrative for the music. The teacher can provide the puppets or students can make their own in art class. When narrations are completed and refined, assign each group to a particular grade; that is, Mrs. Brown's first grade, Mr. Sanchez's first grade, and so on. Each group performs their narration and puppet play for their assigned grade.

4. Give each group the words to a known song and a grid corresponding to that song. In an appointed amount of time, group members are responsible for placing the rhythms of their song into the squares on the grid.

5. Have students listen to other rags and analyze their forms.

6. Have students write and perform their own personal "blues."

7. Have students listen to other blues recordings. Encourage them to write about and share their reactions to how the individual is expressing himself or herself.

Movement and Children

To children, the use of movement can be one of the most natural vessels for musical expression. Children are born into this world as kinesthetic and tactile learners. They begin to discover their environment through touch and movement. While at play, they climb, hop, toss balls, chase one another, and take part in organized singing games that involve rhythmically complex hand clapping and movement of the entire body.

With carefully designed movement activities in the classroom, children can become more aware of how they can use their bodies to express a variety of musical concepts and feelings. In addition, they will find that their musical heritage includes a wide variety of music in which movement plays an integral part.

Emile Jaques Dalcroze (1865–1950), a Swiss music theory instructor, was a pioneer in using movement to attain musical goals. Dalcroze is credited with encouraging musicians and teachers to include movement as an integral part of the development of musicianship in students. His approach contributes to self-understanding by helping students become aware of and develop the expressive possibilities of their bodies. As part of his approach, a vast range of feeling is recognized and cultivated through the use of creatively designed movement activities.

Dalcroze realized that people interpret differently what they hear; as a result, the movements of each student express individual interpretations. In this chapter, a focus on internalizing the basic music concepts of rhythm, melody, harmony, dynamics, and form is brought to fruition through movement improvisation, singing games, and folk dance, using elements of Dalcroze's eurhythmics as a basic foundation.

PREPARING FOR MOVEMENT ACTIVITIES

The Movement Environment

Movement activities should take place in an area that is free of obstacles that might cause harm or inhibit children's freedom. If possible, desks and chairs should be pushed to the side or against the walls of the classroom so that an open space is available. A clean floor should be free of splinters or rough areas that might be damaging to children's feet, hands, arms, and other body parts. If available, a carpeted room should be used.

Dressing for Movement

Because of the many and varied experiences that children encounter during the school day, some administrators and classroom teachers recommend that children dress casually, in loose-fitting sweat suits or jeans and tennis shoes. This style of dress works well when doing movement activities. Teachers may want to inform parents ahead of time that their children will be engaging in movement activities on a regular basis.

Individual Spaces

Each child should be assigned a personal space for movement activities. Classroom rules must be established and enforced by the teacher to avoid bumping, hitting, or other bodily contact which could cause problems.

BEGINNING MOVEMENT ACTIVITIES

Initial experiences in movement should be approached in a relaxed and spontaneous manner. Children should be encouraged and guided by a creative and uninhibited teacher. It is important that the teacher clearly establish defined goals and objectives, such as those listed below, so that some direction and continuity will take place in the movement program. Through movement children can:

1. develop and stimulate their imagination and creative gifts
2. discover and understand musical learnings involving melody, rhythm, form, harmony, texture, tempo, and dynamics
3. realize that different styles of music call forth different physical responses
4. realize a common vocabulary that can be transferred from one style of dance to another, regardless of the culture or time period from which the dance originated
5. demonstrate an understanding of improvisation as a major musical tool for expressive response
6. create interpretive accompaniments for listening activities
7. discover how the various parts of the body can be used to create images, feelings, and moods
8. strengthen coordination of gross and fine motor skills
9. come to a greater understanding and awareness of balance, spatial relationships, and their own self-image

Children, at different age levels and in different environments, perceive environmental phenomena in different ways. When beginning movement activities, teachers should take into consideration the environment as reflected through the eyes, the sensitivities, the perceptions, and the understandings of the children involved. For example, younger children will truly imagine they are in a bakery as they say and move their fingers to "Five Brown Buns."

FIVE BROWN BUNS

Chant: (♩ ♪♪, jazzy feeling)

Five Brown Buns in a Bakery Shop	(Hold up 5 fingers)
Five Brown Buns with Sugar on the Top	(With other hand "shake" sugar onto buns.)
Along Came a Man with a Penny in His Hand,	(Pointer finger comes from behind back, looks at "buns.")
Took One Bun and Away he Ran.	(Pointer finger "runs" back to back)
Four Brown Buns	repeat same actions
Three Brown Buns	" " "
Two Brown Buns	
One Brown Bun	
***With real emotion and crying!	
No Brown Buns	

Note: Say the last verse slowly as you boo-hoo; then, when it says "And away he ran," speed up.

Children continue to be intrigued with the movement of animals, of clouds, of trees blowing in the breeze. They show interest in the flying of birds and the hopping of grasshoppers and rabbits. In developing creative movement activities for their class, teachers should begin with these interests so that their students' initial movement experiences are natural and enjoyable. The following list provides simple, beginning images that children can easily relate to and, with guidance, transfer to movement.

Images of Childhood

snowflakes falling gently from the sky
a bird flying through the sky
a child skating on ice
a soldier marching
leaves falling from a tree
wind blowing
horses galloping
frogs hopping
turning a rope
a train engine tooting along the track
throwing a ball
walking like an elephant
rocking a baby
jumping over a puddle of water
a flower growing
swinging
batting a ball
blowing up a balloon
stirring food
chopping wood
walking on hot coals
directing a symphony
taking a shower
digging a hole
saying good-bye and hello
sawing wood
hammering nails
knocking on a door

After students have demonstrated their abilities to comfortably reflect on and reenact some of the above childhood images, the teacher can have them string responses of images together into patterns to create stories that are communicated through movement. "The Circus" provides an example of how images can be joined to tell a story. These images are italicized to highlight places where creative movement might occur.

The Circus

The children were *sound asleep*. One by one *they awoke*. They *stretched their arms and their legs* in preparation for a very active school day. As they *dressed themselves*, making sure to *wash their face, brush their teeth, and comb their hair*, they *shook in excitement*, because this was the day they were to go on a field trip to the circus. After *quickly eating a big bowl of cereal* with bananas and *drinking a glass of cold milk*, they *slipped off to school*. The stairs that led to the second floor classroom *were climbed with ease* this morning; promptness in getting to class was essential.

As the children *sat in their seats*, the teacher called each of their names. This was a signal for them *to line up at the door. Down the two flights of stairs* they went and *onto a big yellow school bus* which waited to take them to the circus. Soon the bus was on its way. How bumpy the road was! It *shook the children forward*. It *shook them backwards*. It *shook them up*, and it *shook them back down again*. Finally, they arrived at the circus.

Excitement was everywhere as the *ringmaster appeared on a podium* to announce the day's events. *Roller skaters* from the Land of Derby led the list of events. They were followed by the *leap frogs* from the Land of the Toads. An *elephant* from the jungle *stepped slowly* on stage as a group of mice from the Land of Cheese *scampered nervously* through the crowds. *How exciting* it all was! When the last event was finished, the children knew it was time to leave. What a wonderful day it had been.

Children should be asked to form images or pretend to be only those things that they have experienced previously. Because of limited knowledge or exposure, it is difficult for many students to mimic successfully the movement of some animals or images. Consequently, the teacher should include live presentations, discussions, pictures, or creative descriptions of unfamiliar images that will be recreated through movement. For example, before a teacher directs a group of students to move like unfamiliar zoo animals, it would be advisable for students to visit a zoo and observe the movements of these selected animals. The field experience should be followed by an in-class discussion of what was seen, such as:

1. Name an animal that you observed at the zoo.
2. Describe the animal. What color was it?
3. Was it large or small?
4. Was the animal heavy or light in weight?
5. Did the animal have four legs, two legs, wings?
6. Did the animal move fast or slowly?
7. Can you move like the animal moved?

In brief, the teacher should present to children a logical sequence of questions and experiences that will help them become comfortable with the task of creating through movement. After children have had ample opportunities to imitate the movements of phenomena contained within a familiar environment, the teacher can begin to help children understand basic musical elements through movement activities. Skills and vocabulary unique to the area of movement can also be developed.

CATEGORIES OF MOVEMENT

Many different movements can easily be observed by simply watching children at play. Walking, jumping, running, walking on tiptoe, hopping, galloping, bending, sliding, twirling, creeping, and crawling are examples of movements that children engage in while at play. All of these movements can be put into one of two categories: locomotor movements and nonlocomotor movements.

Locomotor Movements

Locomotor movements occur when children move from one place to another. Examples of locomotor movements include walking, jumping, running, jogging, hopping, and leaping. The following list provides the name and description of some of the most commonly used locomotor movements:

Walking	Walking is the most familiar of all fundamental movements. A walking action occurs when an individual steps forward, backward, or sideways, keeping one foot on the floor at all times. An alternation of the left foot, then the right foot, results in walking.
Running	Springing steps involving the alternations of both feet, moving at a much faster tempo than occurs when walking
Jumping	A spring from the ground, both feet landing together
Hopping	A spring from the ground on only one foot
Leaping	A running forward thrust of the body upward into the air, one leg far forward, the other extending backward

Galloping and skipping are examples of combinations of two locomotor movements. Galloping, for example, combines the movements of walking and leaping. Skipping is based on a combination of walking and hopping.

Nonlocomotor Movements

Nonlocomotor movements include movements performed from a stationary position of the body. Twisting, bending, stretching, and curling are examples. Descriptions of common nonlocomotor movements are provided here:

Bending	Flexing the torso
Rocking	Transferring the body weight from one side to the other
Stretching	Reaching or extending the limbs of the body to the furthest extent possible
Swinging	Moving a part of the body in an arc or circle, from a fixed position
Turning	Rotating the entire body on its axis
Twisting	Rotating the torso from side to side

Students should be guided by the teacher to explore both locomotor and nonlocomotor movements. Activities such as the "apple orchard experience" can be used to reinforce children's knowledge of these categories. Have children pretend they are in an apple orchard. They should be directed to:

1. reach as high as possible to pick an apple from the tree
2. bend over to pick up several apples that have fallen to the ground
3. twist their body around to pick up apples that have fallen on the ground around them
4. turn around and toss an apple to a friend
5. walk, run, or skip back home

"How Do You Do Everybody" is a song containing both locomotor and nonlocomotor movements. Have students form a circle and sing "How Do You Do Everybody." Invite them to suggest different locomotor and nonlocomotor movements as they sing and move to this singing game.

HOW DO YOU DO EVERYBODY

Words and music by René Boyer-Alexander

How do you do ev'-ry bo-dy, how do you do, do, do? How do you do ev'-ry bo-dy, how do you do, do, do? I know you and you know me. Clap three times and we'll walk mer-ri-ly. *Walk, walk, walk, a-round the room we go. Walk, walk, walk, a-round the room we go. Walk, walk, walk, a-round the room we go. Rea-dy now, with our hands let's say hel-lo.

*Have students suggest other ways they might move around the room (e.g., skipping, jogging, crawling, marching).

MOVEMENT AND SPACE

Space surrounds the body on all sides. Every movement in which a child engages takes place in that space. Opportunities to explore and experience the surrounding space help children grow in perceptual understanding and self-awareness. Children should participate in movement activities that require them to (a) place themselves in specific locations, (b) become familiar with the size and availability of the space around them, and (c) understand the possibilities for moving in that space. Several options are available when determining the directions in which children may move in space. They may move forward, backward, up or down, side to side, and diagonally. They may turn, move inward or outward, or move over or under. An activity that reinforces movement in different directions might involve the following:

Have students walk to the steady beat of the drum. During the activity, the teacher could scratch or rub the drum to signal to the children that they are to change direction. If students were walking forward, a change in sound produced by scratching the rim of the drum would be a signal for them to walk backwards or sideways. Thus, listening and following directions become an integral part of the movement activity.

In addition to choosing a variety of directions, children should also choose body levels. There are three basic levels to explore: high, medium, and low. Guide students through the Melodic Direction Exercise as a beginning activity for understanding direction of their own body parts.

MELODIC DIRECTION EXERCISE

↑	8	Where my hair grows	8	On my head is
	7	On my head	7	Freddie Flea
	6	Pass my nose	6	Now he's climbing
	5	Pass my tummy	5	Down on me
	4	Up on me	4	Pass my tummy
	3	Now he's climbing	3	Pass my knee
	2	Freddie Flea	2	On the ground
	1	On the ground is	↓ 1	"Take that you flea!"

Other activities that will reinforce a student's awareness of body levels include having the children bend their knees completely, causing the entire body to lower itself. This is an example of a low body activity.

Crawling is also a good low-level activity. Moving while lying flat on the floor is, of course, the lowest level possible. A middle level activity can be achieved by moving in a relatively upright position with the arms no higher than shoulder level. A high level activity involves the extension of the limbs as far as they can reach into the space above the mover. Standing on tiptoe and pretending to reach for the stars is an example of a higher level activity. The game "statues" can be used to reinforce awareness of body levels. The teacher directs the children to walk, run, skip, or gallop to a rhyme or song they are chanting or singing. Recordings can also be used to accompany the movement activity. When a signal is given, or when the music stops, the children should "freeze" in place.* Children should be encouraged to vary the levels at which they freeze. The rhyme can be chanted while children are playing the statue game:

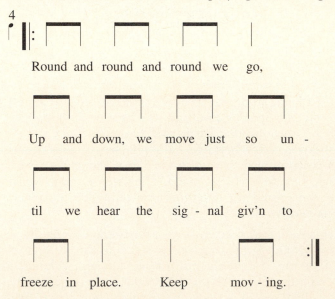

*The freeze signal can be given at any time during the chanting of the rhyme.

Once children have explored the major movement directions and the levels that might accompany those directions, the teacher should direct them in the different ways they can travel from one point to another using straight or curved pathways. Examples of these pathways are represented in the diagram.

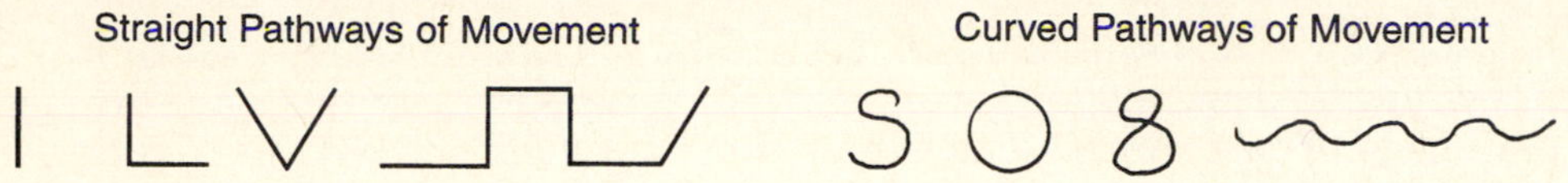

Straight Pathways of Movement   **Curved Pathways of Movement**

| ⌐ V ⎍ ⎍ /   S ◯ 8 〰〰〰

Straight lines and angles become two of the most obvious movement possibilities when following straight paths. When following curved paths, the use of semi-circles, full circles, and other twisted configurations can assist in the development of creative designs or patterns that ultimately become a larger form or whole. Ask children to form groups and create different designs or shapes, such as those suggested here.

Straight Lines	*Curved Lines*	*Combinations*
square	#8	ice cream cone
rectangle	flower top	#2
triangle	#6	#5
#7	#3	pie
#1	rainbow	umbrella
#4	mushroom cap	

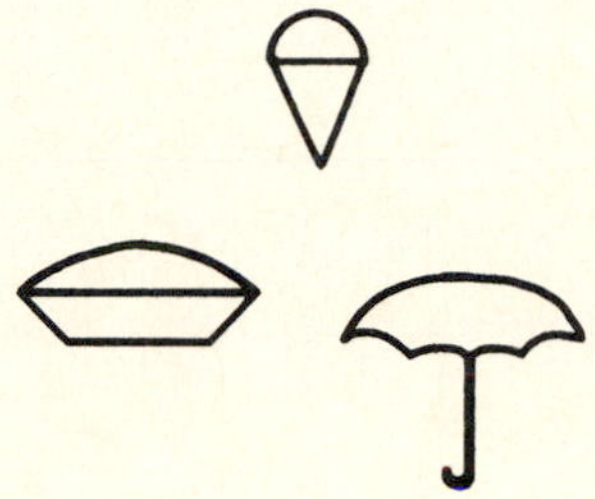

MOVEMENT AND IMPROVISATION

Children should be challenged to create movements that are void of metered pulse. This type of natural improvisation is recommended for initial experiences in movement. The poem "Joey" provides an opportunity for students to improvise through movement. Students should be assigned to different groups that represent Joey, the sun, the corn, the cock, and the wind. Each group should demonstrate, through movement, the story of Joey. After students are comfortable with the sequence of movements, rhythm instruments or other sound effects can be added to enhance the overall effect of the dramatization.

JOEY

By Shel Silverstein

Joey Joey took a stone
And knocked
Down
The Sun!
And whoosh! it swizzled
Down so hard,
And bloomp! it bounced
In his backyard.
And glunk! it landed
On his toe!
And the world was dark,
And the corn wouldn't grow,
And the wind wouldn't brow,
And the cock wouldn't crow,
And it always was Night,
Night,
Night.
All because
Of a stone
And Joe.

MOVEMENT AND DYNAMICS

Many different levels of intensity are involved in every movement. Levels of intensity depend on three major factors: weight, muscular tension, and the inner intensity of movement. Combinations of these three factors can result in the expression of a wide spectrum of dynamic levels. Soft, hard, delicate, strong, light, heavy, angry, silent, and loud are a few examples of adjectives that can, with the use of appropriate weight, muscular tension, and inner intensity, be communicated through movement. Children should be given opportunities to develop a body sensitive to dynamic changes. To accomplish this, ask children to demonstrate, through movement, their responses to such questions as:

1. If you were a feather floating down from the sky, how would you move?
2. If you were an angry giant, how would you react?
3. Can you shout without making a sound?
4. Can you be a dancer on top of a music box?
5. How can you show the silence before a storm?

Provide students with many creative stories that they can act out through silent movement. Direct them to pay special attention to the dynamics of the movements as they reflect the actions in the story. "The Bad, Old Troll" could serve as a useful example.

The Bad, Old Troll

Once upon a time, in the forest, there lived a bad, old troll, who walked back and forth, back and forth, looking very mean and angry. Suddenly, he stopped in his tracks and listened carefully to a sound he had heard in the woods. He listened for a few moments and was finally satisfied that it was a deer, hunting for food in a nearby area. He yawned, stretched out his arms, and decided it was time for his afternoon nap. He lay down near the entrance of his cave and fell asleep. Meanwhile, several children arose from behind some bushes. They peeked around every side and then quietly tiptoed toward the sleeping troll. Carefully and slowly they walked around him looking at his nose and pointing to his ugly toes. The troll continued to sleep soundly. Playfully, one of the older boys decided to jump over the troll. He jumped once. He jumped twice and then three times. The younger children were in great fear that the troll would be awakened. The older boy turned to the other children and dared them to jump over the troll's legs. The last child accidentally tripped, and this awakened the troll. The children screamed and ran in different directions. The troll ran after them, but, being old, he couldn't catch them.

CIRCLE GAMES

Children's movement experiences should include circle games, which add variety to the movement program at the elementary level. In fact, during the primary years, the circle game serves not only as a setting in which children can express themselves, but also reinforces the development of specific learnings and helps them acquire self-management skills. Circle games, and their counterpart, folk dance, also help students fulfill the ninth Content Standard, "Understanding music in relation to history and culture." Clearly, the introduction of folk dance allows students the opportunity to explore, in a non-threatening way, diversity in musical lifestyles that exist throughout our global society. The following examples are representative of only a few of the many circle games commonly used at the primary level.

Looby Loo

For the song "Looby Loo," act out movements as specified by the words in the text of the song. During the chorus, the children skip around the circle hand in hand.

American Folk Song

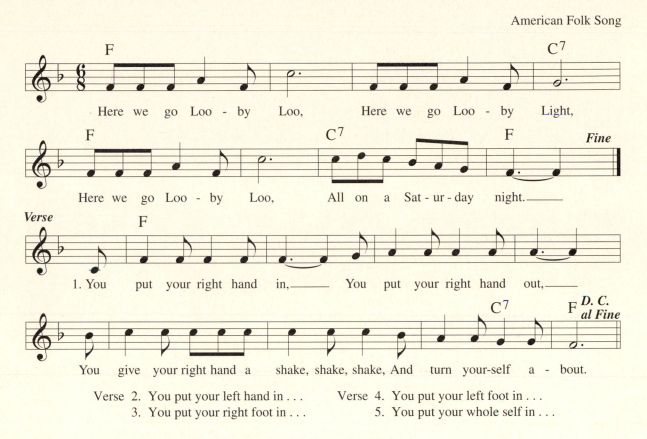

Here we go Loo - by Loo, Here we go Loo - by Light,
Here we go Loo - by Loo, All on a Sat - ur - day night.

Verse
1. You put your right hand in,____ You put your right hand out,____
You give your right hand a shake, shake, shake, And turn your-self a - bout.

Verse 2. You put your left hand in . . .
3. You put your right foot in . . .

Verse 4. You put your left foot in . . .
5. You put your whole self in . . .

Mulberry Bush

Children move hand in hand around the circle while singing the chorus of "Mulberry Bush." During each verse, children must stop and demonstrate, through pantomime, the chores designated.

English Game Song

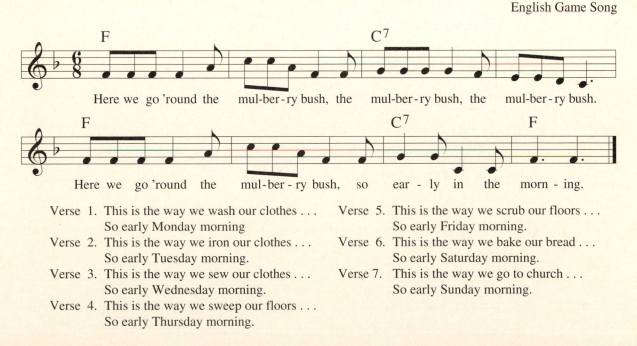

Here we go 'round the mul-ber-ry bush, the mul-ber-ry bush, the mul-ber-ry bush.
Here we go 'round the mul-ber-ry bush, so ear-ly in the morn-ing.

Verse 1. This is the way we wash our clothes . . .
So early Monday morning

Verse 2. This is the way we iron our clothes . . .
So early Tuesday morning.

Verse 3. This is the way we sew our clothes . . .
So early Wednesday morning.

Verse 4. This is the way we sweep our floors . . .
So early Thursday morning.

Verse 5. This is the way we scrub our floors . . .
So early Friday morning.

Verse 6. This is the way we bake our bread . . .
So early Saturday morning.

Verse 7. This is the way we go to church . . .
So early Sunday morning.

Circle 'Round the Zero

During the game "Circle 'Round the Zero," children stand still in a circle while one child walks or skips around the outside of the circle, stopping back to back behind a second child at the words, "Find your lovin' zero." Beginning with the words, "Back, Back, Zero," the two children bump backs and then turn sideways and bump hips. Next, they face one another and pat hands together on the words, "Front, Front, Zero." Finally, they tap each other's shoulders. The second child now proceeds to seek out a new partner and the game continues.

American Street Song

Cir-cle 'round the ze-ro, Find your lov-in' ze-ro, Back, back, ze-ro,

Side, side, ze-ro, Front, front, ze-ro, Tap your lov-in' ze-ro.

Circle games can also be used with older children. Stone-passing games such as "Al Citron" are common among music of many nationalities. "Draw Me a Bucket of Water" has a number of variations; the version used here was collected by Bessie Smith Jones.

Al Citron

All children are seated in a circle on the floor. Each child has a rock or some other object (sponge, shoe, block) to pass to the person on the right.

Latin American Stone-Passing Game

Al - ci - tron de un fan - dan - go, san - go,

san - go, sa - ba - ré. Sa - ba - ré de la ron -

de - la con su tri - ki, tri - ki trón.

Note: Most of the words are nonsense Spanish words.

Movement
1. All sing the song "Al Citron."
2. Repeat the song and pat lap to the steady beat.
3. First, practice the movement without the rock. Beginning in front of your own body, pretend you are picking up a rock and passing it to the person on your right. I all goes well, there should be another rock in front of you, passed there by the person on your left. Pick up the rock and pass it to your right. Rocks should be picked up on the last beat and passed on the first beat of each measure.

4. When the children are successfully picking up and passing the rocks together on each beat, they can repeat the movements using a real rock.

5. On the measure with "triki, triki, trón," the movements change. The rock is tapped to the right but not released; then it is tapped to the left and back to the right where it is released on "trón":

triki   triki   trón
right   left   right and release

6. To heighten the enjoyment, the song can be sung faster and faster for each repetition.

Draw Me a Bucket of Water

Begin by having children stand in groups of four in a square, each holding hands with their opposite partner. Players 1 and 2 (opposite partners) should hold hands under those of players 3 and 4.

African American Play-Party Game

Arr.: René Boyer Alexander

Movement

1. Phrases 1 through 3: with hands joined, partners "pull the rope" back and forth, like a seesaw, to the beat.
2. Phrase 4: On the words "You go under sister Sally," child no. 1 goes under the arms of players nos. 3 and 4, toward the center of the circle. (Be sure that the children do not let go of hands during this activity.) Repeat three more times until children nos. 2, 3, and 4 are also in the center, all hands still joined.
3. Phrase 5 to the end: Children, as a group, jump up and down on the beat, still holding hands. For further joy and excitement, children can spin clockwise during the singing of these phrases.

FOLK DANCES

Folk dances present special challenges for students in upper elementary grades. As children acquire more physical dexterity and intellectual ability, they are able to perform basic traditional dance steps present in much folk dance in the United States and elsewhere. During their upper elementary years, most children are able to understand the basic elements of movement, realize basic movement vocabulary, and physically implement sequences of well-designed movement patterns. Their skills in coordination, timing, sequencing of movements, and implementing the basic elements of music should be at a level that allows them to participate comfortably in folk dance.

Folk dance involves well-designed sequences of stepping movements. Therefore, before children can begin applying their previously learned skills in movement, they must become acquainted with steps and terminology characteristic of the specific dances they are to experience. For example, among the major types of dances associated with North American folk music are circle, line, and square dances. *Circle dances* can involve dancers in one large circle or in two concentric circles. The *line dance* usually consists of any number of couples who come together in two facing lines, while the *square dance* involves four couples. All three dances often involve a caller who "calls out" the steps and actions that the dancers are to use. To begin a dance, performers are usually in a predetermined position, known as *set formation*. Diagram I represents a typical set formation required for the square dance. Diagram II shows the set formation for line dances.

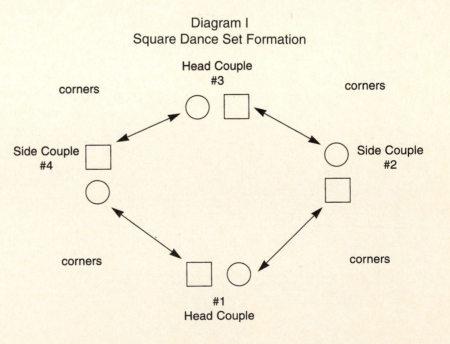

Diagram I
Square Dance Set Formation

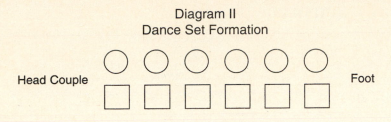

Diagram II
Dance Set Formation

Head Couple   Foot

Traditionally, partners in square dances consist of two individuals of opposite sex. However, in the elementary classroom, it is not necessary to pair boys with girls. Teachers can choose, instead, to have students count off in two's and then assign partners on a number basis. Tags of different colors or shapes could be assigned for students to wear to help in the identification of partners.

When introducing folk dance, the teacher should serve as the model. It is the teacher who must describe and demonstrate the designed steps. Although it is essential that the rote process take place in slow motion and be repeated to ensure success for the students, the teacher should be careful not to cause the learner to lose a sense of the "whole."

"Old Brass Wagon" and "Shake Them 'Simmons Down" are examples of circle dances that clearly suggest, through their texts, directions for dancers to follow. These dances, which are suitable for use in the second, third, and fourth grades, help provide a transition to the more complex dances performed by children in upper grades. If the children are expected to dance to a song that they have learned in class, it is essential that they know the song well before learning the dance steps.

OLD BRASS WAGON

American Dance Song

1. Cir-cle to the left, Old brass wag-on, Cir-cle to the left, Old brass wag-on,
Cir-cle to the left, Old brass wag-on, You're the one, my dar-ling.

2. Circle to the right . . .
3. Ev'rybody in . . .
4. Ev'rybody out . . .

SHAKE THEM 'SIMMONS DOWN

Southern Play-Party Song

1. Cir - cle left, do - oh, do - oh, Cir - cle left, do - oh, do - oh,
Cir - cle left, do - oh, do - oh, Shake them 'sim-mons down.

2. Circle right . . .
3. Boys to center . . .
4. Girls to center . . .
End of each verse: "Shake them 'simmons down!" by raising arms and shaking hands vigorously from high to low.

ACHSHAV

Hebrew Folk Dance

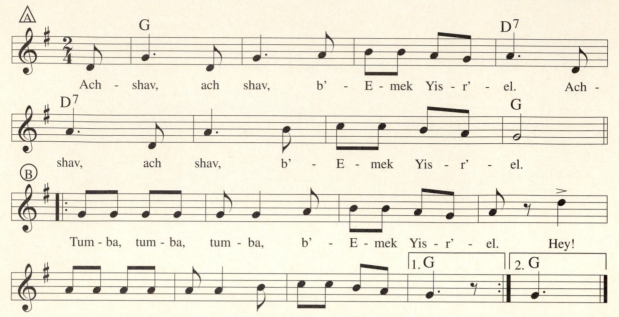

Ach - shav, ach shav, b' - E - mek Yis - r' - el. Ach -

shav, ach shav, b' - E - mek Yis - r' - el.

Tum - ba, tum - ba, tum - ba, b' - E - mek Yis - r' - el. Hey!

Movement instructions

Formation; circle (large enough for children to take eight steps to the center)

A section: Hold hands. With weight on the right foot, place the heel of the left foot forward. Hop, changing weight to left foot, with right foot forward. Do this hop-change movement in the following rhythm:

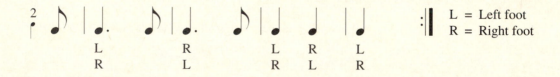

L = Left foot
R = Right foot

B section: Take eight small steps toward the center of the circle, lifting arms for an enthusiastic "Hey!" Lower arms and return to the circle formation by taking eight steps backward. (Repeat the B section.)

Note: This piece is also included in the Recorder section of this book.

The true spirit of moving together can be found in the following folk dance, "Round and Round We Go." Have students form two to three different circles and sing and move to this song. Start the circles at different times in alternate directions to demonstrate how a round can be shown through movement.

ROUND AND ROUND WE GO

Überliedfest

Round and round we go, we hold each oth - er's hands, and

weave our lives in a cir - cle, The day has come, the dance has be - gun.

The following version of "Bingo" is one of North America's favorite folk dances. The text of this dance does not suggest the movements to be used; these movements are outlined below. Have students select partners and form a double circle, facing counterclockwise. Partners should stand side by side and arm in arm, girls on the right.

Formation for BINGO

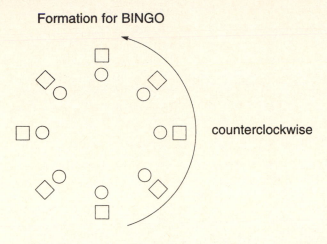

counterclockwise

Part I: All dancers should walk counterclockwise around the circle, singing measures 1–8.

Part II: All join hands to form one large circle, girls on partner's right and still walking counterclockwise, singing measures 9–16.

Part III: Partners face each other and clasp right hands, calling out "B." Partners pass on to a new person with a left-hand hold, calling out "I."

Continue around the circle to a third person for a right-hand hold and shout "N."

On to the fourth person with a left-hand hold, shouting "G."

With a right-hand hold, continue to the fifth person, who becomes the new partner. Shout "O."

Continue the dance from the beginning with new partners, each time moving forward until original couples are again together.

BINGO

East St. Louis Version
Collected by René Boyer-Alexander

The following line dances, "Oh, Susanna" and "A-Hunting We Will Go," can be used to reinforce beginning folk dance steps at the elementary level.

Oh, Susanna

Words	*Movement Directions*
I come from Alabama with my banjo on my knee,	Girls walk forward 4 steps
	Girls walk backward 4 steps
I'm going to Louisiana my true love for to see.	Boys walk forward 4 steps
	Boys walk backward 4 steps
It rained all night the day I left	Girls walk forward 4 steps
The weather it was dry.	Girls walk backward 4 steps
The sun so hot, I froze to death	Boys walk forward 4 steps
Susanna don't you cry.	Boys walk backward 4 steps

Chorus

Oh, Susanna, Oh, don't you cry for me,	Swing partners to the right 8 counts
I've come from Alabama with my banjo on my knee.	Swing partners to the left 8 counts

A-HUNTING WE WILL GO

English Game Song

Oh, a-hunt-ing we will go, A-hunt-ing we will go,

We'll catch a fox and put him in a box, And then we'll let him go.

Chorus

Repeat measures 1–8 using the words: Tra, la, la, la, la, la, . . .

Movements to the verse

Measures 1–4   Head couple moves to the front of the set. Head couple joins hands and skips or slides between the lines to the foot of the set.

Measures 5–8   Head couple returns.

Movements to the chorus

Measures 1–8   All face forward and join hands with partner in skater's position, right hand joined over left. Head couple turns and leads column to foot of set. At foot of set, head couple joins and raises both hands to form an arch. Second couple leads others under the arch, advancing to become the new head couple. Partners should remain on their original side in forming the arch and in passing under the arch.

Repeat the entire dance with each new head couple. The teacher should encourage children to create their own rhymes for line three, such as:

"catch a mouse and put him in a house"

"catch a cat and put him in a hat"

"catch a skunk and put him in a trunk"

"catch a fish and put him in a dish"

A popular square dance that children enjoy performing is "Red River Valley." Form a square made up of four couples. Specify one couple as the "head" couple. The couple to their right is the second couple; the couple directly across from the head couple is couple number three; the fourth couple is to the left of the head couple.

Verse 1

Phrases 1–2   Head couple walks over to the second couple; all join hands and circle four steps to the left, then four steps to the right.

Phrases 3–4   Drop hands, hook elbows and swing opposite partner once around; return to partner and swing once around.

Verse 2

Repeat actions of verse one, with couple 3.

Verse 3

Repeat actions of verse one with couple 4.

Verse 4

Head couple should be back in original position in the square. On the call "allemande left," the boy faces the girl to his left; grasp left hands and circle once completely around until all persons are back facing their own partners.

Begin a "grand right and left": extend right hand to partner, pass him or her by and continue to the next person, extending left hand. Continue in this fashion, grasping first right, then left hand, weaving in and out until each person has returned to the original partner. Girls then reverse direction and all promenade back to their original place.

RED RIVER VALLEY

American Folk Song

Verse 2. Now you lead right on down the valley, (couple no. 1 dances with couple no. 3).
Circle left, then you circle to the right, etc.

3. Now you lead right on down the valley, (couple no. 1 dances with couple no. 4), etc.

4. Now it's allemande left to your corner,
And a right hand to your own.
And when you meet your partner,
Then you promenade her on home.

From *Exploring Music*, Grade 5, by Eunice Boardman, et al., copyright © 1971 by Holt, Rinehart and Winston, Inc. Reprinted by permission of the publisher.

WRITTEN AND PERFORMANCE-RELATED ASSESSMENTS THROUGH COOPERATIVE LEARNING ACTIVITIES: MOVEMENT

1. Animal Game: Ask each group to select an animal they have seen in the zoo or on TV. They should discuss among themselves all aspects of the animal's movements: the way the eyes move, the mouth, the nose, the neck and finally, the body. After a designated time, the first group begins "giving clues" to the other groups, to help them guess what animal they are imitating. Group 1 should begin with eye movements; then mouth movements, and continue adding movements until their animal has been named. For every incorrect guess, a group loses 1 point; a group receives 3 points for guessing correctly. When group 1's animal has been identified, Group 2 presents its animal, and so on until all groups have had a turn. The group with the highest score wins the game.

2. Distribute to each group a descriptive poem of interest to that age level. Ask students to read the poem carefully several times and then create movements that bring out the imagery in the poem.

3. A different short, descriptive story should be given to each group. Have the groups read through their stories and decide what movement they will use to portray the characters, events, and scenery. After a set time span, each group should present its story for the class's enjoyment.

4. Have small groups of students create a square dance to a song of their own choosing and perform for the class.

Organizing Musical Experiences

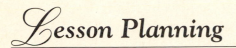

Lesson Planning

Chapter 13

Planning musical experiences for children can be an exciting endeavor. A wide assortment of quality resources are available that will contribute to the preparation of interesting and enjoyable music activities.

Because music is as important as any other subject in the elementary curriculum, it should be included in the daily schedule of every class. The younger the child, the more important it is to provide short lessons daily rather than one long weekly lesson.

While planning musical experiences, the teacher should take into consideration several factors:

1. the characteristics of the group
2. the learnings and skills that should be taught
3. how to teach these learnings and skills
4. how the teacher will know the lesson content was learned
5. the materials that will be needed to teach the content well

CHARACTERISTICS OF THE GROUP

Music materials and activities should center around the interests of the group; interests change from grade to grade and from school to school. Knowing how students relate to one another is also important; how a teacher prepares the class for partner activities may determine their success or failure. An awareness of students who don't work well together for small-group activities is also necessary. In addition, a teacher needs to be particularly sensitive to children who have special needs; with a little forethought and planning, for example, the teacher can provide satisfying activities that will make a child in a wheelchair feel he or she is a part of the group during locomotor activities. Perhaps the most prominent situation that needs the teacher's attention, however, is the problem of differences in levels of musical achievement within a group. The teacher must find ways to meet the needs of those who are behind in music learning while maintaining the interest and growth of those who are ready to progress to the next level.

WHAT SHALL I TEACH?

Goals and Objectives

By formulating goals and objectives, the classroom teacher will be able to provide learning activities that will contribute to musical growth for every child.

Goals.   Goals are broad and concise statements indicating desired terminal outcomes. They are few in number and apply to all children in all grades. Usually, the goals of the music program for a school are predetermined for the teacher; they are expressed in the state music curriculum guide and in a school's philosophy. An example of a goal might read:

> Music experiences should provide students with growth in understanding musical concepts, acquiring musical skills, and developing positive attitudes toward the value of music in a person's life.

General Objectives.   General objectives are more specific than goals in designating desired musical growth over a year's time or month by month. They provide a clear sense of direction for the teacher and are usually expressed in behavioral terms; that is, in terms of what the student will be able to do. General objectives for the school year for grade one might read:

Students will improve their ability to:

a. sing, in tune, short songs with a range of a fourth from mi (3) to la (6)
b. perform accurately (sing, play, move) the steady beat of a song
c. identify and perform ♩, ♫, and 𝄽 and combinations of these rhythms
d. organize music into groups of two by correctly stepping or clapping the accented beat
e. play and improvise simple rhythmic and melodic patterns on classroom instruments.
f. perform music in an expressive manner through the use of loud and soft, fast and slow, and legato and staccato.
g. identify and respond to repetition and contrast in simple music.

It is often helpful to divide learnings, skills, and song materials into monthly blocks so that a teacher can see at a glance the pace needed to present the required material. Generally, the first and last two weeks of school are review times when no new learnings are introduced. The following outline is one way to organize lessons month by month for grade one:

September

By the end of the month, children will improve their ability to:

Singing:	sing phrases to match tones sung by the teacher
	sing review songs from kindergarten:

Star Light, Star Bright	Rain, Rain
One Two, Tie My Shoe	Little Sally Walker
Quaker, Quaker	Where Is Thumbkin
Lucy Locket	Hop Old Squirrel

Moving:	take part in activities related to games, finger plays, and other movements associated with their review songs
	clap, patsch, step, and move in other ways to the beat of familiar songs and recordings
Playing:	play simple rhythmic and melodic ostinati to familiar songs
Listening:	identify extremes of loud and soft, fast and slow, high and low, and smooth and disconnected on recorded music or in songs sung by the teacher. These structural components can be reinforced through singing, moving, playing, and creating.
Creating:	improvise, through expressive, interpretive movement, the sounds heard on recorded music

October

By the end of the month, children will improve their ability to:

Singing:	sing greetings for matching pitches:

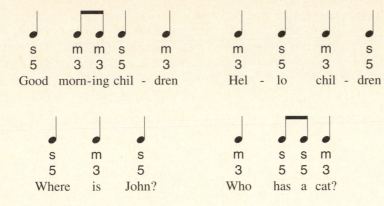

sing songs and phrases containing the minor 3rd as found in:

Star Light, Star Bright   Quaker, Quaker
One Two, Tie My Shoe   Rain, Rain

sing review songs:
Ring Around the Rosy
Other Songs

sing new songs:
Wee Willie Winkle   Mill Wheel
The Clock   Bounce High

Reading: identify the quarter note in various contexts
identify the minor third in various contexts

Writing: notate quarter notes on felt board; practice drawing quarter notes on chalkboard and with crayons on paper
notate so (5) and mi (3) on felt board

Playing: keep steady quarter-note beat using rhythm instruments
perform so—mi on barred instruments
play simple rhythmic and melodic ostinati to familiar songs and to recorded music

Moving: move to quarter-note rhythm heard in songs and recordings
clap quarter notes as notated on charts and felt board
perform actions and games to songs from kindergarten

Listening: identify extremes of loud and soft, fast and slow, high and low, and smooth and disconnected

Creating: same as in September

Specific Objectives.   Specific objectives are precise, clear, and behavioral in nature. They are usually present in day-to-day lesson plans and provide the basis for evaluation of both the teaching and the learning processes. A few examples of specific behavioral objectives for a first grade lesson would be:

a. match the tones la–so–mi (6–5–3) in a variety of combinations after they are sung by the teacher
b. keep a steady beat while bouncing a ball to "One Two, Tie My Shoe"
c. identify silence occurring in a rhythmic pattern by opening the hands when the appropriate notation (𝄽) occurs
d. sing correctly the intervals of a second and a third (so–la or 5–6; mi–so or 3–5) when they appear in patterns on the felt board

Notice that the objective specifies the behavior that a teacher is to perceive so that she or he can evaluate both growth in the student and clarity of presentation. If some children have difficulty in singing the la–so–mi charts, for example, this indicates that either the charts are too difficult and need to be revised (teacher-centered evaluation) or more practice is needed to ensure growth in learning (student-centered evaluation).

Daily Lesson Planning

Preparing daily lesson plans for growth in musical knowledge and skills presupposes that careful long-range planning (preparing goals and general objectives for the entire year) and short-range planning (month-by-month objectives) are already in place. Now the teacher must determine the content and procedures that will best accomplish the desired objectives.

Many types of format can be used for planning a lesson. One of the most basic formats includes:

1. Behavioral Objectives
2. Materials
3. Procedure
4. Summary/Evaluation/Assessment

The following format has seven important areas that will assist the teacher in preparing a more thorough representation of what is to be taught: (1) elements, (2) learnings centering on the structural components of elements, (3) behavioral objectives, (4) materials, (5) procedures, (6) skills, and (7) evaluation/assessment.

Lesson # _____		Date _____	
Element(s)	Materials	Procedures	Skills
Learning			
Behavioral Objectives			
		Evaluation/Assessment	

Elements.   In a balanced lesson, the teacher will usually teach content containing several musical elements from the following list:

a. rhythm
b. melody
c. harmony
d. texture
e. form
f. timbre (tone quality)
g. dynamics
h. tempo

The elements being taught should be clearly stated so that a teacher can see at a glance what area may have been neglected over a period of time.

Learnings. Each element contains a number of structural components to be learned at different stages of a child's development. The teacher must decide which components will be focused on for the first time and which will be reviewed during each lesson. Statements referring to the learning of these components should be succinct, short, and clear. Several examples would include:

Elements	*Learnings*
1. rhythm	a. An eighth note receives half the duration of a quarter note.
	b. Beats in music can be grouped in two's.
	c. A dot to the right of a note extends the length of the note by one-half of its value.
2. melody	a. Some melodies move upward.
	b. An interval is the distance between two successive pitches in a melody.
	c. A note placed on the third line of a staff is called B.
3. timbre	a. A flute is a soprano woodwind instrument.
	b. Rhythms can be expressed through the use of different body sounds, such as clapping and snapping.
	c. Body sounds can be included in a composition.

Behavioral Objectives. One or more behavioral objectives must be written for each structural component to be learned. Behavioral objectives translate components into specific knowledge and skills to be acquired. They tell us exactly what students must do to realize the component being taught. Examples of behavioral objectives were given above under "Specific Objectives."

Materials. Names of songs to be included in the lesson should be indicated, with their page number and source. All too often a teacher goes back to a particular lesson a year or so later and can't remember where the song came from. Recordings, charts, flash cards, and other aids should be clearly indicated; this allows for quick setting up before the lesson. Needed equipment that is not part of the classroom's furnishings should also be noted.

Procedures. Step-by-step procedures should be carefully sequenced for maximum enjoyment and learning. They should contain diversified activities that continually call for student participation and should be well paced to maintain interest. Appropriate pacing is a crucial skill that every teacher needs to acquire. Teachers must be able to move from one musical activity to the next and not spend too much or too little time on any one activity.

Skills. Every music lesson should contribute to the development of some degree of psychomotor, cognitive, and affective skills. These skills include the following:

Psychomotor Skills	*Cognitive Skills*	*Affective Skills*
moving	recalling	attending
listening	interpreting	responding
singing	applying	valuing
playing	analyzing	
reading	synthesizing	
writing	evaluating	
creating		

Students should be involved in extending their abilities in a variety of skills, but not all skills will be included in every lesson. By listing the skills being developed, a teacher can determine quickly how well balanced the lesson is and, over a period of time, what is being neglected. Only psychomotor skills have been indicated in the sample daily lesson plan that follows.

Lesson #_____   Date _____

ELEMENT(S)

Rhythm   Harmony
Melody   Timbre

MATERIALS

1. so-la-mi cards
2. "If You're Happy," p. 8, *Singing With Children*
3. "The Clock," p. 150, *Kodály Method*
4. "Little Sally Water," p. 214, *Kodály Context*
5. "Jig Jog," p. 67, *Music For Fun*
6. ball, rhythm cards, chart, sticks, E and G resonator bells, sleigh bells

LEARNING

1. Songs have a steady beat.
2. Changing rhythms in a song often correspond to the words sung.
3. Songs can rotate between sound and silence.
4. Melodies are made up of successive intervals.
5. Harmony can be added to a song by supporting the melody line with other pitches.
6. The sounds of instruments are distinctive.

BEHAVIORAL OBJECTIVES

By the end of class, children will improve their ability to:

1. match pitches sung by the teacher
2. sing the intervals of a second and a third accurately
3. keep a steady beat when bouncing a ball, using body percussion and playing instruments
4. identify changing rhythms through use of body percussion and notation cards
5. identify silence occurring in a rhythmic pattern by opening hands and notation
6. play a melodic ostinato on bells
7. identify the sound of sticks, sleigh bells, and resonator bells

PROCEDURES

STAND IN A CIRCLE

1. Sing greeting and have students respond:

    so   la   so so mi
    5   6   5   5   3
    How   are   you to-day

    Review la-so-mi (6-5-3) pitches with flash cards

2. Sing review song: "The Clock"
    a. pat and clap the beat while singing
    b. teacher in middle; bounce ball to each student on the beat while singing

SIT

3. Sing "The Clock" again, this time clapping the word rhythms while singing
    a. identify rhythms
    b. perform patterns on chart incorporating these rhythms
    c. give individual packets containing cards with these symbols; clap patterns for children to notate using cards

4. Sing review song: "Jig Jog"
    a. give E and G resonator bells for A section
    b. middle section: sleigh bells
    c. rest of children play sticks on beat
    d. identify timbres by name

STAND

5. Begin learning new song: "Little Sally Water"
6. Sing review song: "If You're Happy"
    a. different children in middle of circle to perform new motion

SKILLS

singing
listening

singing
reading

singing
moving

singing
moving
writing
reading

singing
playing

listening
singing

singing
moving
creating

EVALUATION/ASSESSMENT

by observation

Evaluation/Assessent. If a means other than observation is to be used to evaluate a musical activity, this process should be clearly indicated in the plan. Usually, only student evaluation procedures are recorded. It should be understood, however, that evaluations are always a dual process; they indicate how well the child is progressing and how clearly the teacher is presenting the lesson.

The 30-minute plan for first grade, printed here, is one example of how all seven parts of the daily lesson plan work together for musical growth.

HOW SHALL I TEACH?

Classroom teachers may choose to use an inductive approach to learning, a deductive approach, or a combination of the two. Whichever approach is used, teachers must remember that children learn best through active involvement in the learning process; activities should be child centered.

When using the *inductive approach* to learning, the teacher leads students through a sequence of activities from a part to the whole, from the specific to the general. To learn the music structure ♫ , for example, children are led through a series of specific, carefully sequenced activities until the only thing left is to give the new learning its name. Children might move to the rhythm of two eighth notes by taking short running steps as they listen to an appropriate recording. This might be followed by clapping patterns containing two eighth notes or by playing eighth-note patterns on rhythm instruments. Finally, combinations of quarter- and eighth-note patterns might be compared to see how they relate in terms of sounds per beat; comparisons will be achieved through performing chants and songs containing both quarter- and eighth-note patterns, or through movement: walking and running or clapping and patsching. When the children begin to demonstrate an understanding of the concept that eighth notes (♫) are twice as fast as quarter notes (♩), the new music structure—the eighth note—will be named and its symbol presented to the class. Follow-up activities will be used for reinforcement.

The *deductive approach* is just the reverse in process. The teacher begins with the general and leads children to the specific. The teacher first states what is to be learned (eighth notes), shows the class what symbol represents this structural component of rhythm (♪ and ♫), and explains that two eighth notes are twice as fast as one quarter note. Then the children move from this general awareness of what is to be learned to a series of more specific activities that will contribute to a growth in the understanding of eighth notes. Children can move to the eighth-note rhythm and perform it by clapping, patsching, or playing rhythm instruments. Chants and songs containing the new rhythm are performed, and the new symbol is discovered on the song sheet. Children are led through additional activities involving the use of eighth-note combinations until they can demonstrate, through singing, moving, and performing, that the eighth note is twice as fast as the quarter note.

COOPERATIVE LEARNING

Cooperative learning is a teaching method that involves students with all levels of performance ability working together in small groups to achieve a common goal. In this setting, the same grade is usually earned by all students in the group. If individual grades are given, students are not in competition for those grades. By eliminating grade competition, teachers have discovered that students work more rapidly, produce better results, and interact in a friendlier, more helpful manner than do groups where the highest grade goes to the one who contributes most to the project.

There are a number of different approaches to cooperative learning. One of the easiest to organize and the one favored for the activities in this book involves working in heterogeneous groups of three to five members on some assigned activity having specific objectives.

Evaluation depends on the nature of the activity. The following are some possibilities:

1. Some worksheets, creative projects, listening activities: Each group hands in a single completed sheet and members of the group receive the same grade.
2. Performance skills (each student on the same instrument), flash cards, some worksheets: When the group feels that each member is ready, the teacher observes the individual performance of each student and grades each one separately.
3. Performance skills (each student on a different instrument): When the group feels it is ready, the entire group performs first for the teacher and then for the whole class. All members of a group receive the same grade.

Cooperative learning activities must be carefully organized. Students should understand that they are accountable for both their own learning and the learning of members in their group. Students must also realize that their conduct should not prevent any other group from accomplishing its activity objectives. Group leaders can be appointed who are responsible for keeping group members on task. Objectives, time constraints, and directions should be clearly and concisely indicated on each group's handout.

HOW WILL I KNOW I TAUGHT IT?

Much evaluation of a student's learning, particularly in the primary grades, is achieved through observation. The teacher listens and watches to determine whether a child can match pitches, keep a steady beat, sing so-mi, or move creatively to a recording. These observations can be charted and used as a guide for future lesson planning. The following chart for first grade is an example of how a teacher can keep an accurate, concise record of each child's musical growth in knowledge and skills:

Musical Growth in Knowledge and Skills (Grade One)

1. keeps steady beat
2. matches isolated pitches
3. sings in tune
4. sings from mi (3) to so (5) accurately
5. performs fast and slow
6. performs loud and soft
7. performs legato-staccato
8. moves in time to eighth notes
9. can perform ♫ against ♩
10. identifies repetition
11. identifies melodies moving up and down

Name	1	2	3	4	5	6	7	8	9	10	11
Alexander, Willie J.											
Boyer, Ruth L.											
Johnson, Garreth											
Rubio, Petra											
Smith, Washington											

Growth in learning can also be determined by the type of verbal explanations a student offers, by the accuracy of chalkboard and felt board activities, by the results of improvised and other creative endeavors, by the quality of outcomes from cooperative learning activities, and by responses given on computer or written assignments.

The following written assignments can be used to evaluate growth in the understanding of rhythmic, melodic, harmonic, and formal concepts. Create a number of different worksheets for each idea, using different songs or patterns.

Rhythm

1. On a worksheet, place a series of known rhythm patterns. As the teacher claps one of the patterns, each child draws an arrow to the pattern heard. Example:

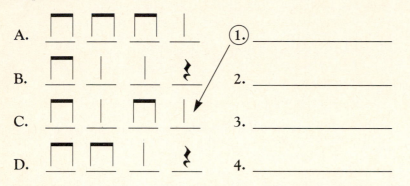

2. On another day, clap one of the patterns in example 1 above. Each child recopies that example on the line beside the no. 1. Continue the clapping and writing until all patterns have been performed and written.
3. Give children a handout containing the rhythms of a known song. Omit the rhythms on some of the beat lines. Children fill in the missing rhythms. Example: "Bow Wow Wow"

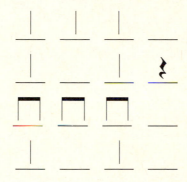

4. Ask the children to write out all the rhythms for a known song. Their handout should contain the beat lines for the song, one phrase per line. Example: "Bow Wow Wow"

——— —— —— ——

——— —— —— ——

——— —— —— ——

——— —— —— ——

5. Have children place accents, bar lines, and the meter sign on a handout containing the rhythms of a known song.
6. On another day, children can mark the counting for the song in no. 5.
7. Place on a handout the rhythms of a known song. Children fill in the missing measures. Example: "Paw Paw Patch"

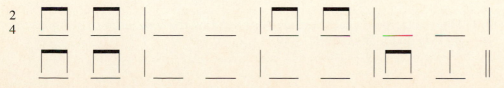

8. Write out each of the phrases of a known song, but place them out of order. Children must number the phrases in correct order. Example: "Ghost of Tom"

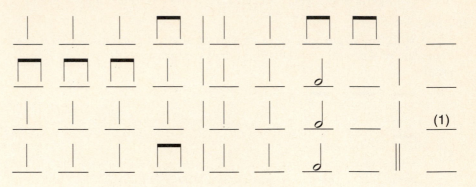

(1)

9. Give the children a handout of a known song containing mixed meters. Children must analyze the song and write in the meters.

Melody

1. Place high and low icons on a handout. If what is heard is high, children color the star; if low, color the starfish.

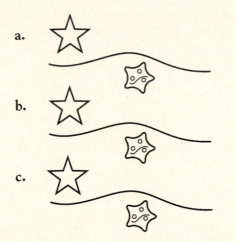

a.

b.

c.

2. On a handout, place the rhythms of a known song. Under each rhythm, children place the solfège names. Example: "Rain, Rain"

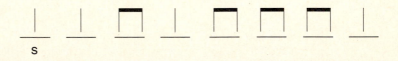

s

3. Write from memory the notes (noteheads) of a known song. Example: "Rain Rain"

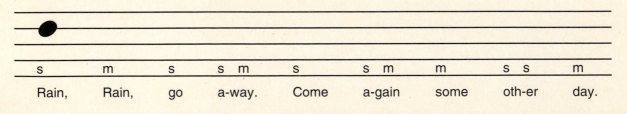

s	m	s	s m	s	s m	m	s s	m
Rain,	Rain,	go	a-way.	Come	a-gain	some	oth-er	day.

4. Draw an arrow to each melody performed by the teacher. Teacher sings the melody on lōō. Example:

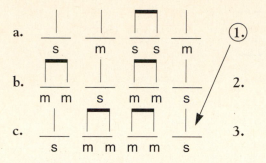

a. | | ⊓ |
   s m s s m

b. ⊓ | ⊓ |
   m m s m m s

c. | ⊓ ⊓ |
   s m m m m s

1. ↘ 2. 3.

5. On a handout, children write in the solfège names for "Bounce High, Bounce Low." Example:

___S___ ___ ___ ___ ___ ___ ___ ___ ___

Bounce   high,   bounce   low.   Bounce   the   ball   to   Shi - loh.

6. Place a known song on a staff. Children must circle one wrong note in each phrase. Example: "Bounce High, Bounce Low"

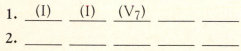

7. Place part of a known song on a staff. Children write in the missing notes.
8. Place notes on a staff. Children identify their absolute note names.
9. Place noteheads on a staff. Children must draw the stems, up or down, according to the rules given.
10. Give children a handout with a blank staff. Under the staff, place absolute note names. Children must draw the notes for each letter indicated and place stems correctly.

Harmony

1. Give children a handout containing different intervals. Children must identify the intervals by size: third, fifth, and so forth.
2. Play a series of I and V₇ chords. On a handout, children indicate which chords were heard. Example:

1. __(I)__ __(I)__ __(V₇)__ ____ ____

2. ____ ____ ____ ____ ____

3. ____ ____ ____ ____ ____

3. On a handout, have children build the triads (or seventh chords) indicated. Example:

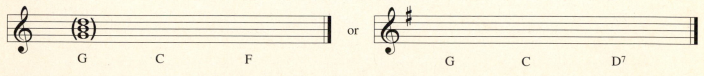

G   C   F   or   G   C   D⁷

Form

1. Write out the rhythms to a known song, one phrase per line. Have children identify the phrases using letters of the alphabet. Example: "Ring Around the Rosy"

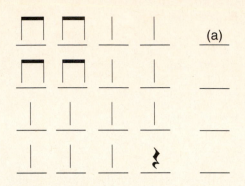

(a)

2. Give children a copy of a song notated on a staff. Children must bracket each phrase first, then identify each phrase by a letter name. Example: "Ring Around the Rosy"

3. Give each child a copy of the song "Cradle Hymn." Children must indicate the first and second endings and cross out unneeded measures.

Many creative activities can be developed as aids for written evaluation. Response charts can be provided to measure growth in musical knowledge. The response charts on the next pages give ideas that can be used both before and after children can read.

Example 1: Grade 1

Directions given verbally.   Listen to the music; then, if the music goes fast, color the leopard; if it goes slowly, color the snail. (Repeat directions for each example played.)

Example 2: Grade 3

Directions. Listen to the pattern I am going to play. Then, in no. 1, circle the pattern heard. (Repeat the directions for each pattern played.)

Example 3: Grade 5

Directions. Listen to the recording of "Anitra's Dance" from *Peer Gynt Suite #1* by Grieg. Circle the correct response. I will play the selection three times. Listen for the form during the second and third playings.

1. Music begins and ends with   chord   scale   few notes

2. Section of the orchestra
   most prominent: strings   brass   woodwinds

3. Percussion instrument
   heard in background
   now and then: cymbals   triangle   xylophone

4. Melody is   legato   staccato   alternates both

5. Dynamics are   continually   continually   neither
                   increasing   decreasing

6. Tempo   continually   continually   neither
                   slows down   speeds up

7. The form is   two parts with some   three parts with some
                   repetition: ABA   repetition: AB

WHAT MATERIALS SHALL I USE?

Usually, each elementary classroom will contain a set of music books for students' use. These series books have excellent teachers' manuals that contain good materials and a number of sequenced lesson plans. The series books for each grade also have a set of tapes and/or CD's for use with singing, moving, and listening activities. The teacher's manual and the teacher's own imagination will provide many ideas for charts, puppets, pictures, and other aids that can be used during the music lesson.

If the school has a music room, teachers should become familiar with its contents. The music specialist is also a good resource person who may have additional song books, games, audiovisual aids, and other materials for the classroom teacher's use. Often educational television offers sequenced music classes that a teacher may want to work into the weekly schedule.

Check the public, school, and university libraries for books, films, and recordings that will be useful for movement and listening activities. Save pictures from calendars, catalogs, and coloring books that can be used to motivate children for learning. Collect song books having materials that will contribute to musical growth. Keep in mind, however, that not all songs and recordings are of equal value; use the best quality available.

Use a variety of song materials. Folk songs of America should be a primary resource because they are the expression of our thoughts, feelings, and culture. Folk songs and games characteristic of all the ethnic groups in our country should be used liberally when planning daily music classes. Use recordings representing many styles, including music by contemporary composers. The best of the popular genres should also be included, such as jazz, blues, country, and rock. They are an important part of our cultural heritage.

Teaching Music in Specialized Areas

Integrating Music Across the Curriculum *Chapter*

14

Every child should have frequent opportunities to respond to music by singing, listening, moving, creating, reading, writing, and playing musical instruments. Simultaneously, however, the use of music in the curriculum as a means to enhance students' knowledge of other subject areas can be used as a powerful educational strategy. The understanding of concepts related to language arts, social studies, and even math and science can be significantly reinforced through carefully designed musical activities.

SOCIAL STUDIES (GRADE 3)

Goal

Students will become knowledgeable about slavery in America and how songs (spirituals) helped slaves escape to freedom in the North.

Objectives

1. Students will learn about Harriet Tubman and how she led slaves to freedom.
2. Students will discover the symbolism in the "drinking gourd" and how it led the slaves to freedom through song.
3. Students will learn that many spiritual songs were associated with escape.

Concepts

Students will be able to:
1. Identify Harriet Tubman and her role as a conductor of the Underground Railroad.
2. Identify how the drinking gourd/North Star assisted slaves in their escape to the North.
3. Identify words in spirituals that helped slaves escape to Freedom.
4. Sing the song, "Follow the Drinking Gourd."

Materials

"Follow the Drinking Gourd" by Jeanette Winter
9×12 sheets of black construction paper
white crayon
glue or glue stick
star stickers
pen

FOLLOW THE DRINKIN' GOURD

Spiritual
Adapted by René Boyer-Alexander

When the sun comes back— and the first quail calls— Fol-low— the

Drink-in' Gourd.— Then the Old Man is a-wait-in for to

car-ry you to free-dom if you Fol-low the Drink-in' Gourd.

Fol-low— the Drink-in' Gourd— Fol-low— the

Drink-in' Gourd,— For the Old Man is a-wait-in' for to

car-ry you to Free-dom if you Fol-low the Drink-in' Gourd.

Procedure

1. Ask students what heroes are and to name some of their heroes.
2. Ask students to name some famous women heroes.
3. Introduce Harriet Tubman, the famous conductor of the Underground Railroad.
4. Read the book *Follow the Drinking Gourd* by Jeanette Winter
5. Tell the students that during the days of slavery, slaves tried to escape cruelty by fleeing North to freedom. They did this with the help of an Underground Railroad. The Underground Railroad was not a train but a group of people who tried to help slaves escape to freedom. People who made up the Underground Railroad were both blacks and whites who were against slavery. Those who maintained this system of escape, which was formed in 1840, hid escaped slaves in their cellars, barns, fields, and even inside tree trunks.

   The slaves usually traveled from location to location or station to station during the night and slept during the day. Many of the slaves escaped unharmed, but many more were killed.

   Harriet Tubman was known as a conductor of the Underground Railroad because it was her job to guide the slaves to freedom. She was very successful in her efforts.

   During the night-time hours, the slaves followed the North Star hoping to find freedom. The North Star is located at the tip of the Big Dipper. The slaves called the Big Dipper a drinking gourd because of the shape of the constellation.

A song was created to help the slaves on their journey to freedom. It was called, "Follow the Drinking Gourd." Hidden secretly in the lyrics of this song were directions for following the Underground Railroad.

   a. passengers = escaped slaves
   b. stations   = homes where slaves hid
   c. conductors = people who helped guide the slaves
   d. agents   = people who offered the slaves clothes, food, and shelter

6. Sing through the lyrics of the drinking gourd song using the whole song approach.
7. Create an art project:
   a. Fold sheet of construction paper
   b. On the cover, have the students create a title.
   c. Open it up. On the top half, the students will write out the refrain from the song "Follow the Drinking Gourd" (words will be on the board).
   d. On the bottom half, using seven sticker stars, the students will create their own drinking gourd and connect each star using a white crayon.

Assessment

The assessment will be authentic, and the teacher will assess the students' finished art project, participation during discussion and singing, and recalling information by answering questions after reading the story and listening to the information that the teacher has shared about the Underground Railroad.

MATHEMATICS (GRADES 1 AND 2)

Description

Students will learn how math and rhythm in music are related. Students will understand how mathematical addition is applied to rhythm.

Goal

Students will learn the value of quarter, half, whole, and eighth notes and how to add them.

Objectives

Students will add musical notes together and come up with a real number as the answer. Students will create different addition problems with the answers using musical notes as the product.

Concepts

Students will be able to understand addition as it applies to music.

Materials

Paper, pencil, sheet music

Procedure

1. Introduce students to the concept of addition and music.
2. Give an example of an addition problem using both real numbers and musical notes.

3. Review the four basic note values with students.
4. Demonstrate a couple of problems on the board. Show the students how they can add a quarter note to a half note and come up with an answer of 3.
5. Give the students a couple of problems to do on their own.
6. Go over the problems with the students, calling on them to write their answers on the board.
7. Now have the students create their own problems and provide the answers to them.
8. Review with the students why addition is used in music and its importance.

Assessment

1. Have students work five additional problems using notes.
2. Have students create ten different addition problems using notes to create the answers.
3. Students will orally describe why math is important to music.

A number of songs and chants will help children learn the basic facts about mathematics. A typical counting chant that children never tire of repeating is:

One, two, buckle my shoe,
Three, four, shut the door.
Five, six, pick up sticks.
Seven, eight, lay them straight.
Nine, Ten, a big fat hen.
Eleven, twelve, dig and delve.
Thirteen, fourteen, maids a-courting.
Fifteen, sixteen, maids in the kitchen.
Seventeen, eighteen, maids in waiting.
Nineteen, twenty, my plate is empty.

The "Welcome Song" offers numerous possibilities for reinforcing a student's ability to practice math concepts in a fun way.

WELCOME SONG

Composed by René Boyer-Alexander

Other math concepts—count backward from 8. Count by 2s; count by 3s; add 4 every time (1, 5, 9, 13, 17, 21, 25).

LITERATURE (GRADES 5 AND 6)

Goal

Students will be introduced to an African folk tale whose main characters are two daughters whose personalities are opposite.

Objectives

1. To become familiar with the African folk tale *Mufaro's Beautiful Daughters*.
2. To evaluate the characters in the story and compare their attitudes to people they know.
3. To become familiar with names of rhythmic instruments that may be used to enhance the telling of the story.

Concepts

Students will be able to:

1. Recognize good and evil in characters in a folk tale
2. Recognize and select instruments that can enhance the meaning and presence of specific moods in character
3. Listen to a story and respond by playing assigned instruments in a timely manner during specific cues

Materials

Book: *Mufaro's Beautiful Daughters*, an African folk tale.
Instruments: small gong, drum, guiro, triangle, maracas, woodblock, cowbell

Procedure

1. Tell the class that people tend to pass stories along to one another from one generation to the next. These things that are passed along, such as stories and music, become part of our folk heritage. *Mufaro's Beautiful Daughters* is an African folk tale that has been passed from one generation to the next because of what the story is trying to teach to us as individuals.
2. Read the story.
3. Discuss the characters in the story.
4. Assign rhythmic instruments to each of the characters. Read the story again and add the instruments.

Great King	gong or cymbal
Mufaro	a short rhythm played on a hand drum
Manyara	Guiro or ratchett
Nyasha	triangle or finger cymbal
snake	maracas or cabasa
boy	woodblock
old woman	cowbell

Assessment

The teacher should assess the student's ability to identify their assigned instrument by name, play the instrument at the appropriate time, and read with expression.

MUFARO'S BEAUTIFUL DAUGHTERS: AN AFRICAN FOLK TALE

Retold by René Boyer-Alexander

A long time ago, in Africa, a small village lay across a river from a city where a Great King lived.

A man named Mufaro lived in this village with his two daughters, Manyara and Nyasha. Both daughters were very beautiful.

Even though she was very beautiful, Manyara was always in a bad and hateful mood. She teased her sister and was mean to her.

Nyasha, on the other hand, was a happy and loving person. She found much pleasure in tending to her garden where she grew sunflowers, yams, and vegetables.

One day Nyasha noticed a small garden snake beneath a yam vine. She named it Nyoka. She was kind to the snake and complimented it on the fine job it did keeping away creatures who would spoil her garden. In turn the snake was kind to her.

One day, the Great King announced his desire to marry. He called for all the beautiful daughters of the land to be presented to him.

Manyara sneaked away in the middle of the night because she wanted to be the first to present herself.

As she traveled to the palace she met a small boy. She was very rude to him. She met an old woman to whom she was also very mean and nasty.

The next morning, Nyasha, her father, and a great wedding party, traveled to the city.

On their way, Nyasha encountered a small boy whom she thought was hungry. She gave him a yam.

She met an old woman who gave her directions. Nyasha was appreciative and said "Thank you."

Whether they realized it or not, both daughters were being secretly tested by the Great King for their kindness and ability to give. The King was interested in finding out which one was worthy to become his Queen.

Without a doubt, Nyasha was chosen to marry the Great King because she had proven herself to be kind and giving.

Poetry

Children study a variety of poems and are often asked to write poetry as part of their English assignment. A simple form used in many English classes is the Japanese haiku, often cast in a five-seven-five syllable form:

Shimmering water,
Always moving back and forth—
Busy but quiet.

Children can set their haiku and other original poems to music that the whole class can then perform. Simple accompaniments can be added.

Poems can also be presented as choral readings to develop an awareness of register, tempo, dynamics, and thick versus thin textures:

ONE STORMY NIGHT

Two little kittens	All
One stormy night,	
Began to quarrel,	
And then to fight.	
One had a mouse,	Girls
The other had none;	Boys
And that's the way	All
The quarrel begun.	
I'll have that mouse,"	First boy
Said the bigger cat.	Three boys
"*You'll* have that mouse?	First girl
We'll see about that!"	
"I *will* have that mouse,"	First boy
Said the eldest son;	Three boys

"You *sha'nt* have the mouse,"	First girl
Said the little one.	Three girls
The old woman seized	Girls
Her sweeping broom,	
And swept both kittens	Boys
Right out of the room.	
The ground was covered	All
With frost and snow:	
And the two little kittens	
Had nowhere to go.	
They lay and shivered	Second boy
On a mat at the door	
While the old woman	Second girl
Was sweeping the floor.	
And then they crept in,	All girls
As quiet as mice,	
All wet with the snow,	All boys
And as cold as ice,	
And found it much better,	All
That stormy night,	
To lie by the fire	
Than to quarrel and fight.	

CULTURAL STUDIES/LITERATURE/DRAMA/POETRY/SCIENCE (GRADES 5 AND 6)

The Power of Rhythm

This unit of study focuses on the integration of arts across the curriculum. The music and folklore of Africa have served as a foundation for much of the music and literature that we listen to and read about today. Most students find it fascinating to explore and experience the music of this country, especially its rhythms.

LESSON 1

Objectives

To recognize through listening, the complex rhythmic structure present in most African-based music
To understand the role of a griot in African society
To develop and perform a rhythmic structure similar to that found in Africa
To recognize the drum as integral to African folk-based music
To identify and creatively present selected African-based proverbs
To identify rondo form
To explore the use of African-based rhythms, instruments, and folk tales through a simple musical play

Materials

Unpitched percussion instruments or home-made instruments
"Jingo Ba," A Nigerian Drumming Song

Procedure

1. Tell students that they are about to become acquainted with the power of rhythm as expressed in the music and folk material of Africa.
2. Build a rhythmic ostinato by layering in a variety of rhythmic instruments, starting first with the steady beat on a pair of rhythm sticks or claves. (Sug-

gestions: If percussion instruments are not available, have students make some. Telephone directories, paper plates, and boxes can serve as interesting percussion instruments. Grooved sides of containers like dish washing soap bottles, soda cans with rice or other seeds, and gallon water containers can create wonders.) Children should be encouraged to make shakers, scrapers, rattles, and other percussion instruments to use throughout these lessons. An orchestration that uses percussion instruments may look like the following:

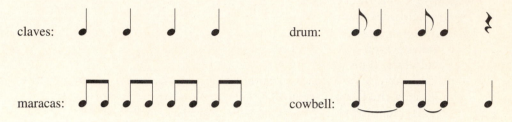

3. Once students are comfortable with the ostinato, using the whole song approach, teach "Jingo-Ba," a Nigerian Drumming Song.

Collected and transcribed by René Boyer-Alexander

Jin - go   Jin - go   ba!   Jin - go   Jin - go   ba!   Jing -

o ———   Jin - go   Ba,   Ba,   Ba.   Jing - o   ba,   ba,   ba

4. Have students listen to "Jingo-Ba" on a recording. *Olatunji Drums of Passion* (0 7464-08210-2), published by Columbia, is a recommended source. Describe some of the kinds of rhythmic instruments heard on the recording. Have students compare the recording to their performance of "Jingo-Ba."
5. Duplicate the following information sheet and hand out to all students. Have students take turns reading aloud, "African Music and Its Influence in America."

AFRICAN MUSIC AND ITS INFLUENCE IN AMERICA

For generations the music of Africa has influenced the musical styles of countries around the world, but none as much as in America. Spirituals, blues, jazz, "pop," and rap have been greatly influenced by the syncopation, question/answer form, tonal structure, and techniques of improvisation found in the music and performance techniques of Africa.

Percussion instruments are widely used in African music. The complex drumming techniques needed to play African rhythms and to communicate the "language of the drum" takes many years of practice. Children begin study to become master drummers at a very early age. It is a most honored position in African society.

---

6. Tell students that the term *griot* refers to an individual who is expert in the music, poetry, storytelling, and social customs of communities within West Africa. *Griots* possess extensive memories. They travel from place to place sharing information with other tribal communities. The *griot* is a very important person in helping to preserve the cultural heritage of the people of Africa.

7. Have the students recreate a scene where a *griot* is communicating to a tribe. Inform them that people from many cultures use *proverbs*, or sayings, to help their children understand real-life situations. These proverbs are usually passed down from one generation to the next.

   Have students practice speaking and/or acting out the following African proverbs in a creative way.
   a. One falsehood spoils a thousand truths.
   b. The ruin of a nation begins in the homes of its people.
   c. He who cannot dance will say: "The drum is bad."
   d. He who hunts two rats catches none.
   e. Knowledge is better than riches.
   f. The teeth are smiling, but is the heart?
8. Take time to explain what each of these proverbs might mean. Transfer their meaning to current situations that the children are experiencing.
9. Divide the class into six groups and assign each group a proverb. Provide each group enough time to dramatize or pantomime their proverb. Encourage creativity!
10. Assign students to play the above rhythmic ostinato parts learned earlier in this Lesson I. Have them play their assigned patterns simultaneously for eight measures. During the last measure, all instruments should join together to play a common rhythmic pattern similar to the following. (This pattern, which is played in unison by all instruments, will serve as an ending to the rhythmic statement.)

   Use this eight-measure pattern that is being played by rhythmic instruments as an A section to a rondo form. The groups that have prepared a creative dramatization can now alternate between each A section of rhythmic instruments to create a wonderful rondo.

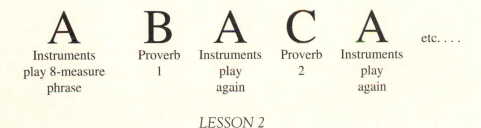

A	B	A	C	A	etc. . . .
Instruments play 8-measure phrase	Proverb 1	Instruments play again	Proverb 2	Instruments play again	

LESSON 2

Objectives

To become acquainted with a piece of African American poetry that reflects African roots.
To sequence previously learned activities into an organized performance.

Materials

The poem, "Danse Africaine" by Langston Hughes
A variety of drums, Orff instruments, gong
Video camera

Procedure

1. Read to the class the poem "Danse Africaine" by Langston Hughes. Have them suggest creative ways to bring this poem alive (perhaps adding a drumming type accompaniment or including the first verse of this poem in a musi-

cal production). Perhaps this poem can serve as an introduction to a piece they will create called, "The Griot Silently Speaks."

The low beating of the tom-toms,
The slow beating of the tom-toms,
Low. . . . Slow
Slow . . . low-
Stirs your blood.
Dance!

2. Let the students know that Langston Hughes was one of America's greatest African American poets. He wrote many poems that reflected the richness of the African American culture. His poetry addressed the injustices against the African American race. One of the outstanding characteristics of Langston Hughes' poetry is the influence of music, especially blues, jazz, and spirituals that influenced his writings. Let them know that Langston Hughes grew up in Lawrence, Kansas, but later attended school in Cleveland, Ohio, where he wrote his first poems. Walt Whitman and Carl Sandburg were two of his greatest role models.
3. Review "Jingo-Ba" and the African proverb activity done in Lesson 1.
4. Decide, as a class, on a program order that would include all the above activities. Have the children review the entire sequence as though they were performing for a live audience.

Summary/Evaluation

Videotape the performance and have the students review their work.

LESSON 3

Behavioral Objectives

To discover the African American folk tale as a major source that can be used for creative music making and dramatization.
To experience incorporating musical themes, costumes, and props within a folk tale to make a musical drama.

Procedure

1. Tell students that folk tales were and still are an important part of African culture. *Griots* told many stories. Usually stories were accompanied by drummers and other musicians as well as dancers. There were opportunities for everyone to participate.
2. "The Fierce Creature" is an example of a folk tale from Africa. Assign students parts in this play and have them act it out.

A FOLK TALE FROM AFRICA
"The Fierce Creature"
Retold and arranged by René Boyer-Alexander

Introduction

(During the opening lines, rhythms are heard. They are performed by a variety of rhythmic instruments played by students. Simultaneously, the following phrases are being spoken by the group.)

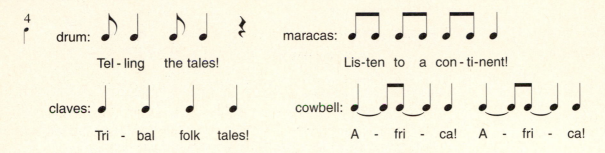

Storyteller: I shall tell you a story from Eastern Africa. It was told to me by the tall **Massai** who live in the high country of Kenya. It is the story of the "Fierce Creature." (Gong)

Storyteller: Ladybug came crawling along, looking for a place to rest.

(Play Ladybug Theme I) She entered the house of the Hare. When the Hare came home, she noticed strange marks on the ground in front of her house.

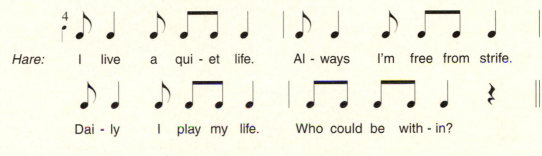

(Insert Hare Theme which is played by a soprano recorder)

Storyteller: Ladybug did not want to be eaten by the Hare so she answered in a fierce voice.

Ladybug: (Insert Ladybug Theme II) I am a terrible warrior, deadlier than the leopard. I crushed all the monkeys to earth and trampled the mighty rhinoceros.

Storyteller: Hare was most frightened. She didn't know what to do, so when Lion came by, searching for meat (Insert Lion's Theme), Hare stopped him.

Hare: There is a fierce creature in my house, Lion. Can you help me? Can you help me?

Animal Chorus: Who is   in   the Hare's house?   (3X) Get out!   Get out!

Ladybug: (Insert Ladybug II Theme) I am a terrible warrior, deadlier than the leopard. I crushed all the monkeys to earth and trampled the mighty rhinoceros.

Storyteller: Lion was most frightened. (Shake jingle bells) He didn't know what to do, so when Elephant came by, on his way to soak in a big mud hole (Elephant's Theme), Hare stopped him.

Hare: There is a fierce creature in my house, Elephant. Can you help me? Can you help me?

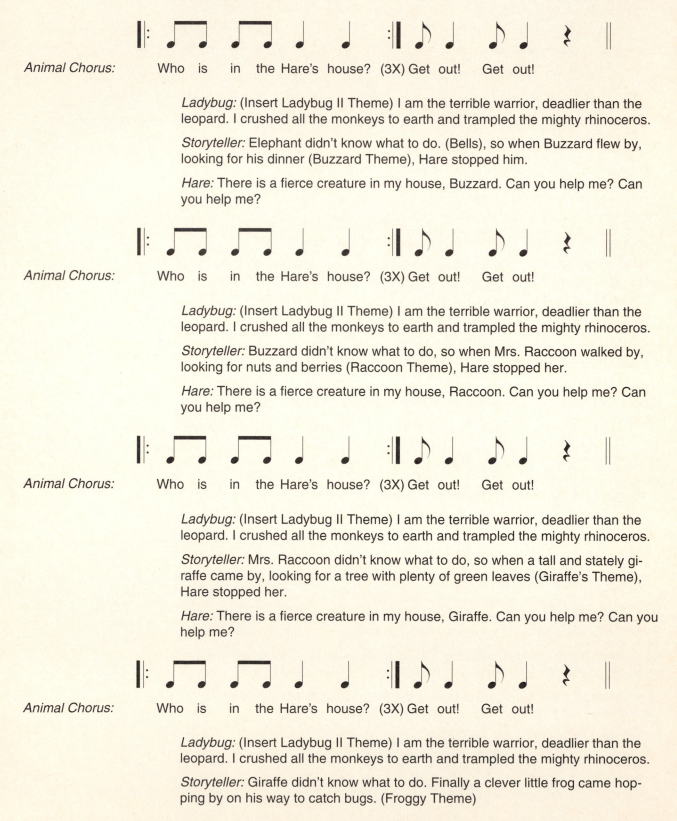

Animal Chorus: Who is in the Hare's house? (3X) Get out! Get out!

Ladybug: (Insert Ladybug II Theme) I am the terrible warrior, deadlier than the leopard. I crushed all the monkeys to earth and trampled the mighty rhinoceros.

Storyteller: Elephant didn't know what to do. (Bells), so when Buzzard flew by, looking for his dinner (Buzzard Theme), Hare stopped him.

Hare: There is a fierce creature in my house, Buzzard. Can you help me? Can you help me?

Animal Chorus: Who is in the Hare's house? (3X) Get out! Get out!

Ladybug: (Insert Ladybug II Theme) I am the terrible warrior, deadlier than the leopard. I crushed all the monkeys to earth and trampled the mighty rhinoceros.

Storyteller: Buzzard didn't know what to do, so when Mrs. Raccoon walked by, looking for nuts and berries (Raccoon Theme), Hare stopped her.

Hare: There is a fierce creature in my house, Raccoon. Can you help me? Can you help me?

Animal Chorus: Who is in the Hare's house? (3X) Get out! Get out!

Ladybug: (Insert Ladybug II Theme) I am the terrible warrior, deadlier than the leopard. I crushed all the monkeys to earth and trampled the mighty rhinoceros.

Storyteller: Mrs. Raccoon didn't know what to do, so when a tall and stately giraffe came by, looking for a tree with plenty of green leaves (Giraffe's Theme), Hare stopped her.

Hare: There is a fierce creature in my house, Giraffe. Can you help me? Can you help me?

Animal Chorus: Who is in the Hare's house? (3X) Get out! Get out!

Ladybug: (Insert Ladybug II Theme) I am the terrible warrior, deadlier than the leopard. I crushed all the monkeys to earth and trampled the mighty rhinoceros.

Storyteller: Giraffe didn't know what to do. Finally a clever little frog came hopping by on his way to catch bugs. (Froggy Theme)

Hare: There is a fierce creature in my house, Froggy. Can you help me? Can you help me?

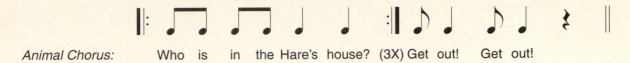

Animal Chorus: Who   is   in   the   Hare's   house?   (3X) Get   out!   Get   out!

Ladybug: (Insert Ladybug II Theme) I am the terrible warrior, deadlier than the leopard. I crushed all the monkeys to earth and trampled the mighty rhinoceros.

Froggy: I, the hideous leaper, have come.

Ladybug: (Trembling, softly) Oh . . . .!

Froggy: I am slippery, slimy green.

Ladybug: (Trembling louder) Oh . . .!

Froggy: Great big warts cover my body.

Ladybug: (Screaming with a high pitched voice) Ohhhhhh!!!. . .

Help . . . Help . . . Let me out of here . . . .!!!!!

(Shaking sounds from instruments, a gradual crescendo)

(Ladybug runs out and away from the house while screaming)

Froggy: Kindly excuse me my fine, feathery, furry friends. I believe I just saw a fierce creature come crawling out of Hare's house. I, the terrible warrior, will pursue him, for my supper is long past due.

(Entire ensemble plays themes.)

Use puppets, or have students design their own masks and costumes to represent each of the characters in "The Fierce Creature."

Have students design a set. Use this set as a background for a performance of this folk tale for parents, friends, and other members of the community.

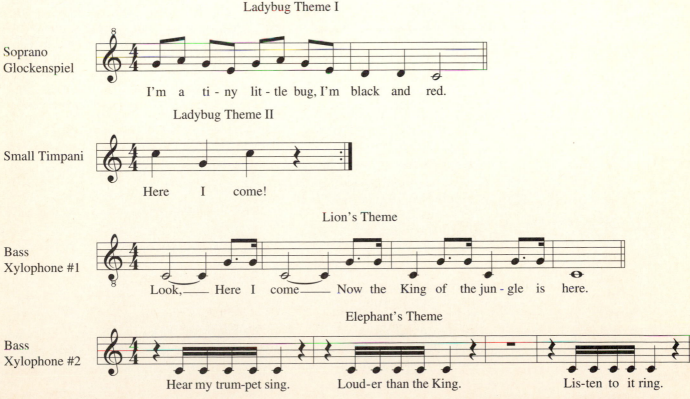

Buzzard Theme

Soprano Metallophone

fly - ing   glid - ing   fly - ing - glid - ing

Note: Slide mallets smoothly from the bottom C to the top C, and then reverse.

Racoon's Theme

Alto Xylophone

Two   black   eyes
What   sur - prise
Look - ing   for   my   sup - per.

Giraffe's Theme (Repeat 4Xs)

Soprano Xylophone

wood-block

Froggie's Theme (Repeat 3Xs)

Alto Xylophone

Note: With the exception of the "Hare's Theme," continue to play each old animal theme when the new animal theme is introduced. This layering technique will result in a wonderful sounding orchestration for this African folk tale.

SELECTED PIECES OF MUSIC FOR INTEGRATED ACTIVITIES

Many songs and instrumental works are available to add to the students' understanding of important events in U.S. and world history, science, and physical education. A few suggestions, given here, will show the richness of musical selections available.

U.S. and World History

People
Abraham, Martin, and John   Holler
   (commemoration of the assassinations
   of Lincoln, King, and Kennedy)
A Lincoln Portrait   Copland
An American in Paris   Gershwin
Appalachian Spring   Copland
   (pioneer couple in Appalachian Mountains)

American Indian
Breezes Are Blowing   Luiseno
Duck Dance   Seminole
Grinding Corn   Hopi
Ho, Ho, Watanay   Iroquois

Indian Lullaby	Quinault
Open Plain	Arapahoe
Stick Game Song	Paiute
Sun-Dance Song	Sioux
Sunrise Song	Zuni

American Cowboy

Billy the Kid	Copland
Chisholm Trail	
Cowboy's Lament	
Git Along Little Dogies	
Goodbye Old Paint	
Home on the Range	
I Ride an Old Paint	
My Home's in Montana	
Rodeo	Copland

Places

American Salute	Gould
America the Beautiful	Ward/Bates
Grand Canyon Suite	Grofé
Mississippi Suite	Grofé
(people and events associated with the Mississippi River)	
Three Places in New England	Ives
Variations on "America"	Ives

(Events)

Revolutionary War

"Chester" from New England Triptych (hymn adopted as a Revolutionary War marching song)	W. Schuman
"Midnight Ride of Paul Revere" from selections from *McGuffey's Reader*	Phillips

Civil War

Battle Hymn of the Republic (written to inspire Union soldiers)	Howe/Steffe
I Wish I Was In Dixie Land	Emmett
When Johnny Comes Marching Home	Lambert

World Wars

I Left My Heart at the Stage Door Canteen	Berlin
Over There	Cohan
Threnody for the Victims of Hiroshima	Penderecki
War Requiem	Britten
We Did It Before and We Can Do It Again	Friend and Tobias

Railroads

Casey Jones	
500 Miles	West
John Henry	
This Train	
The Train Is A-Coming, Oh Yes	
The Wabash Cannon Ball	

1960s

A Hard Rain's A'Gonna Fall (social evils: war, prejudice, poverty, oppression)	Dylan
Ghetto (poverty)	Baez
Last Train to Nuremberg	Seeger

Like a Rolling Stone	Dylan
(social conventions, authority)	
Turn, Turn, Turn	Seeger
Where Have All the Flowers Gone	Seeger
We Shall Overcome	American Freedom Song
(adaptation of an old hymn used	
during Civil Rights movement)	

Children can be aided in understanding other cultures by singing songs and performing the dances of many countries. Classroom teachers have repeated opportunities to incorporate multicultural music into units highlighting specific countries. These ethnic songs are the most popular and accessible for children:

Africa
Banuwa	Liberia
Everybody Loves Saturday Night	Ghana
Kum Bah Yah	South Africa
Nana Bread	
Nigerian Boat Song	Nigeria
Obwisana	Ghana
Tina Singu	
Tue Tue	Ghana

Canada
Going Over the Sea
Huron Carol
Land of the Silver Birch
Lots o' Fish in Bonavist' Harbor

China
Crescent Moon
Jasmine Flower
Trot, Pony, Trot
Song of the Dragon

Czechoslovakia
Above the Plain
Ifca's Castle
Let Us Sing Together
Waters Ripple and Flow

England
Bell Horses
Greensleeves
Gypsy Rover
Hey, Ho! Anybody Home?
Hot Cross Buns
London Bridge
Muffin Man
There Was a Jolly Miller

France
Frère Jacques
The Happy River
In the Moonlight (Au clair de la lune)
Pat-A-Pan
A Rat and the Cat

Germany
All Things Bright and Beautiful
Little Cabin in the Wood
Music Alone Shall Live
My Hat
O Christmas Tree
Silent Night

Israel (Hebrew)
Artsa Alinu
Hanukkah
Hava Nagila
Zum Gali Gali

Mexico
Counting Song
De Colores
Don Gato
El Rorro
La Bamba

Japan
Bento-Uri
Japanese Rain Song
Sakura
Teru Teru Bozu

Russia
Birch Tree
Minka
The Peddler
Russian Slumber Song

Scotland
Aiken Drum
Charlie Is My Darling
Did You Ever See a Lassie?
Skye Boat Song

Some children's recordings contain songs dealing with mathematics, such as the Hap Palmer records: *Learning Basic Skills Through Music*. These include "The Number March" and "Triangle, Circle, Square." Other Palmer records containing aids to learning math are *Math Readiness—Vocabulary and Concepts*, *Math Readiness—Addition and Subtraction*, and *Singing Multiplication Tables*.

Science

Music can be an added dimension in the world of science. Whether studying birds, animals, weather, or sound, a variety of recordings can be used to enhance the science lesson. Some appropriate recordings include:

Carnival of the Animals	Saint-Saëns
Clouds	Debussy
Dance of the Mosquito	Liadov
Flight of the Bumble Bee	Rimsky-Korsakov
Four Seasons	Vivaldi
From the Diary of a Fly	Bartok
Happy Farmer	Schumann
Lightning	Glass
Little Windmills	Couperin
The Planets	Holst
Sea Piece with Birds	Thomson
To the Rising Sun	Torjussen
Wild Horseman	Schumann

Recordings that can be used with a lesson on sound and how it is produced might include:

Ancient Voices of Children	Crumb
Composition for Synthesizer	Babbit
Dripsody	Le Caine

Electronic Study No. 1	Davidovsky
Ionization	Varèse
Piece for Tape Recorder	Ussachevsky
Poème Electronique	Varèse
Variations for Flute and Electronic Sound	Carlos

Physical Education

A variety of music materials are available for use with physical fitness activities. Developing coordination and muscle strength are easier when activities are set to music. Some useful recordings are:

Clap, Snap, and Tap	Brazelton
Fitness Fun for Everyone	Jervey
Multicultural Rhythm Stick Fun	Stewart
Musical Ball Skills	Greiger and Popper
Perceptual-Motor Rhythm Games	Capon, Hallum, and Glass
Rhythm Stick Activities	Glass and Hallum
Synchronized Lummi Sticks	Hughes
Tinikling	Kazan

Related Arts

Relating the arts through the use of common principles is an effective way to help children develop an understanding of artistic concepts. The use of such principles as repetition-contrast, simplicity-complexity, tension-relaxation, balance, and motion can provide variety to music class presentations while highlighting important aspects of music, art, and literature.

One way to approach the study of repetition and contrast in related arts is to ask children to close their eyes and imagine a "nose," any nose—on a friend, an elephant, a pig. We all know what a nose is, even though it may come in different shapes and sizes, depending on who's "wearing" it. The arts have things in common also, even though what is common may take on different aspects in a painting than in a poem or a song. Have children experiment with different aspects of repetition and contrast. Provide a variety of shapes (▷ ○ □) of different sizes and colors. Ask students to create art by arranging the shapes on paper with very little contrast present. Students may choose one color and shape in varying sizes:

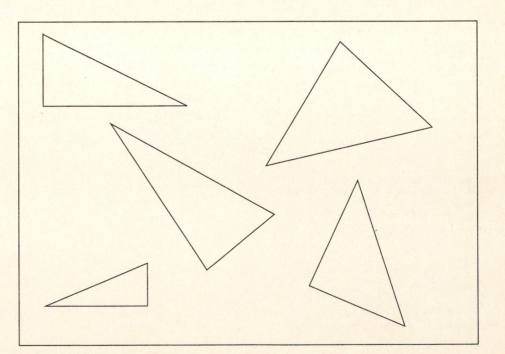

Then have students experiment with maintaining some repetition but increasing the amount of contrast.

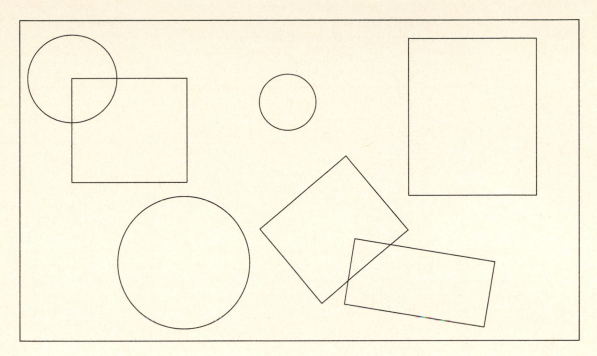

Students can look for repetition and contrast in objects in their environment and in the design in their clothing. Provide examples of repetition and contrast in a variety of folk art, such as beaded moccasins, quilts, and ceremonial masks. Paintings are also rich sources containing good examples of repetition and contrast, such as:

Three Musicians	Picasso
Coca Cola	Warhol
Composition with Red, Blue, Yellow	Mondrian
Broadway Boogie Woogie	Mondrian
Casiopée	Vasarely
Homage to the Square	Albers

Students can apply the principles of repetition and contrast to poetry by studying a variety of poems and identifying where these principles occur. Read the poem "The Wind" by Robert Louis Stevenson. Ask students where repetition occurs. How would the poem change if we removed the repetition? Is there a balance between repetition and contrast in this poem?

THE WIND

I saw you toss the kites on high
And blow the birds about the sky;
And all around I heard you pass,
Like ladies' skirts across the grass—
    O wind, a-blowing all day long,
    O wind, that sings so loud a song!

I saw the different things you did,
But always you yourself you hid.
I felt you push, I heard you call,
I could not see yourself at all—
    O wind, a-blowing all day long,
    O wind, that sings so loud a song!

O you that are so strong and cold,
O blower, are you young or old?
Are you beast of field and tree,
Or just a stronger child than me?
O wind, a-blowing all day long,
O wind, that sings so loud a song!

Provide other good poems that contain clear examples of repetition and contrast, such as:

Poem	Langston Hughes
African Dance	Langston Hughes
House on the Hill	E. A. Robinson
Lazy Jane	Shel Silverstein
The Clam	Shel Silverstein
Serenade	H. W. Longfellow
The Tide Rises, the Tide Falls	H. W. Longfellow
Swift Things Are Beautiful	E. J. Coatsworth

Children will enjoy creating their own poems that show their understanding of the use of repetition and contrast.

Students should be invited to sing a song containing a clear example of repetition and contrast. A good beginning song might be the Czechoslovakian folk song "Above the Plain." After they have learned the song, students should identify how phrases 1 and 2 are contrasting, with one melody line rising and the other falling. Phrases 3 and 4 are exactly the same. Show the repetition and contrast in this song by using letters of the alphabet: abcc.

ABOVE THE PLAIN

Czech Folk Song

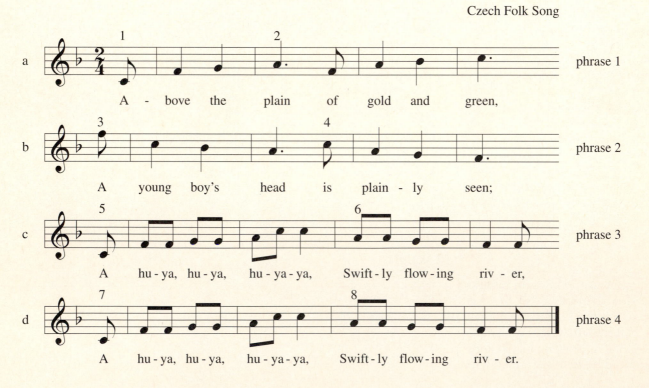

Other songs having clear examples of repetition and contrast are:

Sarasponda
Twinkle, Twinkle, Little Star
Twelve Days of Christmas
Some Folks   Foster
On the Road Again   Nelson
To a Wild Rose   MacDowell

INTEGRATION OF THE ARTS

Music, visual art, and poetry can be integrated into a variety of lessons in the general classroom:

1. When studying units in social science, students can perform the songs and dances of a country, view a video demonstrating the country's music, study the country's visual art (paintings, sculpture, architecture), read poems or stories about the country, or write their own poems and short stories about some interesting characteristic of the country.
2. Students can make individual collages about themselves and the country (or one of the countries) of their ancestry. They can perform a song from each of the countries represented in the class and read poems or stories about those countries. Some students may even have native dress or other native objects that they can show to the class.
3. Instead of making collages, as in number 2, students can be organized into groups representing the country of their origin. Each group is responsible for completing a mural portraying characteristics of their country. White or brown butcher or wrapping paper works well for the murals.
4. When studying a topic in the natural sciences (weather, animals, plant life, insects), students can sing songs whose words address the topic, read or write poems about the topic, and use the topic in an art activity.

WRITTEN AND PERFORMANCE-RELATED ASSESSMENTS THROUGH COOPERATIVE LEARNING ACTIVITIES: SPECIALIZED AREAS

1. Give each group a short story. The group should read through the story and decide what kind of sound effects (body sounds, instruments) would enhance it. The story should be practiced and then performed for the class. (Language Arts)

2. After studying a particular country in social studies, each group should prepare a short drama incorporating information about such things as the history, geography, customs, arts, and food of the country. Each drama can be presented to the class. (Language Arts/Social Studies)

3. The murals suggested under the title "Integration of the Arts" can be organized as a cooperative learning activity. Each mural should include some aspect of the country's musical life. (Social Studies)

4. Give each group a folk dance characteristic of a particular country or countries being studied. Group members must work out the movements and be ready to perform the dance for the class. (Social Studies)

5. Give each group a different set of materials, each set containing a picture of an art work, a poem, and a known song. Students must study each art form to discover in what ways repetition and contrast (or balance, motion, or tension/relaxation) are present. When finished, they can present their conclusions to the class. (Related Arts)

LEARNERS WHO PRESENT VARIATIONS IN THE MUSIC SETTINGS

In most classrooms there are students with a wide range of abilities. Some students grasp concepts quickly, and others require a great deal of assistance and a much longer time. Some students are well behaved, and others need structure and support to achieve acceptable behavior. Some students feel comfortable with their peers, and others struggle to feel at ease. Especially in the music classroom, students who excel in math and science may have difficulty singing a song or clapping a simple rhythm in front of their peers. On the other hand, music may come easily for a student who has difficulty in reading or understanding why $13 - 7 = 6$. Variations in students' readiness and abilities contribute to the wonder of individuality. When these differences come together within a classroom of students, the range of diversity becomes obvious.

Although students with special needs, gifted and talented students, and ethnically diverse students are indistinguishable from their peers in most ways, their learning needs can be quite demanding and, consequently, present a challenge to the teacher. This chapter provides teachers with guidelines and suggestions for working with the complex and often perplexing diversities that may confront them when planning for students who vary in their ways of accessing and experiencing knowledge in their environment.

MAINSTREAMING

Mainstreaming arose from the Individuals with Disabilities Education Act (IDEA), a federal law passed in 1975. It mandated that all children receive a free, appropriate public education regardless of the level of severity of their disability. It provides funds to assist states in the education of students with disabilities and requires that states make sure that these students receive an individualized education program based on their unique needs in the least restrictive environment possible. IDEA also provides guidelines for determining what related services are necessary and outlines a "due process" procedure to make sure these needs are adequately met.

INCLUSION

In recent years, the term *inclusion* has been used extensively to describe a process and philosophy associated with the mainstreaming law, but it is not synonymous with the term *mainstreaming*. Mainstreaming is viewed as a benchmark through which students "earn" their way back into the classroom, but inclusion establishes the student's "right" to be there in the first place. Services and supports are brought to the regular classroom as needed.

The latest legal addition to inclusion, the Individuals with Disabilities Education Act Amendments of 1997, was signed into law by President Clinton on June 4, 1997. A primary implication of the 1997 amendments is the need for all educators to share in the responsibilities for services provided to all students, including those with disabilities. "The IDEA Amendments reflect a step beyond compliance in pursuit of quality." The amendment allows educators to plan for at-risk students even though they are not disabled.

The current inclusive movement clearly challenges all teachers to look beyond mainstreaming to find inclusive strategies to meet students' individual needs. In an inclusive setting it is crucial to invite parents, teachers, community members, and students to join together to be a part of a new culture. Each person should be encouraged to participate to the fullness of his or her capacity—as partners and as members.

WHO ARE LEARNERS WHO PRESENT VARIATION?

Students who are in need of instructional adaptations to make learning take place adequately are candidates for inclusion. These students, although the same as their peers, come to the attention of the teacher because they require a variation in the presentation of materials being taught them. For example, every class, no matter how homogenous, has its "bright" and "not-so-bright" students and its troublemakers or behavior problems. In addition, there are students who, at one time or another, will be disabled physically because of broken or nonfunctional limbs. Consequently, it is necessary for teachers to have some knowledge of the basic characteristics of students with special needs if they are to be adequately prepared to help them develop to their highest potential while in the classroom.

Students who require special adaptations in how their information is presented fall into three major categories: (a) those who have special needs due to learning disabilities, (b) the gifted and talented, and (c) ethnically diverse students.

Students with Special Learning Needs

These students include those who are challenged by mental, physical, sensory, linguistic, or emotional disabilities, such as behavior disorders, attention deficits, mental retardation, speech and language disorders, vision and learning disabilities, and physical and health limitations.

Students who have special learning needs usually have average or above average intelligence and succeed at many tasks. However, because of a variance in how they access information, they experience difficulty in areas of the curriculum dependent on attention, perception, and memory. They find themselves challenged when it comes to receiving and trying to process information. Their memories may be poor, or they may have insufficient skills for communicating information to others. Some students who are challenged mentally are passive learners who fail to become actively involved in the assigned task. Many are frustrated. When given a music book, for example, they may simply stare at the page without actively studying its content.

Despite adequate intelligence, students who are challenged because of their inability to process and communicate experience learning problems. They appear to achieve, but their performance falls short of expectations. Academically, these students often enter school with poor listening or speaking skills. In the early grades, skills such as reading and spelling may be difficult.

Students who struggle in the learning environment are often characterized by their high level of activity. They are constantly moving about and, as a result, have difficulty paying attention to school tasks. Others, while not overactive, may be impulsive and easily distracted. Students who have special learning needs do not have obvious physical problems; in appearance, they are indistinguishable from their classmates. However, some students may have motor control problems, such as running, skipping, or jumping poorly. Fine motor skills required for playing a triangle or claves may be troublesome. Perpetual motor difficulties are often evident in these students' rhythmic abilities; they may not be able to keep a simple, steady beat. With proper training they can overcome many of these difficulties.

Students who have special needs can be helped to build an integrated visual and verbal repertoire. They should have the opportunity to communicate internalized experiences, and they must be able to develop learning skills on all levels—reception, organization, and expression. Carefully planned procedures based on the specific needs of the student who has special needs are important. Limitations should be placed on the student's space, time, choices, materials, workload, and discussion opportunities. Parameters and borders will help the students organize their activities more effectively.

Students with Behavior Disorders

Students with behavior disorders are often described by teachers as being rowdy, unruly, disruptive, and even aggressive. Although most students with behavior disorders have adequate intelligence and hearing, vision, and physical abilities, they often show unsatisfactory achievement in academic skills. The term *behavior disorder* includes a wide range of disabilities. One of the most common diagnoses for elementary school children that deserves discussion is attention deficit–hyperactivity disorder.

Classroom teachers, as well as music specialists, should be able to recognize specific behaviors connected to attention deficit–hyperactivity disorder, often referred to as *ADHD*, because this disorder creates many problems for children. In school, these children have difficulties with listening, paying attention, and sitting still. Some of these children may have trouble learning—a problem that can be compounded by a specific learning disability that is not part of their attention deficit disorder or their hyperactivity. Diagnostic criteria for the ADHD student include:

1. often fidgets with hands or feet or squirms in seat
2. has difficulty sitting still when required to do so
3. is easily distracted
4. has difficulty waiting a turn
5. often blurts out answers before being recognized
6. has difficulty finishing an assignment
7. has difficulty paying attention
8. often shifts from one uncompleted activity to another
9. has difficulty playing quietly
10. often talks excessively
11. often interrupts others
12. often does not seem to listen to what is being said
13. often loses things necessary to complete a task
14. often involves self in physically dangerous activities without considering possible consequences
15. is usually quite intelligent
16. usually succeeds in school and other life activities*

Usually, ADHD does not interfere with a student's desire or ability to engage in musical experiences. In fact, children who have this disorder are often some of the most creative in a music setting.

The more severe of the behavior disorders are serious emotional disturbances: These students generally require special services and are not included in regular classroom instructional programs. However, some instructional programs allow most students with relatively mild behavior disorders to be taught successfully in the mainstream.

*Note: The above criteria are taken from *A Parent's Guide to Attention Deficit Disorders* by Lisa J. Bain. Copyright © 1991 by The Children's Hospital of Chicago. Used by permission of Dell Books, a division of Bantam Doubleday Dell Publishing Group, Inc.

Mentally Challenged Students

In the educational setting, general ability is established by comparing the performance of one student with that of others of the same age. Those who fall within the lowest two to three percent are considered mentally challenged. Within this group of students are several levels of abilities. Most of these students have the ability to learn some music skills.

Mentally challenged students are generally delayed in most, if not all, academic subject areas. They are characterized by having a slower rate of learning and greater difficulty with reasoning tasks. They usually have difficulty focusing attention and transferring information and skills learned in one setting to another situation. Tasks involving abstract reasoning and problem solving pose special problems, but some students are highly creative in music. Sometimes frustration results from repeated failures and a lack of expressive communication skills, but music offers a means for success and expression.

Students with Speech and Language Disorders

Communication problems are primary with students who have speech and language disorders. A student's speech may be difficult for others to understand, or language development may be delayed. Students who have difficulty in understanding and expressing ideas appropriate to their age may be experiencing language problems. Those with adequate language but poor sound production, fluency, or voice quality may be candidates for special services in communication.

Because music includes activities that continually reinforce rhythmic competencies through speech activity and singing, students with speech and language disorders often improve considerably through this medium. Reading lyrics to songs and working on breath control to sing a phrase without breaking the flow offer positive feedback to students who find it difficult to speak or read a complete sentence or paragraph fluently.

Students with Sensory Deficits

Sensory deficits include difficulties with processing information through any of the sensory pathways but usually are most evident in vision and hearing. Students who experience vision difficulties may be blind or partially sighted; those with hearing disorders may be deaf or have impaired hearing. In either case, students who are challenged visually or aurally must be assisted to learn through the senses still available to them. These students, whose impairments may range from mild to severe, may exhibit a wide range of abilities and thereby present a variety of problems to the classroom teacher. Visually impaired students may have difficulty in mobility and in reading print or other visual materials; those with hearing problems may experience difficulty in language development and oral communication.

Both the degree of the disability and the specific characteristics of the student influence the nature and the extent of his or her success in the classroom setting. Students who are challenged visually are taught to rely on unaffected senses, such as hearing and touch. For example, they may learn to read braille or develop their listening skills. For the hearing impaired, adjustments to the music environment are more difficult, because music is an aural art. However, many students with hearing impairments feel vibrations and can participate successfully in most group activities, including movement and dance, which are crucial for normal development.

Students Who Are Challenged by Physical and Health Disabilities

Students who are challenged with disabilities are a heterogeneous group. They represent a variety of conditions and diseases: cerebral palsy, paralysis, epilepsy, diabetes, and AIDS, to name a few. Some physical and health problems are congenital, meaning that they are present at birth through disease, injury, or accident. Physical and health problems may have grave, little, or no effect on the school performance of the student. Some students require no special adaptations, while others require special instruction in many areas such as mobility, communication, and basic skills. Dependency on others is one of the greatest problems of these students.

Students who are challenged with physical and health disabilities may participate fully in regular classroom activities. Those with limited physical mobility, such as being confined to a wheelchair, may take a less active role. Some with chronic health problems may have special needs due to prolonged absences. Nevertheless, students who are challenged physically and those with health impairments can learn successfully in a totally inclusive learning environment. For many of these special students, their physical problems have little effect on their ability to learn.

The music classroom provides an environment in which students are involved in a variety of music-making tasks. These tasks often involve small- and large-group activities, thus providing opportunities for handicapped students to work with their peers.

Gifted and Talented Students

Like students who have special needs due to a learning disability, gifted and talented students are among those who present variations in the learning setting. According to Section 902 of Public Law 95-561—the Gifted and Talented Children's Act of 1978—"The term *gifted and talented children* means children and, whenever applicable, youth who are identified at the preschool, elementary, or secondary level as possessing demonstrated or potential abilities that give evidence of high performance capabilities in areas such as intellectual, creative, specific or leadership ability, or in the performing and visual arts. . . . Their special abilities often require special attention and teaching techniques." Children who are gifted are often described as being unusually bright. They may formulate concepts quickly and excel in many areas. Some gifted students are creative; others may have special abilities in specific areas such as art, music, drama, and sports. To develop to their fullest potential, gifted and talented students must have provisions made for their special learning needs.

Ethnically Diverse Students

Students who are from ethnically diverse backgrounds also present a different type of challenge. Ethnically diverse individuals are those reared in cultures that are at variance with that of the school or different from the dominant American culture. These students usually face at least two sets of expectations: those of the home and those of the school. Many times these expectations are contradictory. Included within this group are minority, culturally different, and bilingual or non–English-speaking students. Some have special learning needs; others do not. If, however, communication is difficult, learning problems may result, thus making it necessary for a mainstream approach to teaching.

INCLUSION IN THE MUSIC CLASSROOM

Developing Sensitivity

Music adds an important dimension to the emotional and aesthetic growth of all children, regardless of physical or mental limitations. This makes the music program a prime area in which inclusion can take place successfully. However, successful inclusion in the music classroom depends on a combination of variables that must be addressed before proper learning can take place. First and foremost, the teacher must be sensitive to and understanding of students who present variations in their learning styles. To help develop sensitivity in themselves and in their students, teachers should:

1. be open and honest with students from the beginning. Don't avoid answering questions. Hold class discussions that will allow students to ask questions and explore feelings.
2. discuss with the class conditions that challenge members in our society. This will help in the development of positive attitudes as well as instill a sense of responsibility within all children in the mainstream setting.
3. view, with the class, filmstrips and films on individuals who are challenged. Many instructional materials are available that will help acquaint students with the needs of students who need extra help.
4. emphasize similarities rather than differences.
5. be honest with yourself. Find help if you need assistance or advice.

Planning Musical Experiences

When practicing total inclusion, the teacher should take into consideration where each student is developmentally. After a careful review of each child has taken place and needs have been identified, the teacher can implement appropriate teaching goals and strategies that address the special needs of the students involved. An *individualized education program,* or IEP, which includes developmental skills in music, helps serve this purpose. An IEP provides the classroom teacher and the music teacher with a statement of (a) the present level of educational performance of the mainstreamed child; (b) annual goals, including short-term instructional objectives; (c) the specific educational services that will be provided to the student, and the extent to which the student will participate in regular educational programs; (d) the projected date for initiation and anticipated duration of such services and appropriate objective criteria; and (e) evaluation procedures and schedules for determining, on at least an annual basis, whether instructional objectives are being achieved.

The General Music Assessment Form that follows provides the teacher with a format for assessing students in the area of general music. Cognitive, affective, and psychomotor activities that address levels of basic musical competencies in singing, rhythmic activities, moving, playing instruments, listening, and creating should be included as major components of the assessment form.

Beginning goals for students in the inclusive general music classroom are similar to those for all students in music. Learning in music begins with students becoming aware of sound and being able to attend to sound as perceived through visual, auditory, and/or kinesthetic senses. For example, the student can sit with the teacher at the piano, an Orff instrument, an autoharp or drum and can touch the piano, another instrument, or the teacher's hand, to feel the vibrations. The student can learn when there is music and when it is absent, when the sound is high and when it is low; can feel a rhythmic pulse, and can make sounds and experience how sounds feel. Sound vibrations can be felt by the body and through the body's contact with the floor or with instruments. A deaf student can learn to feel music in a room and respond to it.

Instruction, especially in the mainstream, should focus on the overall meaning of music as an expressive art form rather than on numerous nonmusical purposes. Teachers should always develop programs that regularly include a variety of musical experiences that involve children in speech and sound production, gross and fine motor movement, eye-hand coordination, rhythmic perception and production, socialization and cooperation, concentration and memory work, and creative as well as recreative fulfillment.

GENERAL MUSIC ASSESSMENT FORM

Rarely
Sometimes
Frequently
Usually
Always

R S F U A   **JOY**
R S F U A   1. Student willingly participates in musical experiences.
R S F U A   2. Student appears to enjoy musical activities
R S F U A   3. Student engages in musical activities (singing, listening, playing instruments) during leisure time
R S F U A   4. Student requests musical activities for self and/or class

R S F U A   **VOLUME**
R S F U A   1. Student distinguishes between loud and soft
R S F U A   2. Student identifies gradual changes in volume
R S F U A   3. Student controls volume in performances

R S F U A   **DURATION**
R S F U A   1. Student distinguishes between long and short sounds
           2. Student maintains steady beat by:
R S F U A   Clapping
R S F U A   Moving (walking, tapping toe, etc.)
R S F U A   Playing percussion instruments
           3. Student identifies changes in tempo (speed of the beat) by:
R S F U A   Clapping
R S F U A   Moving
R S F U A   Playing instruments
R S F U A   4. Student repeats rhythmic pattern
R S F U A   5. Student maintains pattern as accompaniment

R S F U A   **PITCH**
R S F U A   1. Student distinguishes between high and low sounds
R S F U A   2. Student identifies direction of melodic movement
           3. Student produces short melodic fragments
R S F U A   On instruments
R S F U A   Vocally
R S F U A   4. Student distinguishes between stepwise and skipwise movements
R S F U A   5. Student distinguishes between large and small skips

R S F U A   **TIMBRE**
R S F U A   1. Student distinguishes between many classroom and environmental sounds
R S F U A   2. Student distinguishes between sounds of musical instruments
R S F U A   3. Student matches picture and sound of common instruments
R S F U A   4. Students names common instruments by sight
R S F U A   5. Student names common instruments from the sound

R S F U A   **FORM**
R S F U A   1. Student recognizes repeated sounds and sound patterns
R S F U A   2. Student recognizes phrase endings
R S F U A   3. Student recognizes repeated and contrasting sections within a composition

R S F U A   **STYLE**
R S F U A   1. Student distinguishes between different popular and classical styles
R S F U A   2. Student expresses a preference for a specific style

MUSICAL ADAPTATIONS FOR USE IN THE "INCLUSIVE" SETTING

Although musical experiences designed to help reinforce musical learnings in the music classroom are similar to those used in the nonmainstream classroom, teachers must devote more time to preparing special materials that will make the formulation of concepts possible for all students.

Rhythm Activities in the Mainstream

Perhaps one of the most irresistible yet effective rhythmic activities that engage all students is "Going on a Bear Hunt." The teacher should encourage student participation by inviting them to alternate hands on their laps while echoing the following lines after the teacher. (The teacher should perform this activity with much expression.)

BEAR HUNT

I'm goin' on a bear hunt (Alternate hands on lap)
I'm not afraid
I've got my trusty camera
And my film by my side.
All right?
O.K.?
Let's go!
I see a wheat field.
Can't go over it.
Can't go around it.
I'll have to go through it. (Swish hands together 16 times)
I see a bridge.　　　　　(Thump chest 16 times)
I see a mud hole.
I see a stream.　　　　　(Swim, using strokes, 16 times)
I see a tree.　　　　　　(Place one fist on top of another and climb)
I see a cave.　　　　　　(Slow down as students enter the imaginary cave)
What is this?
IT'S A BEAR!!!　　　　　(Scream!!!)

When teaching students to identify basic beat or pulse, the teacher may choose to provide colorful charts, similar to the ones provided here, that contain symbols representing pulse and rhythm, rather than the musical notation itself. Have students look at the pictures and say the words in rhythm.

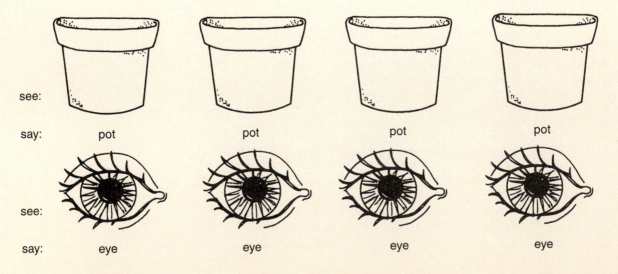

see:

say:　　pot　　　　　pot　　　　　pot　　　　　pot

see:

say:　　eye　　　　　eye　　　　　eye　　　　　eye

Teachers can use symbols that hook together to represent ♫, as in the "flower" and "glasses" shown here.

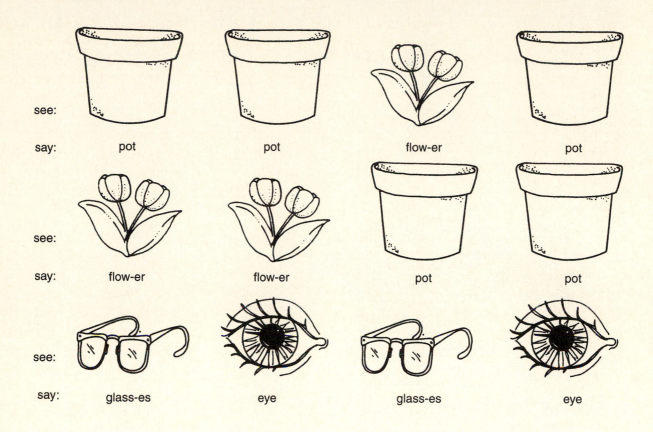

see:

say: pot   pot   flow-er   pot

see:

say: flow-er   flow-er   pot   pot

see:

say: glass-es   eye   glass-es   eye

Once students are comfortable with combinations of these patterns, stick notation can replace the pictures.

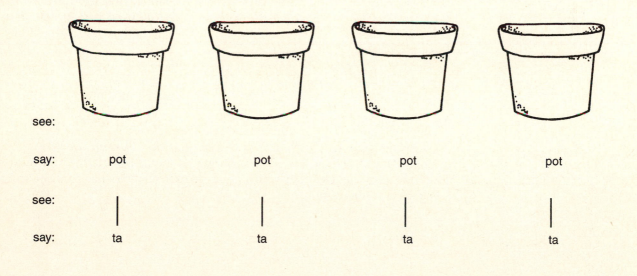

see:

say: pot   pot   pot   pot

see:

say: ta   ta   ta   ta

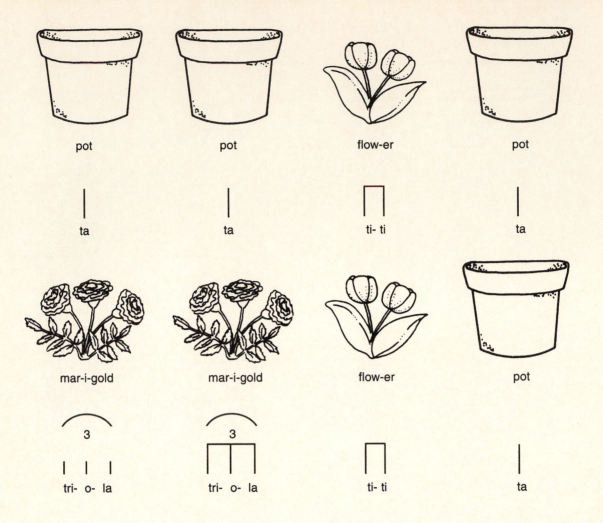

Adapting the rhythm lesson in this way will help those students who need visual reinforcement to prolong their attention span. Gifted and talented students could be asked to find other symbols that could be used to represent the basic pulse and its division. They could then create charts that could be used by their classmates.

Simple echo clapping is particularly helpful in assisting children to develop aural skills. Combining rhythm with words or chant, as in the examples provided, should follow echo clapping for a more challenging task. The use of chants, rhymes, and nonsense syllables offers a nonthreatening activity in which students can demonstrate selected musical competencies.

Students who have difficulty with coordination can keep the basic pulse on a drum, indicated by X below. More advanced students can clap the entire rhythm. They can also suggest other words or nonsense syllables that can be used to accompany a given rhythm.

NAME GAME

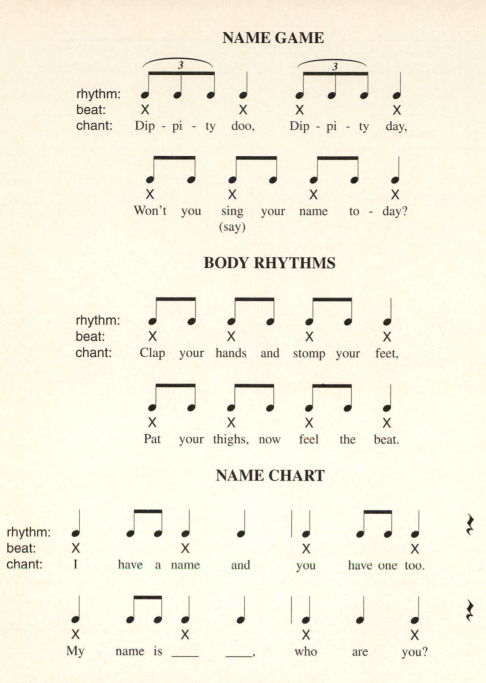

rhythm:
beat: X   X   X   X
chant: Dip - pi - ty doo, Dip - pi - ty day,

beat: X   X   X   X
       Won't you sing your name to - day?
                (say)

BODY RHYTHMS

rhythm:
beat: X   X   X   X
chant: Clap your hands and stomp your feet,

beat: X   X   X   X
       Pat your thighs, now feel the beat.

NAME CHART

rhythm:
beat: X   X   X   X
chant: I   have a name and you have one too.

beat: X   X   X   X
       My name is ___ ___, who are you?

The regularity of the rhythm established in the above examples can be transferred to a rhythmic game as in "Train, Train, Choo Choo Train." The game allows all students to create movement patterns with their bodies, play a rhythm pattern using body percussion, play rhythm instruments, or improvise vocally. Students should be organized in a circle. As the entire class repeats the chant, each member of the group takes a turn creating a pattern through playing, moving, or singing.

Children's Game   Collected by René Boyer Alexander

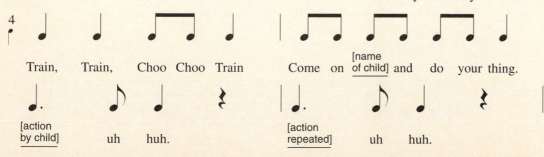

Train, Train, Choo Choo Train   Come on [name of child] and do your thing.

[action by child] uh huh.   [action repeated] uh huh.

If there is a nonambulatory student in the class, a movement activity similar to the one described above can be accomplished by any or all body parts that have a range of motion. In addition, a wheelchair can be pushed, pulled, and turned by others, in rhythm to the music.

The use of chant is usually helpful to mainstream students, especially to those who are learning disabled and those who are challenged due to speech and language disorders. The rhythmic flow of the words provides helpful exercises for these students, and should be included in the music classroom on a regular basis. More advanced students should be guided to add pentatonic melodies to rhythms or chants. Ostinati patterns or varying complexities can also be created and transferred to Orff instruments.

Using rap in the music class is another tool for involving students in music activities. The following raps have been widely accepted by upper elementary school students in an all-inclusive setting.

JUST GIMME THE BEAT

Composed by René Boyer-Alexander

A ROLL CALL GAME

A Section

Sha - boo-ya!   Sha,   Sha,   Sha - boo-ya, Roll Call

Have students form a circle.

Repeat the chant. Use this as an A section to a rondo form.

Have each student alternate with the A section to create their own B section. Tell them to fill in the sentences with something they love to do. Examples have been given.

B Section

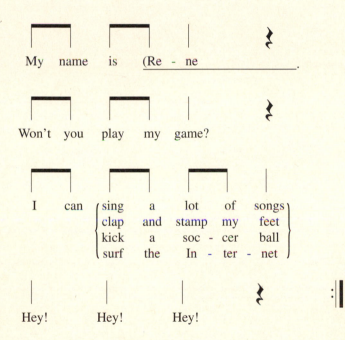

My   name   is   (Re - ne_____.

Won't   you   play   my   game?

I   can   {
sing   a   lot   of   songs
clap   and   stamp   my   feet
kick   a   soc - cer   ball
surf   the   In - ter - net
}

Hey!   Hey!   Hey!

Note: To challenge gifted students, have them attempt to repeat, sequentially, what each of their peers can do.

Singing Activities

When selecting song material that will be used in the mainstream music setting, the teacher should choose songs with much repetition and imitation. Rote teaching is preferable in the initial stages of a child's singing experiences. This process enables a student to learn the song quickly. On the other hand, interpretations of music symbols are difficult for many children in the mainstream and should be delayed. Constant reinforcement of the song at school and at home is recommended. The syllable "loo" can be used to facilitate the learning of a new melody. It removes the obstacles of speech which prove difficult for those who have speech or memory problems. The following songs include repetition, and their movement activities are easy to perform.

HEAD AND SHOULDERS

Collected by René Boyer-Alexander

Head and shoul - ders ba - by One, two,

three. Head and shoul - ders ba - by, One, two,

three. Head and shoul - ders, Head and shoul - ders, Head and shoul - ders ba - by.

One, two, three!

Note: Clap the following rhythmic ostinato throughout:

Let's Take a Walk*

Formation: Children line up behind the teacher.
Directions: The teacher should begin to sing, "Let's Take a Walk." Students should be invited to sing along as they take an imaginary walk with the teacher. When they arrive at a beautiful flower garden, they should take turns naming flowers they see. Students can also take a walk to the zoo, the farm, or through the school and other places where they can easily identify specific items, colors, and shapes.

*In the case of a non-ambulatory student, change the word "walk" to "ride."

LET'S TAKE A WALK

Composed by René Boyer-Alexander

Let's take a walk through the flowers to - day, through the
flowers to - day, through the flowers to - day.
Let's take a walk through the flowers to - day and
see what we can see.

On another day, sing "Animals in the Zoo." Assign students to small groups and
have them imitate the way different animals move.

ANIMALS IN THE ZOO

Composed by René Boyer-Alexander

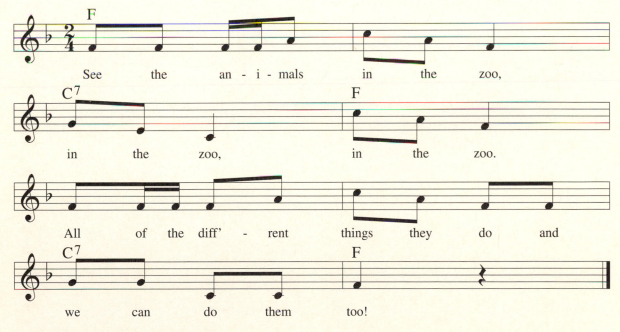

See the an - i - mals in the zoo,
in the zoo, in the zoo.
All of the diff' - rent things they do and
we can do them too!

2. Elephants, tigers, and the big baboon
   Did a little dance by the light of the moon.
   They stepped to the left and then to the right;
   Moved and grooved in the full moon light.

3. An old gorilla and some chimpanzees
   Did a little rhythm on their furry knees.
   The bear, the monkey, and the lion king
   All got up and did their thing.

LOOK AT ME

Words and music by René Boyer-Alexander

Song charts provide an invaluable tool for mainstreamed students learning to sing. The pictorial representations of the words help to develop students' memories. Again, however, extra preparation on the part of the teacher is necessary. The charts should be colorful and large enough to attract the children's attention. The visuals below provide examples of charts that can be used to teach the song, "If I Had a Hammer." Only one card at a time should be made visible to the students. If all cards are shown at the same time, the element of surprise will be lost and attention will be divided in several directions.

Hammer Song Charts

IF I HAD A HAMMER

Words and music by
Lee Hays and Pete Seeger

1. If I had a hammer,____ I'd hammer in the
2. If I had a bell,____ I'd ring it in the
3. If I had a song,____ I'd sing it in the
4. Well, I've got a hammer,____ And I've____ got a

morn - ing,____ I'd ham - mer in the eve - ning,____
morn - ing,____ I'd ring it in the eve - ning,____
morn - ing,____ I'd sing it in the eve - ning,____
bell,____ And I've____ got a song,____

all o - ver this land; I'd ham - mer out
all o - ver this land; I'd ring____ out
all o - ver this land; I'd sing____ out
all o - ver this land; It's the ham - mer of

dan - ger,____ I'd ham - mer out a warn - ing,____
dan - ger,____ I'd ring____ out a warn - ing,____
dan - ger,____ I'd sing____ out a warn - ing____
jus - tice,____ It's the bell____ of____ free - dom,____

I'd ham - mer out
I'd ring____ out
I'd sing____ out love be - tween my broth-ers and my sis - ters,
It's the song a - bout

All____ o - ver this land.____

Teachers should be cautious about choosing songs that are written in too high a range. Children, especially those who are mildly retarded and those who have speech and language disorders, are usually uncomfortable when asked to sing using the head voice; they prefer the chest voice. Compromises in pitch, similar to the medium to low pitch arrangements found in the following songs, should be made if successful singing experiences are to take place.

THE GREATEST LOVE OF ALL

Music by Linda Creed

Words by Michael Masser

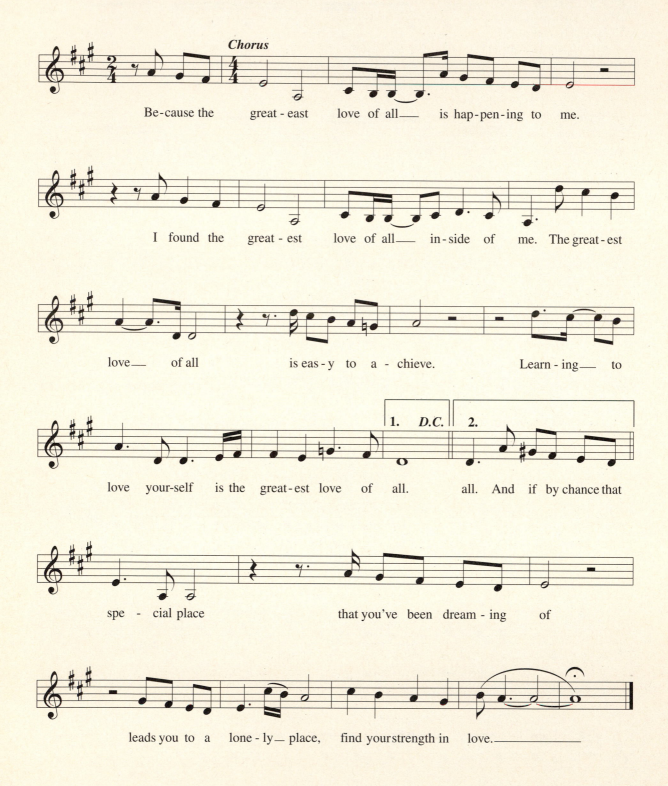

mat - ter what they take from me, they can't take a-way my dig - ni - ty.

Chorus

Be - cause the great - east love of all— is hap-pen-ing to me.

I found the great - est love of all— in-side of me. The great - est

love— of all is eas - y to a - chieve. Learn - ing— to

1. D.C. 2.

love your-self is the great - est love of all. all. And if by chance that

spe - cial place that you've been dream - ing of

leads you to a lone - ly— place, find your strength in love.———

Listening Activities

Listening can serve as a therapeutic device for many special learners. A child who needs to exert great amounts of energy can be asked to move to music that is energetic in its composition. On the other hand, music that leaves a calming or relaxing effect may be needed for some students. All listening lessons should be kept to a two- to three-minute maximum. If possible, attractive charts should accompany the listening lesson.

A list of pieces that are recommended for listening by students in an all-inclusive setting is:

Out of Africa (Motion Picture Soundtrack)
"Circle of Life" from the *Lion King* (Motion Picture Soundtrack)
"What a Wonderful World" (Sung by Louis Armstrong)
Adagio for Strings by Samuel Barber
Piano Concerto No. 2 by Sergei Rachmaninoff
Rhapsody on a Theme by Paganini by Rachmaninoff
Schindler's List (Motion Picture Soundtrack)
Dances with Wolves (Motion Picture Soundtrack)
"If You Believe" and "Home" from *The Wiz* (Musical)
Scenes from Childhood by Robert Schumann
"Earthbeat" by Paul Winter
"Changes" by R. Carlos Nakai (Native American Flute Music)
"Claire de Lune" by Claude Debussey
1st Arabesque Children's Corner Suite by Claude Debussey

When listening, children should be asked to focus on only one learning at a time, and that learning should involve gross discriminations on the part of the student. For example, the teacher might ask students: Is the music being sung, or is it being played on an instrument? What instrument do you hear playing? Is the music loud or soft? Is the music fast or slow? To ask questions that require students to recognize finer discriminations beyond their ability could lead to loss of attention or even frustration.

Playing Instruments

Playing instruments will often motivate the most reluctant of challenged students to respond to music. Every student should be given an opportunity to explore the variety of timbres that exist among selected percussive instruments. When using rhythm instruments, it might be helpful to assign those that shake, such as maracas or jingle bells, to students who have problems with coordination. Melody instruments, including the Orff barred instruments, are well designed for use in a mainstream setting. The teacher can add or remove bars to accommodate the readiness level of the player. Allowing students to compose and perform pentatonic songs on a variety of barred instruments creates a feeling of success because use of the pitches of the pentatonic scale permits mistake-free improvisation and creativity.

Music teachers should consider color-coding particular instruments, if it makes learning the instrument easier for a selected mainstreamed child. The technique of color-coding is particularly helpful, for example, when playing chords on an autoharp or when picking out keys on the piano. Eventually, notation on the staff can be coordinated with the colors of the keys or bars on the instruments, so that the mainstreamed child will begin to understand the symbols involved in reading music.

Where an instrument is placed depends on the physical limitations of the mainstreamed student. Instruments and mallets can be fastened with a Velcro band, tape, or elastic bandage to a body part when the ability to grasp is limited. Two-sided carpet tape, foam curlers, or rubber balls can also be added to handles to help a child grasp the instrument. If an instrument needs to be fastened to a wheelchair or desk, adhesive, plastic, or masking tape should secure it firmly.

Pretzel-shaped teething rings or rubber door stops are easy to grasp and help students to strum instruments, such as the autoharp.

The holes for a particular note on recorders can be blocked off with soft wax or tape so that a child need only pick up the instrument and blow. Several children can blow to accompany a song, or one child can play a single note at the proper point in a song being performed by the group.

CLASSROOM MANAGEMENT IN AN ALL-INCLUSIVE SETTING

A variety of management techniques should be taken into consideration to allow for positive experiences for children in an all-inclusive setting.

1. How students are arranged in relation to each other can affect their academic performance, classroom behavior, and social interactions. Students who have a tendency toward impulsive or erratic behavior will find that an assigned space helps them to control themselves, especially during activities involving movement. Assigning seats to students who are challenged visually or aurally will help them be more responsive. These students should be placed in close proximity to the teacher and to the chalkboard so that they can hear and see.

2. Classroom rules and routines can help to structure the learning environment. Most students need guidelines for behavior and benefit from consistently enforced rules. Rules should be simple, clearly stated, and easily enforceable by the teacher. They should be explained to students and reviewed frequently.

3. The 20-minute music class should consist of a variety of musical activities, each activity being no more than two to three minutes long. The attention span of children must be given primary consideration.

4. Directions given by the teacher should be succinctly stated and easy to understand.

5. The teacher should use a variety of teaching modalities; visual, auditory, and kinesthetic experiences should be included in daily planning.

6. Evaluation strategies in the all-inclusive classroom should be approached in a positive fashion. For example, students might be allowed to retake a test until a sufficiently high score is achieved. Evaluation of individual progress, rather than group achievement at a specific grade level, is preferred.

7. Activities assigned to the challenged child should be less complicated and capable of completion in a shorter amount of time than those assigned to regular students.

8. Communicate on a regular basis with parents/guardian. The child should be persent at some of these meetings.

WRITTEN AND PERFORMANCE-RELATED ASSESSMENTS THROUGH COOPERATIVE LEARNING ACTIVITIES: LEARNERS WHO PRESENT VARIATIONS IN THE MUSIC SETTING

1. Have students work in small groups to create their own raps for the song, "Just Gimme the Beat."
2. Place students in groups of four or five. Ask them to create a rhythmic ostinato, using body percussion, voice sounds, and/or rhythmic instruments to accompany the song, "Just Gimme the Beat."
3. Have groups of students review the English found in "Just Gimme the Beat." Discuss problems with the grammar and elicit reasons why such grammar is used. Suggest how correct grammar would affect the overall style of the speech piece.
4. Distribute a piece of paper to each student. The paper should be large enough for students to trace their bodies. Assign a partner to each student. Each partner is to trace the other. Students should add eyes, ears, a mouth, and a nose to their drawings and be encouraged to draw colorful clothes. After the project is completed, students should have an opportunity to introduce themselves to the class and to tell a little about themselves.

Parents/Student/Teacher

1. Sit together and outline exactly what will be expected of the student. Have all parties sign indicating agreement
   a. what should he/she know.
   b. what should he/she be expected to do.
2. Meet periodically to review the above agreement.

Glossary

absolute pitch names   names of the musical alphabet: ABCDEFG

accent   a symbol placed above or beneath a note head to emphasize the sound of that note: >

accidentals   symbols that are used to alter a pitch in some way: #, ♭, ♮

adagio   tempo marking indicating that the music should proceed slowly

afuche   See cabasa

agogo bells   two conical, metal bells, each having a different pitch and struck with a small rod to produce a ringing sound

alla breve   cut time or 2/2

allegro   fast pace

alto   the lowest of female voice classifications

anacrusis   an incomplete measure of one or more notes found at the beginning of a composition; also known as pick-up notes

andante   walking, moderate pace

asymmetrical   a meter that does not meet the guidelines of duple, triple, or quadruple meters: 7/8 or 5/4

augmented triad   a triad containing two major thirds

autoharp   a strumming instrument used to accompany songs and other musical compositions

baritone   a male voice classification which lies between the bass and tenor ranges

bar line   a vertical line used to separate accented groups of rhythms and/or pitches

bass   the lowest of male voice classifications

bass or F clef   a symbol used for notating relatively low pitches

beat   the underlying, unchanging, repeating pulse found in most music

beat note   the note designated by the time signature to receive one full beat within the measure

behavioral objective   a statement which contains the specific understanding or skill that is desired of a learner as well as the process through which a learner will be led to achieve the understanding or skill

binary   a composition which is divided into two sections, the second being different from the first; written as AB or binary form

bongo   two small, connected drums usually played by placing them between the knees and hitting them with various parts of the hand

brass family   a family of instruments whose basic instruments include the trumpet, trombone, French horn, and tuba

brush strum   a downward movement of the right hand across the strings of the guitar, using the backs of the fingernails

cabasa   a rhythm instrument consisting of metal beads encircled around a large wooden spool

canon   a device whereby the melody of one part is strictly imitated from beginning to end in a second voice or even a third or fourth voice

capo   a device which can be attached to the guitar neck to raise the pitch of the strings, making transposition to a key easier to achieve

castanets   two semi-hollow disks of wood attached to a stick by a cord

changing meters   meter signatures which change often, even from one measure to the next, in the same piece; mixed meters

chant   a single, unaccompanied, melodic line; monophonic music

chest register   that part of the vocal range governed by a set of throat muscles which control lower register singing

chord   the simultaneous sounding of three or more pitches

chordal   See homophonic.

chord inversion   a triad or seventh chord whose root is not at the bottom of the chord

chromatic scale   a scale whose tones are one half-step apart, resulting in twelve semitones

circle dances   dances involving one large circle or two concentric circles

claves   two wooden cylinders containing hollow spaces that resonate when struck together

clef sign   a symbol indicating the relative highness or lowness of the pitches notated

coda   a passage added to the last major section of a form

common time another name for the 4/4 time signature: ℂ

compound interval intervals which are larger than an octave

compound meter a time signature whose upper number is a multiple of three and whose beat note can be divided into three equal parts, creating a ratio of 3:1

conducting patterns hand and arm patterns, used by music directors, which represent the time signature

conga drum a long, cylindrical drum which is open at the bottom and played by striking the head with the palms of the hand

contour the direction or shape of a melody

contralto the lowest range of the alto voice

countersubject a second theme, found in some fugues, that follows the statement of the first theme

cowbell a metal instrument that is struck with a mallet or metal bar

crescendo a gradual increase in volume

cut time another name for the 2/2 time signature: ¢

cymbals two metal disks struck together using a vertical movement

Da capo al fine a common symbol (D.C. al fine) used to direct the performer to repeat a piece of music from the beginning to the term *fine*, where the piece ends

decrescendo a gradual decrease in volume

deductive approach an approach to learning that leads students through a sequence of activities from the general to the specific

descant a countermelody or second melody that is sung higher than the original melody

diaphragm a large muscle which lies across the body under the lungs; with an up-and-down motion, it supplies the impetus which becomes the foundation of the entire breathing system

diatonic stepwise

diatonic sequence a succession of pitches moving in an ascending or descending, stepwise manner:

ABCDEFG

diminished triad a triad consisting of two minor thirds

diminuendo a gradual decrease in volume

dominant seventh a four-toned chord built on the fifth degree of the scale; the added seventh above the root gives it its name

dot a dot following a note or rest which adds to that note or rest one-half of its value; a dot on top of or beneath a note will cause the note to be shortened in duration

double bar line two bar lines that designate the end of either a musical section or the complete work

downbeat the first beat in a measure

duple meter a time signature having a top number divisible by two: 2/4, 2/8, 2/2

duration the length of sound or silence of a designated note or rest

duration syllables nicknames used to designate different rhythmic structures

dynamics the degree of volume in a musical composition, ranging from very soft to very loud

elements the musical dimensions that undergird all music: rhythm, melody, harmony, texture, form, timbre, dynamics, and tempo

enharmonic terms used to designate two pitches having the same sound but different letter names

fermata a musical sign indicating that the note should be held longer than its normal duration: ⌒

fifth the top tone of a triad

finger cymbals two metal disks, held by the fingers, that are struck together using a vertical movement

flat a symbol used to lower the pitch of a note one-half step: ♭

followers those who follow the lead voice in a canon

form the structure or design of a piece of music

fugue a polyphonic composition based on a theme, called the subject, which is stated unaccompanied at the beginning of the piece, and then is taken up imitatively in other voices, called the answers, in close succession

general objectives statements that are usually expressed in behavioral terms indicating what the student will be able to do over a year's time or month-to-month

glissando rapidly sliding up or down with the voice or on an instrument

glockenspiel a small, metal, barred instrument belonging to the Orff Instrumentarium

goals broad and concise statements indicating desired terminal outcomes

gong a disk-shaped, metal instrument struck with a soft mallet

grand staff the combination of treble and bass clefs

grave tempo marking meaning as slowly as possible

guiro a hollow gourd with horizontal grooves cut across its surface. It is scraped or hit with a small wooden stick

half step the smallest interval used in most of the music of Western civilization

hand drum   a cylindrical drum head which is held by the rim

hand signs   designated hand signals which are used to reinforce the inner hearing of intervals

harmonic interval   an interval consisting of two pitches that are sounded simultaneously

harmonic minor scale   a minor scale consisting of the following whole- and half-step sequence:

WHWWH(W+H)H

harmony   the simultaneous interaction between pitches in a melody and sounds in an accompaniment

head register   that part of the vocal range governed by a set of throat muscles which affect upper register singing

homophonic texture   a texture consisting of a succession of chords that support a melody

icon   pictorial representation used to designate something other than itself, depending on its context

improvisation   a musical extemporization for voice or other instruments, performed without much preparation

inductive approach   an approach to learning that leads students through a sequence of activities from the specific to the general

interlude   a passage added to the interior of a composition. It connects one section to another more smoothly than would occur if absent.

introduction   passage occurring at the beginning of a musical work, before its major sections

irregular meters   a meter that does not meet the guidelines of duple, triple, or quadruple meters: 7/8 or 5/4

jingle clogs   an instrument possessing one or more pairs of metal disks loosely attached to a handle

key note   starting note of a scale or home tone of a key

key signature   a sign placed at the beginning of a song, immediately following the clef sign, which tells the performer the names of the sharps or flats occurring in the music

koto   13-stringed zither, native to Japan

largo   very slow pace

leader   the beginning voice in a canon

ledger lines   extra lines that are added above and beneath the staff to accommodate additional pitches

legato   a smooth, corrected progression from note-to-note

line dance   a dance consisting of any number of couples who come together in two facing lines

locomotor movement   moving from one place to another

major scale   a sequence of tones consisting of the following whole- and half-step relationships: WWHWWWH

major triad   a triad which consists of the intervals of a major third on the bottom and a minor third on the top

maracas   gourds which contain dried seeds that produce a rattling sound when shook

measure   the space between two bar lines

melodic interval   the distance in pitch between two notes sounded consecutively

melodic minor scale   a minor scale formed by raising the sixth and the seventh degrees of the natural minor scale by a half step when ascending and cancelling the alteration when descending

melody   a linear succession of sounds and silences ordered in time

metallophone   barred instruments made out of metal that belong to the Orff Instrumentarium; the tone of the metallophone possesses a high resonating quality

meter signature   See time signature.

mezzo-soprano   a soprano with a medium-high voice range

Middle C   a name given to the C located in the middle of the grand staff or the C located approximately in the middle of the piano keyboard

minor scale   a scale built on the sixth tone of the major scale; there are three different minor scales. (See natural, harmonic, and melodic minor scales.)

minor third   an interval consisting of three half steps

minor triad   a triad consisting of the intervals of a minor third on the bottom and a major third on the top

mixed meters   meter signatures which change often, even from one measure to the next, in the same piece; changing meters

mode   an arrangement of the 8 tones of the octave according to a fixed pattern, such as the major or the minor mode

moderato   tempo marking designating a medium speed

monophonic texture   a single, unaccompanied melodic line

musical alphabet—ABCDEFG—   the first seven letters of the alphabet ABCDEFG used to name musical pitches

musique concrète   music containing the recording of natural sounds altered electronically

natural   a symbol used to cancel a previous sharp or flat: ♮

natural minor scale   a minor scale consisting of the following whole- and half-step sequence: WHWWHWW

neumatic notation   a style of writing music which uses neumes instead of standard notation

nonlocomotor   movements originating from a stationary position of the body

notes   musical symbols representing sounds or pitches which are usually placed on a staff

ostinato   a rhythmic, melodic, or harmonic pattern that repeats; used primarily as an accompaniment

ottava   Latin term for octave

parallel keys   a major and a minor key which possess the same key note rather than the same key signature

part method   See phrase method.

partner songs   two or more different songs which share an identical harmonic structure and can be performed simultaneously

patsching   the hitting or patting of the knees or thigh; used as a readiness activity for mallet techniques

pentatonic   a scale consisting of a sequence of five tones within the octave

percussion family   the largest family in the symphony orchestra; includes instruments of both definite and indefinite pitch.

phonation   the process of producing sound

phrase   a musical line which contains a coherent grouping of pitches, similar to a sentence in language, which contains a coherent grouping of words

phrase method   an imitative process used in teaching songs that are longer, more complex, and not easily learned after one or two hearings; part method

pick-up   the incomplete measure of one or more notes found at the beginning of a composition; also called an anacrusis

pitch   the relative highness or lowness of a musical sound

polyphonic texture   two or more independent melodic lines sounding simultaneously, causing harmony to result between the horizontal lines

polyrhythms   combinations of two or more independent rhythms, occurring simultaneously, whose metrical accents do not coincide

portamento   a sliding technique used when playing the trombone

prestissimo   a tempo marking designating a pace that is as fast as possible

presto   very fast pace

primary chords   the tonic, subdominant, and dominant chords

program music   music intended to suggest images, incidents, or people

quadruple meter   a time signature having a top number divisible by four: 4/4, 4/8, 4/2

range   highest-to-lowest pitch in a melody, or that which defines the capacity of a voice or instrument

ratchet   a miniature, machine-like instrument that produces a raspy, grinding sound

refrain   the same melody and words sung after each verse of a song

registers   the different portions of the vocal range which are marked by differences in vibration rate

relative keys   a name given to a major and a minor key using the same key signature

repetition   repeating the same note or notes on the staff

resonator bells   individual metal bars tuned to each tone of the chromatic scale; each bar is mounted on a block of wood and resonates when struck by a mallet

rests   music symbols used to represent silence

rhythm   varied lengths of sound or silence over an underlying beat

rhythmic ostinato   short, repeated rhythm patterns used to accompany speech, songs, other rhythms, instrument playing, or movement

rhythm sticks   long, narrow, cylindrical pieces of wood which are hit together to produce sound

rondo   a form consisting of an original theme which always returns after each digression or contrasting theme; usually symbolized by ABACA or ABACABA

root   the tone upon which a chord is built; its bottom tone

rote learning   an imitative process through which children learn to speak, sing, or move

round   a canon in which each performer returns to the beginning of the song after its conclusion

sand blocks   blocks of wood, covered with sand paper, which are rubbed against one another to produce sound

scale   an orderly ascending or descending arrangement of pitches within the limits of an octave

secondary chords   chords built on the second, third, sixth, and seventh scale degrees

section   the result of musical phrases being combined into a larger unit

sequence   a fragment of a melody being repeated immediately at a different pitch level

set formation a predetermined position in line, circle, and square dances

seventh chord a chord containing four pitches

sforzando a musical symbol requiring a sudden, strong accent on the note above it: *sf*

sharp a symbol which raises the pitch of a note one-half step: ♯

simple meter a time signature in which the upper number is a 2, 3, or 4 and the beat note is divisible into two equal parts, creating a ratio of 2:1

skip a distance larger than an interval of a second between two consecutive pitches

slapstick a paddle-like instrument made of two pieces of wood hinged together; when slapped together, the sound of a whip results

sleigh bells bells attached to a handle or a piece of material; when shook, they produce a jingling sound

slur a curved line connecting two or more notes having different pitch names

solfège syllables syllables which represent scale tones: do, re, mi, fa, so, la, ti

solmization a technique that involves assigning solfa syllables to scale tones

soprano the highest of female voice classifications

specific objective precise and clear objectives usually present in day-to-day lesson planning and providing the basis for evaluation of both the teaching and the learning processes

speech drone a low, single-pitched tone produced by children who have difficulty in matching pitches

square dance a dance, involving four couples, whose set formation is a square

staccato a reduction in the value of notes which have a dot placed over or under them

staff five parallel lines and four spaces upon which musical notation is written

step the movement of a pitch on the staff from a line to the next space directly above or below; or from a space to the next line directly above or below

stick notation a shorthand form of rhythmic notation

string family a family of instruments whose basic instruments include the violin, viola, cello, string bass, and harp

strophic a form consisting of any number of A sections, depending on the number of stanzas in the text being used

structural components subsets of musical elements

sweep strum a downward movement of the right-hand thumb across the strings of the guitar

symphony orchestra a grouping together of the four major families of instruments—brass, woodwinds, strings, and percussion—the dominant family being the string family

syncopation a rhythm resulting from a change in placement of the normal metrical accent

tambourine a round rim of wood with several pairs of metal disks attached to it. It is shook or hit against the body or hand.

temple blocks hollowed gourds of varying sizes which are attached to a frame. Each gourd produces a different pitch when struck with a mallet.

tempo the speed of the basic, underlying beat of a composition, ranging from very slow to very fast

tenor the highest male voice classification

ternary a three-sectional composition in which the second section is different from the first, but the third section is the same or similar to the first section, symbolized as ABA

tessitura the most comfortable singing range of the voice

texture horizontal and vertical elements which come together to add depth or substance to a musical composition

theme and variations a composition in which the theme is repeated again and again but has been altered in different ways for each succeeding repetition

third the middle tone in a triad

tie a curved line that joins two duration symbols of the same pitch. The first note is held for its own duration as well as the duration of the note to which it is tied.

timbre distinctive qualities of sound distinguishing one sound source from another; tone color

time signature two numbers, found at the beginning of a musical work, that represent how many beats there are to a measure and what note or rest receives the beat

tone color distinctive qualities of sound distinguishing one sound source from another; timbre

tonguing a technique used in producing pitches on wind instruments

transposing the technique of rewriting a song in a key different from that in which it was originally written

treble or G clef a symbol used for notating relatively high pitches

triad a chord containing three notes, including a root, a third, and a fifth

triangle a triangular piece of metal suspended from a cord. It is struck by a metal stick to produce a high pitched, ringing sound.

triple meter   a time signature having a top number divisible by three: 3/4, 3/8, 3/2

triplet   a note value that is divided into three equal parts

upbeat   the last beat in a measure

verse   different words and sometimes a different melody sung between repetitions of the refrain of a song

vibra-slap   an instrument which vibrates when slapped by the hand or hit against the body

whole-song method   an imitative process used to teach songs that can be sung in their entirety by students after one or two hearings

whole step   a combination of two half steps

woodblock   a semi-hollow, rectangular-shaped piece of wood that, when hit with a wooden mallet, provides a resonated knocking sound

woodwind family   a family of instruments in which the basic instruments are divided into three major groups: double, single, and no reed; major instruments include piccolo, flute; clarinet, oboe, English horn, bassoon, and contrabassoon

xylophone   a barred instrument, made out of wood, that belongs to the Orff Instrumentarium

Chapter Correlation for National Standards for Arts Education

CONTENT STANDARDS

Chapter	1 Sing Alone and with Others	2 Perform on Instruments	3 Improvise Melodies/ Accompaniments	4 Composing/ Arranging
2 Rhythm		✓✓	✓	
3 Melody	✓✓✓		✓	✓
4 Timbre			✓	
5 Expressive Elements	✓			
6 Form	✓	✓	✓	✓
7 Texture	✓	✓✓		✓
8 Harmony	✓✓✓		✓	
9 Singing Voice	✓✓✓			
10 Playing Instruments		✓✓✓	✓✓✓	
11 Listening				
12 Movement	✓			✓
13 Lesson Planning				
14 Integration				
15 Mainstreaming	✓	✓	✓	✓

✓✓✓ – extensive exposure;
✓✓ – moderate exposure;
✓ – minimal exposure

5 Reading/ Notating	6 Listening/ Analyzing	7 Evaluating Music and Performances	8 Understanding Relationships between Music and Other Disciplines	9 Music History and Culture
✓✓✓	✓✓	✓		
✓✓✓	✓	✓		
	✓✓✓	✓		
✓✓✓		✓		
✓	✓✓✓	✓		
	✓	✓		
	✓	✓		
	✓	✓		
	✓	✓		
	✓✓✓	✓		
	✓✓	✓		
		✓		
		✓	✓✓✓	✓✓✓
✓	✓	✓		

GENERAL MUSIC SERIES

Share the Music, 2000
McGraw-Hill School Division
Two Penn Plaza
New York, NY 10121-2298
(800) 442-9685

The Music Connection
SilverBurdett and Ginn Company
250 James Street
Morristown, NJ 07960
(800) 631-8001

NATIONAL STANDARDS FOR ARTS EDUCATION

Dance, Music, Theatre, Visual Arts
What Every Young American Should Know and Be Able to Do in the Arts
ISBN 1-56545-036-1
Music Educators National Conference, 1806 Robert Fulton Drive, Reston, VA 22091
(1-800-336-3768)

MELODY AND RHYTHM INSTRUMENTS

Peripole-Bergerault
Sylvia Perry
2041 State Street
Salem, OR 97301
(800) 443-3592

West Music Company
Judy Pine
1212 5th Street PO Box 5521
Coralville, IA 52241
(800) 397-9378

Sonor Percussion, C/O Horner
Robert W. Cotton
Lakeridge Industrial Park
Sycamore Drive
Ashland, VA 23005
(804) 798-4500

Sweet Pipes, Inc.
Laura Bergin
6722 Brentwood Stair Road
Fort Worth, TX 76112
(817) 446-3299

MMB Music, Inc.
Norm Goldberg
3526 Washington Avenue
St. Louis, MO 63103-1019
(314) 531-9635

Oscar Schmidt International
230 Lexington Drive
Buffalo Grove, IL 60090
(800) 323-4173

Rhythm Band
Bob Bergin
PO Box 126
Fort Worth, Texas 76101-0126

Remo, Inc.
Lloyd McCausland
28101 Industry Drive
Valencia, CA 91355
(805) 294-5600

Music In Motion
Mary Ann Stewart
783 North Grove #108
Richardson, TX 75081
(972) 231-0403

RESOURCES AND INFORMATION

Available by writing or calling:
Music Educators National Conference
1806 Robert Fulton Drive
Reston, VA 22091   Toll Free: 800-336-3768

Cooperative Learning

Title: Cooperative Learning in Music
Description: A summary of cooperative learning principles, with practical examples for use in general music and performance classes as well as in collegiate musicianship and methods classes. Contains an extensive bibliography, from which more information about cooperative learning can be obtained. By Phyllis R. Kaplan and Sandra L. Stauffer. 1994. 112 pages. ISBN 0-56545-051-5.

Title: Cooperative Learning in the Music Classroom (video)
Description: This videotape will be a useful resource for creating cooperative learning lessons and for showing how this technique can bring new excitement to the classroom. Footage from conference presentations as well as live classroom footage is used to explain the concept of cooperative learning—which includes dividing the class into small groups and working on musical activities together—and its importance and effectiveness. Focuses on musical experiences, but useful for teachers of any subject. Featuring Phyllis Kaplan and Lenore Pogonowski. VHS. 1992. 29 minutes. ISBN 1-56545-014-0.

General Music

Title: Strategies for Teaching Middle-Level General Music
Description: Compiled and edited by June M. Hinckley and Suzanne M. Shull. 1996. ISBN 1-56545-084-1.

Title: Strategies for Teaching K-4 General Music
Description: Compiled and edited by Sandra L. Stauffer and Jennifer Davidson. 1996. ISBN 1-56545-081-7.

Title: Teaching General Music: A Course of Study
Description: A model for developing a strong program of instruction for teaching courses in general music from preschool to high school, including performing/reading, creating, listening/describing, and valuing; offers objectives and procedures within each topic. Developed by the MENC Task Force on General Music Course of Study. 1991. 40 pages. ISBN 0-940796-98-8.

Listening

Title: The London Symphony Orchestra Music Explorer (video)
Description: An award-winning video featuring the London Symphony Orchestra, conducted by Sir Colin Davis, performing twelve definitive pieces of classical music, including Bach's Brandenburg Concerto no. 2, Mahler's Symphony no. 1, and Shostakovich's Symphony no. 10. An accompanying 65-page book by Richard McNicol offers detailed guidance for understanding, analyzing, and enjoying these works. Winner of the "best video and print resource" from the International Education Television Awards. Recorded in stereo. Distributed in the United States exclusively by MENC. For middle level and high school students. Additional materials to help teachers in the United States teach to the National Standards are available on MENC's home page (www.menc.org). 1996. 90 minutes. ISBN 0-952534-73-8.

Title: The World's Greatest Music (video with teacher's guide)
Description: Provides all the materials necessary for building lessons around some of the most respected pieces from the standard repertoire for orchestra, including works by Rossini, Ravel, Mozart, Grieg, and others, performed by the Mineria Symphony Orchestra. The accompanying teacher's guide includes composer profiles, listening guides, suggested student activities, advanced projects, form and style analyses, and a glossary of terms. Suitable for the upper elementary through high school levels. Teacher's guide by William V. May, Vanissa Braswell Murphy, Cecile Johnson, and Bonnie Blu Williams. 1988. VHS. 60 minutes. ISBN 0-940796-58-9.

Multicultural

Title: Sounds of the World/ Music of Eastern Europe: Albanian, Greek, and South Slavic
Description: Recorded in the United States by immigrants dedicated to keeping alive their homeland traditions. Includes three high-quality stereo cassettes containing narration, interviews, and music examples along with a specially prepared teacher's guide with historical and musical background information, pictures of instruments, and suggestions for using materials with elementary, secondary, and college level students. Originally produced for public radio by ethnomusicologist Karl Signell. Selected as an Honorable Mention Folk Recording by the American Folklife Center, Library of Congress. Teacher's guide by Patricia Shehan Campbell. 1990. ISBN 0-940796-70-8.

Title: Sounds of the World/ Music of Latin America: Mexico, Ecuador, Brazil
Description: Recorded in the United States by immigrants dedicated to keeping alive their homeland traditions. Includes three high-quality stereo cassettes containing narration, interviews, and music examples along with a specially prepared teachers' guide with historical and musical background information, pictures of instruments, and suggestions for using materials with elementary, secondary, and college level students. Originally produced for public radio by ethnomusicologist Karl Signell. Teacher's guide by Dale Olsen, Charles Perrone, and Daniel Sheehy. 1987. ISBN 1-56545- 053-1.

Title: Sounds of the World/ Music of East Asia: Chinese, Korean, and Japanese
Description: Recorded in the United States by immigrants dedicated to keeping alive their homeland traditions. Includes three high-quality stereo cassettes containing narration, interviews, and music examples along with a specially prepared teachers' guide with historical and musical background information, pictures of instruments, and suggestions for using materials with elementary, secondary, and college level students. Originally produced for public radio by ethnomusicologist Karl Signell. Teacher's guide by William M. Anderson, with Terry Liu and Ann Prescott. 1989. ISBN 0-940796-69- 4.

Title: Sounds of the World/ Music of the Middle East: Arab, Persian/Iranian, and Turkish
Description: Recorded in the United States by immigrants dedicated to keeping alive their homeland traditions. Includes three high-quality stereo cassettes containing narration, interviews, and music examples along with a specially prepared teachers' guide with historical and musical background information, pictures of instruments, and suggestions for using materials with elementary, secondary, and college level students. Originally produced for public radio by ethnomusicologist Karl Signell. Selected as an Outstanding Folk Recording by the American Folklife Center, Library of Congress. Teacher's guide by Sally Monsour with assistance from Pamela Dorn. 1990. ISBN 0-940796-73-2

Title: Sounds of the World/ Music of Southeast Asia: Lao, Hmong, Vietnamese
Description: Recorded in the United States by immigrants dedicated to keeping alive their homeland traditions. Includes three high-quality stereo cassettes containing narration, interviews, and music examples along with a specially prepared teachers' guide with historical and musical background information, pictures of instruments, and suggestions for using materials with elementary, secondary, and college level students. Originally produced for public radio by ethnomusicologist Karl Signell. Selected as an Honorable Mention Folk Recording by the American Folklife Center, Library of Congress. Teacher's guide by Patricia K. Shehan. 1986. ISBN 1-56545-054-X.

Title: Making Connections: Multicultural Music and the National Standards
Description: This book and compact disc set is a valuable resource for music educators who want to develop a school music program with more culturally diverse music and also incorporate the National Standards. The book provides twenty-one lesson plans from African American, Asian (Balinese), Mexican American, and Native American traditions with discussion on how each lesson meets specific content and achievement standards for grades K-12. Historical background for each tradition is given, as well as music examples, illustrations, and extensive resource lists. Music for classroom listening for thirteen of the lessons is featured on the Making Connections Companion Recording compact disc, which includes African American children's game songs and gospel music, Balinese vocal gamelan music, Mexican American mariachi music, and Native American music. 1997. ISBN 1-56545-108-2.

Title: Making Connections: Multicultural Music and the National Standards (book)
Description: 1997. 144 pages. ISBN 1-56545-106-6.

Title: Making Connections Companion Recording (CD)
Description: 1997. 40 minutes. ISBN 1-56545-107-4.

Title: Music Resources for Multicultural Perspectives
Description: A two-CD sampler of the world's musical riches, including music from North America, Latin America and the Caribbean, Europe, Sub-Saharan Africa, the Middle East, South Asia, East Asia, and Southeast Asia. These compact discs, which can be used with the acclaimed MENC publication Multicultural Perspectives in Music Education, 2nd ed., contain nearly 100 minutes of music. The selections were chosen for use as a classroom resource by the editors of Multicultural Perspectives, William M. Anderson of Kent State University and Patricia Shehan Campbell of the University of Washington. An updated version of the first edition cassettes, including 12 new selections. A must-have for general music teachers! 1998. ISBN 1-56545-112-0.

Title: Bringing Multicultural Music to Children (video)
Description: A look at innovative ways to teach young students about the music of other cultures. This video features noted music professors René Boyer-Alexander, Patricia Shehan Campbell, Han Kuo-Huang, David McAllester, and Marvelene Moore sharing ideas for early elementary multicultural music education at MENC conferences and symposia. Included are songs and chants from Africa, China, and Jamaica; and music from Native Americans, African Americans, and the Maori of New Zealand. 1992. VHS. 27 minutes. ISBN 1-56545-009-4.

Title: Multicultural Songs, Games, and Dances
Description: From the Organization of American Kodaly Educators. This OAKE (Kodaly Association) research collection contains 24 songs, games, and dances from thirteen nations. Pronunciation guides are included. 1995. 30 pages.

Title: Teaching the Music of African Americans (video)
Description: Cultural historian Bernice Johnson Reagon and ethnomusicologist Luvenia A. George discuss the roots of African-American music and the cultural and historical influences the church has had on its development. Included are performances and a segment on Afro-Cuban music by ethnomusicologist Daniel E. Sheehy. Not intended for classroom viewing. 1991. VHS. 25 minutes. ISBN 0-940796-92-9.

Title: Teaching the Music of Hispanic Americans (video)
Description: Ethnomusicologists Dale A. Olsen and Daniel E. Sheehy discuss the development of Hispanic-American music and offer demonstrations of Andean raft pipes and Mexican mariachi ensembles. Music educator Linda O'Brien-Rothe explains important aspects of mariachi music, including the instruments, playing techniques, and rhythms. Not intended for classroom viewing. 1991. VHS. 26 minutes. ISBN 0-940796-95-3.

Title: Teaching the Music of Asian Americans (video)
Description: Ethnomusicologist Kuo-Huang Han traces the development of Chinese music through its changing cultural and historical periods. Includes demonstrations of Chinese opera, folk songs, simple chants, and instruments, as well as lesson ideas. Presented by Han and Patricia Shehan Campbell. Not intended for classroom viewing. 1991. VHS. 37 minutes. ISBN 0-940796-94-5.

Title: Teaching the Music of the American Indian (video)
Description: Getting past the stereotype and discovering the true American Indian lifestyle and music is the focus of this video. It includes discussions by ethnomusicologists David P. McAllester and Edwin Schupman on the role of the music educator in multicultural education, explanations of materials available for teaching, and music examples. Not intended for classroom viewing. 1991. VHS. 37 minutes. ISBN 0-940796-93-7.

Readings

Title: Elementary General Music: The Best of MEJ
Description: A set of effective how-to ideas for elementary general music teaching. Articles focus on five subjects: "A Philosophical Framework for Elementary General Music Teaching"; "Classroom Management, Instructional Pacing, and Organization"; "Active Learning"; "Performance"; and "Partnership with Elementary Teachers." Edited by Betty W. Atterbury. 1992. 136 pages. ISBN 1-56545-013-2.

Title: Toward Tomorrow: New Visions for General Music
Description: From MENC's Society for General Music. Noted music educators and other leaders in education share their visions for the future of general music in this volume, which is based on presentations and discussions at the October 1993 symposium held by SGM and MENC. Featuring essays looking toward "tomorrow" from various perspectives; articles addressing specific areas, such as assessment, technology, and cultural diversity; and reflections and applications for the classroom. Edited by Sandra Stauffer. 1995. 144 pages. ISBN 1-56545-080-9.

Singing

Title: Singing in General Music (video)
Description: From MENC's Society for General Music: a discussion of the importance of singing in general music from noted vocal experts and demonstrations of techniques for teaching singing, including those involving posture, breath control, vocal exploration, range, singing in tune, developing confidence, and more. Actual classroom footage is featured. 1994. VHS. 26 minutes ISBN 1-56545-047-7.

Title: I Love America (video)
Description: A live performance of some of America's most beloved patriotic songs. Featuring Robert Merrill, the U.S. Air Force Band, and the Singing Sergeants, conducted by Captain Amy R. Mills. A wonderful resource for sharing "America's music" with students of all ages in the classroom. Produced by GMZ, Inc. 1991. VHS. 36 minutes.

Special Learner

Title: TIPS: Teaching Music to Special Learners
Description: Tips for using props, visual aids, instruments, rhythm activities, dance movements, and song stories to help children with special needs understand and enjoy music. Compiled by Gail Schaberg. 1988. 48 pages. ISBN 0-940796-56-2.

Technology

Title: Synthesizers in the Elementary Music Classroom
Description: Provides classroom music teachers with helpful suggestions for incorporating electronic instruments into the existing curriculum. Presents background information on the functioning and acquisition of electronic instruments. Includes suggested performance experiences, purchasing information, lesson plans, and activities such as singing, listening, playing instruments, and composing. Appropriate for the elementary level, K-6. By Jackie Wiggins. 1991. 64 pages. ISBN 1-56545-005-1.

Title: TIPS: Technology for Music Educators
Description: Students can create music and communicate in musical ways by using synthesizers, video-discs, and electronic keyboards. Presents ideas for using these new technologies as learning vehicles. Compiled by Charles G. Boody. 1990. 48 pages. ISBN 0-940796-72-4.

Title: An Overview of Electronic Musical Instruments (video)
Description: Presents ideas for using electronic instruments for teaching composition, arranging, and musical acoustics through demonstrations by composer, performer, and educator Don Muro. Offers examples using synthesizers, samplers, drum computers, digital effects processors, and vocoders in a variety of music styles. Produced by Michael Kovins, Joseph Muro, and Don Muro in association with Korg U.S.A. Released in cooperation with MENC. 1991. VHS. 32 minutes. ISBN 0-940796-88-0.

"Old Mother Twitchett," in B. F. Wright. *The Real Mother Goose*. New York: Checkerboard Press. Macmillan Publishing Co., 1944.

Woody Guthrie, "This Land Is Your Land" New York: Copyright 1956, 1984, 1958, 1986 by The Richmond Organization and 1970 by Ludlow Music Inc. Reprinted by permission.

Judith Eisenstein, "O Hanukkah," in *Getaway to Jewish Music*. Wyncote, PA: Recommended Rabbinical College. Reprinted by permission.

Jester Hairston, "Oh, Rocka My Soul." New York: Bourne Co., 1950. Reprinted by permission.

J. S. Bach, Chorale, "Ermuntre dich, mein schwacher Geist." In W. Duckworth, *Creative Approach to Music Fundamentals*, Third Edition. Belmont, CA: Wadsworth Publishing Co., 1989.

"Arirang," in *Holt Music Book*, Grade 6. Orlando, FL: Holt, Rinehart and Winston, 1984.

"San Sereni" from *Sail Away*, edited by Eleanor Locke. Copyright 1988 by Boosey & Hawkes, Inc. Reprinted by permission.

"Candles of Hanukkah," in J. O'Brien, *Creative Music Fundamentals*. Upper Saddle River, NJ: Prentice Hall, Inc., 1985.

"Au Clair de la Lune," in Dallin, *Heritage Songster*, Dubuque, IA: William C. Brown Company, Publishers, 1980.

"Tinga Layo," in *Musical Growth in the Elementary Classroom*, Fifth Edition. Oyster Bay, NY: M. Baron Company, 1943.

"Nighttime," in Lois Choksy, *The Kodály Method: Comprehensive Music Education from Infant to Adult*. Upper Saddle River, NJ: Prentice Hall, Inc., 1974.

"The Clown," in *Music in Our Town*. Morristown, NJ: Silver Burdett Company, copyright 1966. All rights reserved.

"Jig Jog, Jig Jog," in Birkenshaw. *Music for Fun, Music for Learning*, Stainer & Bell Ltd., London, and Galaxy Music Corporation, New York.

"Hoo Hoo," from *New Songs and Games* by Ethel Crowninshield, published by The Boston Music Co., 116 Boylston St., Boston, MA. 02116 and used by permission.

"Come Boating with Me," music by John Wood, words by Lansing Macdowell. In V. Russel, *Songtime* 4. Toronto: Holt, Rinehart and Winston of Canada, 1960. Reprinted by permission.

Sakura, "Cherry Bloom," in *Holt Music Book*, Grade 3. Orlando, FL: Holt, Rinehart and Winston, 1984.

"When That I Was a Tiny Little Boy." In Swanson and Sannerud, *Music Through Folk Song*. Belmont, CA: Wadworth Publishing Company, 1977.

"Marching," in Lois Choksy, *The Kodály Method: Comprehensive Music Education from Infant to Adult*. Upper Saddle River, NJ: Prentice Hall, Inc., 1974.

"Jolly Miller" from 150 *American Folk Songs*, edited by Peter Erdei. Copyright 1974 by Boosey & Hawkes, Inc. Reprinted by permission.

"Poor Little Kitty Cat," in Lois Choksy, *The Kodály Context: Creating an Environment for Musical Learning*. Upper Saddle River, NJ: Prentice Hall, Inc., copyright 1981. Reprinted by permission.

"Hansel and Gretel Dance." Schott's Sohne, Mayence, 1895.

"Magic Penny." Words and Music by Malvina Reynolds. Copyright 1955, 1958 by Northern Music Co. Rights Administered by MCA Music Publishing. New York, NY: International Copyright Secured. Made in U.S.A. All rights reserved.

"Now Let Me Fly," in Lois Choksy, *The Kodály Method: Comprehensive Music Education from Infant to Adult*. Upper Saddle River, NJ: Prentice Hall, Inc., 1974.

"Oranges and Lemons," from *Sally Go Round the Sun* by E. Fawke. Used by permission of the Canadian Publishers, McClelland and Stewart, Toronto.

"Turn! Turn! Turn!" ("To Everything There Is a Season"). Words from the *Book of Ecclesiastes*, adaptation and music by Pete Seeger. The Richmond Organization, copyright 1962 Melody Trails, Inc., New York, NY. Used by permission.

"Laughing Song," in Lois Choksy, *The Kodály Method: Comprehensive Music Education from Infant to Adult*. Upper Saddle River, NJ: Prentice Hall, Inc., 1974.

"The Young Man Who Wouldn't Hoe Corn," in Lois Choksy, *The Kodály Method: Comprehensive Music Education from Infant to Adult*. Upper Saddle River, NJ: Prentice Hall, Inc., 1974.

"By'm By" from *The American Songbag* by Carl Sandburg, copyright 1927 by Harcourt Brace Jovanovich, Inc., and renewed 1955 by Carl Sandburg. Reprinted by permission of the publishers.

"The Little Dappled Cow" from 150 *American Folk Songs*, edited by Peter Erdei. Copyright 1974 by Boosey & Hawke, Inc. Reprinted by permission.

"Scarborough Fair," in Burakoff and Lettick, *Sweet Pipes Soprano Recorder Book I*. Levittown, NY: Sweet Pipes, 1980. Reprinted by permission.

"If I Had a Hammer" (The Hammer Song), words and music by Lee Hays and Pete Seeger. The Richmond Corporation. Copyright 1958 (renewed 1986) and 1962 Ludlow Music, Inc., New York, NY. Used by permission.

"Draw Me a Bucket of Water." Written and adapted by Bessie Jones. Collected and edited by Alan Lomax. TRO-© Copyright 1972 Ludlow Music, Inc., New York, N.Y. Used by permission.

"The Greatest Love of All," words by Michael Masser, music by Linda Creed. Copyright 1977 by Gold Horizon Music Corp. and Golden Torch Music Corp., divisions of Filmtrax Copyright Holdings, Inc. International Copyright Secured. Made in U.S.A. All rights reserved.

Poem beginning "My stomach growls" from *Only the Moon and Me* by Richard J. Margolis. (J.B. Lippincott) Text copyright 1969 by Richard Margolis. Reprinted by permission of HarperCollins Publishers, Inc.

Langston Hughes, "Dreams," in *Don't You Turn Back*. Reprinted by permission of Harold Ober Associates Incorporated. Copyright 1932 by Alfred A. Knopf, Inc. Copyright renewed 1960 by Langston Hughes.

"Joey" from *Where the Sidewalk Ends* by Shel Silverstein. Copyright 1974 by Evil Eye Music Inc. Text only reprinted by permission of HarperCollins Publishers, Inc.

Robert Louis Stevenson, "The Wind," in *A Child's Garden of Verse*. Frank Watts, Inc., Oxford University Press, 1966.

Index

Absolute pitch names, 56–60
Accelerando, 123
Accents, 13–15
Accompaniment
    chordal, 183–190
        on keyboard instruments, 270
    harmonic, using resonator bells, 233
Adult voices, 199, 200
Agogo bells, 223
Alla breve, 28
Alphabetical pitch names, 56–60
Alto voice, 111, 200
Anacrusis, 43–45
Answers (in fugues), 168
Articulation, 128
Asymmetrical meter, 34–35
Attention deficit–hyperactivity disorder (ADHD), 353
Augmented triad, 193
Autoharp, 258–260

Bar line, 14
Baritone voice, 111, 201
Barred instruments, 234–235
    playing, 236
Bass clef, 55
Bass viol, 112
Bass voice, 111, 200
Bassoon, 115, 116
Beat
    accents and, 13–15
    strategies for teaching, 7–8
Beat note, 28
Behavior disorders, students with, 353
B-flat clarinet, 116
Binary form, 142, 143–144
Body sounds, 111. See also Vocal sounds
Bongo drums, 224
Bordun, 182–183, 239
Bow (string instruments), 112, 113
Brass instrument family, 114–115
Breathing, 106
    diaphragmatic, 210
    support of singing tone and, 208

Cabasa, 224
Call charts, 274–275
    using abstract representations, 277–281
    using abstract symbols, 287–288
    using pictures, 275–277
    using words, 281–287
Canons, 165
    rhythmic, 44
Capo, 266
Castanets, 224
Cello, 112
Changing meter, 35–36
Chant, 162–164
Chest register, 201–202
Children's voices
    correcting speech drone, 206
    older students, 204
    primary years, 203–204
    upper elementary years, 204
Chimes, 118
Chordal accompaniment, 183–190
    on keyboard instruments, 270
Chordal texture. See Homophonic texture
Chords, 183. See also Chordal accompaniment
    dominant, 186–189
    inversions of, 191–193
    primary, 186–188
    progressions of, 192
    secondary, 186, 189
    seventh, 190
    subdominant, 186
    tonic, 186
    triads, 185, 193–194
Chromatic scales, 90–91
Circle dance, 306
Circle games, 302–306
Clarinet, 115, 116
Classroom management, inclusive settings and, 371–372
Claves, 224
Clavichord, 267
Clef signs, 55
Codas, 152–154
Common time, 28
Compound intervals, 68
Compound meter, 31–34
Conducting patterns, 16–17, 33
Conga drum, 225
Contour
    of melody, 62–64
    of phrases, 137–138, 139, 140, 141
Contrabassoon, 115, 116

Contralto voice, 201
Cooperative learning activities, 319–320
Countersubjects (in fugues), 169
Cowbell, 225
Crescendo, 126
Cristofori, Bartolommeo, 267
Curriculum integration
    with literature, 332–335
    with mathematics, 331–332
    multicurricular applications, 335–345
    with physical education, 346
    with related arts, 346–349
    rhythm applications in, 335–342
    with science, 345
    with social studies, 329–331
Curwen, John, 214
Cut time, 28
Cymbals, 225

Da capo al fine, 154, 155, 156
Dalcroze, Jaque Émile, 294
Dal segno al fine, 154, 157
Decrescendo, 126
Deductive teaching, 319
Definite pitch percussion instruments, 118
Descants, 167–168, 179–180
Diaphragmatic breathing, 210
Diatonic sequences, 69–70
Diminished triad, 193
Diversity, classroom, 351
Dominant chord, 186–189
Dotted notes, 25–27
Dotted rests, 25
Double bar, 14, 142
Double bass, 112
Double-reed woodwinds, 115, 116
Downbeat, 16
Drums
    bongo, 224
    conga, 225
    hand, 226
Duple meter, 28
Dynamics, 123–127
    markings, 126–127
    symbols, 126

Educate America Act, 2
Eighth notes, 8–10
Electronic keyboards, 271
Electronic sounds, 110–111
English horn, 115, 116
Enharmonic equivalents, 72–73
Environmental sounds, 106, 107
Ethnically diverse students, 351, 355
Evaluation
    General Music Assessment Form, 356, 357
    of student achievement, 320–327

Exercises, vocal, 202–203

F clef, 55
Female voices, 111, 200
Fermata, 132
Finger cymbals, 225
First tenor voice, 201
Flat sign, 70
Flute, 115–116
Folk dances, 306–311
Followers (in canons), 165
Form, 135
    sectional, 142–151
Forte, 267
French horn, 114
Fugues, 168–169

G clef, 55
General Music Assessment Form, 356, 357
Gifted and Talented Children's Act, 355
Gifted and talented students, 351, 355
Glockenspiel, 234–235
Goals 2000, 2
Gong, 225
Grand staff, 56
Guiro, 226
Guitar, 261–266
    chord chart, 266

Half notes, 17
Half rests, 17
Hand drum, 226
Hand signs, 214, 216
Harmonic intervals, 183
Harmonic minor scales, 81
Harmony, 174
    building aural awareness of, 174
    preparation for, 174–177
Harpsichord, 267
Head register, 201–202
Homophonic texture, 169–171
    harmony and, 174

Icons, as musical symbols, 7
Improvisation (movement), 301–302
Inclusion
    candidates for, 352–355
    vs. mainstreaming, 351
Indefinite pitch percussion instruments, 119
Individualized education program (IEP), 356–357
Individuals with Disabilities Education Act (IDEA), 351
    amendments of 1997, 351–352
Inductive teaching, 319
Instrumentarium. See Orff instruments
Instruments
    barred. See Barred instruments

goals for use of, 223
Orff. *See* Orff instruments
playing in mainstreaming classroom, 371
rhythm, 108–110, 223–231
Interludes, 152–154
Intervals
harmonic, 183
melodic. *See* Melodic intervals
minor thirds, 193, 215, 217, 238
sixths, 178–179
thirds, 178–179, 193
Introductions, 152–154
Inversions (chords), 191–193
Irregular meter, 34–35
Italian tempo markings, 123

Jingle clogs/taps, 226

Keyboard instruments, 118
chordal accompaniment for, 270–272
electronic, 271
playing, 267–269
Keys
major, 75–79
minor, 79–87
parallel, 87
transposing, 92–93
Key signatures
for major scales, 75–79
for minor scales, 83
Kodály, Zoltán, 214, 215

Leaders (in canons), 165
Learning theory, music education and, 3–5
Ledger lines, 54–55
Legato, 128
Lesson planning
factors to consider in, 313
formats for daily plans, 316–319
goals and objectives in, 313–315
group characteristics in, 313
Line dance, 306
Listening activities
call charts and, 274–288
goals for, 274
guidelines for, 274–275
in mainstreaming classroom, 371
organizing, 275
rhythm charts and, 291–292
shadow box dramatizations and, 289–290
Literature. *See* Curriculum integration
Locomotor movements, 297–298

Mainstreaming, 351, 355–357
listening activities for, 371
playing instruments in, 371
rhythm activities for, 358–363
singing activities for, 364–370

Major scales, 74–79
Major third, 193
Major triad, 193
Male voices, 111, 200
Mallets, correct use of, 236
Maracas, 226
Mathematics. *See* Curriculum integration
Measure, 14
Melodic intervals, 65–68. *See also* Sixths; Thirds
compound, 68
whole and half steps, 69–70
Melodic minor scales, 82
Melody, 51, 61
accidentals in, 70–72
contour, 62–64
instruments, 232–236. *See also* Orff Schulwerk lessons
intervals in. *See* Melodic intervals
repetition in, 64–65
skips in, 64–65
steps in, 64–65
transposing, 92–93
Mentally challenged students, 354
Metallophone, 234–235
Meter, alla breve, 28
Meter
asymmetrical, 34–35
changing, 35–36
common time, 28
compound, 31–34
cut time, 28
duple, 28
irregular, 34–35
mixed, 35–36
quadruple, 28
signatures. *See* Time signatures
simple, 28–31
triola, 36–37
triple, 28
triplets, 36–37
Mezzo-soprano voice, 111, 200
Middle C, 56
MIDI computer language, 271
Minor scales, 79–87
Minor third, 193, 215, 217, 238
Minor triad, 193
Mixed meter, 35–36
Monophonic texture, 162–164
Movable do
clef, 221
system, 214
Movement activities
beginning, 295–297
categories of, 297–298
circle games, 302–306
dynamics, 302
folk dances, 306–311
goals and objectives for, 295

Movement activities (*continued*)
    improvisation, 301–302
    movement and space, 299–301
    preparing for, 294
Musical alphabet, 56–60
Musical notation. *See* Notation
Musique concrète, 279

National Education Standards Improvement
      Council, 2
Natural minor scales, 79
Natural sign, 70
Neumatic notation, 163
Neumes, 163
Nonlocomotor movements, 298
No-reed woodwinds, 115
Notation
    accidentals, 70–72
    asymmetrical meter, 34
    bar line, 14
    clef signs, 55
    compound meter, 31
    dotted notes, 25
    dotted rests, 25
    double bar, 14, 142
    eighth notes, 8
    enharmonic equivalents, 72–73
    half notes, 17
    half rests, 17
    using icons to represent, 7
    introducing musical symbols, 9–10
    irregular meter, 34
    ledger lines, 54–55
    neumatic, 163
    note stems, 60–61
    ottava, 54–55
    quarter notes, 8
    quarter rests, 11
    repeat sign, 45, 154–157
    simple meter, 28
    sixteenth notes, 17
    sixteenth rests, 17
    slur, 130
    staff, 53–55
    standard, 9
    stick notation, 9
    tie, 23
    whole notes, 17
    whole rests, 17
Notes. *See* Alphabetical pitch names; Notation
Note stems, 60–61

Oboe, 115, 116
Orchestral sounds, 112–118
Orff, Carl, 234
Orff instruments (Instrumentarium), 234–235
    and bordun, 182

chordal accompaniment and, 186
    playing barred, 236
Orff method, 234–236
Orff Schulwerk lessons, 236–242
Ostinati
    melodic, 178, 241
    polyrhythmic, 42–43
    rhythmic, 12, 237
Ottava, 54–55

Parallel keys, 87
Part method, 212–214
Partner songs, 166–167, 179–181
Patsching, 6, 239
Pentatonic scale, 87–90, 215, 238
Percussion instrument family, 118
Phrase method, 212–214
Phrases, 135–142
Physical/health disabilities, students with, 354–355
Piano (softly), 267
Pianos. *See* Keyboard instruments
Piccolo, 115–116
Pick-up note, 43–45
Pitch, 51–53
    organized *vs.* unorganized, 61–62
Pizzicato, 112
Polyphonic texture, 164–169
    harmony and, 174
Polyphony. *See* Polyphonic texture
Polyrhythmic ostinati, 42–43
Polyrhythms, 42–43
Portamento, 114
Primary chords, 186–188
Program music, 285
Progressions (chord), 192
Pulse. *See* Beat

Quadruple meter, 28
Quarter notes, 8–10
Quarter rests, 11–12

Ratchet, 226
Recorder (instrument)
    duets for, 254–255
    fingering chart for, 257
    playing, 243–253
    trios for, 255–256
    types of, 243
Refrain, 145
Registers, vocal. *See* Vocal registers
Relative minor keys, 83
Repeat sign, 45, 154–157
Repetition, in melody, 64–65
Resonator bells, 232–233
Rests, 11–12
    half, 17
    sixteenth, 17
    whole, 17

Rhythm, 6
    accents, 13–15
    activities
        in mainstreaming classroom, 358–363
        notation for, 10
    beat, 7–8
    conducting patterns, 16–17
    instruments
        use in classroom, 223–231. *See also* Orff
            Schulwerk lessons
        tone color of, 108–110
    patsching, 6, 239
    polyrhythms, 42–43
    using speech to reinforce, 13, 21
    strategies for teaching, 8–11
    syncopated, 38–41
    time signatures, 15–17
Rhythmic canon, 44
Rhythmic ostinati, 12
Rhythm sticks, 227
Rhythm syllables, 8, 10
Ritardando, 123
Rondo, 142, 146–148
Rosin, 113
Rote learning method, 211
Rounds, 165,
    teaching, 177

Sand blocks, 227
Saxophone, 116
Scales, 73
    chromatic, 90–91
    major, 74–79
    minor, 79–87
    pentatonic, 87–90, 215, 238
Secondary chords, 186, 189
Second tenor voice, 201
Sectional forms, 142–151
Sections. *See* Sectional forms
Sensory deficits, students with, 354
Sequences, 157–159
Set formation, 306–307
Seventh chords, 190
Shadow box dramatizations, 289–290
Sharp sign, 70
Simple meter, 28–31
Singing
    activities, in mainstreaming classroom, 364–370
    competency, 199
    correct posture for, 209–210
    goals for, 199
    by note, 214–221
    objectives and guidelines for elementary years,
        210–211
    part method, 212–214
    phrase method, 212–214
    by rote, 211
    by whole song method, 211–212

Single-reed woodwinds, 115
Sixteenth notes, 17–19
Sixteenth rests, 17
Sixths (interval), 178–179
Skips, in melody, 64–65
Slapstick, 227
Sleigh bells, 227
Slur, 130
Social studies. *See* Curriculum integration
Solfège syllables, 214
Solmization, 214, 215–221
Soprano recorder. *See* Recorder
Soprano voice, 111, 200
Sound imagery, 109
Special needs students, 352–355. *See also* Inclusion,
        352–355; Mainstreaming individualized educa-
        tion program for, 356–357
Speech and language disorders, students with, 354
Speech drone, 206
Square dance, 306
Staccato, 128
Staff, 53–55
    grand, 56
Stems, 60–61
Steps, in melody, 64–65. *See also* Melodic intervals
Stick notes, 8
Stopping (horn technique), 114
String bass, 112
String instrument family, 112–113
Strophic form, 142, 149–151
Subdominant chords, 186
Subjects (in fugues), 168
Symphonic instruments, 112–118
Symphony orchestra, 112
Syncopation, 38–41

Tambourine, 118, 227
Teaching materials, 327
Teaching methods, 319–320. *See also* Lesson planning
Temple blocks, 228
Tempo, 121–123
Tempo markings, 123
Tenor voice, 111, 200, 201
Ternary form, 142, 145–146
Tessitura, 203
Texture
    harmony and, 174
    homophonic, 169–171
    monophonic, 162–164
    polyphonic, 164–169
Theme and variations, 142, 148–149
Thirds (interval), 178–179, 193, 215
    minor thirds, 193, 215, 217, 238
Tie, 23–25
Timbre, 106
Time signatures, 15–17
Timpani, 118
Tone color. *See* Timbre

Tonguing (recorder technique), 243
Tonic chord, 186
Transposing, 92–93
Transverse woodwinds, 115–116
Treble clef, 55
Triads, 185, 193–194. *See also* Chords naming, 194
Triangle, 118, 228
Triola, 36–37
Triple meter, 28
Triplets, 36–37
Trombone, 114
Trumpet, 114
Tuba, 114

Upbeat, 16

Valves (brass instruments), 114
Verse, 145
Vibra-slap, 228
Viola, 112
Violin, 112
Vocal mechanism, 200
Vocal ranges, 111

helping children to find, 206–208
Vocal registers, 201–202
    helping children to find and work with, 208–209
Vocal sounds, 111
Voice. *See also* Singing
    adult, 199, 200
        classifications of, 200–201
    child's, 203–209
    exercises for, 202–203
    female, 200
    male, 200
    mechanism of production, 200
    problems with, 208–209
    registers. *See* Vocal registers

Whole notes, 17
Whole rests, 17
Whole song method, 211–212
Wind chimes, 228
Wood block, 118, 229
Woodwind instrument family, 115–117

Xylophone, 234, 235